MINISTRY OF CULTURAL AND ENVIRONMENTAL ASSETS
NATIONAL COMMISSION FOR THE CELEBRATION OF THE QUINCENTENNIAL
OF THE DISCOVERY OF AMERICA

NUOVA RACCOLTA COLOMBIANA
ENGLISH EDITION

ISTITUTO POLIGRAFICO E ZECCA DELLO STATO
LIBRERIA DELLO STATO
ROMA

MINISTRY OF CULTURAL AND ENVIRONMENTAL ASSETS
NATIONAL COMMISSION FOR THE CELEBRATION OF THE QUINCENTENNIAL
OF THE DISCOVERY OF AMERICA

NUOVA RACCOLTA COLOMBIANA

CHRISTOPHER COLUMBUS'S DISCOVERIES IN THE TESTIMONIALS OF DIEGO ALVAREZ CHANCA AND ANDRÉS BERNÁLDEZ

INTRODUCTION AND NOTES BY
ANNA UNALI

Translated into English by
GIOACCHINO TRIOLO
LUCIANO F. FARINA - Ohio State University

ISTITUTO POLIGRAFICO E ZECCA DELLO STATO
LIBRERIA DELLO STATO
ROMA

Originally published as *Le scoperte di Cristoforo Colombo nelle testimonianze di Diego Alvarez Chanca e di Andrés Bernáldez*
Translation © 1992 by Gioacchino Triolo and Luciano F. Farina

© ISTITUTO POLIGRAFICO E ZECCA DELLO STATO - LIBRERIA DELLO STATO

NATIONAL COMMISSION FOR THE CELEBRATION OF THE
QUINCENTENNIAL OF THE DISCOVERY OF AMERICA

Scientific Committee for the Nuova Raccolta Colombiana:

PAOLO EMILIO TAVIANI, president; ALDO AGOSTO; GABRIELLA AIRALDI; OSVALDO BALDACCI; GIUSEPPE BELLINI; ALBERTO BOSCOLO †; FRANCO CARDINI; LUISA D'ARIENZO; GAETANO FERRO; FRANCESCO GIUNTA; ILARIA LUZZANA CARACI; GEO PISTARINO; FRANCESCO SISINNI.

ENGLISH EDITION OF "THE NUOVA RACCOLTA COLOMBIANA"

Published and printed by Istituto Poligrafico e Zecca dello Stato - Libreria dello Stato

Edited and translated by The Ohio State University

Volume Editors:

L. F. FARINA and C. K. ZACHER

Editorial Board:

L. F. FARINA; D. O. FRANTZ; J. B. GABEL; C. D. KLOPP; A. N. MANCINI; C. C. SCHLAM; C. K. ZACHER

INTRODUCTION

Two fundamental works about the Columbian period, Diego Alvarez Chanca's Letter, *sent to the municipality of Seville in February 1494, and the* Memoirs of the Catholic Sovereigns' Reign, *composed by Andrés Bernáldez before 1513, are presented together in this volume not only because Chanca's work was heavily consulted by Bernáldez but also because both works deal in a special way with Columbus's second voyage to Hispaniola, a fundamental stage of Columbus's enterprise.*

These two writings, while exhibiting a substantial connection, reflect different historical perspectives, since Chanca's report is the product of his direct experience, whereas the Memoirs *relies on other authors' works.*

Bernáldez was the parish priest of Los Palacios, a small town near Seville, who for his own pleasure undertook to compose an historical work in order to preserve the most important events of his time, which to a great extent coincided with the Catholic Sovereigns' reign. Thus, the Memoirs *chapters dedicated to describing the enterprises of Columbus overseas constitute only a part, even if an extremely remarkable part, of his entire writing.*

This study stresses, among the subjects discussed in this extensive volume, the themes relating to the discovery of the new lands and their exploration by the Spanish and the Portuguese. It additionally points to themes that shed light upon the times and environment of the protagonists of maritime expeditions along Africa's Atlantic coast and toward lands of the East and West.

In analyzing the chapters of the Memoirs *which treat the events described by Chanca, I have especially highlighted the modifications Bernáldez made to Chanca's original.*

The other works consulted by the parish priest of Los Palacios for his treatment of events which took place during the latter part of the second voyage are only partly known.

*By his own admission we know that the narrative of the events following the period described by Chanca is based on Columbus's own writings and this seems to be confirmed in the recently published letters [*Cartas-Relaciones*] of the* Admiral to the Spanish King and Queen. *Besides, among his sources, Bernáldez cites the voyage accounts by other people who had joined Columbus on the second expedition to the Indies, not mentioning, however, any one in particular.*

Although Bernáldez's work must then be considered a composite derived from several sources, it nonetheless appears to have at the same time great historical importance because it reflects both an un-official perspective (in terms of what Bernáldez chooses to report) along with his personal considerations, which emerge here and there as a comment on the information he presents.

The Letter *of Diego Alvarez Chanca, sent from Hispaniola via Antonio Torres to Seville's* Cabildo *[Mayor], has totally different characteristics from the* Memoirs. *First of all, it should be stressed that, except for Columbus's own testimony, the Andalusian physician's report, along with that of Michele da Cuneo, are the only documents concerning the second expedition in which events are related by participants. In judging it, the breadth of the themes dealt with must be considered along with the accuracy of the narrative, which focuses on an investigation of the sensations and the feelings about Nature, as well as the natives and the established relationship with them, including the first difficult permanent period on the island when Columbus's thinking was tested.*

*Until now, Chanca has clearly held for historians a position of secondary importance among chroniclers of journeys across the Atlantic, so much so that in the monumental series (*Nuova Raccolta*) of source material edited by Cesare de Lollis, in 1892, on the occasion of the fourth centenary of the discovery of America, the text of the* Letter *does not appear. The attention given by De Lollis to the report sent to the Sevillian municipality is mainly limited to the parallelisms and the differences found in its description of events as compared to other chroniclers.*

In the one hundred years elapsed since the fourth centenary Italian Raccolta, no edition of Chanca's writings has been published in Italy. Only on the occasion of this Nuova Raccolta *for the fifth centenary does the Sevillian physician's work become available, in the present volume, both in its Spanish original and in English translation.*

Chanca's Letter *has to be considered a document of great historical significance for understanding the complex discovery and colonization of the Indies, not only because it contains direct testimony of the events but also because it is the result of the experience of a doctor-physicist trained in medical science, a scientific field that in those decades recorded a profound transformation that would lead to the dissection of the human body and the elimination of the existing barrier between experimentation and theory in the first half of the 1500's.*

Among contemporaries this work had a large following, and it seems to have been considered highly trustworthy, in view of the fact that Bernáldez preferred it to Columbus's own writings.

Presenting this work in the original and in English translation serves the purpose of both enriching our knowledge of particularly important events in Western history, such as the exploratory journeys to the West, and offering at the same time some new elements about the environment in which Columbus's expeditions originated and took place.

ANNA UNALI

The transcription of the Letter *is by Consuelo Varela (*Cartas de Particulares a Colón, *J. Gil and C. Varela eds., Madrid 1984, 155-176).*

The transcription of the Memorias del reinado de los Reyes Católicos *is by M. Gómez Moreno and J. de M. Carriazo (Madrid 1962).*

The translation from Spanish is by Anna Unali and Rosa Vaccaro Turiella.

The geographical references are taken from Nuova Raccolta Colombiana, *Vol. I and II.*

As this work is being published, the editor turns a deferential thought to the memory of her Maestro, Professor Alberto Boscolo†.

DIEGO ALVAREZ CHANCA

"LETTER" TO THE *MAYOR* OF SEVILLE

Muy magnífico Señor: Porque las cosas que yo particularmente escrivo a otros, en otras cartas, no son igualmente comunicables como las que en esta escritura van, acordé de escrivir distintamente las nuevas de acá y las otras que a mí conbiene suplicar a Vuestra Señoría.

E las nuevas son las siguientes: que la flota que los Reyes Católicos, Nuestros Señores, enbiaron de España para las Indias e gobernación del su Almirante del mar Océano Cristóval Colón por la divina promisión, partió de Cáliz a veinte e çinco de Setiembre del año de *** años con tiempo e viento convenible a nuestro camino, e duró este tiempo dos días en los cuales pudimos andar al pie de cincuenta leguas; y luego nos cambió el tiempo otros dos, en los cuales anduvimos muy poco o nada.

Plogo a Dios que pasados los dos días nos tornó buen tiempo, en manera que en otros dos llegamos a la Gran Canaria, donde tomamos puerto, lo cual nos fue necesario por reparar un navío que hazía mucha agua, y estovimos ende todo aquel día; e luego otro día partimos, e fizonos algunas calmerías, de manera que estovimos en llegar al Gomero cuatro o cinco días, y en la Gomera fue neçesario estar algún día por fazer provisiones de carne, leña e agua la que más pudiesen por la larga jornada que se esperava hacer sin ver más tierra. Ansi que en la estada d'estos puertos y en un día después de partidos de la Gomera, que nos fizo calma, que tardamos en llegar fasta la isla del Fierro, estobimos diez y nueve o veinte días; desde aquí por la bondad de Dios nos tornó buen tiempo, el mejor que nunca flota llevó tan largo camino, tal que partidos del Fierro a treze de Otubre dentro de veinte días ovimos bista de tierra, y viéramosla a catorze o quinze si la nao capitana fuera tan buena velera como los otros navíos, porque muchas vezes los otros navíos sacavan velas, porque nos dexavan mucho atrás.

En todo este tiempo ovimos mucha bonança, que en él ni en todo el camino no ovimos fortuna salvo la bíspera de San Ximón que nos vino una que por cuatro oras nos puso en harto estrecho.

Most magnificent Lord: since the kind of news I privately write to other people, in other letters, is not the same as that which suits this report, I have decided to write of recent events and other information separately, addressing myself humbly to your Lordship.

The news is: the fleet which the Catholic Sovereigns, Our Lords, sent from Spain to the Indies under the command of their Admiral of the Ocean Sea, Christopher Columbus, left Cádiz, by the grace of God, on the 25th of September of the year *** [sic]. The weather and the wind were favorable to our journey for two days, during which we were able to maintain a fifty-league speed. For the following two days, however, the weather changed and we travelled very little or not at all.

As it pleased God, after those two days good weather broke out again so that in another two days we arrived at The Grand Canary where we had to land and refit one of the vessels that was taking on a good deal of water. We stayed there one full day and left on the following, but the sea was so calm that it actually took four or five days to reach Gomera. We had to stay in Gomera for some days in order to stock as much meat, wood and water as possible for the long voyage, which was to unfold far from sight of any land. So, counting the time spent in those ports and also the day after we left Gomera when we had no wind, which made us late in getting to Hierro Island, it took us 19 or 20 days. From then on, we had favorable weather, the best a fleet has ever had during such a long journey. We left Hierro on the 13th of October and in twenty days we sighted land. We would have sighted it in fourteen or fifteen days if the flagship had been a good sailing vessel like the others; many times the other ships lowered their sails so as not to leave us far behind.

During all of this time the weather was good and neither then nor during the whole trip were there storms except on Saint Simon's night, when one troubled us for four hours.

El primero domingo después de Todos Santos, que fue a tres días de noviembre, cerca del alba dixo un piloto de la nao capitana: «¡Albriçias, que tenemos tierra!». Fue el alegría tan grande en la gente que hera maravilla oír las gritas y plazeres que todos hazían, y con mucha razón, que la gente venía ya tan fatigados de la mala vida y de pasar agua, que con muchos deseos sospiravan todos por tierra. Contaron aquel día los pilotos del armada, desde la isla de Fierro fasta la primera tierra que vimos, unas ochocientas leguas, otros sietecientas e ochenta, de manera que la diferencia no hera mucha, e más trezientas que ponen de la isla de Fierro fasta Cáliz, que heran por todas mill e ciento; ansí que no siento quien no fuese satisfecho de ver agua.

Vimos el domingo de mañana sobredicho, por proa de los navíos, una isla, y luego a la man derecha paresçió otra. La primera hera la tierra alta de sierras por aquella parte que vimos, la otra hera tierra llana, también muy llena deárboles muy espesos; y luego que fue más de día començó a apareçer a una parte e a otra islas, de manera que aquel día heran seis islas a diversas partes y las más harto grandes. Fuimos endereçados para ver aquella que primero aviamos visto, allegamos por la costa, andando más de una legua buscando puerto para sorgir, el cual todo aquel espacio nunca se pudo hallar. Hera en todo aquello que paresçía d'esta isla, todo montaña muy hermosa y muy verde, fasta el agua, que hera alegría en mirarla, porque en aquel tiempo no ay en nuestra tierra apenas cosa verde. Después que allí no hallamos puerto acordó el Almirante que nos volbiésemos a la otra isla que paresçía a la mano derecha, que estaba d'esta otra cuatro o çinco leguas; quedó por entonçes un navío en esta isla buscando puerto todo aquel día para que cuando fuese neçesario venir a ella, en la cual halló buen puerto e vido casas e gentes, e luego se tornó aquella noche para donde estava la flota que avía tomado puerto en la otra isla, donde deçendió el Almirante e mucha gente con él, con la vandera real en las manos, adonde tomó posesión por Sus Altezas en forma de derecho.

En esta isla avía tanta espesura de arboledas que hera maravilla, e tanta diferencia de árboles no conoçidos a nadie que hera para espantar, d'ellos con fruto, d'ellos con flor, ansí que todo hera verde. Allí hallamos un árbol cuya hoja tenía el más fino olor de clavos que nunca vi, y hera como laurel salvo

Around dawn on the first Sunday after All Saints day, the third of November, a steersman of the flagship yelled "Hurrah! Land ho!" There was such general gaiety among the men that it was amazing to listen to everyone's well justifiable shouts and exclamations of joy: so tired of the dire living conditions and for having crossed water for so long, they all strongly desired land. That day the pilots of the fleet counted about 800 leagues between Hierro and the first land sighted; others counted 780. Really, the difference was not remarkable. Moreover, considering the 300 leagues between Hierro and Cádiz, they amounted to 1100 in all, so many that I do not know who would not be tired of seeing water.

That Sunday morning, from the bows of the ships we could see an island and just after that on our right a second one. The former, at least the side we observed, had very high mountainous land, while the latter was flat and quite dense with vegetation. As soon as dawn came, several islands began to appear from both sides. Over all, that day, six islands were seen in different directions and most of them were quite large. We set course to observe the one we had seen first and sailed along its coast for more than one league to find a port in which to anchor, but one could not be found all along that part of the coast. The visible side of the island was all mountainous, very beautiful and green down to the water, and it made us merry, for in that season there is hardly anything green in our country. Since we could not find port there, the Admiral decided to shift toward the other island which had appeared on the right and was four or five leagues away from this one. However, he left at the first island, for all of that day, one spare vessel, to keep on looking for a port in case it would have been necessary to return there. Finally, a port was found and houses and people were seen there. At once, that very night, the vessel returned to the fleet, which had landed on the other island where the Admiral, royal flag in his hands, had disembarked along with several men and taken possession in conformity with traditional right.

On this island there were woods so dense it was amazing to look at them and especially stupefying were the many species of trees unknown to everyone-some with fruits, others with flowers, and all was green. There we found a tree whose leaves had the most pleasant clove scent I ever before smelled. It was

que no hera ansí grande; yo ansí pienso que hera laurel su espeçia. Allí avía frutas salvaginas de diferentes maneras, de las cuales algunos, no muy sabios, provavan y del gusto solamente tocándoles con las lenguas se les hinchavan las caras, y les venía tan grande ardor y dolor que pareçían que raviavan, los cuales se remediavan con cosas frías. En esta isla no hallamos gente nin señal della; creímos que hera despoblada, en la cual estovimos bien dos oras, porque cuando allí llegamos hera sobre tarde.

E luego otro día de mañana partimos para otra isla que paresçía en baxo d'ésta, que hera muy grande, fasta la cual d'ésta que abría siete o ocho leguas. Llegamos a ella hazia la parte de una gran montaña que pareçía que quería llegar al çielo, en medio de la cual montaña estava un pico más alto que toda la otra montaña, del cual se vertían a diversas partes muchas aguas, en especial hazia la parte donde íbamos. De tres leguas paresçió un golpe de agua tan gordo como un buey, que se despeñava de tan alto como si cayera del cielo; paresçía de tan lexos que ovo en los nabíos muchas apuestas, que unos dezían que heran peñas blancas e otros que hera agua.

Desque llegamos más açerca vídose lo çierto, y hera la más hermosa cosa del mundo de ver de cuán alto se despeñava e de tan poco logar naçía tan gran golpe de agua. Luego que llegamos cerca mandó el Almirante a una caravela ligera que fuese costeando a buscar puerto; la cual se adelantó y, llegando a la tierra vido unas casas, e con la barca saltó el capitán en tierra e llegó a las casas, en las cuales halló su gente; y luego que los vieron fueron huyendo, e entró en ellas, donde halló las cosas que ellos tienen, que no avían llevado nada, donde tomó dos papagayos muy grandes y muy diferençiados de cuantos se avían visto.

Halló mucho algodón hilado e por hilar e cosas de sus mantenimientos e de todo traxo un poco; en especial traxo cuatro o cinco huesos de braços e piernas de ombres. Luego que aquello vimos, sospechamos que aquellas islas heran las de Caribe, que son abitadas de gente que come carne umana, porque el Almirante por las señas que le avían dado del sitio

similar to the bay tree, though not as big; I therefore think it was of the laurel species. There were different kinds of wild fruits that a few men incautiously tasted. No sooner had they tasted them with their tongues than their faces swelled up and they developed such a strong burning and pain to appear seized with rabies, which could be cured by means of cold things. On this island we could not find people or traces of them; we thought it unpopulated, and there we remained for two hours, since evening was approaching when we got there. Then, the following morning, we left for another island visible from the southernmost tip of this one. It was very large, seven or eight leagues away. We arrived along the side of a big mountain that seemingly reached the sky; in its middle there was a peak taller than all the others and from which many small streams flowed down in different directions, especially toward the side we were approaching. At a distance of three leagues appeared a gush as big as a buey[1], falling from so high that it almost seemed to descend from the sky; having been sighted from quite a distance, aboard the ships many bets were placed, either claiming they were white tops or water falls.

When we got closer, the truth was discovered and it was the most wonderful thing in the world to see from how high the water was falling, and from what a narrow space so great a volume of water originated. As soon as we approached, the Admiral ordered a light caravel to sail along the coast to find a port; while pushing forward and approaching land a few dwellings were spotted. The captain landed in a boat and reached the cabins in which the inhabitants lived, but the latter, as soon as they saw him and the others, fled. He then went into their homes and found all their belongings, since they did not take anything away, and from there he took two very large parrots most different from any seen before.

The captain found a good deal of unspun cotton, yarn and edible provisions and of everything he took samples. In particular, he took away three or four human arm and leg bones. When we saw this, we suspected these islands were inhabited by the Caribs, human-flesh-eating people. Also, the Admiral, based on information about that place he had been

---

[1] *Buey* is a measure for spring water. The waterfall here described is still in existence: [La Soufrière.]

destas islas, el otro camino los indios de las islas que antes avían descubierto, avía endereçado el camino por descubrirlas, porque estavan más cerca de España y también porque por allí se hazía el camino derecho para venir a la isla Española, donde antes avía dexado la gente, los cuales, por la bondad de Dios e por el buen saber del Almirante, venimos tan derechos como si por camino sabido e seguido viniéramos.

Esta isla es muy grande y por el lado nos pareció que avía de luengo de costa veinte e çinco leguas; fuemos costeando por ella buscando puerto más de dos leguas. Por la parte donde íbamos heran montañas muy altas; a la parte que dexamos pareçían grandes llanos, a la orilla de la mar avía algunos poblados pequeños e luego que veían las velas huían todos. Andadas dos leguas allamos puerto y bien tarde. Esa noche acordó el Almirante que a la madrugada saliesen algunos para tomar lengua e saber que gente hera, no embargante la sospecha e los que ya avían visto ir huyendo, que hera gente desnuda como la otra que ya el Almirante avía visto el otro viaje.

Salieron esa madrugada ciertos capitanes; los unos vinieron a ora de comer e traxeron un moço de fasta catorze años, a lo que después se sopo, e él dixo que era de los que esta gente tenían cativos. Los otros se dividieron, los unos tomaron un mochacho pequeño, el cual llevaba un ombre por la mano, e por huir lo desamparó; éste enbiaron luego con algunos dellos; otros quedaron, e d'éstos, unos tomaron çiertas mugeres naturales de la isla e otras que se vinieron de grado que heran de las cativas.

D'esta compañía se apartó un capitán no sabiendo que se avía avido lengua con seis ombres, el cual se perdió con los que con él iban, que jamás supieron tornar, fasta que a cabo de cuatro días toparon con la costa de la mar, e siguiendo por ella tornaron a topar con la flota. Ya los teníamos por perdidos e cornidos de aquellas gentes que se dizen los caribes, porque no bastava razón para creer que heran perdidos de otra manera, porque iban entr'ellos pilotos marineros, que por la estrella saben ir e venir hasta España; creíamos que en tan pequeño espacio no se podían perder.

given by the natives of the islands he had discovered during the previous voyage, wanted to set course toward those islands to discover them, since they lay closer to Spain and also since that was the most direct way to get to Hispaniola, where he had previously left some men. So, thanks to divine goodness and the Admiral's skill, we arrived so expeditiously that it seemed we were travelling through an already known and tested route.

This island[2] is very large giving us the impression that that side of its coast was 25 leagues long, and we sailed it along in for more than two leagues in search of a port. In the part we headed for there were many high mountains, whereas the area we were leaving showed large plains. Along the seacoast there were small clusters of hamlets whose inhabitants would all flee as soon as they noticed our coming. After two leagues, far into the night, we found a port. That night the Admiral decided that the following morning a few of the men would land to find out what kind of people they were, although it was assumed, since a few of them had been seen while fleeing, that they were naked people like those the Admiral had seen during his previous trip.

That morning a few of the captains went ashore. Some got back at meal time, bringing a boy of about fourteen, who, according to what was later learned and what he himself said, had been one of a number kept prisoners by those people. Others parted; some of them took and kept a little boy whose hand had been held by a man before he abandoned him in order to flee. Others yet, who stayed there, captured some native women of that island, whereas other women prisoners went with them quite willingly.

From that group, a captain and six men departed, unaware that information had already been gathered. He, and all those with him, lost their way and were not able to come back until four days later when they happened upon the seacoast and, following it, got back to the fleet. We had by then considered them eaten by the natives, being illogical to think they could disappear for other reasons when among them there were able pilots and sailors who, by looking at the stars, could get to Spain and return to these islands; we therefore held that in such a limited area they could not have lost their way.

[2] Guadeloupe.

Este día primero que allí deçendimos andavan por la playa junto con el agua muchos ombres e mugeres mirando la flota e maravillándose de cosa tan nueba, e llegándose alguna barca a tierra a hablar con ellos diziéndolos «taino, taino», que quiere dezir 'bueno', esperaban en tanto que no salían del agua, junto con él moran, de manera que cuando ellos querían se podían salvar. En conclusión, que de los ombres ninguno se pudo tomar por fuerça ni por grado, salvo dos que se seguraron e después los traxeron por fuerça. Allí se tomaron más de veinte mugeres dellas cativas y de su grado se venían otras naturales de la isla que fueron salteadas y tomadas por fuerça. Ciertos mochachos cabtivos se vinieron a nosotros huyendo de los naturales de la isla que los tenían cabtivos.

En este puerto estovimos ocho días a causa de la pérdida del sobredicho capitán, donde muchas vezes salimos a tierra andando por sus moradas e pueblos que estavan a la costa, donde hallamos infinitos huesos de ombres e los cascos de las cabeças colgados por las casas a manera de vasijas para tener cosas.

Aquí no parescieron muchos ombres, la causa hera, según nos dixeron las mugeres, que heran idas diez canoas con gentes a saltear a otras islas. Esta gente nos pareçió más pulítica que la que avita en estas otras islas que avemos visto, aunque todos tienen las moradas de paja, pero estos las tienen de mucho mejor hechura e más proveídas de mantenimientos e pareçe en ellas más industria ansí veril como femenil. Tenían mucho algodón hilado y por hilar y muchas mantas de algodón tan bien texidas que no deven nada a las de nuestra patria.

Preguntamos a las mugeres que heran cativas en esta isla que qué gente hera ésta; respondieron que heran caribes. Después que entendieron que nosotros aborreçíamos tal gente por su mal uso de comer carne de ombres, holgaban mucho y si de nuevo traían alguna muger o ombre de los caribes, secretamente dezían que heran caribes, que allí donde estaban todos en nuestro poder mostraban temor d'ellos como gente sojuzgada; y de allí conoçimos cuáles heran caribes de las mugeres e cuáles no, porque las caribes traían en las piernas en cada una dos argollas texidas de algodón, la una junto con la rodilla, la otra junto con los tovillos, de manera que les hazen las pantorrillas grandes e de los sobredichos lugares

That first day when we approached there many native men and women paced along the beach near the water, staring at the fleet in astonishment for such a new thing; and, while some people with the boats went ashore to talk to the natives, these, turning to the sailors, kept on shouting "taino, taino," which means "good," and stood by their dwellings until the Spaniards reached shore in such a way that, had they wanted, they could flee to safety. In conclusion, nobody could be captured, neither by force or voluntarily, except for two of them who felt reassured at first and later needed to be retained by force. More than 20 women were taken in all, including the women prisoners who willingly followed, and some other ones native to the island who were captured and forcefully taken away. Some boys ran to us, escaping from the natives who had kept them prisoners.

We stayed in this port for eight days because of the disappearance of the above-mentioned captain, for whom several times we went ashore, exploring all dwellings and villages that lay along the coast where we found quite a few human bones and skulls hanging inside the houses and used as containers to hold things. Here we could not see many men because, according to what the women told us, ten canoes had left to attack other islands.

These people seemed to us more civilized than those living on other islands we had seen. Although all of them own straw-made huts, these people build them better and appear to be stocked with more food and characterized by a superior type of resourcefulness, both the men and the women. They had much yarn and unspun cotton and many cotton blankets so well woven that they have nothing to envy of those from our country.

We asked the women kept prisoners there what kind of people the natives were and they answered they were Caribs. Upon realizing we detested such people on account of their bad custom of eating human flesh, they were most glad indeed; and whenever we would seize Carib men or women, they would tell us in secret they were Carib and, despite the fact that they all were in our power, they were still showing fear of them acting like enslaved people. From then on we recognized which were Caribs and which were not, since Carib women had on each leg two woven cotton rings: one near the knee, and another at the ankle, so as to enlarge the calves and make the above-named parts very

muy çeñidas, que esto me pareçe que tienen ellos por cosa gentil; ansí que por esta diferençia conoçemos los unos de los otros.

La costumbre d'esta gente de caribes es bestial; son tres islas, esta se llama Turuqueira, la otra que primero vimos se llama Ceyre, la terçera se llama Ayai; estos todos son conformidas como si fuesen de un linage, los cuales no se hazen mal: unos e otros hazen guerra a todas las otras islas comarcanas, los cuales van por mar çiento e çincuenta leguas a saltear con muchas canoas que tienen, que son unas fustas pequeñas de un solo madero. Sus armas son frechas en lugar de hierros, porque no poseen ningún hierro; ponen unas puntas fechas de huesos de tortugas los unos, otros de otra isla ponen unas espinas de un pez fechas dentadas, que ansí lo son naturalmente, a manera de sierras bien rezias, que para gente desarmada, como son todos, es cosa que les puede matar e hazer harto daño, pero para gente de nuestra naçión no son armas para mucho temer.

Esta gente saltea en las otras islas, que traen las mugeres que pueden aver, en espeçial moças y hermosas, las cuales tienen para su serviçio e para tener por mançebas, e traen tantas que en çincuenta casas ellos no pareçieron y de las cativas se vinieron más de veinte moças. Dizen también estas mugeres que estos usan de una crueldad que pareçe cosa increíble, que los hijos que en ellas han se los comen, que solamente crían los que han en sus mugeres naturales. Los ombres que pueden aver, los que son vibos, llévanselos a sus casas para hazer carneçería d'ellos y los que han muertos luego se los comen; dizen que la carne del ombre es tan buena que no ay tal cosa en el mundo, y bien pareçe, porque los huesos que en estas casas hallamos, todo lo que se puede roer todo lo tenían roído, que no avía en ellos sino lo que por su mucha dureza no se podía comer.

Allí se halló en una casa, coziendo en una olla, un pescueço de un ombre. Los mochachos que cativan córtanlos el miembro e sírvense de ellos fasta que son ombres y después, cuando quieren fazer fiesta, mátanlos e cómenselos, porque dizen que la carne de los mochachos e de las mugeres no es

narrow, leading me to think they considered it attractive. Thus, by this characteristic we could distinguish the Caribs from all others.

The Carib people's custom is bestial. There are three islands on which they live: one is called Turuqueira; the other, which we have seen before, is called Ceyre and the third Ayai.[3] All these people are similar, as if from the same ancestry, and they do not harm each other. They make war on all the other islands of the region and go by sea as far away as 150 leagues to accomplish their attack with the many canoes they have, small boats carved out of single tree trunks. Their arms are arrows instead of iron weapons, since they do not own iron; on some they put tortoise bone tips whereas on another island they use saw-toothed thorns from fish, naturally shaped like a saw and very resistant. Against disarmed people, like they all are, these tools can kill or cause severe injuries; however, against people of our country, they are not very dangerous weapons.

They assault the other islands and take with them the women they are able to seize, especially young and beautiful girls whom they keep as servants as well as lovers, and they take so many of them that in the fifty dwellings they had fled from more than twenty imprisoned girls followed us. The same women also reported the Caribs act with unbelievable but true cruelty, eating the offspring generated with the imprisoned women while raising only those conceived by women of their own kind. The men they are able to capture alive are brought into their huts for slaughtering and immediate consumption. They claim human flesh is so exquisite that a similar delicacy does not exist in the world, and this is clearly indicated by the fact that, of the bones we found in their dwellings, all that could be gnawed on had been gnawed on, and all that was left was what could not be eaten, because it was inedible.

There, in one of the huts, a human neck was found boiling in a pot. Young boys once captured have their members cut off and are kept as servants until adulthood, at which time, when the Caribs want to celebrate, they kill and eat them for the reason, they say, that boys' and women's flesh is

---

[3] One of the three islands is Guadeloupe. The other two could be Dominica and Marie Galante.

buena para comer. D'estos mochachos se vinieron para nosotros huyendo tres, todos tres cortados sus miembros. E a cabo de cuatro días vino el capitán que se avía perdido, de cuya venida estávamos ya bien desesperados, porque ya los avían ido a buscar otras cuadrillas po dos vezes, y aquel día vino la una cuadrilla sin saber dellos çiertamente. Holgamos con su venida como si nuevamente se obieran hallado. Traxo este capitán, con los que fueron con él, diez cabeças entre mochachos e mugeres. Estos ni los otros que los fueron a buscar nunca hallaron ombres, porque se avían huido, o por ventura que en aquella comarca avía pocos ombres, porque según se supo de las mugeres heran idas diez canoas con gentes a saltear a otras islas.

Vino él y los que fueron con el tan destroçados del monte que hera lástima de los ver; dezían, preguntándoles como se avían perdido, dixeron que hera la espesura de los árboles tanta que el çielo no podían ver e que algunos de ellos, que heran marineros, avían subido por los árboles para mirar el estrella e que nunca la podieron ver e que si non toparan con el mar fuera imposible tornar a la flota.

Partimos desta isla ocho días después que allí llegamos, luego otro día, a mediodía, vimos otra isla no muy grande que estaría d'esta otra doze leguas, porque el primero día que partimos lo más dél nos fizo calma. Fuimos junto con la costa d'esta isla e dixeron las indias que llevábamos que no hera abitada, que los de caribe la avían despoblado e por esto no paramos en ella.

Luego esa tarde vimos otra, a esa noche, cerca desta isla fallamos unos baxos por cuyo temor sorgimos, que no osamos andar fasta que fuese de día. Luego a la mañana paresçió otra isla harto grande. A ninguna destas no llegamos por consolar los que avían dexado en la Española e no plogo a Dios, según que abaxo pareçerá.

Otro día a ora de comer llegamos a una isla e pareçiónos mucho bien porque pareçía muy poblada, según las muchas labranças que en ella avía. Fuimos allá e tomamos puerto en la costa; luego mandó el Almirante ir a tierra una varca guarne-

not good to eat. Three of these castrated boys came to us. Four days into our stay the captain who had lost his way, and whose return at this point was unhoped for since twice other squads had gone to look for them and this very day one of those had returned unsuccessfully, did return. We rejoiced for their arrival as though they had come back to life. That captain and his men brought along ten other women and boys. Neither they, nor the ones who had gone searching for them, ever did see any men, either because they had escaped or perhaps because in that region there were few men or, again according to what was learned from the women, they had gone with ten canoes to assault other islands.

He and the others with him arrived so fatigued because of the exhausting mountain crossing that seeing them aroused our sorrow. When asked how they had lost their way, they replied that the foliage of trees was so dense that the sky could not be seen, and a few of them, being sailors, had climbed tree tops to get oriented with the stars but were absolutely not able to see the sky. Finally, had they not by chance reached the sea, it would have been impossible for them to come back to the fleet.

We left this island eight days after we had landed there, and right away, the following day, we saw another island to the south, not very large, and probably twelve leagues away, since for almost the entire day we left the sea was completely calm. As we approached the coast of this island the Indian women we brought with us claimed it was uninhabited, saying the Carib people had depopulated it, and therefore we did not stop there.

Later on that evening we saw another island and that night around this island, having found some shallow water, we fearfully anchored and did not dare to resume sailing until daybreak. Then, in the morning, another very large island appeared. We did not land at any of these islands, preferring to bring help to our people whom we had left on Hispaniola, a decision that did not enjoy God's favor, as it will be clearly seen later on.

The following day at mealtime, we arrived at an island[4] that made a good impression on us and seemed quite populated, given the many cultivated fields. We got there and took port on the coast; at once the Admiral commanded that a boat

---

[4] From the successive context and compared to other contemporary reports this island can be identified as Saint Croix.

çida de gente para si pudiese tomar lengua para saber qué gente hera, e también porque avíamos menester informarnos del camino, caso qu'el Almirante, aunque nunca avía fecho aquel camino, iba muy bien encaminado, según en cabo pareçió. Pero porque las cosas dubdosas se deven siempre buscar con la mayor çertinidad que averse pueda, quiso aver allí lengua; de la cual gente que iva en la barca ciertas personas saltaron en tierra e llegaron en tierra a un poblado de donde la gente ya se avía escondido. Tomaron allí cinco o seis mugeres y çiertos mochachos, de las cuales las más heran también de las cativas como en la otra isla, porque también éstos heran de los caribes, según ya sabíamos por la relación de las mugeres que traíamos.

Ya que esta varca se quería tornar a los navíos con su presa que avía fecho, por parte debaxo, por la costa venía una canoa en que venían cuatro ombres e dos mugeres e un mochacho, e desque vieron la flota maravillados se emvebeçieron tanto, que por una grande ora estovieron que no se movieron de un lugar casi dos tiros de lombarda de los navíos. En esto fueron vistos de los que estavan en la barca e aun de toda la flota. Luego los de la barca fueron para ellos tan junto con la tierra que, con el enveveçimiento que tenían, maravillándose e pensando qué cosa sería, nunca los vieron hasta que estovieron muy çerca d'ellos que no les pudieron mucho huir, aunque harto trabajaron por ello; pero los nuestros aguijaron con tanta priesa que no se les pudieron ir.

Los caribes desque vieron que el huir no les aprovechava, con mucha osadía pusieron mano a los arcos, también las mugeres como los ombres, e digo con mucha osadía, porque ellos no heran más de cuatro ombres y dos mugeres e los nuestros más de veinte e çinco, de los cuales firieron dos; al uno dieron dos frechadas en los pechos e al otro una por el costado, e si no fuera porque llevavan adargas e tablachutas e porque los invistieron presto con la varca e les trastornaron su canoa, asaetearan con sus frechas los más dellos. E después de trastornada su canoa quedaron en el agua nadando e a las vezes haziendo pie, que allí avía unos baxos, e tovieron harto que hazer en tomarlos, que todavía cuanto podían tiravan, e con todo eso el uno no lo pudieron

with some men go ashore to learn what kind of people lived there and also because we needed information about which way to follow, even though the Admiral, who had never crossed that way, was very well oriented, as he proved to be in the end. Nevertheless, since doubts should be verified to the utmost degree of certitude, he wanted to obtain there some information. Among the men on the boat, some jumped onto the shore and reached by land a village whose inhabitants had already gone into hiding. Here too they took five or six women and some boys; most of the women in this case too were prisoners of the Caribs, as on the other island, a situation we already expected on the basis of what the women with us had predicted.

And as this boat was heading back to the fleet along with its hold, there arrived from the shore side of the island, along the coast, a canoe with four men, two women and a boy who, upon seeing the fleet, were so dumb-founded and full of wonder that they stayed for a good hour without moving from where they stopped, within two lombard shots from our ships. Their stillness was noticed by those on the boat and also by the whole fleet. Almost immediately then, those on the boat came up on them as the natives stood there, so close to land and in astonishment, struck to the point they did not realize what was happening. As they kept on wondering and trying to understand what it was all about, they did not notice at all that they could no longer flee, although they tried to in every way; but the men from our boat managed to seize them very promptly.

The Caribs, both women and men, when they realized they could not get away, used their bows with great boldness, wounding two assailants; I say with great boldness because they were no more than four men and two women against ours, who were more than 25. They struck one with two arrows in the chest and the other with one in the ribs and, had it not been for the fact that they wore shields and wooden plates and also that there was a collision with the boat which capsized their canoe, they would have hit the majority of them with arrows. Even after their canoe overturned, they remained in the water, either swimming or touching the bottom with their feet since there were some shallows, and our men found it very difficult to overtake them as they were still, as far as

tomar sino mal herido de una lançada que murió, el cual traxeron ansí herido fasta los navios.

La diferençia destos a los otros indios en el ábito es que los de Caribe tienen el cavello muy largo, los otros son tresquilados e fechas cient mill diferençias en las cabeças de cruzes, e de otras pinturas en diversas maneras, cada uno como se le antoja, lo cual se hazen con cañas agudas. Todos, ansí los de Caribe como los otros, es gente sin barvas, que por maravilla hallares ombre que las tenga. Estos caribes que allí tomaron venían tiznados los ojos e las cejas, lo cual me pareçe que hazen por gala, e con aquello paresçían más espantables. El uno d'estos dize que en una isla d'ellos llamada Cayre, que es la primera que vimos, a la cual no llegamos, ay mucho oro, que vayan allá con clavos e conteçuelas para hazer sus [canoas] ⟨cambios⟩ y que traerán cuanto oro quisieren.

Luego aquel día partimos d'esta isla, que no estaríamos allí más de seis o siete oras, fuemos para otra tierra que pareçió a ojo que estava en el camino que avíamos de fazer, llegamos noche cerca d'ella. Otro día de maña⟨na⟩ fuimos por la costa d'ella, hera muy gran tierra, aunque no hera muy continua, que eran más de cuarenta y tantos islones, tierra muy alta e la más d'ella pelada, la cual no hera ninguna ni es de las que antes ni después avemos visto. Parescía tierra dispuesta para aver en ella metales; a ésta no llegamos para saltar en tierra, salvo una caravela latina llegó a un islón d'éstos, en el cual hallaron ciertas casas de pescadores. Las indias que traíamos dixeron que no heran pobladas.

Andovimos por esta costa lo más deste día, hasta otro día en la tarde, que llegamos a vista de otra isla llamada Burequen, cuya costa corrimos todo un día. Juzgávase que ternía por aquella vanda treinta leguas. Esta isla es muy hermosa y muy fértil a pareçer, a ésta vienen los de Caribe a conquistar, de la

possible, releasing their arrows so much so that, despite all of that, one of them was captured only after being seriously wounded by a lance thrust, of which he later died, and was brought so wounded to the fleet.

The difference between these Indians and the others in the way they adorn themselves is that the Caribs have very long hair whereas the others have their hair cut, with a thousand different decorative images on their faces, crosses and other symbols of varying fashion, as each of them likes best; and they do this by means of sharp reeds. All of them, both the Caribs and the others, are without beards, so that only rarely could you find a man who had one. The Caribs captured there had painted eyes and eyebrows, which — it seems to me — they do on purpose in a way to appear more frightful. One of them said that on one of their islands, Cayre,[5] which is the first one we saw and skipped, there is much gold that can be exchanged[6] with nails and trinkets and added that the Spaniards could get as much gold as they wished.

Well then, that day, we left this island, where we had stopped for no more than six or seven hours, and we set course toward another land, which we reached during the night and which at a glance seemed to lie in the direction we were going. The following morning we followed its coast; it was a very broad area consisting of forty or more not contiguous islets, some uncharacteristically mountainous and the majority was without vegetation, as we had noticed was typical for all the islands seen and for those yet to be visited. The kind of dirt they were made of seemed to be of the metal-rich type. We did not approach to go ashore except for a lateen rigged caravel which reached one of these islets and discovered some fishermen's cabins. The Indian women aboard said that they were not populated.

We went along this coast for most of that day until the following evening, when we came in view of another island called Borique,[7] and we sailed along that coast for an entire day. It was surmised that in this part the coast would extend for thirty leagues. It is very beautiful and most fertile in

---

[5] Probably Dominica.

[6] C. Varela's transcription reports both readings *canoas* and *cambios*, pointing out that the first one was erased and the second one added.

[7] Puerto Rico.

cual llevavan mucha gente; éstos no tienen fustas ningunas nin saben andar por mar, pero segund dizen estos carives que tomamos, usan arcos como ellos e si por caso cuando los vienen a saltear los pueden prender, también se los comen como los de Caribe a ellos.

En un puerto d'esta isla estovimos dos días, donde saltó mucha gente en tierra, pero jamás podimos aver lengua, que todos se fuyeron como gente temorizadas de los caribes. Todas estas islas dichas fueron descubiertas d'este camino, que fasta aquí ninguna d'ellas avía visto el Almirante el otro viaje; todas son muy hermosas e de muy buena tierra, pero ésta paresçió mejor a todos.

Aquí casi se acabaron las islas que fazia la parte de España avía dexado de ver el Almirante, aunque tenemos por cosa cierta que ay tierra más de cuarenta leguas antes d'estas primeras hasta España, porque dos días antes que viésemos tierra vímos unas aves que llaman rabiorcados, que son aves de rapiña marinas e no sientan ni duermen sobre el agua, sobre tarde rodeando sobir en alto o después tiran su vía a buscar tierra para dormir, las cuales no podrían ir a caer, segund hera tarde, de doze a quinze leguas arriba; y esto hera a la man derecha donde veníamos hasta la parte de España; de donde todos juzgaron allí quedar tierra, lo cual non se buscó porque se nos hazía rodeo para la vía que traíamos. Espero que a pocos viajes se hallará.

D'esta isla sobredicha partimos una madrugada, e aquel día, antes que fuese noche, ovimos vista de tierra, la cual tampoco hera conoçida de ninguno de los que avían venido el otro viaje, pero por las nuevas de las indias que traíamos sospechamos que hera la Española, en la cual agora estamos.

Entre esta isla e la otra de Buriquen pareçía de lexos otra, aunque no hera grande. Desque llegamos a esta Española por el comienço de ella hera tierra baxa y muy llana, del conoçimiento de la cual aún est van todos dubdosos si fuese la que es, porque aquella parte nin el Almirante ni los otros

appearance; there the Caribs go to plunder its inhabitants, which they carry off in large numbers. The latter neither own boats nor are able to go on the sea; however, according to the Caribs we had captured, they can use bows like them and if by any chance, during their attacks, they happen to be captured they exchange the favor, eating them like the Caribs do with them.

Since we stayed two days in a port of this island, many went ashore, but they were unsuccessful in gathering information, all of the natives having fled as they would from fear of Carib people. All of the above-named islands were discovered during this trip; in other words, the Admiral had discovered none of these during his previous expedition. Though they are all very beautiful and have the most fertile land, this particular one appeared to be the best of all.

This was the last of the islands oriented toward Spain which the Admiral had not yet seen, although we think for sure that there is another land more than forty leagues from these first islands to the west toward Spain. In fact, two days before we sighted land, we saw some frigate[8] birds that are predatory sea birds that do not stop or sleep on the water and that at night, making some turns, fly up high and then find their way to land and sleep, and since it was late they could not be more than twelve or fifteen leagues from shore. This happened to our right toward Spain, the side from which we were coming and consequently we all thought that there had to be land there, although we did not linger to look for it as it would have made us prolong the way we had to travel. I hope it will be found during one of the next crossings.

From this above-named island we left one morning and, that day, before night fell, we saw yet another land not known to any of those who had come on the first voyage; yet, according to information given by the native women with us, we suspected it was Hispaniola, where we are now.

Between this island and Borique there appeared in the distance another one, though not large. Since getting to Hispaniola we have seen, in that part, a low and very flat land, so that all were doubtful whether it indeed was the one that actually is, because neither the Admiral nor the ones

---

[8] For the translation of the term *rabiorcados* in Italian *fregate*, see *Nuova Raccolta Colombiana*, Note 35, Vol. I, pt. 2.

que con él vinieron avían visto, e aquesta isla, como es grande, es nombrada por provinçias, e a esta parte que primero llegamos llaman Haití, y luego a la otra provinçia junta con esta llaman Xamaná e a la otra Bohío, en la cual agora estamos; ansí ay en ella muchas probinçias porque es gran cosa, porque segund afirman los que la han visto por la costa de largo, dizen que abrá doszientas leguas, a mí me pareçe que a lo menos abrá çiento e çincuenta, del ancho d'ella hasta agora no se sabe.

Allá es ido cuarenta dias ha a rodearla una caravela, la cual no es venida hasta oy. Es tierra muy singular, donde ay infinitos ríos grandes e sierras grandes e valles grandes rasos, grandes montañas; sospecho que nunca se secan las yerbas en todo el año. Non creo que ay invierno ninguno en esta nin en las otras, porque por Navidad se fallan muchos nidos de aves, d'ellas con páxaros e d'ellas con huevos.

En ella ni en las otras nunca se a visto animal de cuatro pies salvo algunos perros de todas colores como en nuestra patria, la hechura como unos gozques grandes; de animales salvajes no ay. Otrosi, ay un animal de color de conejo e de su pelo, el grandor de un conejo nuevo, el rabo largo, los pies e manos como de ratón; suben por los árboles; muchos los an comido, dizen que es muy bueno de comer; ay culebras muchas, no grandes; lagartos aunque no muchos, porque los indios hazen tanta fiesta d'ellos como haríamos allá con faisanes, son de tamaño de los de allá, salvo que en la hechura son diferentes, aunque en una isleta pequeña, que está junto con un puerto que llaman Monte Cristo, donde estovimos muchos días, vieron muchos días un lagarto muy grande que dezían que sería de gordura de un bezerro, e atán complido como una lança e muchas vezes salieron por lo matar e con la mucha espesura se les metía en la mar, de manera que no se pudo aver d'él derecho.

Ay en esta isla y en las otras infinitas aves de las de nuestra patria, e otras muchas que allá nunca se vieron; de las aves domésticas nunca se a visto acá ninguna, salvo en la Çurruquia avia en las casas unas ánades, las más d'ellas blancas como la nieve e algunas negras, muy lindas, con crestas rasas, mayores que las de allá, menores que ánsares.

who had been there before with him had seen that part of the island and, since it is very large, it has different names for the various regions. Where we first arrived they call Haiti, whereas the other land area right next to it is called Samana, and the one in which we are now, Bohío. So, in it there are many provinces, for it is a very wide territory, to the point that those who have seen its coast claim it could be two hundred leagues long and it seems to me that it is at least one hundred and fifty, and its width is not yet known.

A caravel that left forty days ago to circumnavigate has yet to return. It is a very unusual land, with a great many wide rivers, big mountain chains, ample and treeless valleys and high peaks. I suspect the vegetation does not dry up at all during the year. I do not think there is any winter in this territory or in the others, since at Christmas there can be seen many nests, some with birds, others with eggs.

Neither here nor in the other islands have ever been seen any four-footed animals, except for a few multi-colored dogs, similar to those we know and much like the big curs; there are no wild animals. There is instead a furry animal like the rabbit, the same size as a newly-born rabbit, with a long tail and with fore and hind legs like those of mice, and it climbs trees. Many people that have eaten it say it is indeed tasty. There are several kinds of snakes, but not big ones, and lizards, though not numerous because the Indians like them a lot, as much as we like pheasants in our country. They are of different shape but of the same size as our lizards, except at a small island near a certain port called Monte Cristi, where we stopped for several days and where a large-sized lizard was often seen and described to be the size of a young calf and had the shape of a lance. Many attempts to kill it were thwarted by the dense vegetation where it could hide by the sea and never be caught.

On that island, and on the others, there are very numerous birds like ours and many others we had never seen before. We also never did see any domestic birds, except in Curruquia, where around the dwelli gs were spotted a few geese, mostly white as snow but some black, very gracious with low combs, larger than those of our country, yet smaller than wild ducks.

33

Por la costa d'esta isla corrimos al pie de cient leguas, porque hasta donde el Almirante avía dexado la gente abría en este compás, que será en comedio o en medio de la isla. Andando por la provinçia d'ella llamada Xamaná en derecho echamos en tierra uno de los indios qu'el otro viaje avían llevado, bestido e con algunas cosillas qu'el Almirante le avía mandado dar.

Aquel día se nos murió un marinero vizcaíno que avía sido herido de los caribes, que ya dixe que se tomaron por su mala guarda, e porque íbamos por costa de tierra, diose lugar que saliese una barca a enterrarlo, e fueron en reguarda de la barca dos caravelas çerca con tierra.

Salieron a la barca, en llegando en tierra, muchos indios, de los cuales algunos traían oro al cuello e a las orejas, querían venir con los cristianos a los navíos, e no los quisieron traer porque no llebaban liçençia del Almirante; los cuales desque vieron que no los querían traer, se metieron dos d'ellos en una canoa pequeña e se binieron a una caravela de las que se avían açercado a tierra, en la cual los reçibieron con su amor e traxéronlos a la nao del Almirante; e dixeron, mediante un intérprete, que un rey Fulano los enbiaba a saber que gente héramos e a rogar que quisiésemos llegar a tierra porque tenían mucho oro e le darían d'ello e de lo que tenían de comer; el Almirante les mandó dar sendas camisas e bonetes e otras cosillas e les dixo que porque iba adonde estaba Guacamari non se podría detener, que otro tiempo abría que le pudiese ver, e con esto se fueron.

No çesamos de andar nuestro camino fasta llegar a un puerto llamado Monte Cristi, donde estuvimos dos días para ver la disposiçión de la tierra, porque no avía pareçido bien al Almirante el logar donde avía dexado la gente para hazer asiento.

Deçendimos en tierra para ver la dispusiçión; avía cerca de allí un gran río de muy buen agua, pero es toda tierra anegada e muy indispuesta para abitar.

Along the coast of this island we sailed at a hundred-league speed,[9] since, from there to the place where the Admiral had left the men, the distance should have been such that the place would have been at approximately the central part or in the middle of that coast of the island. While going around Samana, we quickly sent ashore one of those Indians taken during the first voyage, who was dressed up and given some small insignificant things that the Admiral had ordered him to distribute.

That day died the Biscayan sailor who had been wounded earlier by the Caribs and who, as I already indicated, was struck for not having been sufficiently alert. Since we were sailing along the coast a boat was able to reach shore to bury him and two caravels kept watch over the boat near the coast. Many Indians approached the boat as it reached shore. Some, wearing bits of gold on their necks and ears, wished to go with the Christians to the vessels but were refused because they did not have permission from the Admiral. When they realized they were being rejected, two of them went in a canoe to one of the caravels that had approached land and which received and brought them benevolently to the flagship. They said, by means of an interpreter, that a certain k ng was sending them to learn what kind of people we were and to beg us to come ashore, because they owned much gold which they would share with us as well as whatever food they had. The Admiral commanded us to give them blouses and caps and other trinkets and answered that he could not stop since he was heading to where Guacanagarí was and that there would possibly be another occasion to meet him. Thus, off went the Indians.

We did not deviate from our course until we got to a port called Monte Cristi[10] where we stopped two days to study the configuration of the territory, since the Admiral considered unsuitable for a settlement the place where he had left the men.

As we went ashore to review the area and its surroundings we found close at hand a large river with very good water; however, it was all marshy land and minimally suitable to live in.

[9] Chanca in this passage confuses leagues with miles: it should be understood to be a one hundred-mile speed.

[10] Monte Cristi, on the northern coast of the Dominican Republic [Hispaniola].

Andando veyendo el río e tierra, hallaron algunos de los nuestros en una parte dos ombres muertos junto con el río, el uno con un lazo al pescueço y el otro con otro al pie; esto fue el primero día. Otro día siguiente hallaron otros dos muertos más adelante de aquello; el uno d'éstos estava en disposiçión que se le pudo conoçer tener muchas varbas. Algunos de los nuestros sospecharon más mal que bien, e con razón, porque los indios son todos desbarvados, como dicho he. Este puerto está del lugar donde estava la gente cristiana doze leguas.

Pasados dos días alçamos velas para el lugar donde el Almirante avía dexado la sobredicha gente en compañía de un rey d'estos indios que se llamava Guacamari, que pienso ser de los prinçipales desta isla. Este día llegamos en derecho de aquel lugar, pero hera ya tarde e porque allí avía unos baxos, donde el otro día se avía perdido la nao en que avía ido el Almirante, no osamos tomar el puerto çerca de tierra fasta que otro día de mañana se desfondase e pudiesen entrar seguramente; quedamos aquella noche no una legua de tierra. Esa tarde, viniendo para allí de lexos, salió una canoa en que paresçían çinco o seis indios, los cuales venían a prisa para nosotros. El Almirante, creyendo que nos seguravan hasta alçarnos, no quiso que los esperásemos, e porfiando llegaron hasta un tiro de lombarda de nosotros, e parábanse a mirar e desde allí desque vieron que no los esperávamos dieron buelta e tornaron su via.

Después que surgimos en aquel lugar sobredicho, tarde, el Almirante mandó tirar dos lombardas a ver si respondían los cristianos que avían quedado con el dicho Guacamari, porque también tenian lombardas, los cuales nunca respondieron, ni menos paresçían huegos ni señal de casas en aquel logar, de lo cual se desconsoló mucho la gente e tomaron la sospecha que de tal caso se devía tomar.

Estando ansí todos muy tristes, pasadas cuatro o çinco oras de la noche, vino la misma canoa que esa tarde avíamos visto e venía dando bozes, preguntando por el Almirante: un capitán de una caravela donde primero llegaron; traxéronlos a la nao del Almirante, los cuales nunca quisieron entrar hasta que el Almirante los hablase, demandaron lumbre para lo conoçer e después que lo conoçieron entraron. Hera uno dellos

While they continued to observe the river and the land, a few of our men found on one side two dead men near the river, one with a rope around his neck and the other with a rope around his foot. This happened the first day. The next day they found, a little further beyond, two more dead men, one of whom was in a position that revealed he had a long beard. Some of our men had more negative than positive feelings, and rightly so, since none of the Indians have beards, as I already stated. This harbor is twelve leagues away from the place in which the Christians lived.

Two days later we hoisted sails to reach the place where the Admiral had left his previously-mentioned people with a chief of these Indians called Guacanagarí, who I think is one of the most important rulers of this island. That day, we directly reached that location, but since it was already dark and given the presence of some shallows just where, the day before, the ship on which the Admiral travelled had been lost, we did not dare to take port near the coast until the next morning when the depth could be surely known and passage quite safely possible. That night we stopped less than one league from land. That evening, coming from faraway a canoe with five or six Indians appeared to be heading hurriedly toward us. The Admiral, thinking it would follow us as long as we did not move, had no intention to wait for them, whereas they, persisting, arrived within a stone's throw of us and stopped to observe, and from that position, realizing we were not waiting for them, turned around and kept on their way.

After we dropped anchor right there, in the evening, the Admiral ordered two lombard shots to be fired to check whether the Christians, left behind with the above-named Guacanagarí, would respond, since they too had some lombards. There was no response and neither fires nor signs of dwellings were found in that place, which generated a lot of concern in all of us, as we suspected what everyone should in such a circumstance.

Great sadness was all-encompassing, and four or five hours into the night the same canoe we had seen earlier that evening was approaching noisily. As it drew nearer the first of the caravels, they asked its captain for the Admiral. Taken to the Admiral's vessel, they did not want to go aboard until the Admiral had talked with them. They asked for a light to be shone on him so they would be able to identify him and, as

primo del Guacamari, el cual los avía embiado otra vez después que se avían tornado aquella tarde. Traían carátulas de oro que Guacamari enbiava en presente, la una para el Almirante e la otra para un capitán que el otro viaje avía ido con él. Estovieron en la nao hablando con el Almirante en presençia de todos por tres oras, mostrando mucho plazer; preguntándoles por los cristianos qué tales estaban, aquel pariente dixo que estaban todos buenos aunque entre ellos avía algunos muertos de dolençia e otros de diferençia que avía conteçido entre ellos, e que Guacamari estava en otro lugar ferido en una pierna e por eso no avía venido, pero que otro día vernía, porque otros dos reyes llamados el uno Caonabó y el otro Mariení avían venido a pelear con el e que le avían quemado el logar, e luego esa noche se tornaron diziendo que otro día vernían con el dicho Guacamari, e con esto nos dexaron por esa noche consolados.

Otro día en la mañana estovimos esperando que viniese el dicho Guacamari e entretanto saltaron en tierra algunos por mandado del Almirante e fueron al lugar donde solían estar, e halláronle quemado un cortijo algo fuerte con una palizada, donde los cristianos abitavan, e tenían lo suyo quemado e derribado e ciertas vernias e ropas que los indios avían traído a echar en la casa. Los dichos indios que por allí pareçían andaban muy cahareños que no se osaban allegar a nosotros, antes huían, lo cual non nos pareçió bien, porque el Almirante nos avía dicho que en llegando a aquel lugar salían tantas canoas d'ellos a bordo de los navíos a vernos que no nos podríamos defender d'ellos e que en el otro viaje ansí lo fazían; e como agora veíamos que estaban sospechosos de nosotros no nos pareçía bien, con todo halagándolos aquel día e arrojándolos algunas cosas, ansí como cascabeles e cuentas, ovo de asegurarse un su pariente del dicho Guacamari e otros tres, los cuales entraron en la barca e traxeronlos a la nao.

Despues que preguntaron por los cristianos dixeron que todos heran muertos, aunque y nos lo avia dicho un indio de los que llevabamos de Castilla que lo avian hablado los dos indios que antes avian venido a la nao, que se avian quedado al bordo de la nao con su canoa, pero no le aviamos creido.

soon as they recognized him, they climbed aboard the vessel. One of them was a cousin of Guacanagarí who had sent them back again after returning that evening. They brought golden masks that Guacanagarí sent as gifts: one for the Admiral and another for the captain who had gone with him during the previous trip. They remained on the ship conversing with the Admiral, in the presence of everyone, for three hours, showing much satisfaction. To an inquiry about the Christians, Guacanagarí's cousin answered that they were all well, except for the fact that among them some had died because of illness and others because of altercations which had arisen among them. He also said that Guacanagarí was in another place, wounded in the leg — and that was the reason he had not come, but that he would come the following day — because two other chiefs, Caonabó and Marieni, had attacked him and set fire to his village. Not much later that night, they left, promising to return the following day with Guacanagarí himself, leaving us behind, less worried for the night.

The following morning, as we were expecting Guacanagarí, some men, by the Admiral's order, had gone ashore to reach the place where the Christians had settled, a fortified encampment with a palisade in which they lived. It had been burnt to the ground and all belongings had been burnt and destroyed but for few woven pieces of fabric and cloth which the Indians had brought to throw into the houses. All of the Indians who could be seen there seemed very suspicious, did not dare to approach us, and indeed fled at first — not a good sign — since the Admiral had told us that, as they had done during the first voyage, many of their canoes would meet our approaching ship on one side to see us and that we could not defend ourselves against them. Noticing then that they remained suspicious toward us — again not a positive note — we nonetheless tried to flatter them by passing out such things as harness-bells and seed-pearls. We were thus able to reassure a relative of the above-named Guacanagarí and three others, who got in the boat and were brought to the ship.

When asked for information about the Christians, they answered that all of them had died, news which had already been told to us by an Indian of the group we had brought back from Castile who had talked to the two Indians who had earlier come with their canoe to the side of the ship; however, we had not believed him.

Fue preguntado a este pariente de Guacamari quien los avia muerto, dixo que el rey de Canoabo y el rey de Mayreni e que le quemaron las cosas del lugar e que estaban d'ellos muchos heridos e tambien el dicho Gucamari estaba pasado un muslo, y el que estaba en otro lugar y que el queria ir luego alla a lo llamar; al cual dieron algunas cosas e luego se partio para donde estaba Guacamari.

Todo aquel día los estobimos esperando, e desque vimos que no venían, muchos tenían sospecha que se avían ahogado los indios que antenoche avían venido, porque los avían dado a veber dos o tres bezes de vino e benían en una canoa pequeña que se les podría trastornar.

Otro día de mañana salió a tierra el Almirante e algunos de nosotros e fuemos donde solía estar la villa, la cual nos vimos toda quemada e los bestidos de los cristianos se hallavan por aquella yerva. Por aquella ora no vimos ningún muerto. Avía entre nosotros muchas razones diferentes; unos, sospechando que el mismo Guacamari fuese en la traiçión e muerte de los cristianos, otros les pareçía que no, pues estava quemada su villa, ansí que la cosa hera mucho para dubdar.

El Almirante mandó catar todo el sitio donde los cristianos estaban fortaleçidos, porqu'él los avía mandado que desque toviesen alguna cantidad de oro que lo enterrasen. Entretanto que esto se hazía, quiso llegar a ver acerca de una legua do nos paresçía que podría aver asiento para poder hedificar una villa porque ya hera tiempo, adonde fuimos çiertos con él mirando la tierra por la costa, fasta que llegamos a un poblado donde avía siete o ocho casas, las cuales avían desamparado los indios luego que nos vieron ir, e llevaron lo que pudieron e lo otro dexaron escondido entre yervas junto con las casas, que es gente tan bestial que no tienen discreçión para buscar lugar para abitar, que los que viben a la marina es maravilla cuand bestialmente hedifican, que las casas en derredor tienen tan cubiertas de yerba e de humidad que estoy espantado como viben.

En aquellas casas hallamos muchas cosas de los cristianos, las cuales no se creían que ellos oviesen rescatado, ansí como una almalafa muy gentil, la cual no se avía descogido de como la llevaron de Castilla, e calças e pedaços de paños, e una ancla

This relative of Guacanagarí was asked who had killed them and he answered that it had been Chief Caonabó and Chief Mariení, that they had burnt all their belongings, that many of them had been wounded, and also that Guacanagarí himself had been wounded in the thigh and was in a different place; he added that he wanted to go there right away to call on him. To him were given some things just before he went away to go where Guacanagarí was.

That entire day we waited for them, and when we realized that they were not returning, many suspected that the Indians who had come the previous night had drowned, since they had been given wine to drink two or three times and they were on a small canoe which could easily have capsized.

The following morning, the Admiral and a few of us went ashore to see the place i. e. the camp which we saw burnt down and where we found the Christians' clothes strewn on the ground. At that time we did not see any corpses. We were of several different opinions: some suspected that Guacanagarí himself was guilty of a betrayal and of the Christians' deaths; others were not of the same opinion since his own village had been burnt down, a fact that justified doubting he had done it.

The Admiral ordered to search the whole place where the Christians had dug in, because he had left instructions, once they would have taken a certain amount of gold, to hide it in the ground. While this was done he wanted to go and explore within a radius of one league to learn whether there might be a suitable place to build a town, since it had to be done. So I and some others went along with him, exploring the territory along the coast, and reached a village of seven or eight huts that had been deserted by the natives when they saw us coming, after taking with them what they could and leaving the rest hidden in the grass near the huts. These people are so savage that they have no rationality in seeking out a place to live, so that it appears strange to see how primitively those who live along the sea built their houses, which are all so overtaken by weeds and humidity that I am amazed at how they can possibly survive.

In those huts we found so many things belonging to the Christians that it was unrealistic to think they had been given in exchange, in particular a mantle so elegant that one could not explain why it had been brought from Castile. Also found

de la nao qu'el Almirante avía allí perdido el otro viaje, e otras cosas de las cuales más se esforçó nuestra opinión; y de acá hallamos, buscando las cosas que tenían guardadas en una esportilla mucho cosida e mucho a recabdo, una cabeça de ombre mucho guardada. Allí juzgamos por estonçes que sería la cabeça de padre o madre o de persona que mucho querían; después he oído que ayan hallado muchas d'esta manera, por donde creo ser verdad lo que allí juzgamos, desde allí nos tornamos.

Aquel día venimos por donde estaba la villa, y cuando llegamos hallamos muchos indios que avían asegurado y estavan rescatando oro, tenían rescatado fasta un marco, hallamos que avían mostrado donde estaban muertos onze cristianos, cubiertos ya de la yerva que avía creçido sobre ellos, e todos hablaban por una boca que Caonabó e Maireni los avían muerto, pero con todo asomavan quexas que los cristianos, uno tenía tres mugeres, otro cuatro; donde creemos que el mal que les vino fue de çelos.

Otro día de mañana, porque en todo aquello no avía logar dispuesto para nosotros poder hazer asiento, acordó el Almirante fuese una caravela a una parte para mirar lugar conveniente, e algunos que fuimos con el a otra parte, a do hallamos un puerto muy seguro e muy gentil disposiçión de tierra para abitar, pero porque estava lexos de donde nos deseávamos que estava la mina de oro, no acordó el Almirante de poblar sino en otra parte que fuese más cierta si se hallase conviniente dispusiçión.

Cuando venimos d'este lugar hallamos venida la otra caravela que avía ido a la otra parte a buscar el dicho lugar, en la cual avía ido Melchior e otros cuatro o cinco ombres de pro; e yendo, costeando por tierra salió a ellos una canoa en que venían dos indios, el uno hera hermano de Guacamari, el cual fue conoçido por un piloto que iba en la dicha caravela, e preguntó quién iba allí, al cual, dixeron los ombres prençipales, dixeron que Guacamari les rogaba que se llegasen a tierra donde él tenía su asiento con fasta çincuenta casas.

were trousers and a piece of cloth and an anchor from the ship which the Admiral had lost during the previous expedition and other things. All of this concerned us even more as we found there, among the things they preserved, in a small, very refined and hidden basket, a human head which had been kept with care. We inferred that it was the head of a father, a mother or a very dear person, only to later learn that many of these were found similarly preserved. I therefore think what we guessed was true and we left there.

That day we set out for the village and, when we got there, we found many Indians who feeling reassured had retrieved the gold, almost a *marco* of it. We came to learn from them where eleven dead Christians were, already covered by overgrown grass, and all of them, unanimously, claimed that Caonabó and Marieni had killed them. At the same time they gave indications of quarrels among the Christians, since some of them had three women, others four. Therefore we believe their misfortune was caused by jealousy.

The following morning, since in all that territory was not discovered a fitting place for us to be able to settle, the Admiral decided that a caravel would go one way to find such a suitable place, whereas others, and I too, who went with him in another direction, found a very safe port and a terrain configuration more apt to live in;[11] however, since it was far from where we hoped to find the gold mine, the Admiral discarded the idea of settling that area in favor of some other one that would provide greater safety if it could be found on an appropriate terrain.

When we came back from there, we were preceded by the caravel which had gone in the other direction on a similar quest and on which had sailed Melchior and another four or five experienced men. As they were going along the coast, a canoe headed toward them with two Indians, one of whom was recognized as the brother of Guacanagarí by one of the pilots that was on the above-mentioned caravel. After asking who was on board and learning the names of the main sailors, they revealed that Guacanagarí was begging them to go ashore to his village of some fifty cabins.

---

[11] It is certainly the location of present day Cap Haitien.

Los dichos prençipales saltaron en tierra con la varca e fueron donde él estaba, el cual fallaron en su cama echado faziendo del doliente ferido; fablaron con él preguntándole por los cristianos; respondió conçertando con la mesma razón de los otros, que hera qué Caonabó e Marieni los avían muerto e que a él avían ferido en un muslo, el cual mostró ligado; los que entonçes lo vieron ansí les pareçió que hera verdad como él lo dixo. Al tiempo del despedirse dio a cada uno d'ellos una joya de oro, a cada uno como le pareçió que lo meresçía. Este oro fazían en fojas muy delgadas, porque lo quieren para fazer carátulas e para poderse asentar en betún que ellos fazen, si así no fuese no se asentaría. Otro hazen para traer en la cabeça e para colgar en las orejas e narizes, ansí que todavía es menester que sea delgado pues que ellos nada d'esto hazen por riqueza salvo por bien pareçer.

Dixo el dicho Guacamari por señas, o como mejor pudo que porque él estava ansí herido que dixesen al Almirante que quisiese venir a verlo. Luego qu'el Almirante llegó, los sobredichos le contaron este caso. Otro día de mañana acordó partir para allá, al cual lugar llegaríamos dentro de tres oras porque apenas abría dende donde estávamos allá tres leguas; ansí que cuando allí llegamos hera ora de comer, comimos antes de salir en tierra; luego que ovimos comido mandó el Almirante que todos los capitanes viniesen con sus varcas para ir en tierra, porque ya esa mañana antes que partiésemos de donde estávamos avía venido el sobredicho su hermano a hablar con el Almirante e a darle priesa que fuese al lugar donde estaba el dicho Guacamari.

Allí fue el Almirante a tierra e toda la más gente de pro con él, tan atabiados que en una cibdad prençipal parecieran bien; llevò algunas cosas para le presentar, porque ya avía reçibido dél alguna cantidad de oro e era razón le respondiese con la obra e boluntad qu'él avía mostrado. El dicho Guacamari ansimismo tenía aparejado para hazerle presente. Cuando llegamos hallámosle echado en su cama, como ellos lo usan, colgado en el aire, fecha una cama de algodón como de red. No se levantó salvo dende la cama hizo el semblante de cortesía como él mejor sopo, mostró mucho sentimiento con lágrimas en los ojos por la muerte de los cristianos e començó a hablar en ello mostrando, como mejor podía, cómo unos murieron de dolençia e cómo otros se avían ido a Caonabó a buscar la

The leaders went ashore in the boat to where Guacanagarí was and found him on his pallet in the posture of one who suffers from wounds. They talked to him, asking about the Christians; he answered, confirming the reasons adduced previously by the others, namely that Caonabó and Marieni had killed them and had also wounded him in his leg which he was showing still bandaged. Those Spanish who saw him in this way had the impression that what he had said was true. At the moment of their departure he gave each of them a golden jewel, depending on how important they appeared to him. They work this gold into very thin layers because it is used to make masks as well as necklaces that require joining pieces together that otherwise would not hold. They also process some into artifacts to wear on their head and hang on their ears and in the nostrils; so it is imperative that it be thin, considering they do not do this to show wealth, but to look good.

Guacanagarí said with signs or as best he could that because he was wounded they should suggest to the Admiral to come and visit him. As soon as the Admiral arrived these Spaniards told him what they had discovered. The following morning, he decided to head for that place and we arrived there in three hours because it was only three leagues away from where we were. When we got there it was mealtime and we ate before going ashore. As soon as we finished eating, the Admiral ordered all captains to come with their boats and go ashore, because already that morning, before departing, Guacanagarí's brother had come to talk to the Admiral and to urge him to go to the chief's village.

There the Admiral went ashore along with most of the leaders and so well-dressed that they would have drawn praise even in a great city. He brought a few gifts to exchange because he had already received from the chief a goodly amount of gold and it would thus be reasonable that he reciprocate with actions and disposition equal to the Indian's. Yet, Guacanagarí all the same had arranged to give him some gifts. When we arrived, we found him lying in his hammock, made of a kind of cotton net, as is their custom, and hanging in the air. He did not get up, but from the bed he addressed us with a gesture of courtesy as best he could and showed deep emotion to the point of tears for the Christians' deaths, and began talking about that, saying, as best he could, that a few died

mina del oro e que allí los avían muerto, e los otros que se los avían venido a matar allí en su villa. A lo que pareçían los cuerpos de los muertos no avía dos meses que avía acaeçido. Esa ora él presentó al Almirante ocho marcos e medio de oro e çinco o seis çintos labrados de pedrería de diversas colores, e un bonete de la misma pedrería, lo cual me pareçe deven tener ellos en mucho.

En el bonete estaba un joyel, lo cual le dio en mucha beneraçión. Paréçeme que tienen en más el cobre que el oro.

Estávamos presentes yo y un çurugiano de armada; entonçes dixo el Almirante al dicho Guacamari que nosotros héramos sabios de las enfermedades de los ombres que nos quisiese mostrar la herida; él respondió que le plazía, para lo cual yo dixe que sería neçesario, si pudiese, que saliese fuera de casa, porque con la mucha gente estaba oscura e no se podría ver bien, lo cual él fizo luego, creo más de empacho que de gana, arrimándose a él salió fuera. Después de asentado llegose el çurugiano a él e començó a desligarle; entonçes dixo al Almirante que hera ferida fecha con «çiba», que quiere dezir con piedra. Después que fue desatada llegamos a tentarle. Es cierto que no tenía más mal en aquélla que en la otra, aunque él hazía del raposo que le dolía mucho. Ciertamente no se podía bien determinar porque las razones heran ignotas, que çiertamente muchas cosas abía que mostravan aver venido a él gente contraria.

Ansimismo el Almirante no sabía qué se hazer; pareçióle, e a otros muchos, que por estonçes fasta bien saber la verdad que se debría disimular, porque después de sabida, cada que quisiesen se podía d'él reçibir enmienda. E aquella tarde se vino con el Almirante a las naos, e mostráronle cavallos e cuanto aí avía, de lo cual quedó muy maravillado como de cosa estraña a él; tomó colaçión en la nao e esa tarde luego se tornó a su casa. El Almirante dixo que quería ir a abitar allí con él e quería fazer casas y él respondió que le plazía, pero que el lugar hera malsano porque hera muy húmido, e tal hera

because of illness and others had gone to Caonabó's territory to find the gold mine in the city, and they were killed there, while the rest had been seized and killed in their own camp. Judging from the appearance of the corpses, two months had not passed since the event. At that point he presented the Admiral with eight and a half *marcos*[12] of gold and five or six ornate belts with differently colored stones and a headgear adorned with the same type of stones, which they seem to hold in high esteem. On the headgear there was a jewel which he gave to the Admiral with great deference. It appeared they might appreciate copper more than gold.

I and a surgeon of the fleet were at the meeting; therefore, the Admiral said to Guacanagarí that we were experienced in human illnesses and that he should show us his wound. He indicated that this pleased him. I therefore suggested it would be necessary, if he could, to get out of the house, since, the many people in it made it dark and he could not be examined well. He did so right away, more, I think, out of embarrassment than real want, by leaning on me, and came outside. After he was seated, the surgeon approached him and started taking the bandages off, while Guacanagarí explained to the Admiral that it was a wound made by *ciba*, which means stone. When the leg was unbound, we gathered to examine it. It was obvious he felt no more pain in it than in the other leg, although he cleverly tried to show it hurt him very much. Given the unclear original circumstances, nothing could be established with certainty, especially when there were for sure many indications that he had been attacked by some enemy.

Similar indecision affected the Admiral and the others, who, at least temporarily, and as long as the truth was not known, felt they had to pretend then only to be able to ascertain things later and — if needed — obtain satisfaction from him. And that evening he came with the Admiral to the ships, where he was shown horses and all else there was, showing great amazement, as if confronted by a new thing; he ate on the ship before going back that evening to his quarters. The Admiral had expressed his wish to go live near him and his intention to build houses, and he learned that the chief was

---

[12] A half-pound unit of measure that was used for gold and silver. The Castilian pound was 430 grams.

él por çierto. Esto todo pasaba estando por intérpretes dos indios de los que el otro viaje avían ido a Castilla, los cuales avían quedado vibos de siete que metimos en el puerto, que los çinco se nos murieron en el camino, los cuales escaparon a uña de caballo.

Otro día estuvimos surtos en aquel puerto e quiso saber cuándo se partería el Almirante, le mandó dezir que otro día. En aquel día vinieron a la nao el sobredicho hermano suyo e otros con él e traxieron algún oro para rescatar, ansimesmo el día que allá salimos se rescató buena cantidad de oro. En la nao avía diez mugeres de las que se avían tomado en las islas de Caribi, eran las más d'ellas de Boriquen. Aquel hermano de Guacamari habló con ellas; creemos que les dixo lo que luego esa noche pusieron por obra, y es que al primer sueño muy mansamente se echaron al agua e se fueron a tierra de manera que, cuando fueron falladas menos, iban tanto trecho que con las varcas no pudieron tomar más de las cuatro, las cuales tomaron al salir del agua: fueron nadando más de una gran media legua.

Otro día de mañana embió el Almirante a dezir a Guacamari que le embiase aquellas mugeres que la noche antes se avían huido e que luego las mandase buscar. Cuando fueron hallaron el lugar despoblado que no estaba persona en él. Aí tornaron muchos fuerte a afirmar su sospecha, otros dezían que se abría mudado a otra poblaçión, que ellos ansí lo suelen hazer.

Aquel día estovimos allí quedos porque el tiempo hera contrario para salir. Otro día de mañana acordó el Almirante, pues que el tiempo hera contrario, que sería bien ir con las barcas a ver un puerto la costa arriba, fasta el cual abría dos leguas, para ver si abría dispusiçión de tierra para hazer abitaçión; donde fuemos con todas las barcas de los navíos, dexando los navíos en el puerto. Fuimos corriendo toda la costa e también éstos no se seguravan bien de nosotros; llegamos a un lugar de donde todos eran huidos. Andando por él fallamos

very pleased because of that, although the place was unhealthy being very humid — and so it certainly was. All of this was being communicated through two Indian interpreters who had been taken to Castile during the first expedition; in fact they were the only ones left alive of the original seven taken aboard and who barely avoided death (five had died during the journey).

The day after we dropped anchor in that port, Guacanagarí wanted to know when the Admiral would be leaving and was informed it would happen the following day. During that day, his brother, along with others, came to the ship and brought a certain amount of gold to make exchanges and did the same the very day of our departure when again a goodly amount of gold was exchanged. On the ship there were ten women, who had been taken from the Carib islands, most of whom were from Borique. Guacanagarí's brother spoke with them; we suspect he told them what was put into effect that very night. That is, during the first sleep, they very cautiously jumped into the water and fled to land. By the time we realized it, they had covered such a long distance that our boats were not able to recapture more than four of them and that happened when they were getting out of the water. They had swum more than a good half a league.

The following morning, the Admiral sent word to Guacanagarí that he had to return those women who on the previous night had gotten away and that he should send at once to search for them. When the messengers got there they found the place deserted with no one around. Consequently, many people's suspicions were reinforced; others claimed that they perhaps had moved on with another population, as was traditionally done. That day we stayed there because the weather was unfavorable for sailing.

Since the weather was unpropitious even the following morning, it was decided that it was more opportune to go with the boats to study a port farther along the coast, two leagues away, and verify whether the area was suitable for settlement. We then moved on with all the boats, leaving the ships in the port. We sailed up the entire coast and saw that the natives were still afraid of us, and from one place they had all fled. Exploring its surroundings, we found near the houses, up on high grounds, an Indian wounded by a sharp cane.

junto con las casas, metido en el monte, un indio ferido de una vara de una ferida que resollava por las espaldas, que no avía podido huir más lexos. Los d'esta isla pelean con unas varas agudas, las cuales tiran con unas tiranderas como las que tiran los mochachos las varillas en Castilla, con las cuales tiran muy lexos asaz çertero, es çierto que para gente desarmada que pueden hazer harto daño. Este nos dixo que Caonabó e los suyos lo avían ferido e avían quemado las casas a Guacamari; ansí qu'el poco entender que los entendemos e las razones equívocas nos an traído a todos tan afuscados, que fasta agora no se a podido saber la verdad de la muerte de nuestra gente. E no hallamos en aquel puerto dispusiçión saludable para hazer avitaçión.

Acordó el Almirante nos tornásemos por la costa arriba por do avíamos venido de Castilla porque la nueva del oro hera fasta allá. Fuenos el tiempo contrario que mayor pena nos fue tornar treinta leguas atrás que venir desde Castilla, que con el tiempo contrario e la largueza del camino ya heran tres meses pasados cuando deçendimos en tierra.

Plugo a Nuestro Señor que por la contrariedad del tiempo que no nos dexó ir más adelante, ovimos de tomar tierra en el mejor sitio y dispusiçión que pudiéramos escoger donde ay mucho buen puerto e gran pesquería, de la cual tenemos mucha neçesidad por el careçimiento de las carnes. Ay en esta tierra muy singular pescado más sano qu'el de España. Verdad sea que la tierra no consiente que se guarde de un día para otro porque es caliente e húmida, e por ende luego las cosas introfatibles ligeramente se corrompen. La tierra es muy gruesa para todas cosas, tiene junto un río prençipal e otro razonable asaz cerca de muy singular agua, hedificase sobre la ribera d'él una cibdad Marta, junto qu'el lugar se deslinda con el agua de manera que la meitad de la cibdad queda çercada de agua con una barranca de peña tajada tal que por allí no ha menester defensa ninguna; la otra meitad está çercada de una arboleda espesa que apenas podrá un conejo andar por ella; es tan verde que en ningún tiempo del mundo fuego la podrá quemar; hase començado a traer un braço del río el cual dizen los maestros

Injured all over up to his shoulders, he had been unable to get farther away. The people of this island fight with sharp canes which they throw with slings, just like the ones the boys in Castile use to throw little canes in a most precise manner and quite far away; they can certainly cause serious injury to unprotected people. This person told us that Caonabó and his supporters had wounded him and burned the houses of Guacanagarí; thus, the little that could be understood and the contradictory evidence created much confusion that we have no clear truth about our people's death.

That port did not seem suitable for a settlement. The Admiral decided we should keep sailing along the coast in a straight line in the direction we followed coming from Castile, since the information about the gold indicated it was in that part. The weather was so against us that we found it more difficult to cover thirty leagues [13] than the entire crossing from Castile. Because of the unfavorable weather and the length of the journey, three months had already elapsed when we went ashore.

It pleased Our Lord, because of the weather impediment which did not let us continue, that we be made to land on the best place and environment that could be found, where there is an excellent port and much fish, which we greatly need because of the scarcity of meats. There are in this place some very peculiar fish, better than those in Spain. It definitely is true that the region does not allow keeping them from one day to another because of its hot, humid climate in which perishable food quickly deteriorates. The earth is very fertile for everything: there is one large river and another nearly as big, with a peculiar water setting; on its banks a city called Marta [14] is being built inside the area delimited by the water, so that half of the city is surrounded by water and by a rocky precipice of such a shape that no defense is needed. The other half is bounded by woods so dense that scarcely a rabbit could penetrate and so green that in no season will a fire ever be able to burn it down. Work had started already to divert a branch of the river that, as experts put it, will go through

---

[13] Again, it should be miles.

[14] La Isabela.

que trairán por medio del lugar e asentarán en él moliendas e sierras de agua e cuanto se pudiere hazer con agua. An sembrado mucha hortaliza, la cual es çierto que creçe más en ocho días que en España en veinte.

Vienen aquí continuamente muchos indios y caçiques con ellos, que son como capitanes dellos, e muchas indias; todos vienen cargados de «ages» que son como navos muy exçelente manjar, de los cuales fazemos acá muchas maneras de manjares en cualquier manera; es tanto cordial manjar que nos tiene a todos muy consolados, porque de verdad la vida que se traxo por la mar a seido la más estrecha que nunca ombres pasaron, e fue ansí neçesario porque no sabíamos qué tiempo nos haría o cuánto permitiría Dios que estoviésemos en el camino, ansí que fue cordura estrecharnos, porque cualquier tiempo que viniera pudiéramos conservar la vida. Rescatan el oro e mantenimientos e todo lo que traen por cabos de agujetas, por cuentas, por alfileres, por pedaços d'escudillas e de plateles. A este age llaman los de Caribe «nabi», e los indios «hage».

Toda esta gente, como dicho tengo, andan como naçieron, salvo las mugeres d'esta isla traen cubiertas sus vergüenças, d'ellas con ropa de algodón que les çiñen las caderas, otras con yervas e fojas de árboles. Sus galas d'ellos e d'ellas es pintarse, unos de negro, otros de blanco e colorado, de tantos visajes que en verlos es bien cosa de reir; las cabeças rapadas en logares con vedijas de tantas maneras que no se podría escrevir. En conclusión, que todo lo que allá en nuestra España quieren hazer en la cabeça de un loco, acá el mejor d'ellos vos lo terná en mucha merçed.

Aquí estamos en comarca de muchas minas de oro, que según lo que ellos dizen no ay cada una d'ellas de veinte o veinte e çinco leguas; las unas dizen que son en Niti, en poder de Caonabó, aquel que mató los cristianos; otras ay en otra parte que se llama Cibao, las cuales, si plaze a Nuestro Señor, sabremos e veremos con los ojos antes que pasen muchos días, porque agora se fiziera, sino porque ay tantas cosas

the settlement: saw mills and everything else that is possible to do with water will be built on this river. They have sown many vegetables that clearly grow more in eight days here than in twenty in Spain.

Many Indians arrive here continuously and with them the caciques, who are like their captains, and many Indian women; all are laden with *age* [sic],[15] which are like rutabagas, an exquisite dish that we cook here in many different ways. It is a most nutritious food that has given much relief to all of us as indeed our living conditions during the crossing have been the most difficult ever borne by men. In fact, since it was unknown what kind of weather we would have and/or for how long God wanted us to continue sailing, it was good prudence to resort to rationing our food in such a way that we could save our lives no matter how harsh a weather we would find. The Indians exchange gold and food and all they own for buckles, seed-pearls and pins, for pieces of bowls and dishes. The Carib people call this food *nabi* and the Indians *aje(s)* (yams.)

All of them, as I mentioned, go naked like they were born, except for the women of this island, who keep their waists covered by means of either a piece of cotton fabric which girds their hips or weeds and tree leaves. As an embellishment, both men and women paint themselves, some in black, others in white and red, in such an imaginative way that seeing them will make one truly laugh; and their heads are shaved in patches with such various lock patterns that it is impossible to describe. In sum, all that in Spain we might wish to do on a mad man's head would here on the best of them be an object of refined attention.

We are here near a district with many gold mines that, in their opinion, are not more than twenty or twenty-five leagues away; they say some are found in Niti[16] in the territory of Caonabò, the one who killed the Christians; and others are in another area called Cibao.[17] There are mines, Our Lord willing, we will see and explore with our eyes not before long. In fact, we would do it now were it not for the fact we have so many

---

[15] For the *age(s)*, see *Nuova Raccolta Colombiana*, Note 62, Vol. I, pt. 2, 327-28.

[16] Hispaniola, exact interior location not identifiable.

[17] Hispaniola, on the central Cordillera.

de proveer que no bastamos para todo, porque la gente a adoleçido en cuatro o çinco días el terçio della. Creo la mayor causa d'ello a seido el trabajo e mala pasada del camino, allende de la diversidad de la tierra, pero espero en Nuestro Señor que todos se levantaran con salud.

Lo que pareçe d'esta gente es que si lengua toviesemos que todos se convertirían, porque cuanto nos ven fazer tanto fazen en hincar las rodillas a los altares, e el Ave María e a las otras devoçiones e santiguarse. Todos dizen que quieren ser cristianos, puesto que verdaderamente son idólatras porque en sus casas ay figuras de muchas maneras, yo les he preguntado qué es aquello, dízenme que es cosa de «Turev», que quiere dezir cielo; yo acometí a querer echárselos en el fuego e hazíaseles de mal que querían llorar, pero ansí piensan que cuanto nosotros trahemos que es cosa del cielo que a todo llaman «turev», que quiere dezir 'cielo'.

El día que yo salí a dormir en tierra fue el primero día de Henero, el poco tiempo que avemos gastado en tierra a seido más en hazer donde nos metamos e buscar las cosas neçesarias que en saber las cosas que ay en la tierra, pero aunque a seido poco se an visto cosas bien de maravillar, que se han visto árboles que llevan lana y harto fina, tal que los que saben del arte dizen que podrán hazer huenos paños d'ellas; d'estos árboles ay tantos que se podrán cargar las caravelas de la lana, aunque es trabajosa de coger, porque los árboles son muy espinosos, pero bien se puede hallar ingenio para la coger. Ay infinito algodón de árboles perpetuos tan grandes como duraznos; ay árboles que llevan çera en color y en sabor e en arder tan buena como la de avejas, tal que no ay diferençia mucha de la una a la otra; ay infinitos árboles de trementina muy singular e muy fina; ay mucha alquitira también muy buena; ay árboles que pienso que llevan nuezes moscadas, salbo que agora están sin fruto, e digo que lo pienso porque el sabor y olor de la corteza es como de nuezes moscadas. Vi una raíz de gengibre que la traía un indio colgada al cuello; ay también lináloe, aunque no es de la manera del que fasta agora se a visto en nuestras partes, pero no es de dudar que sea una de las espeçias de lináloes que los dotores ponemos; también se a hallado una manera de canela, verdad es que no es tan fina como la que allá se a visto, no sabemos si por ventura lo haze el

problems to solve and we cannot do everything because in four or five days one third of the men fell ill. I think the main cause of this general illness has been the work and the hard crossing in addition to the differences of this land; however, I hope in Our Lord that they will all regain good health.

It appears that these people, if we could communicate with them, would all convert, for they repeat what they see us doing: kneeling down at the altars, saying the Ave Maria and the other prayers, and making the sign of the cross themselves. All claim to want to become Christians since they are really idolaters inasmuch as in their houses there are different kinds of idols. In reply to my question as to what these objects were, they answered it had something to do with *turev*, which means heaven. I tried to throw these into the fire and made them so sorry that they were going to cry; however, they also believe that what we represent is a thing from heaven, for they refer to everything of ours as *turev*/heaven also.

The day I went to sleep on the mainland was the first of January. The little time we spent on land has been consumed in finding a place to settle and in looking for what is needed rather than in discovering what things there were in that territory. Nonetheless, in spite of the short time, we saw many things worthy of amazement: "wool-producing" trees and of great quality, too, so good that those who know the art affirm they could make good clothes with it. There are so many of these trees that the caravels could be loaded with wool, although it is arduous to gather it, for the trees are full of thorns. Yet one can certainly devise a system to gather it. There is very much cotton on evergreen trees, as big as peach trees. There is a wax-producing tree that for color, taste and burning characteristic is as good as the wax of bees, with not much real difference between them. There are numerous turpentine trees, whose product is very distinctive and of fine quality. There is great quantity of tragacanth which is also very good. There are trees that I think produce nutmeg, even if they are now fruitless; I say so on the basis of the taste and smell of their bark, which is much like that of nutmeg. I have seen a ginger root that an Indian wore hanging around his neck. There is also aloe, though it is of a different kind than the type known in our country; no doubt, however, it is one kind of aloe we physicians use.

defeto de saberla coger en sus tiempos como se ha de coger o si por ventura la tierra no la lle a mejor; también se a hallado mirabolanos çetrinos salvo que agora no están sino debaxo del árbol; como la tierra es muy húmida están podridos, tienen el sabor mucho amargo, yo creo sea del podrimiento, pero todo lo otro, salvo el sabor que está corrompido es de mirabolanos verdaderos; ay también almástica muy buena.

Todas estas gentes d'estas islas que fasta agora se an visto, no poseen fierro ninguno; tienen muchas ferramientas, ansí como hachas e açuelas hechas de piedra tan gentiles e tan labradas que es maravilla como sin fierro se pueden fazer. El mantenimiento suyo es de pan hecho de raíces de una yerva que es como entre árbol e yerva; e el age de que ya tengo dicho que es como nabos, que es muy buen mantenimiento; tienen por espeçia, por lo adobar, una espeçia que se llama «axí», con la cual comen también el pescado, como aves cuando las pueden aver, que ay infinitas de muchas maneras. Tienen otrosí unos granos como avellanas muy buenos de comer; comen cuantas culebras e lagartos e arañas e cuantos gusanos se hallan por el suelo; ansí que me pareçe es mayor su bestialidad que de ninguna bestia del mundo.

Después de una vez aver determinado el Almirante de dexar de descobrir las minas fasta primero embiar los navíos, que se avían de partir a Castilla, por la mucha enfermedad que avía seido en la gente, acordó de enbiar dos cuadrillas con dos capitanes, el uno a Cibao y el otro a Niti, donde está Caonabó de que ya he dicho; los cuales fueron e vinieron, el uno a veinte días de henero e el otro a veinte e uno; el que fue a Cibao halló oro en tantas partes que no lo osa ombre dezir, que de verdad en más de çincuenta arroyos e ríos hallaban oro e fuera de los ríos por tierra, de manera que en toda aquella provinçia dize que doquiera que lo quieran buscar lo hallarán. Traxo muestra de muchas partes como en la arena de los ríos e en las hontizuelas que están sobre tierra; créese que cabando, como

Also, a sort of cinnamon was detected, though not as fine as that found in our country; we do not know whether this is due to the fact that it is not harvested at the right time, when it is ripe, or perhaps because the ground does not produce it any better. We also found yellowish myrobolans, except that now we find only those fallen to the ground under the trees and, since the ground is very humid, they are putrefying and have the very bitter taste of decay, I think; however, leaving aside the adulterated taste they are real myrobolans. There is also very good mastic from the mastic tree.

None of the peoples of these islands, of those seen so far, know iron at all; they have many tools, such as stone axes and hatchets, so fine and well-worked that it is amazing to think they can be made without iron. Their food consists of a bread made from a weed root which is half-way between a weed and a tree; it is the *aje* [yam] of which I have already written, similar to the rutabaga plant and an excellent nourishment; they traditionally use it in cooking, along with a spice called *aji*[18] [their pepper], eaten also with fish and birds, when they can catch them. There are great numbers and species of birds. Likewise, they have nuts like hazelnuts which are very good to eat. They eat all snakes, lizards, spiders and worms that can be found all over the land, making these people more similar to animals, as far as I am concerned, more than all others in the world.

After the Admiral decided to renounce the idea of finding the mines before sending off the ships that were to leave for Castile, given the widespread illness affecting so many people, he also decided to send two armed groups of men with two captains to Cibao and to Niti, where the Indian king Caonabó, lived. They went and came back, one on January 20 and the other on the twenty-first. The one who was in Cibao found so much gold in so many places that no man could ever imagine since they indeed struck it in more than fifty brooks and rivers and even outside the rivers, on land. He therefore asserts that in that region wherever one would want to look for gold one would surely find it. He brought samples from many places, from river sands as well as from springs found on that land.

---

[18] See *Nuova Raccolta Colombiana*, Note 64, Vol. I, pt. 2, 333-34.

sabemos hazer, se hallará en mayores pedaços, porque los indios no saben cabar ni tienen con qué puedan cabar de un palmo arriba.

El otro que fue a Niti traxo también nueva de mucho oro en tres o cuatro partes, ansimesmo traxo la muestra d'ello. Ansí que de çierto los Reyes, nuestros Señores, desde agora se pueden tener por los más prósperos e más ricos Príncipes del mundo, porque tal cosa hasta agora no se a visto ni leído de ninguno en el mundo, porque verdaderamente a otro camino que los navíos buelvan pueden llevar tanta cantidad de oro que se puedan maravillar cualesquiera que lo supieren. Aquí me pareçe será bien çesar el cuento; creo que los que me conoçen que oyeren estas cosas, me ternan por prolixo e por ombre que ha alargado algo, pero Dios es testigo que yo no he traspasado una jota los términos de la verdad.

It is thought that through digging, as we are able to do, larger pieces of gold will be found, since the Indians are neither able to dig nor have the tools with which to dig more than a palm deep.

The other captain, who went to Niti, also brought back news of the existence of much gold in three or four areas and in like fashion brought samples of it. In this manner, our Sovereign Lords can now consider themselves to be the most prosperous and wealthiest princes in the world: similar riches have until now neither been seen or read about by anybody in the world. Truly, in a future trip, when the vessels shall return, they will be able to gather such a large quantity of gold that will amaze anyone who shall hear of it. At this point it seems proper to me to put an end to this narration; I know that those who know me when they hear of these things will judge me to have lingered and exaggerated some details but, as God is my witness, I have not distorted in the least the substance of the truth.

ANDRÉS BERNÁLDEZ

MEMOIRS OF THE CATHOLIC SOVEREIGNS' REIGN

CAPITULO CXVIII

Del almirante Cristóval Colón y de la navegación que fizo por el mar Océano fasta que descubrió l s Indias de donde se trae el oro. De la forma que tuvo Cristóval Colón con los indios. De las canoas en que navegan los indios. De la isla Juana. De la isla Española. De la isla de los caribes. De cómo Cristóval Colón tornó a Castilla de su navegación.

En el nonbre de Dios todopoderoso: Ovo un honbre de tierra de Milán, mercader de libros de estanpa, que tratava en esta tierra del Andaluzía, y principalmente en Sevilla, que llamavan Cristóval Colón, onbre de muy alto engenio sin saber muchas letras, muy astuto en el arte de la cosmografia del repartir del mundo. El cual sentió, por lo que de Tolomeo leyó e por otros libros e por su delgadez, cómo e en qué manera el mundo este en que nascemos e andamos está fixo entre la esfera de los cielos; que non llega por nenguna parte a los cielos ni a otra cosa de firmeza a que se arrime, salvo tierra e agua, abraçada en rendondez entre la oquedad de los cielos.

E sentió por qué vía se hallaría tierra de mucho oro, e sentió cómo este mundo e firmamiento de tierra e agua es todo andable en derredor por tierra e por agua, segund cuenta Juan de Mandavilla: Quien toviese tales navíos e a quien Dios quisiese guardar por mar e por tierra, por cierto él podía ir e trasponer por el poniente, de en derecho del cabo de Sant Vicente, e bolver por Iherusalem e Roma, e dende a Sevilla, que sería cercar toda la rendondez de tierra e agua del mundo. E fizo, por su engenio, un mapa mundi desto, e estudió mucho en ello; e sentió que por cualquier parte del mar Océano andando e travesando non se podía errar tierra, e sentió que por cual tierra hallaría más oro.

CHAPTER CXVIII

Admiral Christopher Columbus and the navigation he conducted in the Ocean Sea up to the discovery of the Indies where gold is found. Columbus's attitude toward the Indians. The canoes used by the Indians to navigate. Juana, Hispaniola and the Caribs' island. Columbus's return to Castile.

In omnipotent God's name: there was a man from the land of Milan, a merchant of printed books who worked in the land of Andalusia and principally in Seville under the name of Christopher Columbus, a man of great talent, not particularly cultured although quite skilled in cosmography and the art of world cartography. Based upon what he had read in Ptolemy and in other texts, and by means of his reasoning ability, this man concluded that the earth, where we are born and live, is set within the world, that it does not at any point reach the horizons, that it is not anchored on anything, and is surrounded by land and water in the hollow of the universe.

He conceived a plan and a way by which a land with much gold would be found and by which this world and universe of land and water could be charted all around by land and water. According to John Mandeville's account, whoever owned a fitting ship that would enjoy God's protection on land and sea would certainly be able to sail westward, always in a straight line from Cape St. Vincent, and return afterward, through Jerusalem and Rome, to Seville. And that would amount to travelling in a circle around the whole round earth and the waters of the world. Thanks to his talent, he designed a world map based on this premise and studied it so thoroughly as to formulate the idea that by crossing any part of the Ocean Sea a land would be reached and guessed also that in such land he would find much gold.

E sabiendo que al rey don Iuan de Portogal aplazía mucho el descobrir, él se le fué a conbidar; e recontando el fecho de su imaginación, non le fué dado crédito, porque el rey de Portogal tenía muy altos e fundados pensamientos e marineros muy extremados, que lo non estimaron, e presumían en el mundo non aver otros descubridores mayores que ellos.

Así que Cristóval Colón se vino a la corte del rey don Fernando e de la reina doña Isabel, e les fizo relación de su imaginación; al cual tanpoco no davan mucho crédito, e él les platicó muy de cierto lo que les dezía e les mostró el mapa mundi, de manera que les puso en deseo de saber de aquellas tierras. E dexando a él, llamaron onbres sabios, estrólogos e astrónomos e onbres de la arte de la Cosmografía, de quien se informaron; e la opinión de los más dellos, oída la plática de Cristóval Colón, se falló que dezía verdad; de manera que el rey y la reina se aficionaron a él, e le mandaron dar tres navíos, en Sevilla, bastecidos por el tienpo que él pedía de gente e bituallas, e lo enbiaron en nonbre de Dios e de Nuestra Señora a descobrir.

El cual partió de Palos en el mes de setienbre del año de mill e cuatrocientos y noventa y dos años, e tomó su vía por el mar adelante a las islas de Cabo Verde; e dende, sienpre el ocidente en popa, fazia donde nos vemos poner el sol en el mes de março, por donde todos los marineros creían ser imposible fallar tierra. E muchas vezes los reyes de Portogal enbiaron por aquella vía a descobrir tierras, porque la opinión de muchos era que por aquella vía se hallarían tierras muy ricas de oro, e nunca pudieron hallar ni descobrir tierra alguna; sienpre se bolvían con el trabajo perdido. Y la buena ventura del rey y de la reina, e su merescer, quiso Dios que en su tienpo e días se hallase, e la fallasen e descubriesen ellos.

Ansí, en uno de los tres navíos, iva por capitán Martín Alonso Pinçon, vecino de Palos, grand marinero e onbre de buen consejo para la mar; e desde las islas de Cabo Verde fueron fazia donde era la creencia de Colón, el capitán del armada, e andovieron treinta y tres días hasta que fallaron tierra. E en los postreros días destos, viendo que avían andado más de mill leguas e non descubrían la tierra, las opiniones de los marineros eran muchas, que dellos dezían que ya no era razón de andar más, que ivan sin remedio perdidos e que sería

Then, knowing that King Joao of Portugal cared greatly about explorations, he went to his court to offer his services. Having presented his rational conclusions, he was not believed for the reasons that the King of Portugal had very detailed and erudite information as well as quite skilled seamen who considered his plan unrealizable and who presumed that discoverers greater than themselves did not exist in the world.

So, Christopher Columbus went to the court of King Ferdinand and Queen Isabela, and presented to them what he believed. They also did not put much faith in him, but he persisted, being certain of what he claimed and showed them his globe stimulating in them the desire to know about those lands. After talking with him they sent for learned men with whom they conferred: astrologers, astronomers and experts in the art of cosmography. The opinion of the majority, after hearing Columbus's arguments, was that he was right. Thus, the King and Queen took a liking to him and commanded that he be given three ships at Seville, equipped for the length of time he requested with men and provisions and sent him off to discover in the name of God and of Our Lady.

He left Palos in the month of September of the year 1492 and headed for the open sea off the Cape Verde Islands. Then, always heading in a westerly direction, he set out to follow the setting of the sun in the month of March, the direction where all sailors thought impossible to find land. The king of Portugal had many times sent men to discover lands in that same direction, being then commonly believed that way beyond lay lands very rich in gold. Yet, none was ever found or discovered and so they always returned, after laboring in vain. Instead, for the good luck of the King and Queen and because of their merits, God wished that during their life and their reign, much land be sought, discovered and explored.

The captain of one of the three ships was Martin Alonzo Pinzón, a resident of Palos, a great sailor and a man of sound judgement about the sea. From the Cape Verde Islands they sailed in the direction Columbus, captain of the fleet, considered right to follow and they travelled for thirty-three days before finding land. During the last days, noticing that more than a thousand leagues had been travelled without finding any land, the sailors' opinions were several: some of them claimed that there was no longer reason to go any farther, that they were lost

maravilla acertar a bolver, e desta opinión eran los más; e Colón y los capitanes con dulces palabras los convencieron que anduviesen más e que fuesen ciertos que con ayuda de Dios fallarían tierra.

E Cristóval Colón miró al cielo un día, e vido aves ir bolando muy altas de una parte facia otra, e mostrólas a los conpañeros diziéndoles las buenas nuevas; e dende a día e medio vieron tierra. Y llegados en ella, perdieron después el navío mayor en la Española, que encalló en tierra, en un baxo, e non se perdió nengund onbre. E en la primera isla salieron, e Colón tomó posesión de la tierra en forma, por el rey y por la reina, «con pregón e vandera real estendida», e púsole nonbre la isla de Sant Salvador e llámanla los de allá Guanahani; e allí vieron cómo todas las gentes de aquella tierra andavan desnudas como nascieron, así onbres como mugeres; y allí, aunque huían de las gentes de acá, ovieron de llegar a fablar con algunos de aquellos indios, e diéronles de lo que llevavan, con que los aseguraron.

A la segunda isla que hallaron puso nonbre isla de Santa María, a onrra de Nuestra Señora; a la tercera isla que halló puso nonbre Fernandina, en memoria del rey don Fernando; a la cuarta isla que falló puso nonbre la Isabela, en memoria de la reina doña Isabel; a la quinta isla que halló puso nonbre Juana, en memoria del príncipe don Juan. Y así a cada isla que hallaron nominaron de nonbre nuevo.

E esta isla Juana seguieron el costado della al poniente, e falláronla tan grande que pensaron que tierra firme sería; e como no hallassen villas ni lugares en la costa de la mar della, salvo pequeñas poblaciones, con las gentes de las cuales non podían aver fabla, porque luego huían como los vieron, volvieron atrás a un señalado puerto de donde Cristóval Colón enbió dos onbres la tierra adentro para saber si avía rey o grandes cibdades; los cuales andovieron por la tierra tres jornadas e fallaron infinitas poblaciones, todas de madera e paja, con gentes sin número, mas non en cosa de regimiento, por lo cual se bolvieron; e los indios que ya tenían tomados dixieron por

beyond remedy and that only by an extraordinary feat would they be able to return. Most of them thought so, but Columbus and the captains persuaded them to go farther with convincing words while assuring them that, with God's help, they would sight land.

One day Columbus looked to the sky and saw birds that were flying very high, from one direction to the other, and he pointed this out to his mates, predicting good news to them; indeed, a day and a half later they sighted land. Then, right there at Hispaniola they lost their biggest ship, which ran aground on a shoal, although without losing a single man. They landed on the first island where Columbus took formal possession of the territory in the name of the King and Queen, with the flag and the royal banners unfurled, and named it San Salvador, though its inhabitants call it Guanahani[1] and there they saw how all of the native people went naked as they were born, both men and women. And there, though avoided by fleeing natives our people were able to talk to some Indians and give them of what they had brought, thus reassuring them.

Columbus named the second island he found Santa Maria in honor Our Lady; the third island he found he named Fernandina,[2] to remember the King, Don Ferdinand; the fourth island he named La Isabela,[3] to remember Queen Isabela; the fifth island he named Juana,[4] to remember the prince, Don Juan. In this way he named every discovered island found.

They followed the coast of Juana westward and found it so vast they thought it was mainland. They neither encountered cities nor inhabited places along its coast, except small settlements of people with whom they were unable to communicate, as the natives fled the moment they saw the newcomers. So, they returned to a known harbor, from where Columbus sent two men inland to learn whether there were any kings or big cities. They explored the territory for three days and found most numerous wood and straw villages and innumerable people not subjected to any government. Thus, they returned and the Indians they had already taken communicated with

---

[1] Today's San Salvador.

[2] Long Island, Bahamas.

[3] Crooked Island.

[4] Cuba.

señas que aquélla no era tierra firme salvo isla. E siguieron la costa della al oriente fasta ciento e siete leguas, donde le fallaron fin por aquel cabo; e desde allí vieron otra isla, al oriente, distante desta diez e ocho leguas, a la cual puso nonbre Cristóval Colón la Española.

E fueron allá e seguieron la parte del sententrión así como de la Juana, la cual e todas las otras vieron ser hermosas en demasiado grado; e esta Española mucho más fermosa que todas las otras, ca en ella ay muchos puertos en la costa de la mar, muy singulares, sin conparaciòn, de los buenos, los mejores que en tierra de cristianos se pueden fallar, e muchos ríos buenos e grandes a maravilla.

Las tierras della son altas, e en ellas ay muchas sierras e montañas altísimas e todas muy fermosas, de mill fechuras, e todas andables y llenas de árboles de mill naturas e muy altos, que paresce que llegan al cielo; creo que jamás pierden la hoja, segund por ellos parescía, que era en el tienpo que acá es invierno, cuando todos los más de los árboles tienen perdida la hoja, e allá estavan todos como están acá en el mes de mayo; e dellos estavan floridos, e dellos con sus frutos. E allí en aquellas arboledas cantava el ruiseñor e otros pájaros, en las mañanas, en el mes de novienbre, como hazen acá en mayo; allí ay palmas de seis o siete maneras, que es admiración verlas por la diversidad dellas; e de los otros árboles e frutos e yervas que en ellas ay es maravilla. Ay pinares e vegas e canpiñas grandísimas; ay aves de muchas maneras, e frutas, mas no como las de acá; ay minas de metales e oro, el cual no era estimado de las gentes de allá en su valor.

Paresció al dicho Cristóval Colón e a los que con él fueron, segund la hermosura e grosedad de las tierras, que serían tierras de muy grande estremo e provecho para labrar e plantar e criar las mieses y árboles e ganados de acá de España, e por tales las reputaron y vieron. Y en esta isla Española ay muy grandes ríos e muy dulces; e supieron que avía mucho oro en ellos, e venía en las arenas dellos; y vieron que en los árboles montesinos ni en los otros de allá no avía ninguno que paresciese a los de acá.

Vieron e supieron por los indios cómo en aquella isla avía grandes minas de fino oro, e aun de otros metales.

gestures that this was not a mainland but an island. They followed the East coast of this island for 107 leagues as far as its eastern end, and from there they saw, 18 leagues away, another island to the East that Columbus named Hispaniola.

They went there and followed the northern part of it, as they did at Juana, and it seemed to them extremely beautiful like the others. This Hispaniola they considered by far the most beautiful of all, since there are many ports along the sea-coast not comparable to the others, and among the best that can be found in any Christian land, and also many big rivers amazing to see.

The lands are high and there are several mountain chains with very tall peaks and all very beautiful; they are of a thousand shapes and all passable, enriched by trees of a thousand kinds and so high that they seem to reach the sky. I think the trees never lose their leaves, as shown by the fact that, though it was winter — when here and most anywhere trees should lose their leaves — they all looked as they do in Spain in May and some of them in bloom while others had fruits. In these woods in November the nightingale and other birds sang in the morning, just like Spain in May. There are palm trees of six or seven different types, amazing in their variety, and equally surprising is to see other trees' fruits and plants growing there. Moreover, there are pine groves and valleys and most extensively cultivable lands. There are many bird species and fruits different from those common in our regions. There are metal and gold mines, though gold was not valued by those peoples as it properly should.

It seemed to the above-named Christopher Columbus and to those people who were with him that those lands, with their luxuriance and fertility, would be greatly suitable for cultivation, and profitable if planted and sown to produce harvests as well as trees and also to raise animals imported from Spain. This was how they appraised and valued the island. Also on Hispaniola there are very large and quiet rivers where they learned there was a large quantity of gold lying in the sand. They realized that neither mountain trees nor the other trees resembled those of our country. They saw and heard from the Indians that on that island there were great deposits of pure gold as well as of other metals.

La gente desta isla e de las sobredichas andavan todos desnudos, onbres e mugeres, como nascieron, tan sin enpacho y tan si verguença como las gentes de Castilla vestidos. Algunas mugeres traían cubijado un solo lugar abaxo con una hondilla de algodón e con una cuerda a la cintura, por entre las piernas, no más de lo baxo e la boca de la madre, por onestidad; e otras traían tapado aquello con una hoja sola de árbol, que era larga e propia para ello; otras traían una mantilla texida de algodón recinchada, que cobría las caderas e fasta medios muslos, paresce que por onestidad; e creo que esto traían las mugeres desque parían. Ellos no tenían fierro ni azero ni armas ni cosa que dello se fiziesse, ni de otro nengund metal, salvo de oro. Eran e son gente tan temerosa de la gente de acá, que de tres onbres con armas huyen mill; e no tienen armas sino de cañas e de varas sin fierro, con alguna cosa aguda en el cabo, que puede a los onbres de acá enpecer muy poco; e aunque aquellas armas tenían non savían usar dellas, ni de piedra, que es fuerte arma, porque el coraçón para ello les faltava y falta aun agora.

En el dicho viage acontesció a Cristóval Colón enbiar del navío dos o tres onbres a algunas villas para aver fabla con aquellas gentes, e salir a ellos gente sin número, e después que los vían llegar a cerca fuían todos, e no parava uno con otro. E después que se aseguravan algunos y perdían el temor, eran muy mansos e muy alegres e muy conpañeros, y holgávanse mucho en ver y participar con los de acá. Ellos eran e son todos gente de engenio sin engaño e sin maliscia e muy liberales; e de muy buena voluntad parten lo que tienen los unos con los otros, e conbidan con lo que tienen, e danlo sin escaseza. E los que después de perdido el temor venían a los navíos, mostravan a la gente de acá muy grande amor e caridad, e por cualquier cosa que de los navíos les davan, davan ellos muchas gracias e lo recebían en mucha merced e en reliquias, e davan ellos a los de acá cuanto tenían. Allí acaesció a un marinero, por una agujeta, aver peso de dos castellanos de oro e más; e a otros, por cositas de poco valor así mesmo mucho más, e por blancas nuevas davan por una o dos peso de oro de

The people on this and the named islands, both men and women, went completely naked, just as they were at birth, without showing any embarrassment or shame for this, as naturally as Castilian people go around dressed. Out of virtue some women kept only their lower parts covered with a strip of woven cotton between their legs, supported by a string tied at their waist, which barely covered the vaginal orifice; others yet had it covered only with a tree leaf of the right dimension. Lastly, some of the women, it seems, out of decency, perhaps those who had delivered, wore cotton bands that encircled their waists and fell halfway down their thighs. They did not possess iron or steel, or weapons or objects made by this or other metals, except by gold. They were and are such timid people that three of our armed men could put to flight a thousand of them; and they do not possess weapons except for reeds and canes, without iron, but with sharp points on their tips which in any case can bring little damage to our people. And besides, they did not even know how to use the weapons they had, not even the ones made out of stone which are effective weapons, since they were lacking courage to use them, then and now.

During this trip, Columbus decided to send two or three men from the ships to some villages in order to communicate with those people, and a great number of people appeared. Yet, as soon as the Indians saw the men approaching, all of them would flee and no one would remain. Only after they felt reassured and were no longer afraid did some of them prove themselves to be quite docile, cheerful and affable as well as rather delighted to be observing and participating in all that our men did. They all were and are very capable and quite generous men without deceit or malice; they willingly share with others what they own and give and offer what they have without parsimony. Those who, no longer afraid, got closer to the ships showed our men great friendship and generosity and for any little object given to them by those of the ships they thanked them warmly and accepted it as if it were a great gift or relic, reciprocating with all they owned. So it happened to a sailor there that for a small brooch he was given gold worth two *castellanos* or more; and so it was for others if not to a greater extent for things of little value: for each one or a couple of new copper or silver coins they gave the equivalent of two or three *castellanos* in gold and an

dos o tres castellanos, e una arroba e dos de algodón hilado, que tienen mucho en aquellas tierras.

Non conosció Cristóval Colón, ni los que con él este viage fueron, la crehencia ni seta destas gentes, salvo que les paresció que todos creían en dios de los cielos, e al cielo señalavan, que creían que allí era la fuerça e santidad toda; e pensavan e creían que aquel armada con aquella gente que en ella venía que eran venidos de los cielos e que eran gentes de otro mundo, e con aquel acatamiento e reverencia los recebían en todo lugar después de aver perdido el temor. E esto non porque ellos fuesen tan inocentes e de tan poco entender; que sabed que es gente muy aguda e de sotil engenio, e onbres que navegan todas aquellas mares, que es maravilla la buena cuenta que dan de todo, salvo porque nunca vieron gente vestida, ni semejantes navíos, ni lo oyeron dezir.

Luego como Cristóval Colón llegó a las Indias con su armada, en la primera isla susodicha tomó algunos de aquellos indios, por fuerça, para aver noticia de las cosas de allá; e así fué que, oras por señas e oras por fablas, muy presto se entendieron los de los navíos con ellos; e estos aprovecharon mucho en el viage, que por donde llegavan soltavan e enbiavan algunos, e ellos ivan diziendo por la tierra a grandes bozes: — Venid, venid ver gente que viene del cielo». E los que lo oían, desque se informavan bien dello, ivan otros a lo dezir por toda la tierra de lugar en lugar e de villa en villa, que viniessen a ver tan maravillosa gente que venía del cielo. E así onbres como mugeres todos venían a ver a grand maravilla, así desnudos como nascieron; e después de aver perdido el miedo e los coraçones seguros, todos se llegavan sin temor a los onbres de acá del armada, e les traían de comer e de bever maravillosamente de lo que tenían.

Ellos tenían en todas aquellas islas unas naves con que navegavan, que llamavan canoas; que son y eran de longura de fustas, dellas chicas dellas grandes, salvo que son angostas, porque no es cada una sino de un solo árbol e de un madero, que fazen con piedras de pedernales muy agudos; y tales ay

arroba[5] or two of cotton yarn, of which they have a large amount in those lands.

Neither Columbus nor those who were on that trip with him knew which faith or religion those people had, but it seemed they believed in heavenly gods, and they pointed to the sky, for they believed from there came all power and godliness. They thought and believed that the people of the fleet had come from heaven, that they were people from another world, and with this idea they received them everywhere with submission and reverence, after overcoming their fear. And all of this, not because they were incapable or of limited intelligence — since, it must be understood, they are very clever people and of subtle talent and they are men who sail all over those seas and cause amazement with all their stories and accomplishments — but rather because they had never heard of or seen dressed people or similar ships.

As soon as Christopher Columbus got to the Indies with his fleet, in the first named island he took some of those Indians by force in order to get information about their place. Thus it happened that, sometimes with gestures and sometimes with words, the men of the ships and the Indians soon understood one another. The natives were very useful during the trip, since wherever they arrived they were released and some sent ahead into the territory crying out: "Come, come and see the people who came from heaven." And those who heard it, after gathering additional information, went on to tell others throughout the land from place to place and village to village, so that they might come to see such a wonderful people coming from heaven. Then, both the men and the women came to see such a wonder, naked as they were born. And, once they overcame their fear and were in better spirits, they would all fearlessly approach the men of the fleet, and wonderfully brought them food and drink, or whatever they had.

They had, in all those islands, some boats called canoes in which they sailed; they are and were the same length as *fustas*, some small and others big, though narrow since each of them is built out of a single tree trunk, which they work with very sharp flint stone. There are some as large as an

---

[5] Weight measure equivalent to a quarter of a *quintal*; it roughly corresponds to 10.4 kg.

que son tamañas como una fusta de diez e ocho bancos, mas una fusta no terná con ellas al remo, porque van tan rezias que no es de creer. E con estas canoas navegan las gentes de aquellas islas todas aquellas mares por allí, e tratan sus cosas unos con otros; e algunas canoas avía en que cabían e navegavan sesenta onbres, e otras avía mayores en que cabían e navegavan ochenta onbres, e cada uno con su remo en las manos. E en todas aquellas islas non vieron diversidad en la fechura e color e costunbres de las gentes ni en la lengua, salvo que todos eran las caras e las frentes anchas, las cabeças redondas tan anchas de sien a sien como de la frente al colodrillo, los cabellos prietos e correntíos; gente de medianos cuerpos, de color loros, blancos más que negros, e todos parescía que se entendían e eran de una lengua; que es cosa maravillosa en tantas islas no aver diversidad de lenguas, e podíalo cabsar el navegar, que eran señores de la mar. E por eso en la isla de Canaria non se entendían, porque non tenían con qué navegar, e en cada isla avía una lengua.

Ya dixe cómo Colón andovo en derredor de la isla a que puso nonbre Juana, con su navío, ciento e siete leguas por la costa de la mar por derecha línea; segund lo cual dixo que le paresció ser isla mayor que Inglatierra e Escocia juntas. De la parte del poniente de la isla Juana quedaron dos provincias que Colón no anduvo; a la una llaman los indios Hanan, donde diz que nascen los onbres con cola, enpero yo no creo que sea allí, segund lo señala en el mapa mundi e lo que yo he leído; e si es allí no engorrará mucho en se ver con ayuda de Dios. Las cuales islas e provincias, segund los indios dezían, podían tener cada cincuenta o sesenta leguas de longura.

La isla Española ya dicha, a quien los indios llaman Haití, es entre las otras ya dichas así como oro entre plata. Es muy grande y muy fermosa de arboledas, de ríos, de montes, de canpos; es de muy fermosas mares e puertos; tiene en circuito más que toda España desde Colibre, que es en Cataluña cerca de Perpiñán, por la costa de la mar de España, en derredor de Granada e Portugal e Gallizia e Vizcaya y Fuenterrabía, que es

eighteen-bench *fusta*, but the latter could not compete with them in rowing, since they run so fast that it is hard to believe. They sail among the peoples of those islands and throughout those seas with these canoes trading their possessions with others. Some canoes could fit and sail seventy men; others yet were bigger, with up to eighty men, each one holding an oar. In all the islands they did not notice differences in their features such as the color of the skin or the habits of the people, nor in their language, though they all had broad faces and brows, round heads as wide from side to side as from front to back, with very black and loose hair. People of medium height, dark complexion, more white than black, who seemed all to understand one another and use the same language. It is an astonishing thing that on so many islands there would be no difference in language, and this is probably due to their sailing, since they dominated in that area of the sea. For the same reason, on Grand Canary they did not understand each other, for they did not own boats with which to sail and so on each island there was a different language.

I have already discussed how Columbus sailed with his vessel around Cuba, the island he named Juana, for 107 leagues of coast in a straight line, and which, according to what he himself said, seemed to him to be larger than both England and Scotland together. On the west side of Juana two territories remained unexplored by Columbus: one, called by the Indians Hanan, where it is claimed men are born with tails, though I do not believe it to be true because of what is marked on the world map and what I have read. Were it to be so, on the other hand, it will not be long before, God willing, it will be verified. Those islands and regions, according to what the Indians said, might be fifty or sixty leagues long.

The earlier mentioned Hispaniola, which the Indians call Haiti, is, among the other islands, like gold among silver. It is very large and most beautiful for the woods it has, its rivers, mountains and plains. It has a beautiful sea and good natural ports; its circumference is longer than that of all of Spain from Colibre,[6] Catalonia, near Perpignan, and continuing along the seacoast of Spain, around as far as Granada, Portugal, Galicia,

---

[6] Today Collioure is a French city located in the Department of Eastern Pyrenees, 27 km. southeast of Perpignan.

en cabo de Vizcaya. E ellos andovieron ciento e ochenta e dos leguas en cuadra por derecha línea de ocidente a oriente; e por aquí paresció su grandeza desta Española, que es muy grande isla; e esta isla está en lugar más convenible e mejor comarca para las minas del oro e para todo trato, así de la tierra firme de acá como de la tierra firme de allá.

Tomó asiento Cristóval Colón allí en la Española, Haití llamada por los indios, en una villa a la cual puso nonbre la villa de Navidad; e dexó allí cuarenta onbres con armas e artillerías e bituallas, començada de fazer una fortaleza, e dexó maestros para la hazer; e dexòles que comiesen fasta cierto tienpo.

E dexó allí onbres de los que llevó, especiales e de buen saber y entender para todo; e fué forçado, segund paresció, dexarlos, porque, como se perdió él un navío, non avía en qué viniesen; y esto se calló acá, y se dixo que no quedava sino por comienço de pobladores. E puso su amistad Colón con un rey de aquella comarca donde dexó la gente, e otorgáronse por mucho amigos, como hermanos, e encomendóle Colón aquellos onbres que allí dexaba. E la nao se perdió allí en la Española, cerca de donde dexó los dichos onbres.

Ay allí a la entrada de las Indias ciertas islas que llaman aquellos indios de las islas ya dichas Caribi, que son pobladas de unas gentes que estotros tienen por muy feroces, e han dellos muy grand temor, porque comen carne humana. Estos tienen muchas canoas con las cuales corren todas las islas comarcanas, y roban cuanto fallan y pueden, e llevan presos los onbres e mugeres que pueden, e mátanlos e cámenlos, lo cual es cosa de grand admiración e espanto. Ellos no son más disformes que los otros, salvo que tienen esta mala costunbre; e son gente muy esforçada, e tienen más armas que los otros; que usan arcos e flechas de cañas con un palillo agudo al cabo, o espinas de pescados, por defecto de fierro, que non tienen.

Estos trahen los cabellos luengos como mugeres, e son temidos por feroces entre estos pueblos e islas sobredichas;

to Biscay and Fuenterrabía[7] which is located on the Cape of Biscay. They went on for 182 leagues, each one being four miles, in a straight line from west to east and from this the size of Hispaniola became eviden , being very large and located in a most privileged place and the best region that could be found, given the gold mines and for whatever kind of trade between the mainland on either side.

Christopher Columbus consequently stopped in Hispaniola, called Haiti by the Indians, in a settlement which he called Navidad, and there he left forty men with weapons, artillery, and provisions and with a fort barely initiated and masters to complete it. He left enough provisions for some time and particularly skilled men from those he had brought with him, and with good knowledge and intelligence for what might be needed. Clearly, he was forced to leave them there because, having lost a vessel, it was impossible to take them back. Not a word was said about that and it was claimed they were left there to start a settlement. Columbus befriended a chief of that region where he had left the men, with whom he had established a great brotherly friendship and under whose protection Columbus placed those whom he was leaving there. The ship was lost there in Hispaniola, near the place where he had left the above-mentioned men.

Arriving at the Indies, there are some islands which the Indians of the above-named islands call Caribs, and which are populated by certain people that the other natives consider very ferocious and of whom they are most afraid, for they eat human flesh. They own many canoes which they use to ravage all the islands of the region, stealing whatever they find or are able to steal, and taking prisoner as many men and women as they can that kill and eat, causing amazement and terror. They are not much different from the others, except for this bad custom. They are very courageous and own more weapons than the others; they use reed bows and arrows with sharp wood or fish-bone tips, because of lack of iron which they do not have.

These people wear hair as long as women do and they are feared among the people on the above-named islands be-

---

[7] Fuenterrabìa has kept its ancient name; it is a Spanish city on the Atlantic, between San Sebastiàn and the French border.

e esto es porque todos los otros son gente muy cobarde y muy doméstica e sin maliscia; mas no porque ellos sean fuertes ni las gentes de acá los ayan de tener en más que a los otros. E en las islas destos caribes e en todas las otras susodichas ay oro sin cuento e infinito algodón e muchas especias, especialmente pimienta, que quema e tiene mayor fuerça cuatro vezes que la pimienta que usamos en España, la cual todas aquellas gentes tienen por cosa muy provechosa e muy medecinal. Ay árboles de linaloe e almástiga e ruibarvo e otras muchas buenas cosas, segund paresció al dicho Colón. No avía res de cuatro pies, ni animal de los de acá pudieron ver en cuantas islas desta vez descubrieron, salvo unos gusquejos chiquitos, e en los canpos e montes unos ratones grandes que llaman hutías, que comen, que son muy sabrosos, e cómenlos como acá a los conejos, e en tal precio los tienen. Ay muchas aves, diferentes mucho de las de acá, especialmente infinitos papagayos.

Descubierta la tierra susodicha por el dicho Cristóval Colón, él se vino a Castilla, e llegó a Palos a veinte y tres días del mes de março, año de mill e cuatrocientos y noventa y tres años, e entró en Sevilla con mucha onrra, a treinta e un días de março, domingo de Ramos, bien provada su intención; donde le fué fecho buen recebimiento. Truxo diez indios, de los quales dexó en Sevilla cuatro, e llevó a Barcelona, a enseñar al rey e la reina, seis; donde fué muy bien recebido. E el rey e la reina le dieron grand crédito e le mandaron aderesçar otra armada mucho mayor e bolver con ella; e le dieron título de almirante del mar Océano de las Indias, e le mandaron dar todo lo que él demandó para el viage, e le mandaron llamar don Cristóval Colón, por onrra de la dignidad de almirante.

E él se partió de Barcelona, encomendado a don Juan de Fonseca, arcediano que era estonces de Sevilla, obispo que fué de Badajoz e después de Córdova e después de Palencia e conde de Pernia, que tenía estonces cargo de las armadas

cause of their ferocity; that is so because the others are all very naive and quiet and without malice, and not because they are strong, and we should not consider them superior to the others. In the islands inhabited by Caribs and on all the ones earlier, there is immeasurable gold, a great deal of cotton, and a large amount of spices, especially pepper, which burns, that is four times stronger than the one we use in Spain and is considered by these peoples a very useful and, above all, mainly medicinal product. There are aloe trees and mastic trees and rhubarb and many other good things,[8] as it appeared to the said Columbus. There were no four-footed animals, nor could they see in all the islands they discovered animals similar to those in Spain except for some little dogs and also some rats in the plains and mountains they called *"hutias"*[9] which they eat, being very tasty. They eat them as we do rabbits and they consider them the same way. There are numerous birds, very different from ours and, especially, there is an endless number of parrots.

After discovering these lands, Christopher Columbus returned to Castile and arrived in Palos on March 23, 1493, where he was received with great honors on March 31, Palm Sunday. Having well-demonstrated the truth of his ideas, he entered Seville where he received a warm reception. He brought ten Indians with him, four of whom he left in Seville, taking the other six to show them to the King and Queen in Barcelona, where he was very well received.

The King and Queen gave him great credit and asked him to outfit another, much larger fleet and go back with it to those lands. They granted him the title of "Admiral of the Ocean Sea of the Indies," and ordered that he be given all he might request for the voyage and declared that he be called Don Christopher Columbus, in honor of his title of Admiral.

He left Barcelona under the protection of Don Juan de Fonseca, at that time archdeacon of Seville and, previously, Bishop of Badajoz, Cordoba and Palencia, and Count of Pernia, and who was then in charge of the Armada as well as of

---

[8] With regard to the aloe, mastic, rhubarb and other plants and fruits Columbus found during his first voyage, see the commentaries by P. E. Taviani in *Nuova Raccolta Colombiana*, Vol. I, pt. 2, 334-35.

[9] For *Hutias* see *Nuova Raccolta Colombiana*, Vol. I, pt. 2, 365.

e grandes negocios de Sevilla e desta Andaluzía. E assí con este concierto se vino a Sevilla, donde en breve tienpo fué proveído de la dicha armada e de la gente e vituallas e mantenimientos que para ella fueron menester; e de capitanes e de justicias e de onbres letrados y físicos e onbres de buen consejo, e de armas e de todas las otras cosas que para ella eran menester; e de muy buenos navíos, e de muy buenos e escogidos marineros, e de onbres buenos plateros para saber conoscer e apurar el oro.

important concerns such as Seville and Andalusia. Thus, with these agreements, Columbus arrived in Seville where in a short time he was supplied with the above-mentioned fleet, the needed crew, provisions and all that was deemed necessary to the fleet: captains and magistrates, men of letters, physicians and good counselors, weapons and all the items he needed including good ships, very capable and experienced sailors as well as skilled goldsmiths who might be able to recognize and refine the gold.

CAPITULO CXIX

De la segunda navegación que fizo a las Indias el almirante don Cristóval Colón. De la continuación del viage. De la costunbre de los caribes.

Partió con la gracia de Dios el almirante don Cristóval Colón, por mandado del rey don Fernando e de la reina doña Isabel, con la flota que sus Altezas enbiaron de su España para las Indias, desde Cáliz, a veynte e dos días de setienbre del dicho año de mill e quatrocientos e noventa y tres años, con diez e siete navíos bien aderesçados e con mill e docientos onbres de pelea en ellos, o pocos menos, con viento e tienpo convenible al viaje. E duróles aquel tienpo dos días, en los cuales anduvieron casi cincuenta leguas; calmóles el tienpo otros dos días, en los cuales andovieron muy poco; e luego les bolvió buen tienpo, de manera que en otros dos días llegaron a la Grand Canaria, donde tomaron puerto; lo cual les fué nescesario por reparar un navío que fazía mucha agua, e estovieron allí todo aquel día. E luego otro día partieron, e fízoles algunas calmas, de manera que estovieron en llegar a la Gomera cuatro o cinco días; e allí fué nescessario estar algunos días, donde fizieron provissiones de carne e leña e agua para su larga jornada; assí que en aquellos puertos, e un día que les hizo calma, desque partieron de la Gomera tardaron en llegar a la isla del Fierro veinte días.

Desde allí, por la bondad de Dios, les tornó el mejor tienpo que nunca flota llevó tan largo viage; tal que dentro de veinte días ovieron vista de tierra, e oviéranla en catorze o quinze días si la nao capitana fuera tan buena velera como los otros navíos; e en todo este tienpo nunca ovieron fortuna, salvo la bíspera de sant Ximón e Judas, que ovieron fortuna que les duró cuatro oras, que les puso en harto estrecho. E el primero domingo después de Todos Santos, cerca del alva,

CHAPTER CXIX

The second voyage the Admiral Christopher Columbus made to the Indies. The continuation of that trip. The Caribs' customs.

By the grace of God and charged by King Ferdinand and Queen Isabela, the Admiral Don Christopher Columbus left Cádiz on September 22, 1493, in favorable wind and weather, with the fleet Their Highnesses sent from Spain to the Indies, made up of seventeen well-furnished vessels with 1200 troops on them, or a bit less. The good weather lasted two days during which he sailed about fifty leagues; in the next two days the ships were becalmed so they progressed very little, but soon thereafter the weather was good again, so much so that in two days they reached the Grand Canaries where they did stop as they needed to refit one of the vessels, which was taking on a good deal of water. They remained there for a whole day. Not long after that, during the following day, they departed and, due to intermittent lack of wind, it took four or five days to get to Gomera where they had to stay a few days to stock meat, wood and water for their long trip. So, counting the days they stayed in these ports and the day without wind, it took twenty days to get to Hierro island after leaving Gomera.

From that place, thanks to divine goodness, they had the best weather a fleet ever encountered during such a long trip and, after twenty days, sighted land. Actually, they would have been able to do so in fourteen or fifteen days had the flagship been as good a vessel as the others. In all this time, they never had storms except on Saint Simon and Judas's night when one came up and lasted four hours, troubling them considerably. Around dawn on the first Sunday after

dixo un piloto de la nao capitana: «¡Albricias, que tenemos tierra!». De lo cual todos ovieron mucho plazer.

Contaron aquel día los pilotos del armada, desde la isla del Fierro de Canaria fasta la primera tierra que vieron, unas ochocientas leguas; otros, ochocientas menos veinte, de manera que la diferencia no era mucha; e trezientas que ponen desde el Fierro fasta Cáliz, que son por todas desde los fines de España, que son Cáliz e los puertos del Andaluzía, fasta las primeras tierras de las Indias, mill e cient leguas.

Vieron el domingo de mañana, por proa de los navíos, una isla; e luego a man derecha paresció otra, primera tierra de sierras por aquella parte que vieron; la otra era tierra de árboles muy espesos llena. E luego que fué más de día, començaron a parescer, a una parte e a otra, islas; de manera que aquel día seis islas a diversas partes vieron, e las más harto grandes. E fueron endereçados a la que primero avían visto, e llegaron por la costa andando más de veinte leguas, buscando puerto para surgir, el cual todo aquel espacio jamás se pudo fallar: era todo aquello que parescía desta isla, montaña muy fermosa e muy verde fasta el agua; que era alegría de la mirar, porque en España en tal tienpo apenas ay cosa verde.

Después que allí no hallaron puerto, acordó el almirante que se bolviesen a la otra isla que parescía a la mano derecha, que estava desta otra cuatro o cinco leguas; e quedó por estonces un navío en esta isla primera, buscando puerto todo aquel día para cuando fuese necesario de venir a ella; el cual falló buen puerto e vido casas e gente, y luego se tornó aquella noche para donde estava la flota, que avía ya tomado puerto en la otra isla. Donde descendió el almirante en tierra e mucha gente con él, con la vandera real en las manos, adonde tomó posesión por sus Altezas del rey don Fernando e de la reina doña Isabel su muger, reyes de España, en forma de derecho.

En esta isla avía tanta espesura de árboles, que era maravilla, e tantas diferencias de árboles no conoscidos de nadie, que era para espantar; e algunos de los frutos dellos con color, e dellos verdes, assí que todos los árboles eran verdes. Allí

All Saints day, a steersman of the flagship yelled: "Hurrah! Land Ho!" to general delight.

The pilots of the fleet counted about 800 leagues between Hierro in the Grand Canaries and the first land sighted; others counted twenty leagues less, making the difference irrelevant. And, considering the 300 leagues there are from Hierro to Cádiz, we have 1100 leagues from Spain's borders, Cádiz and the Andalusian ports, to the first lands of the Indies. That Sunday morning they saw an island off the bows of the ships and immediately after on their right appeared a second one, the first mountainous land they saw there, the former being a land with very thick trees. Little by little, as the day went on, more islands were spotted on both sides, so that on that day they saw a total of six islands all around, most of them quite large. Setting course toward the first one sighted, they sailed along its coast for more than twenty leagues, looking for a port in which to anchor, but they could not find one all along that stretch of coast. That side of the island looked like a mountainous area, very beautiful and green down to the sea, a pleasure to see since Spain in that season has hardly any green.

Unable to find port there, the Admiral thought they should set course for another island looming on the right, four or five leagues away; however, at the same time, he left a vessel at this first island [10] for the purpose of seeking a port the entire day in case it became necessary to return there. A good port was found and houses and people were seen before rejoining at once, that very night, the fleet which had already dropped anchor in a port at the other island.[11] There the Admiral went ashore along with many men and, royal flag in his hands, took possession of those lands in the name of their Royal Highnesses of Spain, King Ferdinand and Queen Isabela, his wife, in conformity with traditional right.

On this island the trees were so dense that it was an amazing thing to see as well the high variety of plants unknown to anybody and the many fruits, some red and others green, that contributed to create a luxuriant environment.

---

[10] Dominica.

[11] Marie Galante.

hallaron un árbol cuya hoja tenía el más fino olor de clavos que ser podía, e era como un laurel, salvo que no era assí grande. Allí avía frutas salvaginas de diferentes maneras; e algunos no muy sabios provaron de ellas, de los cuales ovo algunos que del gusto, solamente tocándolas con la lengua, se les finchavan las caras e les venía tan grande ardor e dolor que parescía que rabiavan; los cuales se remediavan con cosas frías. E en esta isla no hallaron gente ni señal della: creyóse ser despoblada; en la cual estovieron por dos oras del día, porque cuando allí llegaron era tarde.

Luego, otro día por la mañana, partieron para otra isla que parescía a vista desta, que era muy grande, fasta la cual avía siete o ocho leguas; e llegaron a ella fazia la parte de una grande montaña, que parescía que quería llegar al cielo; en medio de la cual montaña estava un pico más alto que toda la otra montaña, del cual se vertían a diversas partes aguas muchas, en especial fazia la parte de la flota; que de tres leguas parescía un golpe de agua tan gordo como un buey, que se despeñava de tan alto como si cayera del cielo, e como se parescía de tan lexos, ovo en los navíos muchas apuestas e porfías, que unos dezían que eran peñas blancas e otros que era agua. E desque llegaron más cerca vídose lo cierto, que era m y fermosa cosa de ver e muy maravillosa, de tan pequeño lugar cómo nascía tan gran golpe de agua, e de cuand alto se despeñava.

E luego que llegaron, mandó el almirante a una caravela ligera que fuesse a costear e vuscar puerto, la cual se adelantó; e llegando a la tierra vido unas casas, e con la barca saltò el capitán en tierra e llegó a las casas, en las cuales halló gente. E luego que vieron al capitán e a los que ivan con él fuyeron quellas gentes, e el capitán entró en las casas e falló las cosas que ellos allí tenían, que no avían llevado nada; donde falló e tomó dos papagayos muy grandes e muy diferenciados de cuantos se avían visto, e halló mucho algodón hilado e por hilar e cosas de sus mantenimientos, e de todo tomó un poco; e traxo cuatro o cinco huesos de braços e piernas de onbres. E luego como aquello vieron, conoscieron ser aquellas las islas de los caribes, que son abitadas de gente que comen carne humana.

There they found a tree whose leaves had the finest clove smell imaginable and similar to the laurel, though not as large. There were different types of wild fruits that a few not-so-wise men tasted. No sooner had they done so with their tongues than their faces started to swell up and they experienced great burning and pain to the point of going mad. This condition was remedied using cold things. On this island they did not find any people or traces of them so it was thought to be uninhabited and they remained there for two hours, having reached there early evening.

The following morning, they immediately headed toward another island[12] visible from this one. It was very large and seven or eight leagues away. They reached it near where a great mountain seemed to touch the sky, especially with its middle peak, higher than the others, and rich in water courses branching off in different directions, especially on the side overlooking the fleet. From a distance of three leagues a gush, as mighty as a buey,[13] falling from that height seemed to be forthcoming directly from the sky. Observed from far away, it caused many bets and guesses on the ships, where some identified it as snowy tops, and others claimed it was water. Only by getting closer did they realize what it was, what a wonderful sight to admire and how awesome a gush it was, coming from such a small space and great height!

When they arrived, the Admiral ordered a light caravel to sail along the coast and find a port. It set out to do so. While approaching land, a few huts were sighted and the captain landed in a boat and reached those dwellings where he found people. As soon as the captain and the others were seen, the people fled and the captain entered these huts and found all that they kept there since they did not take anything away. Thus he found and took two parrots, very big and different from those they had seen and he also found a good deal of unspun cotton, yarn and items necessary for their subsistence. Of everything he took a bit, including three or four human arm and leg bones. After seeing the latter, they understood these were Carib islands, inhabited by human flesh-eating

---

[12] Guadeloupe.

[13] "Buey" is a measure for spring water. Explained on p. 15.

E el almirante, por las señas que al otro primero viage le avían dado los indios de las islas que descubrió, del sitio donde están, hizo el viage por allí, por descubrirlas e porque estavan más cerca de España; e tanbién porque por allí se hazía el camino más derecho para la Española, a su parescer, donde antes avía dexado la gente. A la cual, por la bondad de Dios e por el buen saber del almirante, fueron tan derechos como si por un camino seguido e sabido fueran a aquella isla; la cual es muy grande, que por el lado que le vieron paresció que avía de luengo de costa veinte e cinco leguas. Fueron costeando por el lado della, vuscando puerto, más de dos leguas; e por la parte donde ivan eran montañas muy altas, e a la otra parte que dexaron parescían muy grandes llanuras, e por la orilla de la mar avía algunos poblados pequeños; e luego que vían las velas fuían todos. Andadas dos leguas fallaron puerto, ya bien tarde; y esa noche acordó el almirante que a la madrugada saliessen algunos a tierra para tomar lengua e a saber qué gente era, no enbargante la sospecha e lo que ya avían visto.

Salieron esa madrugada algunos capitanes por la tierra, e los unos vinieron a ora de comer e truxieron un moço de fasta catorze años, e a lo que después se supo e él dixo, era de los que aquella gente tenía cabtivos. E los otros se dividieron, e los unos traxieron un muchacho pequeño, el cual tenía un onbre por la mano, e por fuir lo desanparó: este enbiaron luego con algunos dellos, e los otros quedaron; e de los que quedaron unos tomaron ciertas mugeres naturales de la isla, que truxieron, e otras mugeres que se vinieron de grado con ellos, que eran de las cabtivas.

De esta conpañía se apartó un capitán, non sabiendo que se avía avído lengua, con seis onbres, el cual se perdió con ellos, que jamás supieron tornar, fasta que en cabo de cuatro días toparon con la costa de la mar, e seguiendo por ella tornaron a topar con la flota. Ya los tenían por perdidos e comidos de los caribes, porque ya no bastava razón a creer otra cosa, porque entre ellos ivan pilotos marinos, que por la estrella sabían ir y venir fasta España, y creíanse que en tan pequeño espacio non se podían desatinar ni perder.

people. Given the information that had been provided to the Admiral by the Indians of the discovered islands concerning the place where the Caribs lived, he headed toward these places to verify their existence since they lay closer to Spain, and also because he was convinced that passing through them was the most direct way to get to Hispaniola, where he previously had left some men. Thanks to divine goodness and to the Admiral's wisdom, they reached Hispaniola so quickly that it created the impression they already knew the correct course to follow. The island is very large; the side they saw seemed to be 25 leagues long. For more than two leagues they sailed along one of its sides in search of a port. In the direction they sailed there were many high mountains, whereas in the area left behind appeared very large plains with, along the seacoast, some little hamlets whose inhabitants all fled as soon as they saw the sails. Two leagues ahead, when it was already very late, they found a port. That night the Admiral decided that the next morning a few of the men would land to gather information and learn what kind of people they were, notwithstanding their suspicions generated by what they had already seen.

That morning a few of the captains then went ashore and some got back at meal time, bringing along a boy of about fourteen from whom it was later learned, as he himself stated, that he was one of those kept prisoners by the Carib people. The others parted, some taking another little boy — whose hand had been held by a man who left him behind while fleeing — and who was at once sent to the ships, while the others stopped there. Of those who stopped, some captured a few native women of the island whom they brought with them together with other women who voluntarily joined them because they had been prisoners.

From this group, not knowing that the sought information had already been acquired, a captain and six men departed and lost their way, being unable to return until four days later when they came across the seacoast and, following it, reached the fleet. Already, they had been considered missing and eaten by the Caribs, since it was unreasonable to think anything else, for among them were capable pilots and sailors who, by means of the stars, could go to Spain and return, as well as because it was commonly thought that in such a limited area they could neither lose their bearings nor get lost.

Aquel día primero que allí descendieron, andavan por la playa junto con el agua muchos onbres e mugeres, mirando la flota e maravillándose mucho de cosa tan nueva; e llegando alguna barca a tierra, a fablar con ellos, dezían *taibo, taibo*, que quiere dezir *bueno, bueno*; e esperavan, en tanto que no salían del agua, junto con el monte, de manera que cuando ellos querían se podían salvar; e en conclusión, que de los onbres nenguno se pudo tomar por fuerça ni por grado, salvo dos que se asseguraron e después los truxieron por fuerça. Allí se tomaron más de veinte mugeres, dellas de las cabtivas, que de su grado se venían, e otras naturales de la isla, que fueron salteadas e tomadas por fuerça; e ciertos muchachos cabtivos, que se vinieron a la flota fuyendo de los naturales de la isla, que los tenían cabtivos para comer.

En aquel puerto estovieron ocho días, a cabsa de la pérdida del capitán susodicho; donde muchas vezes salió gente de la flota a tierra, a andar por sus moradas e pueblos que estavan a la costa, donde se hallaron infinitos huesos de onbres e los caxcos de las cabeças colgados por las casas, a manera de basijas para tener cosas de servicio de casa; esto era de la gente que comían. En todo este espacio non se vieron muchos onbres, porque diz que eran idos, segund las mugeres dixieron, a saltear con diez canoas a otras islas.

Esta gente desta isla paresció más política que non la de las otras islas que se vieron de por allí, e tenían muy mejores casas, aunque todas eran de paja; e éstos las tenían de muy mejor fechura a más proveídas de mantenimientos, e parescían más industriosos que los otros. Tenían mucho algodón, hilado e por hilar, en sus casas, e muchas mantas del mismo algodón, tan bien texidas que no devían nada a las de Castilla.

Preguntando a las mugeres que eran cabtivas en esta isla que qué gente era ésta que las tenían cabtivas, respondían que eran caribes; e después que entendieron que los castellanos aborrescían tal gente por su mal uso de comer onbres, holgávanse mucho dello; e si de nuevo traían algund onbre o muger de los caribes, secretamente dezían a los de los navíos cómo eran caribes; e aun allí adonde estavan en poder de los castellanos, en los

That first day when they went ashore there and were going down the coast near the water, many men and women were looking at the fleet with great astonishment for what was happening and kept on shouting toward some boats gone ashore to talk with them: "taibo, taibo"[14] which means "good, good;" they waited next to an elevated coast not too far from the water, so as to be able to flee whenever they wished. In conclusion, none of the men either could be captured by force or would surrender willingly, except for two who were trapped and then taken by force. Altogether, they took there more than twenty women prisoners who spontaneously followed and other natives of the island whom they had attacked and seized by force as well as some boys who fled to the fleet away from the natives and those who kept them prisoners to eat them.

They stayed in that port[15] eight days due to the disappearance of the aforementioned captain; and there the men of the fleet went many times ashore to explore the dwellings and hamlets along the coast, where very many human bones and skulls had been found hanging inside the cabins like pottery in which to keep household goods, but they were bones of the people they ate. In all of that area not many men could be seen because, it was claimed, as the women had reported, they had left with ten canoes to attack other islands.

The people of this island appeared more civilized than those of the other islands observed in the area and characterized by far better dwellings, though all straw huts; built better and kept full of stored food they made these people appear more industrious than the others. They had in their living quarters much unspun cotton and yarn with many cotton blankets so well woven they left nothing to be desired when compared to Castilian ones. When the freed women were asked what kind of people kept them prisoners, they answered that they were Caribs, and upon realizing that the Castilians abhorred such people because of their horrible custom of eating human flesh, they greatly rejoiced. Whenever some other Carib man or woman was seized, these women secretly pointed out to those on the boats that they were Caribs, still fearing them

---

[14] Chanca says instead "taino."

[15] The Grand Anse Bay, a little north-east of the southern tip of Guadaloupe.

navíos, mostravan aver temor dellos, como gente muy sojuzgada de ellos; e de allí conoscieron cuales eran caribes e cuales eran de los otros, por el dicho de las mugeres. Porque los caribes traían en las piernas en cada una dos argollas texidas de algodón, la una junto con la rodilla e la otra junto con los tovillos, de manera que les fazen las pantorrillas grandes e de los sobredichos lugares muy ceñidas, e esto paresció que ellos tenían por cosa gentil; así que por esta diferencia conoscieron los unos de los otros, e los caribes ser de más mala costunbre que los otros indios.

La costunbre desta gente de caribes es tal. Son tres islas: esta susodicha se llama Quaruqueria, la otra que primero se vido se llama Quayrique, la otra se llama Ayay. Estos todos son en conformidad como si fuessen de un linage, los cuales non se hazen mal unos a otros, enpero hazen guerra a todas las otras islas comarcanas; los cuales van por mar ciento e cincuenta leguas a los más lexos, a saltear, con muchas canoas que tienen, que son fustas pequeñas fechas de un solo madero cada una, segund dicho es en el capítulo antes deste. E sus armas son frechas, e en los tiros destas frechas, en lugar de fierros, porque ellos non lo poseen, ponen unas puntas fechas de huesos de tortugas; otros ponen unas espinas de un pece, fechas naturalmente de manera de fierro, huecas, bien rezias, que para gente desnuda, como son todos, es cosa que les puede bien ofender e matar; enpero para gente de acá de España no son rmas para mucho ofender.

Esta gente saltea en las otras islas e tráhense las mugeres que pueden aver, en especial moças fermosas, las cuales tienen para sus servicios e para tener por mancebas. Traen muchas, segund se supo, porque más de veinte moças de las cabtivas fueron las que se vinieron a la flota, como dicho es. E dezían que tanbién usavan dellas de una terrible crueldad aquellos onbres caribes, que paresce increíble: que los fijos que en ellas engendravan que se los comían, e que solamente crían los que han en las mugeres naturales, e comen los otros. E los onbres que pueden aver tráhenlos a sus casas, e fazen carnescería dellos cuando quieren, e los que matan por los prender cómenlos luego; e dizen que la carne de los onbres es tan buena cosa que

like people entirely subjected to them even aboard the ships and under Castilian protection. From then on our men could distinguish the Caribs from the others on the basis of what the women said, noticing that the Caribs had on each leg two woven cotton rings: one near the knee and another at the ankles so as to enlarge their calves while constricting the ringed parts, a custom that appeared to be considered a beauty care element. So, from this feature they could distinguish the good ones from the Caribs who had worse customs than the other Indians.

Such is then the Carib people's custom on three islands; the above mentioned island is called Quaruqueira, the one seen earlier is called Quayrique and the last is Ayay.[16] All these people, who do not harm each other and make war only against the other islands of the region, resemble each other as though they had the same ancestry. They go up to 150 leagues out at sea to attack with their many canoes, indeed small *fustas*, each of them made from a single trunk, as reported in the previous chapter. Their weapons are arrows whose tips have tortoise bone instead of iron, that they do not own. Others utilize fish bones for iron-like arrows, empty and very hard, which can clearly wound and kill naked people like all of them are but hardly endanger our people from Spain.

These men attack the area islands, seizing all the women they can, especially young girls whom they keep as servants and as concubines. They capture many, according to what was learned, as already more than twenty of them had come aboard the fleet, as previously noted. All were saying that these Carib men showed great cruelty toward them to a seemingly incredible degree, in fact they reached the point of eating the children conceived by them while raising only the ones born from their women. The men they are able to capture are taken into their huts and slaughtered at their whim, whereas those killed in action are eaten immediately. They claim human flesh is so good that no other edible thing in the world is better. Indeed,

---

[16] It is impossible to identify precisely their present-day names. The above-named island is probably Guadeloupe; the one "seen earlier" should correspond to Dominica or Marie Galante. As for Ayay, Morison erroneously identifies it with St. Croix, because Bernáldez will talk later about St. Croix. In all probability it is Marie Galante.

no ay tal cosa de comer en el mundo. E bien paresció su mal viscio e costunbre, porque en los huesos que en sus casas se hallaron, todo lo que se podía roer todo estava comido, que no avía en ellos sino lo que por su mucha dureza no se podía comer.

Allí se halló en una casa cociendo un pescueço de un onbre; e los mochachos que cabtivavan chicos cortávanles a cada uno su mienbro generativo, e sírvense dellos hasta que son onbres o fasta que quieren, e después fazen fiesta e mátanlos e cómenlos; e dizen que la carne de los mochachos e de las mugeres non es buena para comer ni tal como la de los onbres. E destos mochachos se vinieron fuyendo a la flota tres, con sus mienbros generativos cortados a raíz de las verijas.

En cabo de cuatro días vino el capitán que se avía perdido con los conpañeros; de cuya venida estavan ya desafuziados, porque los avían ido a buscar otras cuadrillas, e aquel día vino la una, e todas vinieron sin saber dellos; e con su venida holgaron mucho los de la flota, como si nuevamente se ovieran hallado. Traxo este capitán e los que fueron con él diez personas, entre mochachos e mugeres; éstos ni los otros que los fueron a buscar nunca hallaron onbres, porque se avían fuído, o porque por ventura avía pocos en aquella comarca, porque avían ido a hurtar, como dixieron las mugeres. Vino el dicho capitán e los que fueron con él tan destroçados del monte, que era lástima de los ver; dezían que se avían perdido por la espesura de los árboles, que era tanta quel cielo non podían ver, e que algunos dellos que eran marineros avían subido por los árboles de noche para mirar el estrella del norte e no la avían podido ver, e si no toparan con la mar fuera inposible tornar a la flota.

Partió de aquella isla la flota ocho días pasados después que allí llegaron; e luego otro día vieron otra isla no muy grande, a ora de medio día, que estava desta obra de doze leguas; e porque el primero día que partieron les fizo calma, fueron junto con la costa desta isla, e dixeron las mugeres indias que aquella isla no era abitada de gente, porque los de Caribe la avían despoblado, e por eso la flota non paró allí.

this bad habit and custom of theirs was well evidenced by the condition of bones found in their homes: hard bare bones was all that was left, as all that could be gnawed on had been gnawed on. There, in one of the huts, they found a human neck still boiling. Traditionally, they cut the male sex organs off imprisoned young boys, forcing them to work until they become adults or until they wish them to, before celebrating, killing and eating them. Another claim is that boys' and women's flesh is different and not as good to eat as that of men. Three of such boys, in fact, their genitals cut to the root, fled toward the fleet.

At the end of the fourth day, the captain who had lost his way with his companions reappeared. Their return was no longer hoped for since numerous squads had gone out searching for them, and even that very day one had come back, but all of them had returned empty-handed. Their arrival was then celebrated by the men of the fleet as if they had come back to life. The captain and those with him brought boys and women, ten people in all. Neither they nor the ones who had gone searching for them ever found men, either because they had all fled or perhaps because there were few of them left in that region since, as reported by the women, they had gone out ravaging. The captain and the others with him arrived so fatigued after the mountain crossing that seeing them aroused sorrow; they explained how they lost their way due to the density of the trees which obscured the sky and recollected how some of them, who were sailors, had climbed trees at night in order to locate the North Star and still could not manage to see it. Had they not reached the sea by chance it would have been impossible for them to rejoin the fleet.

The fleet left this island eight days after it had arrived, and soon sighted — the following day at noon — another very large island[17] twelve leagues away. Since the first day after departing the ships were becalmed, they got closer to the coast of this island which the Indian women said was uninhabited because the Carib people depopulated it, and consequently the fleet did not stop there.

---

[17] Montserrat.

Luego esa tarde vieron otra isla, y esa noche hallaron cerca della unos baxos por cuyo temor surgieron, e non osaron andar fasta que fuesse de día; e luego a la mañana paresció otra isla asaz grande. A nenguna destas no llegaron, por ir a consolar los onbres que avían dexado el otro viage en la isla Española; e no plugo a Dios que los fallasen bivos, como adelante en este libro se dirà.

Otro día, a ora de comer, llegaron a una isla que parescía muy bien e muy poblada; fueron e tomaron puerto en ella. Luego el almirante mandó ir a tierra una barca guarnescida de gente, para si pudiessen aver lengua para saber qué gente era, e para aver informasción del viaje que era menester, no enbargante que el almirante, aunque nunca avía fecho aquel camino, iva muy bien encaminado, segund paresció. E saltaron ciertas personas en tierra de la dicha barca, e llegaron a un poblado donde la gente ya se avía escondido, e tomaron cinco o seis mugeres e ciertos mochachos, de las cuales eran tanbién las más cabtivas, como en la otra isla, porque allí tanbién eran caribes. E ya esta barca se quería tornar a los navíos con su presa, e por parte de baxo por la costa venía una canoa en que venían cuatro onbres e dos mugeres e un mochacho; e desque vieron la flota, maravillados se enbevecieron tanto, que por una grande ora no se movieron de un lugar, casi dos tiros de lonbarda de los navíos. En esto fueron vistos de los que estavan en la barca e de toda la flota; e luego los de la barca fueron a ellos, tan junto con la tierra, que con el enbevecimiento que tenían, maravillándose e pensando qué cosa sería aquélla, nunca los vieron fasta que estovieron muy cerca dellos, que no les pudieron mucho fuir, aunque farto trabajaron por ello; e los de la barca trabajaron con tanta priesa que no se les pudieron ir.

Los caribes, desque vieron que el fuir no les aprovechava, con mucha osadía pusieron mano a los arcos, tan bien las mugeres como los onbres; e digo con mucha osadía, porque ellos no eran más de cuatro onbres e dos mugeres, e eran los de la barca más de veinte e cinco, de los cuales firieron dos onbres: al uno dieron dos frechadas en los pechos e al otro

From there, that evening, they saw another island[18] but came upon some shallows later in the night, so, out of fear, they dropped anchor and dared not move until daybreak. In the morning, soon after appeared another very large island.[19] They did not land on any of these islands, preferring to bring relief to the people left behind at Hispaniola during the first voyage; but it did not please God that they should find them alive, as will be reported later on in this book.

The following day at mealtime, they arrived at an island which seemed very beautiful and well-populated and moored there.[20] Meanwhile, the Admiral ordered a boat with some men to go ashore and learn, if they could communicate, what kind of people were there and also to get information about the course to follow even though, as it turned out, the Admiral, who had never travelled over that way, proved nevertheless very well oriented. From the above-mentioned boat, some men landed and reached a village, where the people had already gone into hiding and captured five or six women and some boys. The majority of these women were prisoners here also as on the other island, since there were Caribs here, too. This boat was about ready to come back to the fleet along with the prisoners when on the southern part, along the coast, they saw an approaching canoe with four men, two women and a boy. As soon as it came into sight of the fleet, they were so filled with wonder and awestruck that for a good part of an hour they stood within close distance, at a couple of lombard shots from the vessels. They were noticed, consequently, by those in the returning boat as well as by the entire fleet; and in a short while once those of the boat were very near them, close to land, being still astonished and novelty-struck to the point of not noticing, in their wonder and strain to perceive what was going on, the approaching Spaniards until they were too close for them to be able to flee, although they tried quite earnestly, but those of the boat moved very fast and did not allow them to take off. When the Caribs realized that they could not succeed in fleeing, with great boldness they took to their bows, both women and men, and I think with great

[18] Nevis.
[19] Antigua.
[20] St. Croix.

una por el costado; e si no fuera porque llevavan adargas e tablachinas, e porque los enbestieron presto con la barca e les trastornaran la canoa, asaetearan os más dellos con sus frechas. Después de trastornada la canoa, quedaron en el agua nadando, e a las vezes haciendo pie, porque por allí avía unos baxos; e tovieron harto que fazer en tomarlos, que todavía trabajavan por tirar; con todo se les iva uno, e no lo pudieron tomar sino mal herido de una lançada, de que murió, el cual truxieron así mal herido a los navíos.

La diferencia destos indios caribes a los otros ya dichos, en elábito, es que los de Caribe tienen el cavello muy largo y los otros son tresquilados e fechas muchas diferencias en las cabeças de cruzes e de otras pinturas en diversas maneras, cada uno como se le antoja, lo cual hazen con cañas agudas. E todos, así los de Caribe como los otros, es gente sin barvas, que por maravilla hallaréis onbre que las tenga, que todas se las pelan o quitan antes que crezcan, de manera que paresce que no les nascen. Estos que allí tomaron venían tiznados los ojos e las cejas, lo cual paresce que hazen por gala, e con aquello parescían cosa espantable; el uno de aquellos dixo, que en una isla de aquellas llamada Carib, que es la primera que se vido, a la cual la flota non llegó, que ay mucho oro, e que si allá fuesen que llevasen açadones e cosas para hazer sus caminos e traerían cuanto oro quisiesen.

Luego aquel día partió de allí la flota, en cabo de seis o siete oras después de aver allí llegado, e fueron a otra tierra que parescía a ojo que estava en el camino que la flota avía de llevar, e llegaron noche cerca della; e otro día de mañana fueron por la costa della, e era muy grand tierra, aunque no era muy continua, que eran más de cuarenta e tantos islones, tierra muy alta, la más della pelada, lo cual no es en nenguna de las que avían visto. E a esta no llegaron para saltar en tierra, salvo una carabela latina que llegó a un islón de aquellos, en el qual hallaron ciertas casas de pescadores.

Las mugeres indias que traían dixieron que no eran pobladas aquellas tierras, e andovieron por aquella costa lo más de aquel día, fasta otro día en la tarde, que llegaron a vista de

courage, being no more than four men and two women against more than 25 in the boat, and wounding two: one was struck by two arrows in his chest and the other by one in the ribs. Had it not been in fact for the protection of their shields and wooden armor and for their sudden collision with the boat which capsized their canoe as well, they would have wounded the majority of them with their arrows. Even after the canoe capsized, they kept on shooting arrows from the water, either swimming or standing since there were some shallows, making it difficult as much as they could to take them. And, despite all of this, one of them got away and could not be captured until after being seriously wounded by a thrusted lance. Thus, they brought him to the ships seriously wounded, where he later died. The difference between these Carib Indians and the others in the way they dress is that the Caribs have very long hair whereas the others have their hair cut and they paint their heads with crosses and other drawings, in different styles, as each likes best, doing so using sharp reeds. And, all of them, Caribs or not, are without beards. It would be a great surprise to find a bearded man since they all either cut or remove it before it grows out, as if they never had a beard. The ones captured there had eyes and eyebrows dyed, apparently as an ornament and to appear more frightening. One of them said that on one of the Carib islands, the first one seen and bypassed by the fleet, there is much gold. In case they did go there they should take picks and other tools to open trails and be able to take as much gold as wished.

Right away, that day, the fleet departed, approaching six hours later another land that seemed to lie roughly on the route to be followed, but reached it at night. So, the following morning they coasted along and found it to be a very large land, though not continuous, since there were more than forty islets. It was also quite elevated and for the most part without vegetation, different from the lands they had until then seen. The ships did not get close enough to go ashore, except for a lateen-rigged caravel that reached one of those islets where some fishermen's huts were found.

With the Indian women aboard claiming those islands were not populated, they kept coasting along most of that day and until the following evening, when they came in view of

otra isla llamada Borique, cuya costa corrieron todo un día, jueves, la cual tenía por aquella vanda treinta leguas, e es muy fermosa e muy fértil; e al parescer a ésta vienen los de Caribe a saltear e conquistar, de la cual llevan mucha gente para comer. Estos no tienen canoas nengunas ni saben andar por mar; enpero usan de arcos e frechas, como los caribes, con que pelean e se defienden; e si por ventura han victoria de los que los vienen a saltear, tanbién se los comen como los caribes a ellos.

En un puerto desta isla estovo la flota dos días, donde saltó mucha gente en tierra; enpero nunca pudieron aver lengua, que todos fuyeron como gente atemorizada de los caribes. Todas estas islas fueron descubiertas deste viage, que en el otro viage nenguna avía visto el almirante; todas parescían muy fermosas islas, e ésta parescía mejor a todos. Aquí se acabaron las islas que ovo fazia la parte de España, atrás de lo que andovieron que avía dexado de ver el almirante en el primero viaje. E aun créese aver alguna isla o islas antes que éstas, cuarenta o cincuenta leguas fazia España; porque antes que viessen tierra los desta flota, vieron unas aves, que se llaman rabihorcados, volar; e son aves de rapiña marinas, e non sientan ni duermen sobre el agua; e viéronlas sobre tarde, rodeando, sobir en alto, e depués seguir su vía de buscar tierra para dormir; las cuales non podìan ya ir a caer, segund era tarde, más de doze o quinze leguas; e esto era sobre la mano derecha de la flota fazia España, de donde todos juzgaron allì quedar tierra, que non se buscó porque se hazía rodeo e tardança para el viage, enpero si las quisieren buscar non las pueden errar.

Desta isla susodicha de Borique partió la flota una madrugada; e aquel día, antes que fuesse noche, ovieron vista de tierra, la cual tanpoco non era conoscida de los del otro viage; enpero, por las nuevas de las mugeres que llevavan, sospechavan que serìa la Española, la que ivan a buscar. E era la mesma Española, Aití llamada por los indios; e entre ella e la otra de Borique, ya dicha, parescía otra isla, aunque non era grande.

another island called Borique[21] which they also sail along that entire day, Thursday, being on that side thirty leagues long, quite beautiful and most fertile. It seems, further, that this island is attacked and pillaged by Caribs who take away many people to eat them. The natives here do not own any canoes nor are they able to travel by sea; however, they use bows and arrows like the Caribs against whom they fight and defend themselves, and, when by chance they happen to overcome the attackers, they eat them like the Caribs do with them.

In a port of this island[22] where many men went ashore, the fleet anchored for two days; however, they could get no information, for all had fled as if chased by the Caribs. All these islands were discovered during this trip since during the previous one the Admiral had visited none of them. All appeared to be very beautiful islands and this one seemed to everyone the best. Thus terminated the string of islands west of our course, toward Spain, which the Admiral had neglected to visit during his first trip. Beyond these, forty or fifty leagues toward Spain, it is thought there are one or more islands, since before sighting land those of the fleet saw a few birds in flight that are called frigates,[23] predatory sea birds which do not stop or sleep on the water. Toward sunset they saw them climbing high, in circles and then following their instinct toward land to rest on. And since it was evening the birds could not go farther than twelve or fifteen leagues in the direction of Spain since the birds' flight was to the right of the fleet. It was indeed generally thought that there had to be unsought land, intentionally so, to avoid a useless detour and a certain delay although they were equally convinced to be able to find it if they wanted to.

One morning the fleet left the said Borique island and the same day, before night, a land also not discovered in the previous voyage was sighted. They suspected it was Hispaniola, that is, the one they were looking for owing to the information given by the women they had brought along. Indeed, it was Hispaniola, called Haiti by the Indians, and between them and the above-named island of Borique, they saw another island but not a large one.

---

[21] Puerto Rico.

[22] Bahía.

[23] For the translation of the term "rabiorcados" with Italian *fregate*, see *Nuova Raccolta Colombiana*, Note 35, Vol. I, pt. 2.

CAPITULO CXX

Cómo llegaron a la Española y fallaron muertos los onbres que avían dexado.

Llegados a la Española el almirante e toda su flota, a donde arribaron por aquel comienço era tierra baxa e muy llana, del conoscimiento de la cual aun estavan todos muy dubdosos si fuesse ella; porque por aquella parte ni el almirante ni los otros que con él avían ido no la avían visto. Esta isla es muy grande e es nonbrada por provincias, e a esta parte por donde llegaron llaman Ahía, e a otra provincia junto con esta llaman Samana, e a otra Boyo, e a otra Cibao, e otras muchas provincias ay, así como acá en España. Por la costa desta isla corrió la flota al pie de cient leguas, porque fasta donde el almirante avía dexado la gente avía este conpás, que sería en comedio desta isla. Andando por en derecho de la provincia llamada Samana, echó el almirante en tierra uno de los indios que el otro viaje avía traído a España, vestido e con algunas cosillas.

Aquel día fallesció el marinero vizcaíno que avía sido ferido de los caribes, ya dichos, que tomaron, e murió por su mala guarda; e porque iva por costa dióse lugar que saliesen en una barca a enterrarlo, e fueron en reguarda de la barca dos carabelas, e acercáronse a tierra e salieron de la barca. E desque salieron, muchos indios, de los cuales algunos traían oro al cuello e a las orejas, querían venir con los cristianos a los navios, e non los quisieron traer porque no llevavan liscencia del almirante; de los cuales, desque vieron que non los querían traer, se metieron dos dellos en una canoa e se vinieron a una de las dos carabelas, en la cual los recebieron con su canoa, e truxiéronlos a la nao del almirante.

Dixieron, mediante un intérprete indio de los que ivan de acá de España, que un rey de aquella provincia los enbiava

CHAPTER CXX

How they reached Hispaniola and found the men, whom they had left there, dead.

Approaching Hispaniola, the Admiral and his entire fleet immediately came to a low and very flat area about which all of them were most doubtful whether it really corresponded to the island they were looking for, since neither the Admiral nor the men who had come with him could recollect ever seeing that part. This island is very large, has different names varying with its regions; the area in which they had arrived was called Ahia, with the one next to it being Samana, then Boyo, Cibao and many different regions just like here in Spain.

The fleet sailed along this island's coast for about a hundred leagues since this was about the distance to the middle part of the island, where the Admiral had left his men. While heading toward the region called Samana, the Admiral had an Indian, one of those taken to Spain during the previous trip, go ashore all dressed up and with small gifts.

That day died the imprudent Biscayan sailor earlier wounded by the terrified Caribs who had captured him. Since they were sailing near the coast, it was possible for them to go ashore in a boat and bury him, with two caravels keeping close watch as it approached and landed. After they landed, many Indians, some wearing gold around their necks and in their ears, wanted to follow the Christians to the vessels but were refused for lack of permission to do so from the Admiral. Two of them, realizing they were not going to be taken, approached one of the two caravels using a canoe and succeeded in being received and led to the Admiral's ship.

By means of an interpreting Indian, one of those returning from Spain, they spoke of a chief of that land who had sent

a saber que qué gente eran, e que les rogava que saliessen a tierra e que daría al almirante mucho oro que tenía, e de comer de lo que tuviesse. E el almirante les mandó dar sendas camisas e bonetes e otras cosillas, e les dixo que porque iva donde estava Guacanari non se podía detener; que otro tienpo avría para que le pudiesse ver; e con esto se fueron.

La flota non cessó su viage fasta llegar a un puerto quel almirante llamó Monte Juan, donde estovieron dos días para ver la dispusición de la tierra; porque non avía parescido al almirante el logar donde avía dexado la gente que estava en un assiento bueno para hazer asiento. E descendieron en tierra, e avía cerca de allí un grand río de muy buena agua; enpero era toda tierra muy anegada e muy indispuesta para abitar. E andando viendo el río e tierra, algunos de los de la flota, fallaron dos onbres muertos junto con el río: esto fué el primero día, e otro día siguiente fallaron otros dos onbres muertos más adelante de aquellos, e el uno dellos estava en desposición que se le pudo conoscer tener muchas barvas; e algunos de los del armada sospecharon más mal que bien, así porque los indios son todos sin barvas, como porque al uno de los muertos fallaron un lazo al pescueço e a otro un lazo al pie. E este puerto está, del logar donde avía quedado la gente cristiana el primero viage, doze leguas.

Pasados dos días, alçaron velas para ir donde el almirante avía dexado la sobredicha gente en compañía del rey de los indios de aquella provincia, llamado Guacanari, que parescía ser de los principales de la isla. Aquel día llegaron en derecho de aquel lugar ya tarde; e porque allí avía unos bajos, donde el otro viage se avía perdido la nao en que avia ido el almirante, no osaron tomar el puerto cerca de tierra fasta que el otro día de mañana se sondase e pudiesen entrar seguramente: quedaron aquella noche una legua de tierra. Esa tarde, yendo para allí, de lexos, salió una canoa en que parescían cinco o seis indios, los cuales venian apriesa para la flota; e el almirante, creyendo que le seguiría fasta alcançarlo, non quiso que los esperasen; e ellos porfiando llegaron fasta un tiro de lonbarda de la flota, e paráronse a mirar; e desque vieron que no los esperavan, dieron buelta. E después que surgieron en aquel dicho lugar sobre tarde, el almirante mandó tirar dos lonbardas a ver si

them to learn what kind of people they were and also to beg them to go ashore, where the Chief would have presented the Admiral with much of the gold he owned as well as share whatever food he had. The Admiral then commanded his men to offer garments and caps and other small objects, adding that since he was going to where Guacanagarí was, he could not linger further and that on a later occasion he would come to meet him, and after that he went off. The fleet did not put an end to its journey until it anchored in a port the Admiral named Mount Juan and where they stopped for two days to study the topography of the area, since the place where the Admiral had left his people had never seemed to him to lay in an area completely suitable to the establishment of a settlement. They went ashore and found a large river nearby with very good water; however, being a marshy land it turned out to be unsuitable to live in. As they continued to survey the area and its river, some men of the fleet found two corpses near the river; this happened the first day. On the next day they found two more dead men a little farther on, with one in a position that revealed he had a dense beard. The sailors' suspicions of something worse ahead was justified by the fact that all Indians have no beard, and two of the dead men were bound with ropes, one around his neck and the other around his foot. This port is twelve leagues away from the place where the Christian people had been left during the first voyage.

Two days went by before hoisting sails to go where the Admiral had left his people in this territory with a chief the Indians called Guacanagarí and who had appeared to be one of the most important rulers of this island. They arrived near such a place late that day, but given the shallows in that precise area where the flagship had been lost during the previous crossing, they did not dare to dock near the land before dawn the next day when they could sound the depth and approach safely. So that night they stopped about a league off the coast. During the evening a canoe with five or six Indians appeared in the far-away distance, heading hurriedly toward the fleet. The Admiral, knowing they would pursue him all the way, did not want to wait for them; and in fact, in their persistence, they arrived within a stone's throw of the fleet and stopped there to observe. Once they realized the ships were not expecting them, they turned back. When in the evening the fleet

responderían los ctistianos que avían quedado a cerca del dicho Guacanari, porque tanbién les avían quedado lonbardas; a lo cual nunca respondieron ni menos parescían, ni señal dellos, nin casas ni el logar donde avían quedado, de lo cual se desconsoló mucho la gente, e tomaron la sospecha que se devía de tomar.

E estando así todos tristes, pasadas cuatro o cinco oras de la noche, vino la mesma canoa que esa tarde avían visto, e venía a la flota dando bozes preguntando por el almirante; e un capitán de una carabela donde primero llegaron tráxolos a la nao del almirante; los cuales nunca quisieron hablar fasta que el almirante les fablase, e demandaron lunbre para lo conoscer, e después que lo conoscieron entraron en la nao. Era el uno privado del Guacanari, el cual Guacanati los avía tornado a enbiar después que se avían tornado aquella tarde; e truxieron dos carátulas de oro que el Guacanari enbiava en presente, la una para el almirante e la otra para un capitán que el otro viage avía ido con él; e estovieron en la nao hablando con el almirante en presencia de todos por tres oras, mostrando mucho plazer. E preguntándoles por los ctistianos que allí avían quedado qué tales estavan, aquel privado dixo que todos estavan buenos, aunque entre ellos avía algunos muertos de dolencia e otros de diferencia que avía avido entre ellos; e que Guacanari estava en otro lugar ferido en una pierna, e que por eso no avía venido, pero que otro día vernía; porque otros dos reyes, llamados el uno Caonaboa e el otro Marieni, avían venido a pelear con él, e que le avían quemado el lugar. E luego esa noche se bolvieron, diziendo que otro día vernían con el dicho Guacanari; e con esto dexaron esta noche consolada la gente del armada, e se partieron.

E otro día de mañana estovieron esperando a Guacanari e nunca vino; e entre tanto saltaron en tierra algunos por mandado del almirante, e fueron al lugar donde solía estar Guacanari, e falláronlo quemado; e un cortijo algo fuerte con una palizada, donde los cristianos abitavan e tenian lo suyo, estava tanbién quemado e derribado, e ciertas bernias e ropas

anchored in that place, the Admiral ordered two lombard shots fired to check whether the Christians whom they had left in an area near the above-named Guacanagarí would return the fire since they had been provided some lombards too; however, there was no response at all to that signal, nor was there any indication, such as houses, or fortifications, where they had been left behind. This very much saddened the searching people who then felt the natural suspicions arising in such a circumstance.

While they were thus sad, four or five hours into the night the same canoe seen earlier that evening approached the fleet, shouting and asking for the Admiral. One of the caravels' captains, the closest to their approach, took them to the Admiral's ship. They absolutely did not want to speak except with the Admiral and asked for more light on him so that he could be recognized and, after seeing him, they went on board the ship. One of them was Guacanagarí's trusted man. Chief Guacanagarí had sent him along with the others a second time after they had returned that evening. They brought two golden masks which Guacanagarí was sending as gifts, one to the Admiral and the other for a captain who had been with him during the first voyage. They remained on the ship conversing publicly with the Admiral for three hours and showed much satisfaction. When the natives were asked about the Christians that had been left there, the chief's relative claimed they all were well except for the fact that some of them had died because of illness and others because of altercations that had arisen among them. He said also that Guacanagarí, with a leg wound, was in another area, and because of it he had not been able to come himself but intended to do so the next day anyway. Two other chiefs, Caonabó and Marianí, had gone to attack him and had set fire to his village. Soon afterwards they left, promising to come back the following day along with the above-named Guacanagarí, thus leaving reassured the people of the fleet for that night.

The following morning while waiting for Guacanagarí, who was not coming, the Admiral ordered some men to go ashore and reach the place where Guacanagarí usually stayed. They found it burned down. Even the camp where the Christians used to live and keep their belongings, though fortified with a palisade, had been burnt and destroyed, as were some

que los indios avían traído a hechar en la casa. E los indios que por allí parescían andavan muy estraños, e non se osavan llegar a los cristianos, mas antes fuían, lo que no parescía bien a los cristianos; e arrojándoles cuentas e caxcaveles e otras cositas ovo de asegurarse un su pariente del Guacanari e otros tres, los cuales entraron en la barca; e truxiéronlos a la nao e preguntáronles por los cristianos, e dixieron que todos eran muertos.

E ya lo avía dicho uno de los indios que llevaron de Castilla, que le avian dicho los indios que avían venido a la nao cómo eran muertos; enpero no le avían creído. E preguntando a este indio pariente de Guacanari, que quién los avía muerto, dixo que el rey Caonoboa e el rey Marieni, e que les quemaron las casas del lugar, e que estavan dellos muchos hetidos, e que tanbién el dicho Guacanari estava herido, pasado un muslo, el cual estava en otro logar, e que él quería ir luego allá, a lo llamar; al cual dieron algunas cosas e luego se partió para donde estava Guacanari, e todo aquel día estovieron esperando e nunca vino.

Otro día salió el almirante a tierra, e algunos con él, e fueron donde solía estar la villa e avían quedado los cristianos, la cual estava toda quemada, e los vestidos de los cristianos se hallavan por aquella yerva. Por aquella ora non se vido nengund muerto, e avía sospecha si el Guacanari los oviese muerto, e otros dezían que cómo avía él de quemar su villa; e el almirante mandó cabar todo el sitio donde los cristianos estavan fortalescidos, porque él les avía mandado que desque toviessen alguna cantidad de oro que lo enterrasen. E entre tanto que esto se hazía, quiso llegar a una legua de ay, donde le avía parescido aver buen sitio para edificar una villa; e llegaron a un poblado donde avía siete o ocho casas, las cuales los indios, luego que vieron ir cristianos, desanpararon, e llevaron lo que pudieron, e dexaron lo otro escondido en las yervas junto con las casas; que era gente tan bestial que no tenían discreción para escoger donde abitar, e los que bivian a la marina era maravilla quand bestialmente bivían, las casas llenas de yervas en derredor e de umedad, que era maravilla cómo bivían.

blankets and clothes which the Indians had brought to throw into the houses. The Indians who could be seen around there seemed very suspicious and afraid to approach the Christians. By throwing them seed-pearls and little bells and other small things, however, Guacanagarí's relative and three others were reassured enough to go on board the boat. They were taken to the ship where, asked about the Christians, they admitted that all of them were dead.

Actually, one of the Indians brought back from Castile had already given news of it since some of the Indians who had come to the fleet had told him how they died; however, he was not believed. When the Indian relative of Guacanagarí was asked who had killed them, he replied that chief Caonabó and chief Marieni were responsible: they had burnt down the huts of that place and wounded many of them including Guacanagarí himself, who was wounded in a leg and had moved elsewhere, and he said that he intended to go at once to call him. So, they gave this Indian a few things and he went off to where Guacanagarí was. They waited for him all that day, but no one came. The following day the Admiral and some others with him went ashore and reached the former settlement area where they had left the Christians, found it burnt to the ground, and saw the Christians' clothes strewn all around. At first they did not see any bodies; some were arguing that Guacanagarí had killed them but others objected, saying that he himself would have had to burn down his own village. The Admiral commanded the men to dig all around the area where the Christians had built their stronghold since they had been given instructions to bury the gold after gathering a sizeable amount. In the meantime, while all of this was happening, he wanted to go exploring within a radius of one league for a place that was seemingly suitable to build a city. They reached a village of seven or eight huts abandoned by the Indians, who fled as soon as they saw the approaching Christians, taking with them what they could and leaving the rest hidden in the tall grass near the huts. These people were most primitive, showing lack of discernment even in selecting the place in which to live, and most astonishing was to see how roughly the people lived who settled near the sea, since around their huts there were weeds and such a high level of humidity as to make one wonder how they could survive.

Fallaron allí muchas cosas de los cristianos, así como una almalafa muy gentil, la cual nunca se avía descogido de como se avía llevado de Castilla, e calças, e una áncora de la nao que el almirante allí avía perdido el otro viage, e pedaços de paño e otras cosas. E aun fallaron, buscando las cosas que tenían guardadas, en una esportilla mucho cosida e mucho a recabdo, una cabeça de onbre mucho guardada; e creyeron que sería la cabeça de alguno que tenían por reliquia, de padre o madre, o de algund rey, por alguna costunbre de la tierra.

De allí el almirante se bolvió, e los que con él ivan, por donde estava la villa, e falló muchos indios que se avían asegurado con los que quedaron allí guardando e cavando, buscando si los cristianos oviessen dexado oro escondido, e con otros cristianos de la flota que allí avían quedado; e avían rescatado con ellos oro fasta un marco, e avían mostrado dónde estavan muertos honze onbres de los cristianos, cubiertos ya de la yerva que avía crescido sobre ellos. E todos aquellos indios hablavan por una boca, que Caonaboa e Matieni los avían muerto; enpero afirmavan e dezían que los cristianos tenían cada uno tres o cuatro mugeres; donde se creyó que el mal que les vino a aquellos cristianos que allí sin dicha ovieron quedado, fué por su desconcierto; e por se enbolver con las mugeres indias los indios de celos los mataron; o por algunas cosas de desaguisados que farían en la tierra se invocaron para los matar.

Otro día, de mañana, porque por todo aquello non avía lugar dispuesto para poblar, el almirante enbió una caravela a buscar por una parte, e él fué por otra; e él falló un puerto muy seguro e en muy buena disposición de tierra para abitar. E cuando bolvió era venida la caravela que avía ido por la otra parte, en la cual avía ido Melchior e otros cuatro o cinco cavalleros,; e yendo costeando en su viaje, salió a ellos una canoa con dos indios, el uno hermano del Guacanari; el cual, conoscido por un piloto que iva en la dicha caravela, les preguntó que quién iva allí, e el piloto le dixo: «Onbres principales del almirante». E el indio les dixo que Guacanari les rogava que saliessen a tierra donde él tenía su aposentamiento, el cual era fasta cincuenta casas. E saltaron en tierra los más principales que ivan en la caravela, con la barca, e fueron a donde estava el Guacanari, el cual hallaron en su cama echado faziendo del doliente. Fablaron con él, preguntándole por los cristianos: respondió,

There they found many of the Christians' belongings, as in the case of a very attractive mantle (never unfolded since it was brought from Castile), trousers, an anchor lost by the flagship there during the first voyage, pieces of cloth, and other things. While searching, they also found among objects kept in a small, very well-crafted and hidden-away basket, a well-preserved human head thought to be the head of a father or mother or some chief locally revered as a relic.

From there the Admiral and those with him returned to the settlement site and found many Indians, reassured by now by those people who had kept watch there and were digging and searching along with other Christians of the fleet to locate where the Christians had hidden any gold. With the Indians' cooperation they retrieved almost a *marco* of gold and discovered the place where eleven dead Christians laid already covered by the grass that had grown over them. All these Indians claimed, unanimously, that Caonabó and Marieni had killed them; however, they also asserted that each of the Christians had three or four women and they therefore thought the evil that ensued among the Christians who had been left there was caused by internal disagreements and also perhaps due to the fact that the Indians might have killed them out of jealousy, for becoming involved with Indian women; or else that the pretext for killing them was provided by some irrational acts possibly carried out by the Spaniards.

The next morning, since there was no suitable place to settle in all that area, the Admiral sent a caravel to search in one direction while he himself went the opposite way. He found a very safe place with an excellent territorial configuration, well suited to live in. When he came back, he found also the caravel that had gone in the other direction with Melchior and four or five other infantrymen who reported that while sailing along the coast, they were approached by a canoe with two Indians aboard, one of whom was Guacanagarí's brother — as recognized by one of the caravel pilots — and who himself asked who they were, and the pilot answered: "Important men of the Admiral." The Indian told them that Guacanagarí begged them to go ashore to his village of about fifty huts. The highest ranking men on the caravel went ashore in a boat and made their way to where Guacanagarí was and saw him laying on a pallet as one who is seemingly suffering.

concertando con la misma razón de los otros, que Caonaboa e Marieni los avían muerto, e que a él lo avían ferido en un muslo, el cual mostró ligado. Los que estonces lo vieron asi les paresció como él lo dixo; al tiempo del despedir, a cada uno dellos dió una joya de oro, a cada uno como le paresció que lo merescía, segund el ábito en que los vido.

Este oro hazían ellos en fojas muy delgadas, para carátulas e para poderse asentar sobre betumen que ellos fazían, e si ansí no fuera non se asentara de otra manera. Hazían para asentar en la cabeça, e para colgar en las orejas e narizes, e para todo lo fazían delgado, e así era menester; e ellos no tenían nada dello por riqueza ni cosa de grand valor, salvo por bien parescer.

Dixo el Guacanari, por señas e como mejor él pudo, que dixiesen al almirante de cómo él estava así ferido, que lo viniesse a ver; e luego como el almirante llegó, luego los sobredichos le contaron todo lo dicho. E otro día de mañana acordó el almirante de ir allá, al cual lugar llegó con los que ivan con él, dentro de tres oras, que la jornada era de tres leguas e aún menos, desde donde estava la flota fasta allí; e cuando allá llegaron era ora de comer, e el almirante comió antes de salir en tierra. E luego mandó que todos los capitanes viniesen con sus barcas para ir en tierra, porque ya esta mañana, antes que partiesen de donde estavan, avía venido el hermano de Guacanari, e avía fablado con el almirante e a darle priesa que fuese a donde estava el dicho Guacanari. Y allí fué el almirante a tierra, e toda la más gente de pro con él, tan ataviados que en una cibdad principal parescieran bien; llevó algunas cosas para le presentar, porque ya avía recebido dél alguna cantidad de oro, y era razón de le responder con la obra e voluntad que él avía mostrado.

El dicho Guacanari tenía asimesmo aparejado para le fazer presente; e cuando el almirante llegó con los capitanes e gente al lugar e casa donde estava Guacanari, falláronlo echado en su cama, como ellos usan, colgada en el aire, fecha de algodón como de red. Non se levantó, salvo desde la cama hizo el senblante de la cortesía como él mejor supo; mostró mucho sentimiento con lágrimas en los ojos por la muerte de los

While talking with him and asking him about the Christians, his answers clearly coincided with the explanation brought forward earlier by the others, that Caonabó and Marien í had killed them and that he himself had been wounded in the leg, which he showed bandaged. What he said seemed trustworthy to those who saw him as he was. At the time to take leave, he presented each of them with a gold ornament, depending on how important they appeared to him to be by their dress.

The Indians work this gold into very thin layers in order to make masks and be able to link together pieces they made which otherwise could not be joined. They worked gold so as to wear it on their heads, hang it on their ears or nostrils, and in every case indeed they worked it thin, as they had to, and did not consider it wealth or a thing of great value but rather only a fine ornament.

Guacanagarí said, by gestures and as best he could, that they report to the Admiral that he was wounded and to please come to see him; and no sooner did the Admiral return that these men conveyed to him all that had been said. So, the following morning he decided to visit in about three hours the village with all the people who were with him since the distance between that place and the fleet was of three leagues or even less. It was mealtime when they arrived, so the Admiral ate before going ashore. At once he commanded that all the captains go ashore in their boats because that very morning, before leaving the place where they were, Guacanagarí's brother had come and had talked to the Admiral, urging him to go to the place where the above-named Guacanagarí lay. The Admiral went ashore there along with all the high-ranking men so well-dressed that they would have been noticed indeed even in an important city. Columbus had brought a few things to donate, having already received from Guacanagarí a substantial amount of gold, making it only reasonable that he reciprocate with equal acts of generosity.

The said Guacanagarí had also pre-arranged to present him with a gift, and when the Admiral arrived, along with the captains and the others, to his place and dwelling, they found him laying on his cot, a cotton net hanging in the air as usual. He did not get up from the bed but showed courtesy as best he could. He also showed great emotion and tears in his eyes for the Christians' death and began to talk about it,

cristianos, e començó a fablar en ello mostrando como mejor podía cómo unos murieron de dolencia e cómo otros se avían ido a Caonaboa, a buscar la mina del oro, e que allí los avian muerto; e los otros, que se los avían venido a matar en su villa. E a lo que parescía en los cuerpos de los muertos, podía aver dos meses que eran muertos e que avía acontecido aquello.

A esa ora presentó al almirante ocho marcos e medio de oro, e cinco o seis cintos labrados de pedrería de diversos colores, e un bonete de la misma pedrería, e en el bonete estava un joyel; lo cual le dió en mucha veneración. Estavan allí presentes el dotor Chanca, médico, vezino de Sevilla, e otro, çurugiano del armada; e dixo el almirante a Guacanari cómo aquellos eran sabios para curar las enfermedades de los onbres, que les quisiese mostrar la herida; e él respondió que le plazía, para lo cual el dicho doctor le dixo que sería nescesario, si pudiesse, que saliese de casa, porque de la gente estava escura la casa e non se podía bien ver, lo cual él fizo luego: creo que sería más de enpacho que de gana, e arrimándose a él salió fuera. Después de asentado, allegó el çurujano e començó de desligarle, e estonces dixo Guacanari al almirante que era ferida fecha con *ceva*, que quiere dezir *piedra*; después que fué asentado, el doctor e el çurujano vieron que no tenía más mal en aquella pierna que en la otra, aunque él hazía del raposo que le dolía. Ciertamente este caso puso a todos mayor sospecha de la que tenían; pero, aun con todo eso, nengund onbre cuerdo se pudo bien determinar para juzgar en este caso e saber la verdad, porque las razones eran tan innotas, que ciertas cosas avía que mostravan aver venido gente contraria; e asimesmo el almirante no sabía que se hazer. Parescióle, e a otros muchos, que por estonces, fasta saber bien la verdad, que se devía disimular, porque después de sabida cada que quisiesse podría tomar dél emienda.

Aquella tarde se vino con el almirante a la flota, e mostráronle cavallos e cuanto allí avía, de lo cual quedó muy maravillado, como de cosa estraña; tomó colasción en la nao, e esa tarde se bolvió a su casa; e el almirante le dixo que quería abitar allí con él e fazer allí casas; respondió que la

explaining, as best he could, how a few had died because of illness and the others, gone to Caonabó's territory to search for the gold mine, had been killed there. The remaining ones were killed right at La Navidad. Judging from the corpses, perhaps two months had passed since the killings had taken place.

Next he most deferentially presented the Admiral with eight and a half *marcos* in gold and five or six belts finished with different colored stones and a head piece adorned with the same stones and, in addition, a jewel. Doctor Chanca, a physician and citizen of Seville and another physician, the fleet's surgeon, were standing there when the Admiral told Guacanagarí that they were skilled in curing human illness and that he should show them his wound. When he answered that it would please him to do so, the above-named doctor pointed out that it would be necessary, if he could, to get out of the hut, since, given the many people and the darkness of the room, it would be impossible to examine carefully his wound. He quickly complied and got out, leaning on the doctor, I think more annoyed, however, than willingly. After he was seated, the surgeon approached him and began to untie the bandage as Guacanagarí was telling the Admiral it was a wound made by a *ceva*, which means stone. While still seated both physician and surgeon realized that he did not feel any more pain in that leg than in the other, notwithstanding his clever acting to show it hurt. This behavior certainly aroused in everyone a much greater suspicion than they already felt; however, despite all of it, no wise man could truly decide and pass judgement on this case, or learn the truth, because the clues were mixed and obscure and indeed various signs indicated that enemies had been there. Even the Admiral did not know what to do. It seemed right, however, to him and many others that, temporarily at least, until the full truth was known, they should simulate belief considering that once they learned the real truth they could get back to him and obtain satisfaction.

That evening he followed the Admiral to the fleet and was shown horses and all else that was brought, exuding great amazement for it as for a strange thing. He ate on the ship before returning that night to his dwelling. The Admiral announced to him that he wished to live there with him and

plazía, pero que el logar era malsano porque era muy úmido, e tal era él por cierto. Esto todo pasava por intérpetres, que eran dos indios de los que avian venido en Castilla que andavan allí con el almirante, que avian quedado de siete que partieron de Castilla, que los cinco se murieron en el camino e aquellos dos escaparon por maravilla, llegando a grand peligro.

Otro día estovieron surtos en aquel puerto, e quiso saber Guacanarí cuando se partía el almirante, e el almirante le mandó dezir que otro día; e aquel día vino a la nao el sobredicho hermano suyo, e otros con él, e truxieron algund oro para resgatar.

En la nao avía diez mugeres de las que se avían tomado que estavan cabtivas en las islas de Caribi, e eran las más dellas de la isla de Boriquen; e aquel hermano de Guacanarí fabló con ellas e les dixo lo que luego esa noche pusieron en obra; e es que al primero sueño muy mansamente se echaron al agua e se fueron a tierra, de manera que cuando fueron halladas menos ivan tanto trecho que con las barcas non pudieron tomar más de las cuatro, las cuales tomaron al salir del agua; fueron nadando una grande media legua.

Otro día de mañana enbió el almirante a Guacanarí que le enbiase aquellas mugeres que la noche antes se le avian fuído, que luego las mandasse buscar; e cuando fueron fallaron el lugar despoblado, que non hallaron persona en él. Aquel día estovo la flota queda, porque el tiempo era contrario para salir; otro día acordó el almirante que de mañana fuesen todas las barcas a buscar puerto, e fueron por la costa fasta dos leguas buscando tierra de buena dispusición para fazer abitación, e tanbién los abitadores indios de por allí no se aseguravan de los cristianos. Llegaron a un lugar donde todos eran fuídos, a donde fallaron, junto con las casas, metido en el monte, un indio herido de una vara de una hetida que resollava por las espaldas, el cual non avía podido fuir más lexos.

Los indios desta isla Española, Aytí por ellos llamada, pelean con varas agudas, las cuales tiran con unas tiranderas como fazen acá los mochachos en Castilla, con las cuales tiran muy lexos e asaz certero, que para gente desarmada puede hazer harto dapño. Este indio herido dixo al almirante que Caonaboa

build some houses. He answered that it would be pleasing although that locality was unhealthy, being very humid and it really was so. All of this was communicated through the two Indian interpreters who had gone to Castile and were now with the Admiral. They were the only ones left of the seven who departed from Castile: five of them had died during the crossing, but these two surprisingly escaped death though they too had been in most critical conditions.

The following day they dropped anchor in that port and Guacanagarí asked when the Admiral would be leaving. The Admiral sent him word that he would leave on another day, so that very day the brother of the above-named chief and others along with him came aboard, bringing a certain amount of gold to trade. There were ten women on the ship of those they had taken, having been prisoners on the Carib islands, and most of them were from Borique. Guacanagarí's brother spoke with them and prompted them to what they soon, that very night, would put into effect: during the first sleep they very cautiously dove into the sea to swim ashore. When this was discovered, they had covered such a long distance that the boats were able to retake no more than four of them, capturing them as they were getting out of the water after swimming for a good half a league.

The following morning the Admiral sent word to Guacanagarí to search for and return at once those women who had fled on the previous night. But when the messengers got there, they found a deserted place; not one was left.

The fleet stayed there that day as the weather was unfavorable for setting sail. The day after the Admiral decided that all the vessels would go out looking for a port in the morning. So, they sailed along the coast for almost two leagues, looking for an area suitable to build some dwellings but the natives appeared suspicious of the Christians there. They arrived at an abandoned place where, near the dwellings, up on high ground, they found an Indian wounded by an arrow. His wounds reached his shoulders, preventing him from getting farther away.

The Indians on Hispaniola, which they call Haiti, fight with sharp arrows which they throw by means of slings, just as the boys here in Castile do. Thanks to the slings, they throw quite a good distance and with great accuracy so that they can certainly cause serious injuries to disarmed people. The wounded

e los suyos le avían herido, e avían quemado las casas de Guacanari,; así que el poco entender que le entendían e las razones innotas tenían confuso al almirante e a todos, que non podían saber de cierto cómo oviese sido la muerte de los cristianos.

No hallaron en aquel puerto dispusición saludable para fazer pueblo; acordó el almirante bolverse por la costa donde avía venido allí de Castilla, porque la mina del oro era fazia allá. Fué el tienpo tan contrario, que mayor pena les fué andar treinta leguas que ir allá desde Castilla; que en el tienpo contrario e largueza del camino ya eran tres meses cunplidos cuando descendieron en tierra.

Plugo a Nuestro Señor que por la contrariedad del tienpo, que non los dexó ir más adelante, ovieron de tomar tierra en el mejor sitio e dispusición que se pudiera escoger, donde avía muy buen puerto e muy grand pesquería, de la cual tenían mucha nescesidad por el carescimiento de la carne, que non avia en toda aquella tierra. Allí eran tierras muy gruesas para todas cosas, y tienen junto un río principal, e otro razonable bien cerca, de muy sengular agua. Allí començó a edificar una cibdad, a la cual puso nombre Isabela. Començóse a edificar una villa sobre la ribera de la mar, en muy lindo lugar, que un corral se deslindava con el agua, con una barranca de peña tajada tal, que por allí non avia menester defensa nenguna; la otra meitad estava cercada de una arboleda tan espesa que apenas un conejo pudiera andar por ella, e tan verde que en nengund tienpo del mundo fuego le podía quemar. Començaron de senbrar ortalizas e muchas cosas de las de acá, e crescían más allá en ocho días que acá en Castilla en veinte.

Fecho allí el asiento e comienço de pueblo, luego el almirante se conosció con los capitanes o reyes de aquella comarca, que ellos llaman allá caciques, e traíanles de sus viandas e venian allí continuamente muchos indios con oro para resgatar, e cargados de maíz, que es un buen manjar, e patatas, que son como nabos, que se crían debaxo de la tierra, de lo cual se hazen muchos manjares, el qual es muy

Indian told the Admiral that Caonabó and his men had wounded him and had burnt down Guacanagarí's dwellings; thus, between the little that could be understood and possibly unknown motivations made for great confusion for the Admiral and for all others involved, since they were not able to learn with certainty how the Christians' deaths had occurred.

In that port they did not find any healthy place in which to establish the settlement, so the Admiral decided to go back along the coast from where he had arrived coming from Castile since the gold mine lay in that direction. The weather was so unfavorable that they had more trouble in sailing for thirty leagues [24] than they had in getting there from Castile. Thus, because of contrary winds and the duration of the crossing, three months had already passed by the time they landed.

As it pleased Our Lord, through the impediment of the weather which did not let them go any farther, they were forced to land in the best place and environment that could ever be picked, with an excellent port and most abundant fish which was greatly needed due to the scarcity of meat in all that area. The fields nearby next to a large river and to another farther away of medium flow and with very special waters were very fertile for any kind of cultivation. There they began to build up a city, which they named La Isabela. They began to build the city on the river bank in a very pleasant place bordering the water on one side and right on a rocky precipice on the other, in such a way that no defense was necessary there. The other half was surrounded by so dense a wood that scarcely a rabbit could go through it and it was so green that a fire would never be able in any season to burn it down. They began to sow many vegetables and plants from our country, which grew more there in eight days than ever in Castile in twenty.

The settlement's foundation was established there and construction actually started. Soon the Admiral met with chiefs or kings of that region, referred to as caciques, as well as many Indians who brought them their own food and came over continually with some gold to trade and laden with nourishing corn and with root-like potatoes which grow underground and are used in many dishes; this is such a wholesome nourishment

---

[24] The text by Bernáldez coincides with Chanca's, who wrongly gives the distance in leagues, meaning miles instead.

cordial manjar con que se mantienen allá las gentes, y el maíz es en lugar de pan; ay otro manjar, que llaman ajes, tanbién se cría debaxo de la tierra; ay otro que llaman caçabí; ay otras muchas maneras de manjares e frutas, todas muy diferentes de los de acá de Castilla.

Lo que desta gente se pudo luego conoscer fué que era gente muy sinple, sin letras; non avían enpacho de andar desnudos como nascieron, ansí honbres como mugeres; las mugeres, por la mayor parte, traian cubiertas sus verguenças recinchada una mantilla de algodón en derredor de las caderas, e otras con fojas de árboles. Sus galas dellos e dellas eran pintarse unos de negro, otros de blanco, otros de colorado e de otras colores, de tantos visages que verlos era para reír; las cabeças, rapadas en logares e en lugares con vedijas de tantas maneras que no se podrían escrivir; e todo lo que fazen acá en la cabeça de un loco, el mejor dellos lo avría allá en muy buena ventura que lo fiziessen en la suya. Lo que luego paresció desta gente fué que, si luego tovieran lengua castellana con que los bien entendieran, luego se querrían tornar cristianos; e cuanto vían que fazían los cristianos todo lo fazían ellos, en fincar las rodillas, poner las manos, dezir el Pater noster e el Ave María e las otras devociones, e santiguarse; e dezían que querían ser cristianos, puesto caso que verdaderamente eran idólatras, porque en sus casas avía figuras de muchas maneras, e todas muy disformes e feas, que parescían al diablo; las quales tanbién traían en las carátulas que se tocavan e en los cintos de algodón; e preguntándoles que qué era aquello decían *turey*, que quiere dezir cosa del cielo. E si les querían tomar aquellas figuras, o disciéndoles que era cosa aborrescible, que lo echasen en el fuego, mostravan por ello tristeza e parescía que tenían en aquello mucha devoción; e asimesmo mostravan e pensavan que cuanto los castellanos tenían, e ellos, todo avía venido del cielo, e a todo llamavan *turrey*, que quiere dezir en su lengua cielo.

Luego que allí asentaron e començaron de fazer población, se tendió gente de los castellanos por aquella comarca, e vieron por la tierra en poco tienpo cosas bien hazañosas que ay en

that for people there it is as basic as corn and they use it instead of bread. There is another kind of food called *age* which also grows in the earth; and a third one called *casabi*; there are many kinds of food and fruit, all very different from those found here in Castile.[25]

What was immediately understandable about these people was that they were very simple, without instruction; the men or the women did not feel any embarrassment in going around naked as at birth. Most of the women kept their pubic area covered up with a cotton fabric girded on their hips, whereas others covered it with tree leaves. Common embellishment to both men and women was the painting of themselves: some used black, others white, red or such showy hues that seeing them made one laugh. Their heads were either shaved in some areas or with spots of hair tangled in so many ways that it is impossible to describe; all that in our country could only be done on a mad man's head the best of them would much prefer to see done on their own heads. What immediately stood out next about these people was that if they will learn the Castilian language and understand it, they soon will wish to become Christians since what they saw the Christians do they imitated, kneeling, clasping hands, reciting the Pater Noster, the Ave Maria and other prayers, and making the sign of the cross. Though claiming they wished to be Christians, really they were idolaters, since in their dwellings there was every sort of image resembling the devil and all of them deformed and ugly, which they reproduce also on their dress-up masks and cotton belts. To the question of what images they were, they answered "*turey,*" which means "thing from heaven." And, when our people tried to take those images away from them, saying they were something abominable to be really thrown into the fire, they showed great sadness and appeared to consider them with great reverence. At the same time, they showed that they believed that all that the Christians, and they themselves, owned came from heaven, and they referred to everything as *turey*, which in their language means heaven. As soon as they established themselves there and began to settle down, a few of the

---

[25] See, in *Nuova Raccolta Colombiana*, Vol. I, pt. 2, 327-28, the notes by P.E. Taviani. The *patatas* which Bernáldez refers to are not yet the potatoes found on the Pacific Ocean side of the Andes (Peru, Ecuador, northern Chile) but the *batate* or sweet potatoes.

aquella tierra; que vieron que ay árboles que llevan lana y harto fina, e tal que los que sabían del arte dezían que se podían fazer buenos paños della; e destos árboles ay tantos que se podrían cargar caravelas de la lana, aunque es trabajosa de coger, porque los árboles son muy espinosos; enpero bien se podría hallar engenio para la coger. Ay, que se vido, infinito algodón de árboles perpetuos que lo dan, e son tan grandes como duraznos; y ay árboles que llevan cera, en color y en sabor, y arde tan bien como la de avejas, tal que no ay diferencia mucha de una a otra. Ay infinitos árboles de trementina muy singular y muy fina; ay mucha alquitira, tanbién muy buena; ay árboles que paresció a los físicos que allí fueron que eran de los que llevavan nuezes moxcadas, salvo que estavan estonces sin fruto, e juzgáronlo ser dello por el sabor e olor de la corteza, que era como de nuez moxcada. Vídose una raíz de gengibre, que la traía un indio colgada del pezcueço; ay tanbién linaloe, aunque no es de la manera del que se á visto acá en Castilla, pero no es de dubdar que no sea una de las especies de linaloe que los dotores ponen.

Vieron tanbién que ay una manera de canela, enpero no tan fina como la que acá vemos, que viene por la via de Alexandria, o lo podría fazer no ser tan fina en defecto de no la saber coger en tiempo, o por ventura curarla así la naturaleza de la tierra; tanbién hallaron mirabolanos cetrinos, salvo que estonces non estavan sino debaxo del árbol, e como la tierra es muy úmida estavan perdidos e tenían el savor mucho amargo, e creyóse que sería del pudrimiento; enpero todo lo otro, salvo el savor que es corronpido, es de mirabolanos verdaderos. E tanbién ay almásciga muy buena, e tanbién primienta muy buena, e quema dos vezes más que la que acá tenemos, e nasce en arbolesillos como de hortaliza; es floxa, no tan dura como ésta que aquí viene por la vía de Alexandría; es mayor un poco. La que tienen los indios por cosa mediscinal e muy buena, e la sienbran e cogen.

Es maravilla de cómo las gentes de todas aquellas islas no poseen fierro de las ferramientas, que tienen de piedras, muy agudas e fechas a maravilla, así como hachas e açuelas e otras ferramientas con que se sirven e fazen sus cosas. Sus mantenimientos son pan de raízes, que Dios les echó e dió en aquella tierra en lugar de trigo, que trigo ni cevada ni centeno ni avena ni escaña ni panizo ni saina ni mijo no ay allá, ni cosa que le

Castilians went inland in that region and quickly saw in those territories very extraordinary things: trees producing quite a valuable wool, which, according to those who knew the trade, was good enough to make quality clothes. The trees are so numerous that many caravels could be loaded with "wool," although it is arduous to harvest, for the trees are full of thorns; still, there is certainly a way to do so. They also saw large amounts of cotton produced by evergreen trees as big as peach trees. There are other trees producing wax equal in color, taste and burning efficiency to that of bees, making for little difference between one and the other. There are quite numerous turpentine trees of a special kind and fine quality; there is a great amount of tragacanth which is also very good; though fruitless at that time, there are trees, according to the scientists who were there and judged by the taste and smell of its bark, that are quite similar to that of nutmeg. They saw an Indian with a ginger root hung on his neck. There is aloe, too, though not of the same kind that can be found here in Castile, but undoubtedly a kind of aloe used by physicians.

They found there also a type of cinnamon (though not as fine as that which can be found in our country) which gets here through Alexandria; the lack of refined quality could be due to unseasonable harvesting or perhaps to the nature of the ground. Moreover, they found yellowish *myrabolans* but at that time with a few fruits fallen to the ground and, the latter being very humid, they had begun to rot and acquire a very bitter taste which they thought resulted from the rotting; however, all the other features, leaving aside the altered taste, are like the real *myrabolans*. There is also a good quality mastic and a highly valued pepper, twice as spicy as the one we have here and it grows on bushes, as vegetables do; it is soft and not as hard as that which reaches here through Alexandria and it is a bit larger. The Indians consider it an excellent medicinal product, so they sow and harvest it.

It is amazing to see how all the people of these islands do not own any iron and use very sharp, wonderfully-made stone tools such as axes and hatchets and other implements fit to do their work. As for food, they have bread made from roots spontaneously sprouting which God gave that land instead of wheat since there is no grain, barley, rye, oat,...panic, sorghum, millet, or similar products. There is some *casabi* harvested in

paresca. Ay caçabi, que cogen en unos racimos como que quieren parescer al panizo, sino que son mucho mayores los granos e más blancos. Ay maíz e ajez e otros manjares e raízes, con que an bivido fasta agora, e otras frutas e mantenimientos salvages e cosas que Dios allí les dió, con que se crian e mantienen e han criado e mantenido desde que Dios nuestro Señor allí los hechó.

Non avía cosa de mantenimiento, fasta aquel tienpo que los castellanos fueron allá a poblar, de los que acá ay, ni que se le paresciese. Non avía fabas ni garvanços ni yeros ni lentejas ni atramuzes, ni res de cuatro pies ni alimañias, salvo unos gozques pequeños e aquellas utías, que son como grandes ratones; e son como entre ratones e conejos, e on muy buenas e sabrosas de comer, e tienen pies e manos como ratón e suben por los árboles; son del tamaño de un conejo nuevo. Los gozques son blancos e prietos e de todas colores. Ay lagartos e culebras, e no muchos, porque los comen los indios e fazen tanta fiesta dellos como fazen acá de perdizes; son los lagartos de allá como los de acá en el tamaño, salvo que en la fechura son diferentes; aunque en una isleta pequeña, que está junto con un puerto que se llama Monte Juan donde la flota estuvo algunos días, se vido un lagarto muchas vezes de gordura de un bezerro e tan conplido como una lança; e muchas vezes salieron por lo matar e no podían con la espesura, e fuía y metíase en la niar. Otrosí comen los indios, allende de comer lagartos y culebras, comen cuantas arañas e gusanos hallan por el suelo; así que paresce que es su bestialidad mayor que de nenguna bestia del mundo.

Llevó el almirante de este viage diez e siete navíos, como dicho tengo, en que ivan cuatro naos y treze caravelas, y mill y trezientos onbres de pelea para quedar allá, prosiguiendo la posesión de la tierra, e para exercitar e saber del oro lo cierto, e adquirirlo para el rey e reina, quier por grado de los abitadores, quier por fuerça. E llevó veinte y cuatro cavallos e diez yeguas e tres mulas, e llevó puercos e puercas berracas e berracos e cabras e ovejas, de todo un poco, para criar; para lo qual la tierra fué muy conforme e aprovechable, e muy más sana que non para los onbres. El almirante avía determinado una vez de enbiar los navíos en Castilla antes de ir a buscar las

bunches, similar to the panic grass bunches, but with much larger and whiter grains. There is corn, *age* and other wild food and roots with which they nourished and kept themselves since God, Our Lord, created them.

Until the time the Castilians arrived there to settle, there was no food-stuff equal or similar to ours. There were no broad fava beans or ceci beans [garbanzos], no vetches, lentils, lupines nor any four-footed animal or other animals except for a few little dogs and the *hutias*,[26] which are like big rats, a bit larger but smaller than rabbits, very good and tasty to eat, with hind and fore legs like those of mice, and they climb trees; in size, they are like small rabbits, whereas the little dogs are white or black, or of other colors. There are lizards and snakes, but not many because the Indians love this delicacy the way our people love partridges. The lizards are similar to ours in size but are of a different shape generally, although on a small island[27] near the port, called Monte Juan,[28] where the fleet had stopped a few days, a lizard as big as a calf and similar in shape to a lance was often observed. Many times they tried to kill it but they were unable to, given the density of the trees and because it fled and went into the sea. Besides lizards and snakes, the Indians also ate spiders and worms found on the ground, making their beast-like behavior greater than that of any other animal in the world.

The Admiral brought seventeen vessels with him on this trip, as I already said, four of which were ships and thirteen caravels, with 1300 soldiers for the settlement, so that he would continue taking possession of territories and explore and learn about the location of gold to take it for the King and Queen, either with the inhabitants' consent or by force. He brought 24 stallions, ten mares and three mules, pigs and sows, calves and goats, sheep and animals of all kind for breeding in that land, which turned out to be very suitable, fertile and much healthier for them than for men. One day the Admiral had decided to send the ships back to Castile before starting the

---

[26] See footnote 8.

[27] Cabra Island.

[28] Evident is Bernáldez's misunderstanding; Monte Juan is Monte Cristi in Chanca, don Fernando Colombo and in Las Casas. Today it is called Monte Cristi.

minas del oro; e cayeron tantos dolientes de los que con él ivan que fué maravilla; e desque esto vido, mientras se curavan e remediavan, enbió dos capitanes con dos cuadrillas de gentes a buscar las minas del oro, segund el aviso que tenían de los indios; la una a Cibao, que es una provincia donde ay mucho oro, e la otra a Aytí, tierras del rey Caonaboa, que era muy poderoso en aquella tierra. Los cuales hallaron muchas demuestras donde se podía hallar mucho oro, e en más de cincuenta ríos e arroyos e fuentes fallaron que avía mucho oro e se podía coger, e troxieron muestras de otras partes, e creyeron que cavando la tierra muy honda se hallaría mucha cuantidad de oro, pues que en las arenas de los arroyaderos del agua se hallava, y pues que los indios no cabavan más en fondo la tierra de un palmo, que no tenían con qué, e lo hallavan.

Esto sabido, el almirante despedió los navíos para acá para Castilla, e dexó allá los que vido que era nescesatio quedar; e enbió el oro que más pudo aver al rey e a la reina. E vinieron los navíos a Cáliz, donde fasta que el obispo don Juan de Fonseca fué non osaron salir a tierra fasta le entregar el oro; y dende en adelante se tuvo esta forma, que todos los navíos que venían de las Indias venían a Cáliz, e allí entregavan todo lo que traían al dicho obispo, fasta que él tuvo otro cargo que sus Altezas le dieron, que fué por enbaxador sobre los casamientos al enperador, a Flandes; e después que el obispo dexó el cargo de las armadas e recebtoría del oro, ovo otras formas e ordenamientos en lo rescebir.

En ese mesmo año de noventa e cuatro, que vinieron los navios de las Indias, dexando en la Española al almirante e la gente castellana, en el pueblo començado a edificar, enbió otra armada don Juan de Fonseca, con refresco para la dicha gente de mucho pan e vino e bituallas, la cual fué a buen tiempo e les fizo mucho provecho. Vinieron en março de mill e cuatrocientos y noventa y cuatro los navios de las Indias, e bolvió el armada con los mantenimientos dende a pocos días.

El almirante non echó en olvido la muerte de los treinta e nueve onbres que le mataron, e fizo su inquisición e supo de los mesmos indios quién los avía muerto. E entró por la tierra e cabtivó infinitos dellos, de los cuales enbió en la segunda vez que enbió los navíos quinientas ánimas de indios e indias, todos de buena hedad, desde doze años fasta treinta e cinco poco más o menos; los cuales todos se entregaron en Sevilla al

search for the gold mines, but many men with him, most surprisingly, had fallen ill. Consequently, during their recovery and remedy-seeking period, he sent two captains along with two squadrons to seek for the gold mines following the indications furnished by the Indians, thus sending one to Cibao, a territory rich in gold, and the other to Haiti, the land of chief Caonabó, who was very powerful in that region. They found many clues related to the locations where a large amount of gold could be found as they verified its existence and availability in more than fifty rivers and springs. They took samples from other areas and, realizing that it lay in the river-bed sands, they surmised that by digging much deeper larger amounts of gold could be found even considering that the Indians, unable to dig deeper than a half a foot for lack of proper tools, still found some.

Learning this, the Admiral sent some vessels to Castile, keeping there those whom he judged necessary to remain there. He sent the largest amount of gold he could obtain to the King and Queen. The ships got to Cádiz where, since the bishop Juan de Fonseca was there, they did not dare go ashore before having handed him the gold. Since then, this procedure became customary: all the ships from the Indies had to go to Cádiz and consign all their cargo to the above-named bishop until he was appointed by their Highnesses ambassador to Flanders at the emperor's court as a consequence of a marriage. After the bishop left his original post and the meeting of the fleets to receive the gold, new ways and regulations to receive it were introduced.

In this same year, 1494, when the ships arrived from the Indies, while the Admiral and the Castilian people had remained on Hispaniola in the settlement they had begun to establish, Don Juan de Fonseca sent another fleet with supplies for the colony: lots of bread, wine and staples, which arrived most timely and were of great benefit to them. The vessels from the Indies arrived in March 1494, and the supply fleet left a few days later.

The Admiral had not forgotten the deaths of his 39 men and kept on trying to understand what might have happened and did learn from the Indians themselves who had killed the colonists. He penetrated inland and captured a great number of natives so, the second time he sent back the ships, he sent along 500 of them, men and women, all of young age, more or less between twelve and 35 years old. All of them were

dicho obispo don Juan de Fonseca, e vinieron así como andavan en su tierra, como nascieron, de lo cual non avían más enpacho que alimañas; los cuales todo vendieron, e aprovaron muy mal, que se murieron todos los más, que los provó la tierra.

Ovo cisma entre el almirante e algunos de los que fueron debaxo de su mando, que le no querían obedescer, e dezían que avían engañado al rey y a la reyna en les dezir de aquel oro que avía tanto, lo cual afirmavan que no era verdad, e que si halgo avia que sería tanto y más el gasto que se ponia en lo buscar como el provecho; e como se engorravan en acertar en las minas, por no ser diestros los castellanos para lo buscar e sacar mucho, creyeron esto acá en Castilla. Ovo muy grandes murmuraciones contra el almirante, e él, como soberano sobre ellos, enbió presos algunos dellos, así como a Formizedo, vezino de Sevilla, que avía ido por maestro para conoscer e apurar el oro, el cual hazía escarnio del oro; e él e otros dezían que aquel oro que aquellos indios poseían e davan al almirante que lo tenían de muchos tienpos e lo avían avido subcesivamente de sus antecesores. E enbió preso a Bernaldo de Pisa, alguazil de la corte, e a otros, e los entregaron en Sevilla presos. E de aqui se siguieron muchas disenciones contra el almirante, e todos a muy grande sinrrazón, segund después paresció la verdad; y esto todo acaesció después que él vino de descubrir la tierra firme de la parte del austrio, donde se engorró e tardó allá cuatro o cinco meses del año de mill e cuatrocientos e noventa y cuatro.

handed over to the above-named bishop, Juan de Fonseca, arriving there in accordance with their country's custom, naked as at their birth, without showing greater embarrassment than animals. All were sold, but yielded very little, since the majority died, afflicted by climate differences.

A conflict arose between the Admiral and some of those under his command: not wanting to obey, they claimed he had deceived the King and Queen, telling them that there were large amounts of gold, when in their opinion it was untrue. As for the amount there actually was, here in Castile they believed, the inevitable expenses in finding it would be equal to or greater than the income that could be earned and besides they wasted time in finding the gold mines, being the Castilians unaccustomed to searching for it and mining it in good amounts. Many insinuations were voiced against the Admiral who, as their chief, sent some of them back as prisoners, including Formin Zedo, a citizen of Seville who had embarked because of his skills in recognizing and selecting gold. He scoffed at that gold, and he and others said that the gold the Indians owned and gave to the Admiral they had already possessed for a long time, having received it in turn from their ancestors. He sent as prisoner also Bernaldo from Pisa, *alquazil* [treasurer] of the court, with others who were turned over as prisoners in Seville. From that moment on there were many criticisms against the Admiral, though all were totally unfounded, if one is to judge by the truth that afterwards came to light. All of this happened after he returned from discovering the continent in the southern part where he stayed for four or five months in the year 1494.

CAPITULO CXXI

De cómo el almirante fué por la tierra a buscar el oro a la provincia de Cibao, e de lo que paresció de la tierra, e de la fortaleza que fizo.

Después de partidos los navíos en que fué la dicha armada, de la cibdad Isabela, començada de fundar, los cuales vinieron debaxo de la capitanía de Antonio de Torres, hermano del ama del príncipe don Juan, que partieron de la dicha cibdad Isabela a tres días de febrero, año de noventa y cuatro, el almirante dió priesa a fortalescer la cibdad e en aderesçar las cosas que para allá convenían, para remediar las vidas e la vivienda de toda aquella gente que allá quedó. Y fecho halgo dello, a doze días de março, se partió con toda la gente que fué menester, de pie e de cavallo, para ir a ver la provincia de Cibao, que está diez e ocho leguas al austrio de la dicha ciudad; e atravesó vegas e puertos, e fué e olló la dicha provincia, e fizo caminos llanos algunos puertos, e fizo allá una fortaleza, en Cibao, en que puso gente e alcaide e maestros para el edeficio, para poder señorear la gente della.

Cibao es nombre de provincia, como ya es dicho, e quiere dezir *pedregal*, porque es áspera tierra de cabeços e montañas muy altos e llenos de tierras pedregosas e ásperas, aunque no mucho, sin árboles, pero non sin yervas, ca es tierra de mucha yerva, la cual es toda como grama y más espesa e más alta que alcacel, e en algunas partes fasta las sillas de los cavallos, y así está continuamente, e espesa, si no la queman; y debaxo de la cual tòdas aquellas montañas e cabeços son llenos de guijarros grandes y redondos, como en una ribera o playa, e todos o la mayor parte son azules. E esta provincia es toda tierra muy fuerte e defensible e tenplada e sanísima, e en ella llueve bien a menudo; al pie de cada

CHAPTER CXXI

The Admiral's land exploration and search for gold in the Cibao region. His impressions about the territory. The fort he built.

On the third of February, 1494, after the ships making up the above-mentioned fleet had left the city of La Isabela — which was just beginning to be built, under the command of Antonio Torres, the brother of Prince Don Juan's wet nurse — the Admiral rushed to fortify the town and set the objectives regarding what was worthwhile to do in order to improve the lives and the dwellings of the people left behind there. Once some of those objectives were met, on March 12, he left with people on foot and others on horseback, setting out for the Cibao region, located eighteen leagues south of La Isabela. He crossed plains and some ports and then arrived and found the said province where he had a few roads built and some passes levelled. He built a fortress there in Cibao, outfitting it with men, a governor and master masons for construction purposes, in order to be able to control the natives.

As I have already mentioned, Cibao is the name of the region which means "stony place," for it is a quite rough type of land with very high peaks and mountains, many stony and steep ground areas, often without trees, but not without vegetation since it is a territory rich in tall grass similar to dog-grass, growing denser and taller than barley. In certain places it touches the horses' saddles and is extremely thick if it is not burned down. Underneath this weed covering all mountains and peaks are many large and round stones, as on a river bank or stony beach, all blue, or at least most of them. This territory is itself fortified and protected, with a temperate and very healthy climate and heavy precipitation. At the foot of

cabeço ay un arroyo o un río, chico o grande segund es la montaña; el agua es delgada e sabrosa e fría, e non cruda, como otras aguas que dañan y fazen mal a la persona; esta agua es como medescinal, que quebranta la piedra de los riñones, e muchas personas se sintieron muy bien e sanos con ella. En todos aquellos arroyos e cabeços ay mucho oro, e todo en granos.

each peak there is a small or large brook or river, depending on the mountain's size. The water is light, tasty and cold; it is not heavy like other waters which damage the human body. This water is of the curative type which dissolves kidney stones, making many people feel much better and healthier after drinking it. In those brooks and throughout those peaks there is a lot of gold, all nuggets.

CAPITULO CXXII

De los granos de oro e esperimentos dél, e de cómo los indios lo coxían.

La fortaleza que el almirante fizo en Cibao llamó de Santo Tomás; e al tienpo que él allí estovo edificándola vinieron muchos indios con gana de caxcaveles e de otras cosillas, de lo cual non se les dava nada fasta que truxiesen oro, e como esto se les dezía corrían a la ribera e en menos de una ora traía cada uno dellos una hoja o un caracol llenos de granos de oro. E un indio viejo traxo dos granos de peso de tres castellanos, que fasta estonces el almirante no los avia visto tan grandes, salvo uno que le avia enpresentado Guacanari, que avia enbiado con el capitán Antonio de Torres al rey y a la reina, con otros menudos que les enbió; enpero los más dellos fueron fundidos creyendo a Formizedo, que estava allá por onbre de mucho saber en el oro, el cual erró en esto de estos granos, porque eran de nascimiento y no fundidos como él dixo. E después se supo lo cierto, que Formizedo sabia muy poco en ello, que tanbién dixo al almirante de unos granos que avía entre los otros, que eran de oro baxo, que avía sido falsificado de latón, de que no supo lo que dixo, e tanbién andava errado, porque supo el almirante que aquello proscedia de la mina donde nasció; ni es de creer que los indios, aunque supieran fundir, que mezclaran el alatón con el oro, pues que tienen en más estima el alatón cient vezes que el oro.

Así que, recebidos los granos del viejo, el almirante le dió un caxcavel, el cual él rescebió en tanta estima como si le dieran alguna buena villa, e dixo al almirante que eran pequeños

CHAPTER CXXII

The gold nuggets, their testing, and the way in which the Indians gathered gold.

The Admiral named the stronghold he had built in Cibao St. Thomas and, during the period he stayed there while it was being built, many Indians came, wishing to obtain harness-bells and other small things, none of which was traded with them without their bringing gold. As soon as they were told to do so, they would run to the river bank and in less than an hour each of them brought back a leaf or a shell full of gold nuggets. An old Indian brought two grains weighing three *castellanos*; up to that moment the Admiral had never seen nuggets bigger than these, except for one Guacanagarí had presented him and which he had sent along with smaller ones to the King and Queen by means of the captain Antonio Torres. Following Formin Zedo's suggestion, who was there in charge as gold expert, the majority of these grains were melted; however, he was wrong about the composition of the nuggets, since they were naturally like that and not melted as he claimed. The truth was later discovered that Formin Zedo knew very little about gold considering that he even had told the Admiral, without good knowledge of what he was talking about, that some of those nuggets were of low-quality gold and that they had been mixed with brass. He was again wrong, as the Admiral learned that the gold came directly from the mine where it had been found; nor can one believe that the Indians, though they knew how to melt, would mix brass with gold since they valued brass a hundred times more than gold.

Thus, upon receiving the two nuggets from the old man, the Admiral gave him a harness-bell which he prized most highly as though he had been presented with a wonderful city,

aquéllos a conparación de otros que avia en su tierra, que era cinco leguas de allí, e figuró en piedras tamañas como nuez, e dixo que tamaños granos de oro avía él hallado e mayores; e otros figuravan que avía granos tamaños como unas piedras que mostravan, tan gordas como naranjas e mayores, e se hallavan algunas vezes. Otros dezían que entre ellos avían visto grano tamaño como una piedra que señalavan, que pesava media arroba; en fin, de lo que se vido fasta estonces ovo grano de ocho castellanos.

Los indios, allende de ser gente bestial, son perezosos e malos trabajadores, porque su ábito lo haze manifiesto; porque en el invierno que allá se siente haze asaz frío, y aunque no ay lana ay mucho algodón, de que se podrían vestir e fazer mucha onrra e repararse; e déxanse andar así como bestias, por pereza sufriendo en sus personas el frío e el calor.

Bolvió el almirante a Isabela desde Cibao; e dexada en concierto la gente, adereçó de ir a descobrir la tierra firme de las Indias, pensando de allar por aquella vía e aguas todavía la grande e muy riquísima cibdad de Catayo, que es del Grand Can.

and he told the Admiral that those samples were small compared with the other ones in his territory five leagues away. He gave them to understand that they were grains big as walnuts, adding that he himself had found some that big and even bigger. Others also gave them to understand that there were grains as big as some stones they pointed to, as big as oranges and occasionally even bigger. Some other ones talking among themselves claimed to have seen a nugget as big as a stone they pointed to and weighing half an *arroba*.[29] Lastly, based upon what they until then had observed, there was a gold grain of eight *castellanos*.

The Indians, besides being primitive people, are lazy and bad workers, and this is evident by their clothes. During the winter there is much cold there and, though there is no wool, they have plenty of cotton that could be used to dress and wear to protect themselves. They live like beasts, enduring cold and hot on their bodies because of their laziness. The Admiral returned to La Isabela from Cibao and, having ensured full harmony among the people, decided to go on and discover the Indies believing he would find, heading that way and beyond those waters, the large and most wealthy city of Cathay, which belonged to the Grand Khan.

---

[29] See footnote number 5.

CAPITULO CXXIII

De cómo fué a descubrir el almirante la tierra firme de las Indias.

Partió el almirante a descobrir la tierra firme de las Indias a veinte y cuatro días del mes de abril del dicho año de mill e cuatrocientos y noventa y cuatro. Dexó en la cibdad por presidentes a su hermano e a un fraile que se dezía fray Buil, e ordenado lo que cada uno avía de hazer; e partió con tres caravelas de vela redonda, e en muy pocos días llegó al muy señalado puerto de Sant Niculao, el cual está en la mesma Española, frontero del cabo del Alfa et O, que es en la Juana, donde él juzgava por tierra firme, fin e cabo de las Indias por el oriente. E enderesçó al dicho cabo e llegó a él, e dexó de seguir la costa del sentenrión, por donde el viaje primero avía andado, e navegó al poniente corriendo la otra costa de la parte del austrio; las cuales costas van ansí anbas al poniente desviándose la una del polo ártico e la otra acercándose a él por el anchura de la tierra, que comiença por angosto e va subiendo el sentenrión. E por la parte del austro, dexando la tierra de la Juana sobre la mano derecha, navegó pensando dar la buelta al derredor e correr, después de ver el cabo, la vía de su deseo, que era buscar la provincia e cibdad del Cathayo, diziendo que la podría hallar por allí, que es en el señorío del Grand Can.

De la cual se lee, segund dize Juan de Mandavilla e otros que la vieron, que es la más rica provincia del mundo, e la más abundosa de oro e plata e de todos metales, e seda e paños e mieses e frutas e ganados; en la cual provincia son todos

CHAPTER CXXIII

How the Admiral went on to discover the Indie's mainland.

The Admiral left to discover the Indian mainland on the 24th day of the above-mentioned year, 1494. He left in charge of the city his brother and Friar Buil, entrusting to each of them specific duties they should attend to. He then left with three square-rigged caravels and in a very few days arrived at the important Saint Nicholas Port,[30] which is located on Hispaniola itself, opposite Alfa et O Cape[31] in Juana [Cuba], which he thought to be the mainland, the beginning and the end of the Eastern Indies. He headed toward the above-named cape, reached it and ceased sailing along the northern coast, as he had done during the first voyage, setting his course west and sailing along the other coast from the south. Both the northern and southern coasts turned westward, one coming from the direction of the Arctic pole and the other going near it on the broad side of the land which begins with a narrow area and gradually widens northward. The Admiral set course from the south, leaving Juana on his right side, thinking to go around and, after looking at the cape, head toward the course he wished, in search of the region and city of Cathay under the rule of the Grand Khan, convinced that he could find it through that route.

About this land one reads, at least according to John Mandeville and others who saw it, that it is the wealthiest region in the world, the richest in gold and silver and all the metals, silk, clothes, harvests, fruit and livestock. In this region

---

[30] Saint Nicolas, Haiti.
[31] Pointe Maisí, Cuba.

idolatrios e gente muy agudísima y nigromántica e sabia en todas artes e cavallerías, e della se escriven muchas maravillas, segund cuenta el dicho Juan de Mandavilla, que lo andovo e vido, e bivió con el Grand Can algund tienpo. Quien desto quisiere saber lo cierto, lea en su libro el ochenta y cinco, e ochenta y siete, e ochenta y ocho capítulos, e allí verán cómo la cibdad del Cathayo es muy noble e rica, e cómo la provinscia suya tiene el nonbre de la cibdad. La cual provinscia e cibdad es en las partidas de Asia, cerca de la tierra del Preste Juan, en la parte que señorea e mira el norte.

E por donde el almirante lo buscava, yo digo que avía menester grande distancia de tienpo para lo hallar, porque el Grand Can antiguamente fué señor de los tártaros, e desde la Grand Tartaria, que es en los confines de Ruxia e Valia. E podemos dezir que se comiença la tierra Tartaria desde Ongaria, que son tierras que están, mirando desde esta Andaluzía, por en derecho de donde sale el sol en el mes de los mayores días del año, e por aquel derecho solían ir los mercaderes en aquella tierra. Que por la vanda que el almirante buscava el Catayo, es mi creer que otras mill e dozientas leguas, andando el firmamento de la mar e tierra en derredor, non llegase allà.

E así ge lo dixe e fize entender yo el año de mill e cuatrocientos e noventa y seis, cuando vino en Castilla la primera vez después de aver ido otra vez a descubrir, que fué mi huésped e me dexó algunas de sus escripturas, en presencia de don Juan de Fonseca, de donde yo saqué e cotegé con otras que escrivió el dotor Chanca, e otros cavalleros que con él fueron en los viages ya dichos, que escrivieron lo que vieron. De donde yo fuí informado e escriví esto de las Indias, por cosa muy maravillosa e hazañosa, que Nuestro Señor quiso demostrar en la buena ventura e en tienpo del rey don Fernando e de la reina doña Isabel, su primera muger.

Así que el almirante, pensando que la Juana era isla, andovo mucho por la costa della, e preguntava a los indios si era isla o tierra firme; e como ellos son gente bestial e piensan que todo el mundo es islas e non saben qué cosa sea tierra firme, ni tienen letras ni memorias antiguas, nin se deleitan en otra cosa sino en comer y en mugeres, dezían que era isla; enpero algunos le dixeron que era isla, mas que no la andaría en cuarenta lunas. E mientras más seguían la costa, más los

all the people are idolaters and very witty, necromantic, and wise in all the arts and the noble traditions. Again, about its people in general many wondrous things have been written, according to John Mandeville, who went there and saw and lived for a certain length of time with the Grand Khan. Whoever wants to know the truth about this should read chapters 85, 87 and 88 in his book and consequently realize that Cathay city is very noble and wealthy and how the region is named after the city. Both region and city lie in the land of Asia, near the territory of Prester John, in the part facing north which belongs to him. Yet I say that, due to the way the Admiral was searching for them, it would necessarily take a long time to find them, since in ancient times the Grand Khan ruled the Tartars as far as the Grand Tartar region which borders on Russia and Valia. We can indeed say that the Tartar region begins with Hungary and that all Tartar lands lie, looking at them from our region of Andalusia, in a straight line in the direction where the sun rises during the month with the longest days of the year, which is the direction merchants used to travel to that land. In my opinion, even sailing 1200 more leagues around the endless sea and land in the direction taken by the Admiral in his search for Cathay, he would not get there.

Trying to make him understand, I told him so in 1496, when he came for the first time to Castile, after having gone for the second time to discover lands, when he was my guest and left me, in the presence of Don Juan de Fonseca, some of his writings, from which I took information I then compared with other texts, including Doctor Chanca's and others' who had gone with him on the above-mentioned voyages and had written down what they saw. From them I learned and wrote about the Indies as something wonderful and remarkable that Our Lord in his goodness willed to happen during the Kingdom of Don Ferdinand and Queen Isabela, his first wife.

The Admiral then, thinking Juana was an island, sailed along a good deal of its coast and kept on asking the Indians whether it was an island or mainland. Since they are primitive people and believe the whole world is made of islands — they do not know what a mainland is, nor are they educated, nor do they have ancient traditions, and they do not enjoy anything else but eating and taking pleasure with women — they said it was an island, with some of them pointing out, however, that

echava la tierra al austro; que él bien pensó de dar buelta a la Juana e bolver al poniente, e dende al setentrión, donde pensava hallar la noble provincia e cibdad riquísima del Cathayo. E ovo por fuerça de seguir aquella vanda, por donde la tierra lo desviava de sí; e descubrió por aquella vía la isla de Jamaica, e bolvió a seguir la costa de tierra firme sesenta días, andando por ella fasta aver pasado a estar muy cerca al Aurea Chersoneso; donde tomó la buelta, por temor de los tienpos e por la grandísima navegación e mengua de mantenimientos.

E allí le vino en mientes que, si próspero se hallara, que provara a bolver a España por oriente, viniendo al Ganges e dende al Sino Arábico, e después por Ethiopía; e después pudiera venir por la tierra a Iherúsalem e dende a Japha, e enbarcar e entrar en el mar Mediterráneo, e dende a Cáliz. El viage bien se podía hazer desta manera, enpero era peligroso de la tierra, porque son todos moros desde Ethiopía fasta Iherúsalem; enpero él pudiera ir por la mar toda vía, e ir desde allá fasta Calicud, que es la cibdad que descubrieron los portogueses; e para no salir por tierra sino toda vía por agua, él avía de bolver por el mesmo mar Océano rodeando toda Libia, que es la tierra de los negros, e bolver por donde vienen los portogueses de Calicud.

Después de aver andado el almirante en este viage trezientas e veinte e dos leguas, a cuatro millas cada una, así como acostunbra en la mar, desde el cabo de Alfaeto se bolvió, e non por el camino por donde avía ido; e cuando pasó por aquel cabo de Alfaeto, que está al comienço de la tierra Juana, puso allí colunas de cruzes, tomando la posesión por sus Altezas; e fué muy bien fecho, pues remanesció ser tan estremo cabo e puerto. Que deveis saver que aquel es estremo cabo de la tierra de oriente por aquella vía, así como es acá el estremo cabo de la tierra firme del poniente el cabo de San Vicente, que está en Portogal; en medio de los cuales cabos anbos se contiene todo el poblado del mundo. Que quien partiese por tierra desde el cabo de San Vicente podría ir sienpre al levante, sin pasar nenguna cosa del mar Océano, fasta llegar al cabo de Alfaeto; e desde Alfaeto, por la contra, venir fasta el cabo de San Vicente por tierra firme, ecétera, a quien Dios ayudase en el viage.

it was an island that could not be covered in 40 moons. The more they sailed along the coast, the more they found land southward, so much so that the Admiral wisely decided to go around Juana and turn westward and later northward, where he believed he would find the noble region and most wealthy city of Cathay. He had no other choice but to follow that course and gradually leave behind that land, and thus he discovered the island of Jamaica whose main coast he followed for sixty days and, going that way, he got very close to the Golden Peninsula [Chersonese] only to reverse himself out of fear of weather conditions and because of the very long voyage and scarcity of provisions.

There it occurred to him that, if helped by luck, he could try to return to Spain via the Orient, reaching the Ganges and then the Gulf of Arabia and then Ethiopia. Afterwards, he could arrive by land at Jerusalem and Jaffa and from there board a ship, cross the Mediterranean and finally reach Cádiz. The voyage could indeed be accomplished that way but travelling by land was dangerous, for all the populations from Ethiopia to Jerusalem are Moorish. Yet, he could have done the whole trip by sea and reached Calicut from there, the city discovered by the Portuguese. In order to avoid land and go entirely by sea, he had to return through the same Ocean, circumnavigating all of Libya [Africa], a land of black people, and go back the way the Portuguese return from Calicut.

Having sailed 320 leagues during this trip, each corresponding to four miles according the seafaring statute, the Admiral went back to Cape Alfa et O but not the same way tracked previously. When he rounded the Cape, located at the beginning of Juana, he planted there some big crosses taking possession of it in the name of Their Highnesses, an excellent move since later it turned out to be both the outermost cape and a port.

It should be pointed out that it was the outermost cape in the east, just as Cape Saint Vicente, in Portugal, in our continent is the outermost cape in the west. Between the two lay all the populated lands of the world. In fact, one who left Saint Vicente could go eastward by land without crossing the Ocean at all and reach Cape Alfa et O, and vice versa, likewise one could come from there to Cape Saint Vicente still on mainland, and so on.. with God's help.

CAPITULO CXXIV

De cómo el almirante llegó a tierra donde los árboles llevan dos vezes fruto, e del pescado e serpientes que hallaron, e de cómo fueron a la isla de Jamaica.

Tornando a proseguir e recontar más por menudo las islas e tierras e mares que el dicho almirante descubrió de aquel viage: Siguió por la mar, como dicho es, dexando la tierra firme a la mano derecha, fasta un puerto muy singularísimo, al cual él llamó Puerto Muy Grande. En aquella tierra los árboles e las yervas llevan dos vezes en el año fruto, e esto se supo e se experimentó por verdad; de los cuales muy suavíssimo olor salía, que alcançava en grand parte a la mar. En aquel puerto non avia población, e como entraron en él vieron, a mano derecha, muchos fuegos junto con el agua, e un perro e dos camas sin personas. Descendieron en tierra e fallaron más de cuatro quintales de peces, en asadores al fuego, e conejos e dos serpientes; e allí muy cerca estavan en muchos lugares puestas al pie de los árboles serpientes, la más asquerosa cosa e fea que los onbres vieron, e todas tenían cosidas las bocas. Eran todas de color de madera seca, e el cuero de todo el cuerpo muy arrugado, en especial en la cabeça, que le descendía sobre los ojos, los cuales tenían beninosos e espantables; e todas eran cubiertas de sus conchas muy fuertes, como un pece de escama, e desde la cabeça fasta la punta de la cola, por medio del cuerpo, tenían unas conchas altas e feas e agudas como puntas de diamantes.

E mandó el almirante tomar el pescado, con que ovo refresco la gente; y después, andando buscando puerto con la barca, vieron

CHAPTER CXXIV

How the Admiral arrived in a land where the trees produce fruit twice a year. The fish and snakes which can be found there. And, how he arrived in Jamaica.

Let us continue in greater detail the account about the islands, lands and seas the said Admiral discovered on that trip. He continued by sea to a very distinctive port which he named Puerto [Muy] Grande.[32] The trees and herbs in that land produce fruit twice a year, it was learned for sure and indeed so verified. These fruits released a most aromatic scent, which spread as far as the sea. In that port there were no people, and when they entered they saw on the right, near the water, many fires, a dog and two pallets without people. After landing they found more than one thousand pounds of fish cooking on the fire, rabbits and two "snakes;" nearby, at the base of the trees, they found snakes in many places, the most repugnant thing the men had seen since all of the "snakes" had their mouths sewn up. They were of the color of dry wood and their skin was very wrinkled (particularly at the head), stretching well over their eyes, making them appear poisonous and dreadful. They were entirely covered with scales, very thick like fish, and from head to the tip of their tail, in the center of their bodies, they had some long, ugly protuberances, sharp as diamond points. The Admiral ordered his men to take some fish on which they fed. Then, while they were looking for a port in a boat, they spotted on top of a high ground many people, who were, after their custom, naked. Upon beckoning them to come near, one of them

---

[32] Bahía de Guantanamo, (Guantanamo Bay).

del cabo de un cerro mucha gente desnuda, a la costunbre de allá; e faziéndoles señal que se allegasen, allegóse uno. E fabló un indio que el almirante llevava por intérpetre, de los que avían venido a Castilla, que entendía ya bien castellano e entendía tanbién a los indios; e el indio estraño fablava desde encima de una peña, e como entendió al otro asegURóse e llamó a la otra gente, que eran obra de setenta onbres, los cuales dixieron que andavan caçando por mandado de su cacique para una fiesta que quería fazer. E el almirante les mandó dar caxcaveles e otras cosillas, e mandóles dezir que perdonasen que él avía tomado el pescado e non otra cosa; e holgaron mucho cuando supieron que no les avían tomado las serpientes, e respondieron que fuese todo en buena ora, que ellos pescarían más a la noche.

Salió de allí otro día, antes que saliesse el sol; seguió al poniente la costa de la tierra, la cual vían ser muy poblada y muy fermosa tierra; e como vían tales navíos, venían a las playas a ver muchas gentes y niños chicos e grandes, trayéndoles pan e cosas de comer, mostrando el pan y las calabaças llenas de agua llamando: «¡Tomad, comed e beved, gente del cielo!». E rogávanles que descendiesen e fuesen a sus casas, e otros venían en canoas a lo mesmo. E así navegaron fasta un golfo donde avía infinitas poblaciones, e las tierras e canpos eran tales, que todas parescían huertas las más fermosas del mundo, e todas tierras altas e montañas. Surgieron alli, y las gentes de las comarcas luego vinieron allí, e traíanles pan e agua e pescado.

E luego otro día siguiente, en amanesciendo, partieron de allí; e andando fazia un cabo, después, determinó el almirante de dexar aquel camino e aquella tierra e navegación en busca de la isla Jamaica, al austrio. E en cabo de dos días e dos noches allegaron a ella con buen viento, e fueron a dar en el medio della, la cual es la más fermosa que los ojos vieron. Ella no es montañosa, e paresce que llega la tierra al cielo; es muy grande, mayor que Secilia; tiene en cerco ochocientas millas, e es toda llena de valles e canpos e prados. Es muy fertilísima, e populatísima ultra modo; que así a la lengua de la mar como en la tierra adentro toda es llena de poblados, e muy grandes

approached. Speaking was an Indian whom the Admiral had as an interpreter, one of those who had come to Castile, and already understood Castilian well, as well as the Indian language. The other Indian spoke standing on a rock and, as soon as he understood what the other one said, felt reassured and called all the others, about seventy men, who said they were hunting by order of their cacique for a feast he was going to hold. The Admiral ordered that they be given some harness-bells and other small things, asking them to forgive him for having taken their fish, and nothing else. The natives cheered a lot upon learning the snakes had not been taken, adding that they hoped the fish was enjoyable and that they would catch other fish that very night.

He left that place before sunrise the next day and sailed westward along the coast of a land which appeared very populated and beautiful. Many people, adult and young, as soon as they would see the ships would go to the beach to watch them, bringing bread and food and pointing to the bread and the gourds filled with water and shouting: "Take, eat and drink, people from the heavens." They would beg them to go ashore and visit their dwellings, while others would approach in canoes. So they sailed as far as a gulf[33] where there were many people, and the fields and the lands looked like the most beautiful gardens in the world with high, mountainous ranges. As they anchored there, the people of those areas soon gathered, bringing them bread, water and fish.

Then, at dawn the next day, they left and set course toward a cape,[34] with the Admiral deciding later to abandon such a course, the land and the sea-lane in order to seek out, southward, Jamaica. After two days and two nights they reached it, thanks to a favorable wind, arriving in the middle part of the most beautiful among the islands eyes had ever seen. It is not mountainous, and creates the impression that the land joins the sky; it is very large, larger than Sicily, with a perimeter of 800 miles, all made up of valleys, fields and meadows. It is very fertile and densely populated, both near the sea and inland, its villages very large and near each other

---

[33] Bahía de Santiago, (Santiago Bay).
[34] Cabo Cruz, Cuba.

e muy cerca unos de otros, a cuarto de legua. Tienen canoas más que en nenguna parte de por allá, e las más grandes que fasta estonces se avían visto, todas de un trosço, como dicho es, enteras de un árbol; e cada cacique de todas aquellas comarcas tiene una canoa grande, de que se prescia e sirve. Como acá un cavallero, que se prescia de tener una nao grande e fermosa, ellos así traen aquellas canoas, labradas en popa e proa, a lazos e pinturas, que es maravilla la hermosura dellas. En una de aquellas grandes midió el almirante noventa e seis pies de luengo e ocho pies de ancho.

— only a quarter of a league away from each other. They have more canoes than anyone else there, the biggest heretofore seen, all carved out of single trunks as they are — as it was pointed out earlier — and built entirely from trees. Each of the caciques of that region owns and uses a big canoe of which he is proud, just as in our country a gentleman takes pride in his big and beautiful boat. They build those canoes, carving and embellishing both the bow and stern with ornaments and paintings, in such a way that their beauty is amazing. The Admiral measured out one of them: it was 96 feet long and eight feet wide.

CAPITULO CXXV

De la isla Jamaica.

Así como el almirante llegó a cerca de la tierra de Jamaica, luego salieron contra él bien setenta canoas, todas cargadas de gente e varas por armas, una legua en la mar, en son e forma de pelear. E el almirante con sus tres caravelas e gente non dió por ellos nada, e segnió todavía el camino de la tierra; e desque esto vieron ovieron miedo e bolvieron fuyendo; e el almirante tuvo forma, con su faraute, como una de aquellas canoas se aseguró e vino a él con la gente; e dióles vestidos e otras muchas cosas, que ellos tovieron en grand prescio; e dióles liscencia que se fuesen. E él fué a surgir a un lugar, que puso nonbre Santa Gloria, por la estrema fermosura de la tierra, porque nenguna conparasción tienen a ella las huertas de Valencia ni de otra parte, e esto es en toda la isla; e durmieron alli aquella noche.

Otro día, en amanesciendo, fueron a buscar puerto cerrado, para despalmar e adobar los navíos; e andando al poniente cuatro leguas, fallaron un sengularísimo puerto, e el almirante enbió la barca a ver la entrada, e salieron a ella dos canoas con mucha gente e le tiraron muchas varas; enpero luego huyeron desque vieron resistencia, e no tan presto que no recebieron castigo. E el almirante entró en el puerto e surgió, e vinieron tantos de indios sobre él que cubrían la tierra, e todos teñidos de mill colores, e la mayor parte de prieto, e todos desnudos a su uso; e traían plumages en las cabeças de diversas maneras,

CHAPTER CXXV

Jamaica.

No sooner had the Admiral approached the land of Jamaica than as many as seventy canoes headed toward him, all of them loaded with people bearing arrows as weapons, one league into the sea, combat ready and making noise. The Admiral, with his three caravels and his people, ignored them and kept on sailing along the coast. The natives grew afraid after this and turned back, fleeing, but the Admiral, through his messenger, was able to reassure the men of one of these canoes who then approached. He gave them clothes and many other things, which they much appreciated, and then let them leave. He went on to anchor in a place which he named Santa Gloria[35] because of that land's beauty, extreme to the point of obliterating any comparison drawn between it and Valencia's gardens or any others, and this is true of the whole island; there they spent the night.

At dawn the following day they went looking for a sheltered port, to reseal and refit the vessels. Traveling westward for four leagues, they found a most distinctive port[36] into which the Admiral sent a boat to survey its entrance, and it was attacked by two canoes... people shooting arrows who, however, soon fled, realizing there was resistance, but not fast enough to avoid any damage. The Admiral entered the port and dropped anchor; a great many Indians gathered, so many that they covered the whole space. All were painted in a thousand colors, mostly black, and were naked according to their custom. They wore on their heads different sorts of plumed

---

[35] St. Anne's Bay, Jamaica.

[36] Puerto Bueno [Good Port], Saint Ann's Bay, Jamaica.

e traian el pecho e el vientre cubierto con hojas de palma, dando la mayor grita del mundo e tirando varas, aunque no alcançavan.

E en los navíos tenian nescesidad de agua e de leña, allende de adobar los navíos; e el almirante vió que no era raçón dexarlos en aquella osadía sin pena, porque otra vez non se atreviesen; así armó todas tres barcas, porque las caravelas non podían llegar a donde ellos estavan, por el poco hondo; e porque conosciesen las armas de Castilla, allegáronse a cerca dellos con las barcas, e tiráronles con las ballestas; e desque los picaron bien e començaron de coger miedo, saltaron en tierra a ellos despeldando tiros. E como los indios vieron que los castellanos descendían a ellos, dieron todos buelta a huir, onbres e mugeres, que non paró nenguno en toda la comarca; e un perro que soltaron de un navío los seguía e mordía, e les hizo grand dapño, que un perro vale para contra los indios como diez onbres.

El día seguiente, antes del sol salido, bolvieron seis onbres de aquellos indios a la playa, llamando e diziendo al almirante que aquellos caciques todos le rogavan que non se fuese, que lo querían ver e traer pan e pescado e frutas; e al almirante le plugo mucho de la enbaxada, e fizieron su amistança e seguro, e vinieron los caciques e muchos indios a él pidiéndole perdón de lo pasado. E truxiéronles muchos mantenimientos, con que refrescó mucho la gente; e estovieron muy abundosos de todo todos los días que alli estovieron, e los indios quedaron muy contentos con las cosas que el almirante les dió; e adobados los navíos e descansada la gente, partiéronse de allí.

tops and their chests and bellies were covered with palm leaves; they were continually uttering the loudest yells in the world and shooting arrows, although they did not reach the vessels.

They needed water and wood aboard the ships besides having to refit them. The Admiral realized it was unreasonable to let the natives dare so much without deterring them from doing so another time and thus armed all three boats, since the caravels could not proceed further because of the shallows. To make the natives well aware of Castilians' weapons, they approached with the boats and struck them with the cross-bows. Being badly hit, they began to be afraid when the men went ashore shooting arrows. The Indians, seeing the Castilians coming toward them, they all, men and women, turned to flee, abandoning completely the territory. A dog, let go from one of the boats, chased and bit them, causing great damage, a dog being equal to ten men against the Indians!

The next day, before sunrise, six of those Indians returned to the beach, calling for the Admiral and saying that all of the caciques begged them not to leave, for they wished to see him and bring him bread, fish, and fruit. At that announcement the Admiral was very pleased and they made peace. The Indians were reassured and the caciques with many others came to him, begging forgiveness for what had happened. They brought a great deal of food which revived our people, who enjoyed an abundance of everything for the entire duration of their stay. The Indians, too, were very pleased with the things the Admiral gave them. After the vessels were refitted and the crews refreshed, they departed.

CAPITULO CXXVI

De muchas islas que se descubrieron.

Partió el almirante con sus tres caravelas de Jamaica, e navegó treinta e cuatro leguas al poniente, fasta el golfo de Buen Tienpo; e allí ovieron los ientos contrarios para seguir la costa adelante de la dicha isla de Jamaica, de la cual su calidad era ya conoscida; e visto que non avía en ella oro ni metal nenguno, aunque de lo otro era como un paraíso e por más que oro tenida, fizieron del viento contrario bueno, e bolvieron e la tierra firme de la Juana con propósito de seguir la costa della; que avían dexado de saber cierto si era tierra firme. E fueron a parar a una provincia que llaman Macaca, que es muy hermosa, e fueron a surgir a una población muy grande, el cacique de la cual ya conoscía al almirante e las caravelas antes que fuesen esta jornada, que allegaron por aquella costa las oídas de la primera vez que el almirante fué a descobrir, que todos los caciques de aquella tierra lo supieron; e fué toda aquella tierra e islas alborotadas de tan nueva cosa e navíos, e todos dezían que era gente del cielo. No enbargante que él no avía navegado aquella costa, salvo la otra de setentrión.

E llegados allí, el almirante enbió presente al dicho cacique, de las cosas que ellos allá tenían en mucho precio; e el cacique les enbió buen refresco, e a dezir cómo lo conoscían al almirante por oídas, e conoscían a su padre de Ximón, indio que el almirante avía traído a Castilla e dado al príncipe don Juan. E el almirante decendió en tierra e preguntó al dicho cacique e a los indios de aquel lugar si aquella era isla o tierra

CHAPTER CXXVI

About the many islands that were discovered.

The Admiral left Jamaica with his three caravels and sailed westward 34 leagues as far as the Montego Bay [37] where, while sailing along the coast, they met unfavorable winds right off Jamaica whose features they already knew. Considering there was neither gold nor any other metal, even though in all other aspects it was like a paradise and valued more than gold, they turned the unfavorable wind into a favorable one and headed back toward Juana with the intention of sailing along its coast since they had given up trying to understand whether it was mainland or not. They stopped in a very beautiful region named Macaca and anchored next to a very large village whose cacique already knew about the Admiral and the caravels before they arrived, since rumors of the first discovery expedition made by the Admiral had reached that coast and spread to all the caciques of that land. Those lands and islands were thrown into disarray by such a new event and by the vessels, and all were repeating that they were people from heaven, even though he had never sailed along those coasts but along the northern one.

Upon arriving, the Admiral sent to the cacique a gift of things that were much appreciated there. The cacique sent him healthy food and also word on how they knew about the Admiral through the reports handed down, being also acquainted with the father of Simon, the Indian the Admiral had taken to Castile to the prince Don Juan. The Admiral went ashore and asked the above-mentioned cacique and the Indians

---

[37] Montego Bay, Jamaica, (Northern Coast).

firme; e él con todos los otros le respondieron que era tierra infinita, de que nadie avía visto el cabo, aunque era isla.

Esta era gente muy mansa e desviados de malos pensamientos. Ay diferencia en grand manera de esta gente desta tierra Juana a los otros de todas las otras islas comarcanas; e eso mesmo ay en las aves e en las otras cosas todas; que todos son de mejor conversación e más mansos.

Otro día partieron de allí e navegaron al sententrión, declinando al norueste, siguiendo la costa de la tierra; a ora de vísperas vieron de lexos que aquella costa bolvía al poniente, e tomaron aquel camino para atajar, dexando la tierra a la mano derecha. Otro día, al salir del sol, miraron de encima del mástel, e vieron la mar llena de islas a todos cuatro vientos, e todas verdes e llenas de árboles, la cosa más fermosa que ojos vieron. E el almirante quisiera pasar al austro e dexar estas islas a la mano derecha; mas acordándosele aver leído que toda aquella mar es así llena de islas, e Juan de Mandavilla dize que en las Indias ay más de cinco mill islas, determinó de andar adelante e seguir e non dexar la vista de la tierra firme de la Juana, e ver lo cierto, si era isla o no; e cuanto más andavan más islas descubrían, e día se hizo anotar e contar ciento e setenta e cuatro islas. E el tienpo para navegar entre ellas sienpre ge lo dió Dios bueno, e corrían los navíos por aquellas mares que parescia que bolavan.

E allegaron, el día de pascua del Spíritu Sancto del año de mill e cuatrocientos e noventa y cuatro años, a posar a la costa de la tierra firme, a un lugar despoblado, e non por destenperança del cielo ni esterilidad de la tierra, en un grande palmar de palmas que parescía que llegavan al cielo. Allí, en la orilla de la mar, salían en la tierra dos ojos de agua, tan gordos que en el agujero cupiera una gorda naranja; e venía esta agua en alto con ínpetu cuando la marea era del cresciente, e tan fría e tan dulce que en el mundo no se podía aver mejor; e este frior no es salvaje, como otros que davan dolor del estómago, salvo sanísimo. E descansaron allí todos en las yervas de aquellas fuentes e al olor de las flores, que allí se sentía muy maravilloso, e al dulçor del cantar de los paxaricos, tantos eran e tan suaves, e a la sonbra de aquellas palmas, tan grandes e tan fermosas que era maravilla ver lo

of that place whether it was an island or a mainland. The cacique, along with all the others, answered that it was a boundless land of which none had ever seen the furthermost limit, though it was an island.

These people were very meek and without a hostile attitude. There is a big difference between these people of Juana and the people of the other islands of the region; the same is true for their birds and everything else. All of the people are more affable and docile.

They left there the next day and sailed northwards, steering northeast to follow the shoreline until evening, when they noticed from afar that it turned westward, and so did they, it being the shortest way, leaving land to the right. The next day at sunrise they looked from the top of the ship's main mast and saw a sea full of islands in all four directions. All were green and full of trees, the most beautiful thing eyes had ever seen. The Admiral wanted to turn southward and leave such islands to his right; however, remembering to have read that all those seas are full of islands and that John Mandeville says that in the Indies there are more than 5,000 of them, he decided to push forward without losing ight of Juana's mainland and verify whether or not it was an island. The more they continued, the more islands they discovered, so he began to take note and counted 174 islands. While sailing among them, God always gave him favorable weather and the ships ran across those seas as if they flew.

On Easter Sunday, day of the Holy Spirit, 1494, they landed in a big palm-grove whose trees seemed to reach the sky, on the mainland coast in a place that was uninhabited, but not because of Heaven's negligence or Earth's sterility. There, on the sea-shore, two water jets gushed out of the earth, so large that in their holes could fit a large orange, with the water shooting up vehemently with rising tide, a water so cold and sweet that nothing better could be had in the world. Its cold temperature is not harmful but very healthy, unlike others which caused stomach pain. They all rested in that place among the green surrounding those springs, amidst the flowery scent that could wonderfully be smelled and the gentle sweetness of the singing sparrows, which were so many and so pleasing, and in the shade of those palms, so tall and beautiful: it amazed them to experience both the one and the other. There was no

uno y lo otro. Allí no parescía gente nenguna, enpero señal avía de andar gente por aquí, que avía ramas de palmas cortadas.

De allí el almirante entró en una barca, e fué con ella e con las otras a ver un rio, al levante de alli una legua, e fallaron el agua dél tan caliente que escasamente se sufría la mano en ella; e anduvieron por la ribera dos leguas sin hallar gente ni casas, e sienpre la tierra era en aquella fermosura, e los canpos muy verdes e llenos de infinitas gruas e tan coloradas como escarlata; e en toda parte por allí avía el olor de las flores e el cantar de los páxaros muy suave, lo cual todo vieron e sentieron en cuantas islas por alli llegaron. E porque eran tantas que no se podrían en sengular contar cada una, púsoles a todas en general el almirante por nonbre el Jardín de la Reina.

E el día seguiente, estando el almirante en mucho deseo de aver lengua, vino una canoa a caça de peces, que así le llaman ellos caça, que caçan con unos peces otros, que traen atadas unas peces por la cola con unos cordeles. E aquellos peces son de hechura de congrios e tienen la boca larga toda llena de fosas, así como de pulpo, e son muy osados, como acá los urones; e lánçanlos en el agua, e ellos van a pegarse a cualquier pece en lugar más ofensivo; e desque se apega cualquier pece destos en el agua, non la desapegarán fasta que la saquen fuera del agua, antes morirá, e es pece muy ligero; e desque se apegan tiran por el cordel muy luengo en que lo traen atado, e sacan cada vez uno, y tómanlo llegando a la lunbre del agua.

Ansí que aquellos caçadores andavan muy desviados de las caravelas, e el almirante enbió las barcas armadas e con arte que no les fuyesen a tierra; y llegados a ellos, les hablaron todos aquellos caçadores como corderos mansos sin maliscia, como si toda su vida los ovieran visto, que se detuviesen con las barcas, porque tenían uno destos peces pegado en fondo en una grande tortuga, fasta que les oviesen recogido adentro en la canoa, e así lo fizieron. E después tomaron la canoa e a ellos con cuatro tortugas, que cada una dellas tenía tres cobdos en luengo, e los truxieron a los navíos al almirante, e allí aquéllos le dieron nueva de toda aquella tierra e islas e de su cacique,

sign of human presence there other than the indication that people passed through those places since some palms had broken off branches.

In that place the Admiral got into a boat and went, along with other boats, to explore a river a league east of there. They found its water so hot that it could hardly be borne by a hand. They followed its bank for two leagues, finding neither people nor dwellings, and as usual the land had the same beauty; the fields were quite green and full of so many pink cranes of such a bright color, almost scarlet, and everywhere there was the scent of flowers and the very sweet sparrows' song. They saw and heard all of this in all the islands they reached. Since the islands were so many that they could not be counted one by one, the captain named them all, as a whole, the Queen's Garden.[38]

The following day, while the Admiral had a great desire to obtain information, a canoe hunting for fish arrived. In fact, they call it hunting, since they hunt the fish using another species of fish tied in the tail with thin ropes. This fish is similar to crabs with a wide mouth full of cavities, like the octopus's, and very aggressive like the uruses (aurochs) in our country. Once thrown into the water, they seize upon any fish in the most harmful way; so when one of them sticks to another fish in the water, it will not let go of it until pulled out of the water, dying before letting go; it is a very light fish. The fishermen pull the very long rope, holding it when one sticks to its prey thus, catching a single fish at a time.

Since those hunters were going far away from the caravels, the Admiral sent out well-armed boats to prevent them from fleeing ashore; when they approached, all those hunters spoke like meek lambs, as though they had known the Castilians all their lives, begging them to stop the boat since they had one of those fishes at the bottom, inside a big tortoise, until they had gathered them into the canoe, and so they did. Then they took the canoe and the fish contained in four three-cubits-long turtles and brought them to the Admiral's ships. There the Indians gave him information about all of that territory, those islands and their cacique, the one who had sent them hunting,

---

[38] Jardines de la Reina, Cuba.

que estavan allí muy cerca, que los avía enbiado a caçar; e rogaron al almirante que se fuese allá e que le harían grande fiesta; e diéronle todas cuatro tortugas, e él les dió muchas cosas de las que llevava, con que fueron muy contentos. E preguntáronles si aquella tierra era muy grande, e respondieron que al poniente no tenía cabo, e dixieron que toda aquella mar al austro e poniente era llena de islas. Dióles licencia, e ellos le preguntaron cómo se llamava, e ellos dixieron el nonbre de su cacique e bolviéronse a su exercicio de pescar.

and said that they lived very close there. They requested the Admiral to go there, adding that they would give him a great welcome. They gave him the four turtles and he presented them with several things he had brought, which made them quite happy. He asked them whether that land was very large and they answered that westward it did not have any end and also said that all that sea southward and westward was full of islands. He dismissed them after asking them their name. They pronounced their cacique's name and went back to fishing.

CAPITULO CXXVII

De la tierra donde los onbres comen perros y los engordan con pescado para ello, e del suavísimo olor de la tierra.

Partió el almirante de allí por entre aquellas islas, por las canales más navegables, seguiendo al poniente, non se desviando de tierra firme; e después de con buen tienpo aver andado muchas leguas, falló una isla grande e al cabo della una grand población; e aunque las caravelas llevavan buen tienpo, surgieron allí y fueron a tierra; mas no hallaron persona alguna, que todos fuieron e dexaron el lugar; creyóse ser gente que se governava de pescados. Allí hallaron infinitas conchas de tortugas, que tenían por aquella playa; allí hallaron juntos cuarenta perros, non muy grandes ni muy feos; non ladravan, parecían estar criados a pescado e cevados; supieron de los indios cómo los comían, e que tienen tan buen sabor como acá los cabritos en Castilla, porque algunos castellanos los provaron; tenían allí aquellos indios muchas garçotas mansas e otras muchas aves.

El almirante mandó que no les tomasen cosa nenguna, e partióse de allí con sus navíos; e luego hallaron otra isla mayor que aquélla e non curaron della, mas endereçaron a unas montañas que vieron muy altas de la tierra firme, que estavan de allí catorze leguas; e allí hallaron una gran población, e el cacique e todos los avitadores de muy buena conversación e de buen trato; e allí dieron buen refresco al almirante e a su gente de pan e frutas e agua. E preguntóles el almirante si aquella tierra andava mucho adelante al poniente, e respondió el cacique, con otros viejos de su tienpo, ca era onbre viejo, que aquella tierra era grandísima, que jamás oyó dezir que toviese cabo; mas que adelante sabrá más de la gente de Magón, de la cual provincia ellos estavan comarcanos.

CHAPTER CXXVII

The territory where men eat dogs and make them fat by feeding them fish. And the most pleasant scent of that land.

The Admiral left there to sail among those islands, through the more navigable channels, going westward without losing sight of the mainland. After traveling many leagues with good weather, he found an island of considerable size with a large village on its outermost point. Though the caravels had favorable weather, he dropped anchor there and the men went ashore. They could not find anyone, however, because all had fled and abandoned that place; it was thought they were fish-eating people. There they found a great many turtle shells that the Indians kept on the beach. Moreover, they found forty dogs altogether, neither very big nor very ugly; it seems they did not bark because they were raised on fish. They learned from the Indians that they ate the dogs and that they have a taste as good as baby goats do in Castile, since some Castilians tasted them. Those Indians also kept there numerous tame lesser egrets and many other birds.

The Admiral ordered his men not to take anything and he left with his ships. They soon after found another island, larger than the former, but ignored it, heading instead toward some high mountains sighted on the mainland fourteen leagues away. There they found a large village whose cacique and all the inhabitants were willing to talk and were well behaved. They gave the Admiral and his people good food to eat including bread, fruit and water. The Admiral asked them whether that land extended much farther westward, and the old cacique, along with others of his same age, answered that the land was very large, that he had never heard it had ends but that the Admiral could learn more from the Magón people, whose region they bordered.

Navegaron al seguirnte día al poniente, siguiendo sienpre la costa de la tierra, e andovieron muchas leguas, sienpre por islas más grandes y no tan espesas como primero; e llegaron a una sierra muy grande e muy alta que andava mucho adentro en la tierra, tanto que no se pudo ver el fin della; e de parte de la mar della avía poblaziones infinitas, de las cuales luego vino a los navíos mucha gente con fruta e pan e agua e algodón hilado, e conejos e palomas e de otras mill maravillas de aves, de otras maneras que no ay acá, cantando por la fiesta, creyendo que aquella gente e navíos venían del cielo; e aunque el indio intérpetre les dezía que era gente de Castilla, creían que Castilla era el cielo, e el rey y la reina señores de aquellos navíos, cuya era aquella gente, estavan en el cielo. Llámase aquella provincia Hornofay.

Llegaron allí una tarde e avían andado mucho, e allí no pudieron surgir, e el viento de la tierra los echava afuera; e estovieron allí toda una noche a la cuerda, pairando, que no les paresció una ora de mano por el suavísimo olor que de la tierra venía e el cantar de los paxaricos, e el de los indios, que era muy maravilloso e contentable. Allí dixieron al almirante que adelante de allí era Magón, donde todas las gentes tenían rabo como bestias o alimanias, e que a esta cabsa los hallaría vestidos; lo cual non era ansí, mas paresce que entre ellos ay este ardid de oídas, e los sinples dellos lo creen ser ansí con su sinpleza, e los discretos creo yo que no lo creerán, porque paresce que ello fué dicho primeramente por burla, faziendo escarnio de los que andavan bestidos; como dize Juan de Mandavilla en el capítulo ochenta y cuatro de su libro, que en las Indias, en la provincia de la Mori, todos andan desnudos como nascieron, que hazen burla de los que andan vestidos, e dizen que es gente que no creen en Dios que fizo a Adan y Eva, nuestros padres, el cual los hizo desnudos, e dizen que de lo que es natural nenguno deve aver vergüença. E así los desta provincia de Hornofay, como ellos todos andan desnudos, onbres e mugeres, hazen escarnio de los que oyen dezir que andan bestidos; e el almirante supo ser burla, que si algunos donde ellos dizen andan vestidos, tanpoco tienen rabos como ellos. Dixieron allí

Sailing westward the next day and always following the coast, they travelled many leagues through fewer but larger islands. They reached a very big and high mountain chain which extended so far into the territory that they were unable to see its end. On the sea-side there were very numerous villages from which many people came at once to the ships with fruit, bread and water, spun cotton, rabbits, doves and thousands of other wonderful birds of various types that we do not have here; they were singing in welcome, believing these men and ships had come from heaven. Although the Indian interpreter told them they were people from Castile, they thought Castile was in heaven and that the King and Queen, owners of those ships, lords and masters of these men, lived in heaven. Ornofay is the name of that territory.

One evening they arrived there after sailing a long distance, but they could not anchor due to the wind off the land which pushed them back. They spent the entire night handling riggings; however, it seemed to them that scarcely an hour had passed, because they were entranced by the extremely sweet scent coming from the land and the sparrows' and the Indians' songs, all wonderful and very pleasant. There the Admiral was told that the Magón people farther ahead had tails like beasts and predatory animals and that because of this the Castilians would find them clothed. This was not the truth. However, it seems this rumor goes around among them with the most naive belief, because of their simplicity, that it really is so, whereas, in my opinion, the cleverest do not believe it as it appears that it all started as a joke to make fun of those wearing clothes. As John Mandeville tells us in Chapter 84 of his book, all the people of the Indies, in the Mori province, go around naked as at birth and make fun of those who are dressed, saying that those people do not believe in God, who created our progenitors, Adam and Eve, naked, stating that nobody should be ashamed of what is natural. Thus, all the people in Ornofay territory,[39] men and women, go around naked and scoff at those who reportedly get dressed, although, just like them, they do not have tails. They also told the Admiral that farther ahead lay innumerable islands and shallows

---

[39] Cienfuegos area, Cuba.

tanbién al almirante, que adelante avía islas inumerables e poco hondo, e que el fin de aquella tierra era muy lexos, e tanto que en cuarenta lunas no le podrían llegar al cabo; e ellos fablavan segund el andar de sus canoas, que es muy poco, que una caravela andará más en un día que ellos en siete.

and that the extremity of that land lay so far away that in forty moons it could not be reached. They were talking of course in terms of the speed of their own canoes, which is very limited, whereas a caravel can sail in a single day as far as the canoes are able to in seven.

CAPITULO CXXVIII

De la mar Blanca.

Partió el almirante de Ornofay el día siguiente, con buen tienpo, con sus caravelas, e cargó de velas, e anduvo muy grande camino fasta que llegó a una mar blanca todo de un golpe, e pasó muchos baxos antes de allegar a ella; la cual era blanca como de leche, e espesa como el agua en que los çurradores adovan los cueros. E luego les faltó el agua e quedaron dos braças de agua, e el viento les sacudió mucho, estando en una canal muy peligrosa para bolver atrás ni para surgir con los navíos, porque no podían virar sobre el ancla, la proa al viento, ni avía hondo para ello, porque sienpre andavan rastrando la cuchilla por el suelo; e andovieron ansí por estas canales de dentro destas islas diez leguas, fasta una isla donde hallaron dos braças e un codo de agua, e largura para estar las carabelas. Allí surgieron e estuvieron con muy grand pena, pensando dexar la empresa e que no harían poco en poder bolver a donde avían partido; mas Nuestro Señor, que sienpre acorre a los humillados e de buena voluntad, les puso esfuerço, e puso en coraçón al almirante que seguiese adelante. E el día siguiente enbió una caravela pequeña al fondo de aquella mar, allí cerca, a ver si hallaría agua dulce en la tierra firme de Juana; que tenían todos los navíos mucha necesidad. Bolvió con la respuesta, que a la orilla de la tierra era el todo muy hondo, e que estava dentro en la mar el arboleda tan espesa que no entraría por ella un gato. Avía por alli tantas islas que eran más espesas que en el Jardín ya dicho, e tantas arboledas al rededor en la orilla de la mar que

CHAPTER CXXVIII

The White Sea.

The next day the Admiral hoisted sail and left Ornofay with his caravels in good weather, sailing on for a long distance until he entered a suddenly whitened sea, overcoming several shoals before entering it. The sea was as white as milk and thick like the water where the tanners tan leather. Soon they were in low waters and stopped in four fathoms-deep water with a wind that strongly shook them as they were sitting in a very dangerous channel, dangerous in any case whether one decides to turn back or to anchor the vessels since they were unable to veer on the anchor with the prow to the wind, nor was there any depth so they were forced to constantly move, with the keel scraping the bottom. They sailed this way for ten leagues through these channels, shifting about the islands up to one where they found a depth of two fathoms and a cubit and enough width to hold the three caravels. There they anchored and remained quite worried, thinking to have to give up their undertaking since it would not be a simple matter to be able to return to where they had left. But, Our Lord, who always assists the needy and the people of good will, infused vigor into them and made ready the Admiral's mind to going ahead. The next day he sent a small caravel to enter the sea around there, to verify whether there was any fresh water in Juana's territory since all the ships needed it very much. It returned with the answer that all around the coast there was a thick layer of mud, and that stretching out into the sea there was so dense a wood that not even a cat could penetrate it. The islands there were many, even more numerous than in the Queen's Garden which I mentioned earlier, and so many woods around the shoreline that they

parescían muros; e junto con aquellas arboledas avía tierra alta e muchas montañas e muy verdes, e en ellas parescían muchas ahumadas e grandes fuegos.

E el almirante determinó de andar adelante, e navegó por aquellas canales entre aquellas islas, las cuales, como dicho es, eran más espesas que en el Jardín de la Reina; e navegó fasta que llegaron a una punta muy baxa de la tierra, a la cual el almirante puso nonbre la Punta del Serafín. Allí ovieron muchos trabajos, que muchas vezes se hallaron con los navíos en seco; e dentro la punta de la tierra bojava al oriente, e se descubrían al setentrión montañas muy altas, lexos de esta punta, e entre medias linpio de islas, que todas quedavan al austro e al poniente. Ovieron alli un viento bueno, e allí hallaron tres braças de agua de hondo; e el almirante determinó de tomar el camino de aquellas montañas, a las cuales llegó otro día seguiente; e fueron a surgir a un palmar muy fermoso e muy grande, a donde fallaron fuentes de agua dulce e muy buena, e señal que alli avía estado gente.

Acaesció allí que, estando forneciendo los navios de lena e agua, salió un vallestero de las caravelas a caça por la tierra con su ballesta, e alexado un poco se halló con obra de treinta indios, e el uno dellos era vestido de una túnica blanca fasta los pies; e se halló tan súpito sobre ellos que pensó, por aquel vestido, que era algund fraile de la Trenidad que iva allí en la conpaña; e después vinieron a él otros dos con túnicas blancas, que les llegavan abaxo de las rodillas, los cuales eran tan blancos como onbres de Castilla en color; estonces ovo miedo e dió bozes, e bolvió fuyendo a la mar. E vido que los otros se estavan quedos, e el de la túnica blanca conplida venía tras dél llamándolo, e él nunca osó esperar, e así fuyendo se vino a los navíos. E el almirante, desque lo supo, enbió allá por saber qué gente era; e cuando fueron no hallaron a nenguno, e creyeron que aquel de la túnica conplida sería el cacique dellos.

El día seguiente enbió el almirante veinte e cinco onbres armados, que andoviesen ocho o diez leguas por la tierra adentro fasta hallar gente; e andando un cuarto de legua fallaron una vega, que andava de poniente a levante en luengo de la costa, e por non saber el camino quisieron atraversar la vega, e nunca pudieron, con tanta yerva e tan entretexida que nunca pudieron andar; e bolvieron cansados como si ovieran andado

appeared like walls. Next to the woods there was a high ground as well as very green mountains with many columns of smoke and big fires.

The Admiral decided to continue on and sailed through those channels among those islands which, as already stated, were more numerous than in the Queen's Garden. He sailed until he reached a very low point in the land, which he named Serafin Pointe. There they met with many troubles, for often their vessels ran aground. The land from Serafin Pointe sloped inland toward the east and north, letting one see in the distance many high mountains, and in between there were no islands for all of them lay south or west. There they enjoyed a good wind and a depth of three fathoms, so the Admiral decided to head toward those mountains, reaching that territory the following day. They anchored near a very beautiful and large palm-grove where they found very good springs of fresh water and indications people had been there.

It happened that while they were supplying the ships with wood and water, an archer from the caravels went ashore to go hunting with his crossbow. As he went farther away, he ran across some thirty Indians, one dressed in a long white robe that reached his feet, and found himself unexpectedly in their midst. Given this garb, he thought the man was a Trinity friar that was there with them. When two other men with below-knee-length robes walked toward him, white as the Castilians are dark, he grew scared and, shouting, turned around, taking off toward the sea. He realized that while the others stood calm, the one with the longer white robe was running after him and calling to him, but he did not dare to stop and so reached the vessels, still fleeing. When the Admiral learned about this, he dispatched some men to discover who they were. Yet, when they got there they could find no one and guessed that the one with the long robe was their cacique.

The next day Columbus sent 25 armed men to explore inland eight or ten leagues deep until they could find people. After traveling a quarter of a league, they found a plain that stretched along the coast from west to east and, not knowing the way, they set out to cross the plain but were not able due to the dense vegetation which prevented their walking. They came back tired, as if they had traveled twenty leagues, and

veinte leguas, e dixieron que por allí era inposible poder andar la tierra, que non avía camino ni vereda.

Otro día fueron otros a luengo de la playa, e fallaron rastro de bestias grandísimas de cinco uñas, cosa espantable, e juzgaron que fuesen grifos; e de otras bestias que juzgavan que faesen leones: tanbién se bolvieron atrás. Allí hallaron muchas parras e muy grandes e cargadas de agraz, que cobrían todos aquellos árboles que era maravilla de lo ver; tomó el almirante de aquel agraz una espuerta llena, e de los troços de las parras e de la tierra blanca de la mar, para mostrar e para enbiar al rey y a la reina. Tanbién allí avía muchas aromáticas frutas, como en los otros lugares susodichos; tanbién avía allí grúas dos vezes mayores que las de Castilla.

Visto el almirante que avía dexado la punta del Serafín, adonde la tierra bojava al oriente, e avía atravesado a las montañas al sententrión, navegó de allí al oriente por la mesma costa, fasta que vido que la una costa e la otra se juntavan e fazían seno, e bolvieron atrás al poniente; e aunque andavan los navíos e gente muy cansada, pensó el almirante navegar al poniente, a unas montañas que avía visto lexos, treinta e cinco leguas de donde avía tomado el agua. E andando las nueve leguas hallaron una playa y muchos indios, e tomaron el cacique dellos, el cual, como ignorante persona que no avía salido de allí de aquellas montañas, le dixo que era la mar muy honda e baxa al sententrión, e muy grande camino de jornadas.

Levantaron sus áncoras e seguieron sus caminos muy alegres, pensando que sería como él les avía dicho, e andando ciertas leguas se hallaron enbaraçados entre muchas islas e en muy poco hondo, de manera que no hallavan canal que los consintiesse pasar adelante; e a cabo de un día e medio, por un canal muy angosto e baxo, por fuerça de anclas e cabestral, ovieron de pasar los navíos por la tierra en seco casi una braça, fasta aver andado bien dos leguas: donde hallaron dos braças y media de agua, en que navegavan los navíos, e andando más adelante hallaron tres braças. Allí vinieron muchas canoas a los navíos, e las gentes dellas dezían que las gentes de aquellas montañas tenían un rey de grande estado; e ellos parece que lo tenían en maravilla el modo e suma de su región e grande estado, diziendo que tenía infinitas provincias, que le llaman santo e que traía túnica blanca que le arrastrava por el suelo.

reported that it was impossible to go inland that way, since there were no roads nor trails.

The following day others went along the beach and found animal tracks which they thought were lions' and therefore they turned right around. There they found a large amount of very tall climbing vines heavy with sour grapes, which entirely covered the trees, truly a wonder to see. The Admiral took a full basket of those grapes and some pieces of vine and a little White Sea sand to send and show to the King and Queen. In addition, there were many aromatic fruits as in the localities treated earlier; and there were a few cranes, twice as big as the ones in Castile.

Since he had left Serafin Pointe where the land turned toward the east and had crossed the mountains on the north side, the Admiral sailed eastward from there along the same coast, until he noticed that both coasts joined, forming a gulf. He then turned back toward the west and even though the ships pressed on and the men were very tired, the Admiral decided to sail westward toward some mountains he had seen far off, about 35 leagues from where he had taken on water. After covering nine leagues, they found a beach and many Indians. The Castilians took their cacique, who, never having left those mountains, had no real knowledge but told them that the sea was very deep, but low in the northern part, and the distance was very great.

They weighed anchor and continued their journey very relaxed, thinking it would be as he had told them, but after a few leagues, they soon found there were quagmires among several islands in a very shallow sea, and they were unable to find a single channel which would let them proceed. After a day and a half in the narrowest low channel they were able, by dint of anchors and ropes, to get the ships past an area full of shoals and water only one-fathom deep, to a place two leagues beyond. There they found two fathoms and a half of water in which the vessels went on and further ahead they found three fathoms. In those places many canoes came toward the vessels and the Indians were saying that the people of those mountains had a particularly important king. It seemed they believed the manner in which he ruled the territory was wonderful for a large state government, saying that he ruled over many regions, that they called him "saint" and he wore a white robe which reached the ground.

E así siguieron aquel camino por la costa de aquella mar, sienpre con tres braças de agua de hondo; e después de navegado cuatro días e pasadas las montañas que quedavan mucho al oriente, e sienpre hallando la costa de la mar así anegada, e arboledas espesas cerca della, como dicho es, que era inposible entrar por ellas; e estando metidos los navíos en un seno por donde otra vez la tierra bolvía al oriente, vieron unas montañas muy altas, allí adonde aquella tierra fazía cabo, lexos dellas veinte leguas. Determinó el almirante ir allá, pues la mar no bogía al sententrión e era de muy grandísimo hondo, como el cacique avía dicho; y dixo que por allí, por donde el almirante quería ir, que en cincuenta lunas no hallaría cabo, e así lo avía él oído dezir.

Navegaron por dentro de muchas islas, e al cabo de dos días con sus noches llegaron a las montañas que avían visto, e fallaron que era un cherseneso, atán grande como el de la Aurea, como la isla de Córcega. Cercáronla toda, e nunca pudieron fallar entrada para ir a la tierra adentro, porque era así la tierra llena de lodo e de arboledas espesas, como lo otro que dicho es; e las ahumadas de gente eran en la tierra adentro muy grandes. E muchos estovieron por allí por aquella costa siete días buscando agua dulce de que tenían necesidad, la cual hallaron en la tierra de parte de oriente, en unos palmares muy lindos; e allí hallaron nícaros e grandísimas perlas, e vieron que allí avría buenas pesquerías si las continuasen.

Después que tomaron agua e leña, navegaron al austro siguiendo la costa de la tierra, y después al poniente siguiendo sienpre la costa de la tierra firme fasta que los llevaron al sureste, e parescía que avía de llevar por aquella vía grande número de jornadas; e al austro vieron toda la mar llena de islas, después de aver andado grand pieça de donde avían partido. E aquí los navíos estavan muy desconcertados, por las muchas vezes que avían tocado en tierra, e las cuerdas e aparejos gastados, e la mayor parte de los mantenimientos muy perdidos, en especial el viscocho, por la mucha agua que fazían los navíos; e toda la gente estava muy cansada e temerosos de mantenimientos, e dubdando que la sazón de los vientos a la buelta les podría ser adversa.

Avían andado fasta allí, desde cabo Alifaet, mill e dozientas e ochenta e ocho millas, que son trecientas e veinte e dos

Thus, they followed that course along that sea coast, always in a three-fathom depth. They sailed for four days, and overshot the mountains, leaving them very far to the east, and kept on finding the seacoast so submerged and the woods around it so dense that, as was stated earlier, it was impossible to penetrate. After having left the ships in a cove where the land turned eastward, they saw some high mountains where that land formed a cape, twenty leagues away. The Admiral decided to go there since the sea did not turn northward and was very deep, as the cacique had said. He had also said that according to hearsay, where the Admiral intended to go it would be next to impossible to find the outermost edge even in fifty moons.

They sailed among many isl nds and in two days and two nights they arrived at the mountains they had sighted. They found it was as big as the Golden Chersonese, and like the island of Corsica. They went all around it but could not find a way to enter and penetrate the territory, since the land was so full of mud and thick with trees, as in other instances mentioned before. Yet, the smoke columns of the local people were quite large. They remained a long time, seven days, along that coast, looking for the fresh water they needed and then found in the eastern part of the territory in some quite nice palm-groves. They found shells and very big pearls and realized that they could successfully gather a lot of them if they kept on fishing.

After gathering water and wood they sailed southward, constantly aligned with the shoreline until they got to the south-east. All indications suggested that the route required many days; after having covered quite a distance in relation to where they had left, they saw to the south a sea full of islands; their ships were by now damaged from the many times they had scraped bottom, and the ropes and other equipment were worn out and most of the food rotten, especially the hard-tack, given all the water taken in by the ships; and, all the men were tired and afraid they would not have enough food or that the winds might be unfavorable to them on the way back.

They had traveled that far[40] from the Cape Alfa et O, 1280 miles or 322 leagues, discovering many islands all along,

---

[40] Ensenada de Cortés, Southwestern Cuba.

leguas, en que avía descubierto muchas islas, segund dicho es, y la tierra firme. Estonces acordó el almirante dar la buelta por otro camino, non por donde avía ido, e bolver por Jamaica, el cual nonbre el almirante le avia mudado e puesto Santiago, e por acabar de redondear toda la parte del austro que les avia quedado por andar. E asi dieron la buelta, pensando poder pasar dentro de unas islas que allí estavan, en las cuales nunca fallaron canal, e les fué forçado bolver atrás, por un braço de mar por donde avían navegado fasta la punta del Serafín, a las islas donde primero avían surgido de la mar Blanca.

as has been said, and also the mainland. Then the Admiral decided to return another way, avoiding the former run to go back through Jamaica, which he had named Santiago, thus completing the southward route that he had to interrupt during the voyage out. Thus, they turned back, thinking they could pass among some of those islands there; however, not finding a channel it became necessary for them to return through an arm of the sea which they had navigated as far as Serafin Pointe,[41] to the islands where they had anchored as they left the White Sea.

---

[41] The locality is today called Punta Gorda.

CAPITULO CXXIX

De los cuervos marinos que vieron, e mariposas e tortugas muy grandes.

Viniendo de buelta, después que ovieron pasado las casas del cacique susodicho una jornada, un día, antes que el sol saliese, vieron venir de mar en fuera, el camino de la tierra, más de un cuento de cuervos marinos todos juntos, e lo ovieron por maravilla de tanta multitud de cuervos; e el día seguiente vinieron a los navíos tantas de mariposas que escurecían el aire del cielo, e duraron así fasta la noche, que las destruyó una grande agua que llovió, e truenos con ella. E tanbién desde donde dexaron la tierra donde dezían que estava el rey santo, para ir al teroneso, a quien de Sant Juan Evangelista pusieron nonbre, bien que en todo el viage vieron que avía muchas tortugas e muy grandes, enpero muy muchas más vieron en estas veinte leguas; ca la mar era cuajada de todas aquéllas, e muy grandísimas, a tantas que parescía que los navíos se querían encallar en ellas, e así bugían entre ellas: tiénenlas los indios en grand precio e por muy buen manjar, e por muy sanas e sabrosas.

CHAPTER CXXIX

The sea crows, butterflies and very large turtles they saw.

While they were returning, one day after they overshot the above-mentioned cacique's dwellings and before sunrise, they saw more than a million sea crows in compact formation flying from the island out to sea. Seeing such a multitude of them was considered truly a wonder. The following day instead so many butterflies came toward the ships that they darkened the sky until night, when they were scattered by heavy rains and thunder. Again, from there, where the king "saint" was reported to live, they left land to reach the peninsula they named San Juan Evangelista.[42] During the whole trip they saw numerous very large turtles, but they saw many more of them in these twenty leagues, so many in fact that the sea was hidden by them. They were very big and in such quantities that the vessels appeared to be stranded, as indeed they experienced difficulties because of them. The Indians particularly appreciated turtles for their meat, being truly a very healthy and savory food.

---

[42] It is difficult to establish precisely whether the San Juan Evangelista Columbus reached is Los Pinos (Pine Island) or the western region of Cuba.

CAPITULO CXXX

De la provincia de Ornofay, e de dónde el almirante fizo decir misa, e del recivimiento que el cacique de aquella tierra le fizo.

Partieron de allí e navegaron por un braço de mar blanco, como es todo lo otro por allí, e muy poco hondo; e andadas ciertas leguas llegaron al cabo de las muchas islas donde avían surgido la primera vez en la mar Blanca; e fué maravilla de Nuestro Señor aportar a venir allí, e milagro, más que non por saber ni engenio de onbre. E dende vinieron fasta la provincia de Ornofay, con no menos peligro del pasado, e allí surgieron en un río, e fornecieron los navíos de agua e leña, para navegar al austro e no bolver por donde avían ido, e dexar el Jardín de la Reina a la mano ezquierda; e así vinieron, e aun no se pudieron escusar de comunicar con muchas islas que fasta estonces no avían visto. Aquí, como dicho es, es la tierra montañosa e fertilísima, de gente mansa en grand manera, e muy abundosa de frutas e de viandas; que de todo les dieron muy grand parte: eran las frutas suavísimas e aromáticas. Allí les truxieron infinitas aves, papagayos e de otras aves, e las más dellas eran mansas e muy grandes, e tan sabrosas como perdizes de acá de Castilla; e tenían el papo lleno de flores que olían más que azahar de los naranjos.

Allí fizo el almirante dezir misa, e fizo plantar una cruz de un grand madero, así como acostunbrava fazer en todos los otros cabos donde llegaron e le parecía que convenía. Era domingo cuando al almirante dixieron misa e él descendió en tierra; e el cacique de allí era onbre muy onrrado e señor de

CHAPTER CXXX

The Ornofay region. The place where Columbus had Mass celebrated. The reception reserved for him by the cacique of that land.

They left there and sailed through an arm of the White Sea, so-called since the entire sea in that area was white and extremely shallow. Traveling some leagues, they arrived at the cape with many islands where they had anchored for the first time in the White Sea.[43] Getting there was an extraordinary feat and a miracle wrought by Our Lord rather than by man's skill and talent. Afterwards they reached the region of Ornofay, with no less danger than before, anchoring near a river where they supplied the ships with water and wood in order to sail southward, and not return the way they had come, as well as to keep the Queen's Garden on their left. And thus they arrived with regret for not being able to visit the many islands they had seen up to that time. Here, as previously stated, there are mountains and a very fertile land, mainly inhabited by very mild people, with most abundant fruit and food. Of all these the inhabitants gave them large amounts; the fruits were aromatic and had a sweet taste. They brought them an infinite number of birds, parrots and other species, the majority of which were docile, of large dimension and as tasty as partridges are here in Castile. Their double chin, when full of flowers, had an odor more intense than orange blossoms.

On this land the Admiral had Mass celebrated and a cross planted made of a big tree, as he usually did on all the other landing points when it was deemed proper. It was on a Sunday

---

[43] La Mar Blanca, (White Sea).

mucha gente e familia, e cuando vido al almirante descendido de la barca en tierra le tomó de la mano, e otro indio de más de ochenta años que venía con él le tomó de la otra mano, faziéndole mucha fiesta; e traía aquel viejo un ramal de cuentas de piedra mármol al pescueço, las cuales ellos tienen allá en grand precio e un cestillo de mançanas en la mano, las cuales luego dió al almirante, así como descendió de la barca, en presente. E el cacique e el viejo e todos los otros andavan desnudos como nascieron, sin nengund enpacho, así como andan en todas aquellas partes de la tierra descubierta por el almirante Colón. Así, por las manos, fueron, e todos los otros indios en pos dellos, fasta donde el almirante fué a fazer su oración e oír misa, donde avía mandado aparejar para ello.

Después que el almirante acabó su oración, el viejo indio, con muy buen senblante e osadía, fizo su razonamiento; e dixo, que él avía sabido cómo el almirante corría e buscava todas las islas e tierra firme de aquellas partes, e que supiesen que allí estavan en la tierra firme de allá; e dixo al almirante que no tomase vanagloria, puesto caso que toda la gente le oviese miedo, porque él era mortal como todos los otros onbres. E començó por palabras e señas, figurando en su persona cómo todos los onbres nascieron desnudos e tenían ánima inmortal, e que del mal de cada mienbro el ánima era la que se dolía; e cómo, al tienpo de la muerte, del despedimiento del cuerpo sentía muy grande pena, e que iva al rey del cielo o en el abismo de la tierra, segund el bien o mal que avía fecho e obrado en el mundo: e porque él conosció del almirante que avía plazer de lo oír, él se alargava más en el razonamiento, con tales señas que todo lo entendía el almirante.

E el almirante le respondió, por intercesión del indio intérpetre que traía, que avía venido a Castilla, el cual entendía muy bien la lengua castellana e la pronunciava, e era muy buen onbre e de muy buen engenio. E respondió que él no avía fecho mal a nenguna persona, ni era venido para hazer mal a los buenos, salvo a los malos; e que antes fazía bienes y mercedes a los buenos, e mucha onrra, e que esto era lo que sus señores, el rey don Fernando y la reina doña Isabel, muy grandes reyes d'España, le avían mandado.

when the Admiral went ashore and had the Service held. The local cacique, a very respectable man and chief of a great number of people and head of a large family, when he saw the Admiral off the boat, took his hand, while another Indian, more than eighty years old, who came with him, took the Admiral's other hand, giving him a great welcome. This old man wore on his neck a "rosary" with beads made of marble held in high esteem by them, and in his hands a small basket of apples which he had presented to the Admiral as soon as he got off the boat. The cacique, the old man and the others were all naked as they were born, without showing embarrassment, as was true in all the lands discovered by Admiral Columbus. Thus they walked, holding each other's hands with all the other Indians behind them to where the Admiral stopped for prayers and Mass in the location he had chosen for the liturgy to be held.

After the Admiral had finished his prayers, the old Indian gave his speech with a pleasant but bold demeanor, saying that he had learned how the Admiral had traveled around through all the islands and to their mainland; that they should know that that was the mainland; and, finally, that the Admiral should not boast because the people showed fear of him, being himself a mortal like all other men. He began with words and gestures, exemplifying with his own body that all men are born unclothed and have an immortal soul which suffers because of the illness of each part; and that the soul, at the time of death, i.e. of its separation from the body, feels great pain as it departs to meet either the king of the heavens or that of the abyss of the earth, depending on the good or evil achieved or performed in the world. Since he sensed that the Admiral was pleased to listen to him, he lingered on with such plain gestures and reasonings that the Admiral understood everything.

The Admiral replied, using as an interpreter the Indian he had with him who had gone to Castile since he understood and spoke the Castilian language quite well and was a good and very talented man. The Admiral answered that he had not done harm to anybody, and had not come to hurt good people but only bad people; that he would rather do good, reward good people and treat them with much honor since that was what his lords, King Ferdinand and Queen Isabela, the most illustrious Sovereigns of Spain, had ordered him to do.

E el indio respondió muy maravillado al intérpetre: «Cómo, ¿este almirante otro señor tiene e obedesce?». E el intérpetre dixo: «Al rey y a la reina de Castilla, que son los mayores señores del mundo». E de aquí le contó al cacique e al viejo, e a todos los otros indios, las cosas que avía visto en Castilla, e las maravillas de España, e de las grandes cibdades e fortalezas, iglesias e gentes e cavallos e alimañias, e de la nobleza e riqueza de los reyes e grandes señores, e de los mantenimientos, e de las fiestas e justas que avía visto, e del correr de los toros, e de las guerras lo que avía sabido. E todo ge lo recontò muy bien e en forma; de lo cual el viejo e los otros se gozaron mucho por lo saber, e lo comunicavan los unos con los otros; e el viejo dixo que él quería venir a ver tales cosas, e determinava de se venir con el almirante, salvo por el inpedimento de su muger e fijos que lloravan, e por esto, por piedad dellos, lo dexó con mucha pena. E el almirante tomó otro mancebo de allí, que truxo sin escándalo de la tierra; el cual, con el otro cacique que traía, que avía tomado, enbió al rey e a la reina, después de venido del viage en la Española.

Todas aquellas gentes isleñas e de la tierra firme de allá, aunque parescen bestiales e andan desnudos, segund el almirante e los que con él fueron este viage, les parescieron ser bien razonables e de agudos ingenios; los cuales todos holgavan e huelgan mucho de saber cosas nuevas, como hazen acá los onbres, que desean saber todas las cosas, que aquello no nasce sino de bivez e agudo engenio; e son aquellas gentes muy obedientes e muy leales a sus caciques, que son sus reyes e señores, e los tienen en muy grande cuenta e onrra. Y luego, donde quiera que las caravelas llegavan, fazían saber, cualesquier indios que ay estoviessen o llegasen, el nonbre de su cacique, e preguntavan por el nonbre del cacique de las caravelas para replicarlo entre ellos, e el uno con el otro lo replicavan porque non se les olvidase; e después preguntavan cómo llamavan a los navíos, e si venian del cielo o de dónde venían. E aunque les dezían que era gente de Castilla, ellos pensavan que Castilla era en el cielo, porque ellos no tienen nengunas letras ni saben de ley ni de estorias, ni saben qué cosa es leer ni leyenda ni escriptura, e por eso están tan ignorantes. Ellos dizen que los de Magón andan vestidos porque tienen colas, por cobijar aquella fealdad, e tienen por enjutia entre ellos andar vestido, como dicho es.

The very astonished Indian replied to the interpreter: "How is it possible that this Admiral has and obeys another lord?" The interpreter said: "The King and Queen of Castile are the most important lords in the world." Then he continued to tell the cacique, the old men and all the other Indians about the things he had seen in Castile and the wonders of Spain: the great cities and fortresses, churches, people, horses and the other animals; the nobility, the wealth of the kings and the great lords; the food, feasts and contests he had seen, the bull ride, and what he had learned about wars. All of this he told very well and correctly. The old man and the others were amused to learn all this and repeated it to each other. The old man said he wished to go see such things and that he would have gone with the Admiral if it had not been for his wife and children who were crying. For this reason, for pity on them, he left him with much regret. Along with the other cacique he had taken with him the Admiral took another young man from there without any difficulty to send to the King and Queen when he would return from the trip to Hispaniola.

All the people of the islands and of the mainland over there, though appearing to be primitive and naked, were, in the opinion of the Admiral and those with him on this trip, endowed with great common sense and sharp talent. They all were and are much delighted to learn new things, just as those who wish to know everything are here, a tendency born solely from lively intellect and sharp talent. All those people are very obedient and loyal toward their caciques whom they consider their kings and lords and whom they hold in great esteem and honor. After that, whenever the caravels went, a local Indian living there or getting there would tell his cacique's name and would ask for the name of the caravel's cacique. They would repeat the name to each other in order not to forget it. Then they would ask how the ships were called and whether they came from heaven. And although they were told they were people from Castile, the natives thought Castile was in heaven since they have no instruction, nor know anything about law, history, what to read, or even what reading or writing is, being therefore quite ignorant. They repeat that the people of Magón wear clothes, because they have tails, in order to hide that ugliness, and that for them it is offensive to wear clothes, as previously stated.

La tierra es tan fértil, en lo que se pudo conoscer por todas aquellas islas e tierras de aquellas mares, que aunque fuesen muchas más gentes, e fuesen cien vezes otros tantos, les sobrarían los mantenimientos. Bien puede se er la tierra adentro aver otros regimientos e otras diferencias e modos de gentes e cosas estrañas, que no puede ser menos, las cuales deste viage non se pudieron ver ni saber. Despidióse el almirante de aquel cacique e de aquel viejo onrrado, su privado o pariente, de Ornofay con mucha amistancia e con muchas obligaciones.

Since the land's productivity level is high, it justified the view that there would be more than sufficient provisions in all those islands and lands in that sea even if the population were much more numerous, indeed even if it were to be a hundred times its number. It is possible as well in the interior of these territories that there may be other forms of government and other differences or particular customs of the people as well as other oddities which could neither be observed nor studied in detail during that trip, as it could not be helped. When the Admiral left the cacique and the venerable old man of Ornofay, his trusted man or relative, he did so with great friendship and heartfelt gratitude.

CAPÍTULO CXXXI

De cómo el almirante se partió de allí, e de lo que andubo; e de cuántas leguas puede andar una carabela; y de cómo aportaron a una isla de muchas poblaciones. Del cacique que se metió con su mujer e cosas en la caravela, para venir con el almirante; e de como volvió a la Española. E de la fin de esta escritura, e de la muerte del dicho almirante.

Partió el almirante de la provincia de Ornofay, del río de Laxar, a que puso nonbre de las Misas. Navegaron al austro, por dexar al Jardín de la Reina, que eran las muchas islas verdes y hermosas, a la mano ezquierda, por el peligro del navegar que primero a la ida avían pasado; vinieron a tener a la provincia de Macaca, por cabsa de los vientos que les resistieron, e allí en toda la provincia los recebieron muy bien. E allí en un golfo muy grande, a donde puso el almirante nonbre Buen Tienpo, allí navegaron al poniente, fasta que llegaron al cabo de la isla, e dende al austro fasta que la tierra bogía al oriente; e ansí, a cabo de ciertos días, vinieron al monte Castalino, e de allí a la punta del Farol, e a la Baxa, que es más a levante onze leguas, a donde haze fin la isla sobredicha. Allí ovieron ciertos días de viento contrario.

Los marineros tienen que, en común navegar de una caravela, en un día son dozientas millas de cuatro en legua, que son en un día natural cincuenta leguas, e un día grande sesenta e dos leguas; destas le acaescieron al almirante e a su gente en este viaje hartas jornadas, segund ellos contavan e escrivió el almirante en el libro que dello fizo. Y non

CHAPTER CXXXI

The trip of the Admiral after leaving the Ornofay region. The leagues a caravel is able to travel. How they landed on an island with many villages. The cacique who boarded a caravel along with his wife and their belongings to go with the Admiral. How the Admiral returned to Hispaniola. The conclusion of this work and the death of our Admiral.

The Admiral left the Ornofay region from the Laxar river, which he renamed the Messe.[44] They sailed southward, leaving to their left the Queen's Garden of many beautiful and green islands, because he feared a trip similar to the previous one on the way over. They stopped in the Macaca region due to the unfavorable winds, and there they were given a warm welcome. In a very beautiful gulf there, which the Admiral named "Good Weather," they sailed westward until they reached the outermost point of the island and then continued southward as long as the land faced east. Thus, they arrived after a few days at Mount Castalino and from there sailed to Farol Pointe[45] and then to Baxa, which lies eleven leagues farther east or where the said island ends. There they had some days of unfavorable wind.

The sailors believe that during regular sailing a caravel travels 200 miles, four per league, i.e. fifty leagues in a normal day and 62 on long days. During this trip the Admiral and his people had many such days, according to what they reported; the Admiral himself discussed this matter in a book. It should not be surprising that during a voyage the wrong route may

---

[44] Jagua, Jamaica.

[45] Morant Pointe, Jamaica.

parescía a maravilla, que navegando se pueda arbitrar el camino incierto, mas antes se prueva por muy verdadero; porque muchas vezes se buelve el navío a las olas, otras veces se buelve atrás a donde partió, e non con el mesmo viento e tienpo, salvo con lo contrario e adverso. E aquí consiste el saber del maestro, e el remediarle al tiempo de la tormenta; ni se tiene por buen piloto o maestro aquel que aya de pasar en una tierra de otra muy lexos sin ver señal de otra tierra alguna, que yerre diez leguas, aunque el tránsito sea de mill leguas, salvo si la fuerça de la tormenta le fuerça e priva el usar del engenio.

Asi que, navegando ellos a la partida del austro, fueron a surgir una tarde a una vaía adonde allí en aquella comarca avía muchas poblazones. E vino un cacique de una grand poblazón, que está en un alto, a los navíos, e trúxoles muy buen refresco, e el almirante les dió a él e a los suyos de las cosas que él tenía e les agradavan; e el cacique preguntó de dónde venían e cómo llamaván al señor de los navíos. E el almirante respondió que él era vasallo de los grandes y muy onrrados rey e reina de Castilla, sus señores, los cuales lo avían enbiado en aquellas partes a saber e descobrir aquellas tierras, e a onrrar mucho a los buenos e obedientes, e a destruir los malos; e esto fué por intervención del intérpete indio que fablava. De lo cual el dicho cacique se holgó mucho, e preguntó muy por estenso al dicho indio de las cosas de acá, e él se lo recontó mucho por estenso, de lo cual el cacique e los otros indios, muy maravillados, se holgaron mucho; e estovieron allí fasta la noche, que se despedieron del almirante.

E otro día partió el almirante de allí, e ya que iva a la vela con poco viento, vino el cacique con tres canoas e alcançó al almirante; el cual venia tan concertado que no es de dexar de escrivir la forma de su estado. La una de las canoas era muy grande, como una grande fusta, e muy pintada; allí venía su persona e la muger e dos fijas, la una de fasta diez e ocho años, muy fermosa, desnuda del todo como allá se acostunbrava, muy onesta; la otra era menor; e dos fijos mochachos e cinco hermanos y ocho criados, y los otros todos devían ser

be followed and at first considered to be the correct one; many times in fact the ship is directed out to sea while other times is reversed in the direction it came from, but not with the same weather and wind, indeed with one contrary and unfavorable. That is when the skill of the experienced man comes into play and is expected to remedy stormy weather. A good pilot or master is not considered such if, in traveling over a great distance from land to land, out in the open sea with no indication of any land, he is off by ten leagues even when the trip is a thousand leagues long, except in the case of an overpowering violent storm that prevents him from making use of his ingenuity.

It so happened that as they sailed southward they anchored one evening in a bay of a region with many villages. A cacique of a very large village set on high ground came to the ships bringing excellent food for them and the Admiral gave him and his people of what he had, things they appreciated. The cacique asked where they were coming from and the ship lord's name. The Admiral replied that he was a subject of his very great and most illustrious lords, the King and Queen of Castile, who had sent him there to know and to discover those lands and to greatly honor the good and obedient people and kill the bad ones. This was communicated with the help of the Indian interpreter, who related all of this. The above-mentioned cacique was most glad to hear this and asked very detailed questions of the Indian interpreter regarding our country. He answered quite extensively and for that the cacique and the other Indians, quite surprised, were greatly delighted. They remained there until night, at which time they took leave of the Admiral.

The Admiral left that place the next day and, since he sailed with little wind, the cacique was able to catch up to him with three canoes. He came with such a retinue that it is impossible not to describe the way it all unfolded.[46] One of the canoes was as large as a big *fusta* and multi-colored. There beside the cacique stood his wife and two daughters: one of almost 18 years of age, very beautiful, completely naked as customary, yet quite chaste; the other daughter was younger. In addition there were two young sons, five brothers, eight

---

[46] This famous episode happened in the area of the present-day Portland Bay, near Kingston, Jamaica.

sus vasallos. Traía él en su canoa un onbre como alférez; éste solo venía en pie en la proa de la canoa, con un sayo de plumas coloradas de fechura de cota de armas, e en la cabeça traía un grand plumage que parecía muy bien, e traía en la mano una vandera blanca sin señal alguna. Dos o tres venían con las caras pintadas de colores de una mesma manera, e cada uno traía en la cabeça un grande plumage de fechura de celada, e en la frente una tableta redonda, tan grande como un plato, e pintadas, así la una como la otra, de una mesma obra e color, que no avía diferencia, así como en los plumages; traían éstos en la mano cada uno un juguete con que tañían. Avía otros dos onbres, así pintados en otra forma; estos traían dos tronpetas de palo, muy labradas a páxaros e a otras sotilezas, el leño de que eran era de muy negro fino; cada uno destos traía un lindo sonbrero de plumas verdes muy espesas e de muy sotil obra, e otros seis traían sonbreros de plumas blancas; e venían todos juntos en guarda de las cosas del cacique.

El cacique traía al pescueço una joya de alanbre, de una isla que es en aquella comarca que se llama Guani, que es muy fino, e tanto que parece oro de ocho quilates; era de fechura de una flor de lis tamaño como un plato; traía al pescueço con un sartal de cuentas gordas de piedra mármol, que tanbién tienen en grande precio. E en la cabeça traía una guirnalda de piedras menudas verdes e coloradas, puestas en orden, y entre medias algunas blancas mayores, a donde bien parescían. Traía más una joya grande colgada sobre la frente, e a las orejas le colgavan dos grandes tabletas de oro con unas sartas de cuentas verdes más menudas; traía un cinto, aunque andava desnudo, ceñido, de la mesma obra de la guirnalda, e todo lo otro del cuerpo descubierto. E asimesmo su muger venía adornada, desnuda, descubierta, salvo un solo lugar de su mienbro, que de una cosilla no mayor que una oja de naranjo, de algodón, traía tapado; traía en los braços, junto con el sobaco, un bulto de algodón fecho en semejança de los brahones de los jubones antiguos de los franceses; traía otros dos, como aquéllos e más grandes, en cada pierna el suyo, como axorcas, tanbién de algodón, debaxo de las rodillas. La hija mayor e más fermosa toda andava desnuda; un solo cordón de piedras muy negras e menudas solamente traía ceñido, del cual colgava una cosa de fechura de yedra, como una hoja della, de piedras verdes e coloradas, pegadas sobre algodón texido.

sirvientes with all the others, probably his subjects. He brought along with him in his canoe a man as ensign; he stood alone upright on the first boat wearing a dress of multi-colored feathers shaped like a tabard and on his head a big, good-looking plume whereas in his hands he held a plain white flag. Two or three of them had their faces painted with similar colors and each of them wore on the head a big plume shaped like a helmet with a round tablet, on the forehead, big as a plate. Both were painted in the same way and were of the same color, so there was no difference as in the case of the plumes. They held an instrument in their hands which they were playing. Similarly, two other men were there but dressed in a different way. They each held a little wooden trumpet, finely-crafted in the shape of birds and other refined designs, made of a very dark, good quality wood. Each was wearing an attractive headpiece of very thick green feathers, of very fine workmanship, and six other men wore headpieces of white feathers. They all stayed very close together, keeping watch over the cacique's things.

On his neck the cacique wore jewelry of thin beaten metal — so polished that it looked like 18-karat gold — found in an island called Guani which is part of that region. It had the shape of a lily flower as big as a plate. In addition, on his neck he wore a string of big marble-like beads also highly valued. On his head he wore a wreath of small green and multi-colored stones strung according to size and with a few large white stones in the middle that stood out very well. Moreover, hanging on his forehead was a big jewel, and, from his ears, two large gold tablets with some strings of smaller green gems. Though he was bare, he wore a belt crafted like the garland on his head and nothing else on his body. His woman was adorned in the same way, but wearing no clothes except for a small cotton cloth around her genital area, covering up a space no larger than an orange leaf. She wore a puffed-out cotton band at the top of her arms, made like the sleeves of the ancient French bodice, and two larger ones but similar, also of cotton, on each of her legs under her knees. The elder daughter, the most beautiful, completely naked, was wearing only a belt of very dark and small stones from which hung something the shape of an ivy leaf, made of green and multi-colored stones set on a cotton fabric.

La canoa grande venía entre las otras dos, e más con una poca de ventaja adelante; e luego como llegó este cacique al bordo del navio, començó de dar a los maestros e gente cosas de su cámara a cada uno; e era de mañana, e el almirante estava rezando e non vido tan aína las dádivas ni la determinación de la venida deste cacique. El cual luego entró en la caravela con toda su gente; e cuando el almirante salió ya tenía enbiados los vasallos que bolviesen a las canoas muy alegres a tierra, e ivan ya lexos. E luego que vido al almirante, se fué a él con cara muy alegre diziendo: — Amigo, yo tengo determinado de dexar la tierra e irme contigo e ver el rey e la reina y el principe su hijo, los mayores senores del mundo, los cuales tienen tanto poder que tienen aca sojuzgadas tantas tierras por ti, que les obedesces e vas por su mandado todo este mundo sojuzgadon, como he sabido destos indios que contigo traes; e que en todo cabo estan las gentes de ti tan temerosas que es maravilla; e a los caribes, que es gente innumerable e muy brava, les has destruido las tierras e casas, e tomadas las mugeres e fijos, e muertos dellos los que no fuyeron. Yo sé que en todas las islas desta comarca, que es infinito mundo de gente innumerable, te temen e han grand miedo, y les puedes fazer mucho mal y dapño, si no obedecen al grand rey de Castilla, tu señor, pues ya conoces las gentes destas islas e su flaqueza y sabes la tierra. Pues antes que me tomes mi tierra e señorío, yo me quiero ir contigo, con mi casa, en tus navíos, a ver los grandes rey e reina tus señores, e ver la tierra más rica e abundosa del mundo, donde ellos están, e a ver las maravillas de Castilla, que son muchas, segund tu indio me ha dicho.

E el almirante, aviendo conpasión dél e de su muger e fijos, ge lo estorvó, viendo su ignorancia, e sana voluntad, e dixo que él lo rccebía por vasallo del rey e de la reina; e que por estonces que se quedase, que aún le quedava mucho para ir a descubrir, e que tiempo avía, de otra buelta, para conplir su deseo; e fizieron su amistad, e así se ovo de quedar con su gente e casa.

El almirante navegó dende el austro e al oriente por aquellas mares, entre otras muchas islas pobladas de aquellas mesmas

The big canoe advanced between the two others, staying a little ahead of them. As soon as this cacique reached the side of the vessel, he began to give each of the officers and the others objects which he owned. It was morning and the Admiral was praying, so he was not very pleased with either this cacique's gifts or with his determination to come. The cacique soon went aboard the caravel along with all his people, but by the time the Admiral showed up he had already asked his subjects to return quickly to shore with their canoes and so they had done. As soon as he saw the Admiral he turned to him with a smiling face and said: "My friend, I have decided to leave my land and go with you to see the King and Queen and their son, the prince, the most important lords in the world, who have so great a power as to control so many lands through you who obey them and in respect of their will keep taking possession of all this world, as I learned from the Indians you bring with you; you whom your people everywhere fear so much that it is amazing; you who devastated the lands of the Caribs — an innumerable and very courageous people — and destroyed their dwellings, taking the wives and children and killing those who had not fled. I know that in all the islands of this region, inhabited by many people, everyone is timorous of you, fearing you since you can cause a lot of hurt and damage if they do not obey the great King of Castile, your lord, since by now you know the people of these islands, their weaknesses and their territories. Therefore, before you take away my land and possessions, I want to come with you on your vessels, along with my family, to meet your great lords, the King and Queen, to see the wealthiest and most productive land in the world, where they live, and the many wonders of Castile, according to what your Indian told me."

The Admiral, having compassion for him, his wife and his children, prevented him from doing so, knowing his ignorance and good faith, and said he considered him a vassal of the King and the Queen, but that for the moment he should stay there because as Admiral he still had much to discover; that there would be other opportunities with his next stop to bring his wish to fruition. They became friends, but the cacique had no choice but stay with his people and his family.

The Admiral then sailed south and east through those seas, among the many islands inhabited by those naked people,

gentes desnudas, segund escrivió el almirante; de las cuales por no hazer mención dexo de escrivir, e basta esto, porque toda la gente era como la susodicha; e cuando bolvió a la Española, de donde avía partido, vino a salir por entre las islas de los caribes, fazia por donde avían ido el segundo viage. Ya no hazían cuenta dél en la Española, ni de sus navíos, sino pensavan que él fuese perdido; e acá en Castilla así mesmo, que avían escripto de la Española cómo non parecía tanto tienpo avía.

Alegráronse con su venida los que lo bien querían; e por la contra, a otros que no le tenían en buena voluntad, les pesó; porque no dexava aprovechar a nenguno ni rescatar cosa alguna, salvo todo para el rey e para la reina, porque avía muy grandes gastos fechos en la demanda; e avía grandes murmuraciones contra él.

Non halló cogido oro, ni ovo quien procurase de lo aver, ni quien lo supiese ni osase buscar, por temor de los indios, mientras él estuvo en el dicho viage. Desque fué venido, luego puso en obra de aver lo más que pudo, e por las discordias que ovo entre ellos fizo justicia de algunos, e enbió presos al rey otros, como atrás es dicho. Los gastos eran muchos, los provechos eran pocos fasta estonces, la sospecha que no avía oro era muy grande, así acá como en Castilla. Ovo falta de mantenimientos; allegó la gente a estar en mucha nescesidad, lo cual remedió de acá don Juan de Fonseca, que tenía cargo de proveerlo. Ovo quien fizo entender al rey e a la reina que sienpre sería muy mucho más el gasto que el provecho, de manera que enbiaron por el almirante; e vino en Castilla, en el mes de junio de mill e cuatrocientos y noventa y seis años, vestido de unas raposas de color de ábitos de fraile de sant Francisco de observancia, e en la fechura poco menos que ábito, e un cordón de sant Francisco por devoción: e troxo consigo algunos indios.

E antes que de allá partiese, avía prendido al grand cacique Caonaboa, e a un su hermano e a un su fijo de fasta diez años, no en pelea, salvo desque los aseguró; e después diz que dixo que los traía a ver al rey e a la reina, para después bolverlos en su onrra e estado. Traía al Caonaboa e a un su hermano de fasta treinta e cinco años, a quien puso por nonbre don Diego, e a un moçuelo sobrino suyo, fijo de otro hermano. E murióse el Caonaboa en la mar, o de dolencia o de poco plazer. Traía

as he wrote, about whom I will not talk, refraining from description since they were all like the others. When he returned to Hispaniola, from which he had left, he went through the Carib islands as far as they had gone during the second trip. In Hispaniola they had already lost any hope of seeing him and his ships again, since they thought he had lost his way. They thought the same thing here in Castile since the ones on Hispaniola had written that the Admiral had not been seen for a long time. Those who wished him well cheered his arrival, whereas those who did not like him were unhappy because he did not let anyone take advantage of the situation or personally profit from taking anything, everything being reserved for the King and the Queen, since his request had involved heavy expenses; consequently, great criticism was leveled against him.

Upon his return he did not find gold already accumulated, nor anyone who worked to that purpose, nor anyone with knowledge of where to find it or even daring to look for it out of fear of the Indians. Soon, after arriving he did his best to obtain the most he could and, because of the disagreements arisen internally, he put some of them to death and others, as is subsequently noted, he sent as prisoners to the King. Great were the expenses, while the profit, until then, was minimal. The suspicion that there was no gold was strong, both there and in Castile. There was a lack of food; the people were in great need: that was remedied from here by Don Juan de Fonseca, who was in charge of supplies. There were those who gave the King and Queen to understand that the costs would always be more than the earnings, and therefore they sent for the Admiral. He arrived in Castile in June, 1496, wearing out of devotion a habit the color of those worn by the observant friars of St. Francis, including the Franciscan sash, that little resembled a dress. Columbus brought with him a few Indians.

Before leaving Hispaniola, Columbus had captured the grand cacique Caonabó, one of his brothers and his almost ten-year old son, not in a battle but by giving assurances, adding later that he had informed them afterwards he was going to take them to see the King and Queen and then deliver them back to their own land and living conditions. He brought Caonabó and one of his brothers of almost 35 years of age, whom he named Don Diego, and also a boy, their cousin, the

un collar el dicho don Diego, hermano del Caonaboa, de oro, que le fazía el almirante poner cuando entrava por las cibdades o logares, fecho a eslabones de cadena, que pesava seiscientos castellanos; el cual yo ví e tomé en mis manos, e tuve por huéspedes en mi casa al obispo don Juan de Fonseca e al almirante e al dicho don Diego.

Truxo el almirante estonces muchas cosas de allá, de las del uso de los indios: coronas, carátulas, cintos, collares e otras muchas cosas entretexidas de algodón, e en todas figurado el diablo en figuras de gato o de cara de lechuza, e donde bide otras figuras, dellas entalladas en madera, dellas fechas en bulto, del mesmo algodón o de lo que era la alhaja. Traxo unas coronas con unas alas, en ellas unos ojos a los lados; e en especial traía una corona, que dezían que era del cacique Caonaboa, que era muy grande e alta, e tenía a los lados, estando tocado, unas alas como adargas e unos ojos de oro tamaños como taças de plata de medio marco cada uno, allí asentados como esmaltados por muy sotil e estraña manera, e allí el diablo figurado en aquella corona; e créese que así se les parecía, y que eran idólatras e tenían al diablo por señor.

Los que de aquellos indios que truxo bivieron, presentó con las cosas e oro que truxo al rey e a la reina, de los cuales él fué muy bien recebido, e ovieron plazer de ver las cosas estrañas e de saber de lo descubierto; aunque el almirante tenía hartos contrarios, que no lo podían tragar por ser de otra nasción e porque sobjuzgava mucho en su capitanía e cargo a los sobervios e adversos. Estovo desta vez acá el almirante, en la corte e en Castilla e en Aragón, más de un año, que con las guerras de Francia no lo podían despachar; e después ovo licencia e flota e despacho de sus Altezas; e estando en la corte se negoció e concertó e se dió licencia a otros muchos capitanes que lo procuraron para ir a descubrir, e fueron e descubrieron diversas islas.

Partió el almirante de buelta a las Indias, en fin de agosto del año de mill e cuatrocientos y noventa y siete, con tres

son of another brother. Caonabó died, however, of an illness or because of the precarious living conditions during the crossing. Don Diego, Caonabó's brother, wore a gold neckpiece made of linked rings which weighed 600 *castellanos* which the Admiral made him wear when entering the cities and other inhabited places. I saw and held it in my own hands, since I hosted the bishop Don Juan de Fonseca, the Admiral and the above-named Don Diego in my home.

The Admiral had brought from Hispaniola many things used by the Indians: crowns, masks, belts, necklaces and many other cotton fabric things. In all of them was depicted the devil in the shape of a cat with an owl's face and other designs as well, a few carved out of wood and a few in relief, made of the same cotton or of the material of which the ornament was made. He brought a few crowns with wings and eyes on the sides. They especially brought a crown, which they said belonged to the cacique Caonabó, very large and high, decorated on its sides and wings with shields and golden eyes as big as silver bowls and of half a *marco* each, which looked almost enameled, reproduced in a very thin and unique way, and the devil was on the crown too. It must be believed that they imagined it in this way, that they were idolaters and that they considered the devil to be their lord.

He presented to the King and Queen, along with the things and the gold he had brought, the surviving Indians. The Sovereigns received him very well and were pleased to see the unusual objects and to learn what had been discovered, despite the fact that the Admiral had many enemies who could not tolerate him, because he was from another country and in his command he proved to be particularly intransigent toward rebels and opponents. This time the Admiral remained here at the Court, in Castile and in Aragon for more than one year, since they were not able to authorize him to leave again because of the war with France. Afterwards, he received permission from Their Highnesses, a fleet and the authorization to leave. During his stay at the Court it was negotiated and decided to give permission to many other captains who made arrangements to go and discover new lands: they left and discovered some islands.

The Admiral returned again to the Indies with three caravels at the end of August 1497. He set course for certain islands

caravelas; e atinó fazia ciertas islas, donde no avía llegado, en las partes del austro, en par de las islas de los caribes; e descubrió e falló la isla de las Perlas, e non quiso que resgatasen, salvo muy poca cosa por demuestra, de que los marineros fueron dél muy malcontentos; porque les avía dicho que de lo que Dios les diese e echase en encuentro en aquel viaje que partiría con ellos; e después dixo que el rey y la reina lo enbiavan a descubrir por aquella vía e non a resgatar; que tienpo avría para bolver a resgatar. E siguió su vía de buelta a la Española, e llegando en ella dió forma en las minas del oro e en las poblaciones, donde trabajó mucho; e falló muy grandes minas de oro, como él creía que las avía, e lo dezia e non era creído de muchos, asi de cavalleros como de marineros e escuderos e gente común, que fazían burla de su fablar.

E fechas minas e dada orden muy agudísima en el buscar del oro, pasó cerca de un año que non pudo hallar la abundancia; e en el año de mill e cuatrocientos e noventa y nueve començó de hallar la abundancia, e en el año de quinientos começó a coger. E como se cogía todo en nonbre del rey e de la reina, aunque pagavan halgo a los que travajavan e andavan en las minas, como el almirante lo recebía e adquería todo, avía muchas murmuraciones contra él; e él se engorró e tardó de enbiar el oro al rey algo más de lo que devía, en tal manera que ovo quien escrivió de allá, o vino acá a dezir al rey e a la reina que encubría el oro e que se quería enseñorear de la isla; e otros, que la quería dar a genoveses, e otras muchas cosas; de lo cual lo menos se deviera de creer que él tal fiziera.

E el rey enbió un governador, que se dezía Bovadilla, a la Española; e enbió por el almirante, el cual el dicho governador enbió en son de preso con el oro que tenia. El cual aportó a Cáliz en el verano del año de quinientos y un años, e presentado al rey con el oro que truxo e dado su descargo, el rey le mandó, porque asi convenía a su servicio, que no entrase jamás en la isla Española; e por los servicios que le avía fecho confirmóle su almirantadgo para sienpre jamás, con sus derechos e rentas; e que andoviese en la corte e estoviese en Castilla, adonde él quisiese. E díxole que en esto creía que le fazía mucha onrra e merced, que lo quitava del peligro de los castellanos, que estavan

200

which he had not previously reached in the southern area, opposite to the Carib islands. He found and discovered the island of the pearls, but he did not allow any trading to take place except for a very few things taken as samples. The sailors were very disappointed at this, since he had told them that whatever thing God would give and offer during that trip he would share with them, but he later pointed out that the King and Queen had sent him along that route to discover, not to make exchanges, for which there would be time later. He followed his return route to Hispaniola and, once there, he imposed order in regard to the gold mines and among the people, committing himself strongly in all of this. He found very large gold mines, such as he had thought there would be, though he had not been believed by many people, gentlemen, sailors, esquires or common people alike who used to scoff at what he said.

After rebuilding the mines and giving most specific instructions to search for gold, about a year went by during which he could not find it in great quantities. But, in 1499 he began to find it in large amounts and in 1500 the collection process was started. Everything was gathered in the name of the King and Queen, though they paid a small amount to those who worked the mines, but since the Admiral received and kept all of it, there were many rumors against him. He became irritated and delayed more than he should have in delivering the gold to the King and Queen, prompting some to write from there or even return to tell the King and Queen that he was hiding gold and wished to become lord of the island and others to report that he wanted to give it to the Genoese — and there were many other things too to which no credence should be given for he could not have acted that way.

The King sent to Hispaniola a governor named Bobadilla. Because of the Admiral's behavior, the above-named governor sent him back as a prisoner with the gold he had. In the summer of 1501 Columbus was taken to Cádiz and presented with the gold he had brought to the King, who removed him from office since it so suited him, ordering Columbus never to return to Hispaniola. For the services he had given, the King confirmed forever his title of Admiral with all rights and annuities and further ordered that Columbus frequent the Court and live in Castile wherever he wished. The King told Columbus that he intended to do him much honor and favor this way, rescuing him from the danger of the Castilians, who were

muy indignados contra él, e que si allá bolviese que non se podría escusar alboroto e escándalo, que sería dar a los indios mal exemplo.

El almirante, vista la voluntad del rey e de la reina, suplicó a sus Altezas le diesen licencia para ir a descobrir por la vía del setentrión el costado derecho de la tierra firme que le avía quedado por descobrir; porque aunque su voluntad fué ir por aquella vía la otra vez, la tierra firme lo avía echado por la otra vanda. E el rey le dió licencia, e fué con tres navíos a descobrir, e ovo en el viage muchos siniestros e fortunas, después de aver pasado allende la Española, que halló las mares muy bravas y non pudo andar tanto cuanto él quisiera; e aunque descubrió en el viage muchas islas, segund él escrivió, su propósito non pudo aver el efecto que deseava. E en algunos puertos, con las fortunas, estovo retraído algunas distancias de tienpo, que le inpedió el descubrir; e del mucho navegar e del mucho trabajo, o del umor de aquellas mares, que de tal manera enpeció los navíos, que se le comieron de broma: e maravillosamente él y la gente escaparon en el uno a una isla cerca de la Española, el navío ya tanbién muy perdido, donde por vía de indios el governador supo dél, e enbió por él e lo truxieron, con la gente que avia ido con él, a la Española; e dende lo enbió en Castilla, e lo truxo Diego Rodrigues, cómitre, vezino de Triana, el año de mill e quinientos y cuatro, a cerca de Navidad.

El cual dicho almirante don Cristóval Colón, de maravillosa e onrrada memoria, natural de la provincia de Milán, estando en Valladolid el año de mill e quinientos y seis, en el mes de mayo, murió, inventor de las Indias, de hedad de setenta años: Dios le ponga en gloria. Subcedióle su hijo mayor, don Diego Colón, en el almirantazgo e rentas e onrra que él por su trabaxo e industria e buena ventura ganó, con los navíos que para ello el rey e la reina le dieron.

very upset with him, and that had he returned to Hispaniola disorders and scandals could not be avoided, setting consequently a bad example for the Indians.

The Admiral, seeing the King's and Queen's will, implored Their Highnesses that he be accorded the authorization to go discovering through a northern route, the right side of the mainland which was left to be discovered, since, although he intended the other time to go that route, the mainland had driven him back to another area. The King gave him the requested authorization and Columbus went to explore with three ships and suffered many accidents and storms during the journey. It so happened that beyond Hispaniola he found very rough seas that prevented him from going as far as he wished and — according to what he wrote — although he discovered many islands in this trip, his intended purpose could not be realized. He was forced by high winds to stop for a certain time in some ports, which prevented him from discovering other islands. The ships were damaged from the long sailing, the many difficulties hidden in the strange water of those seas, as well as consumption by shipworms. Miraculously, he and his people were able to escape on a vessel, though almost in total ruin, to an island near Hispaniola from where, through some Indians, the governor learned about what had happened to him and sent someone to the rescue, thus bringing him to Hispaniola and all his people with him. Later, the governor had him return to Castile where he was taken by Don Diego Rodriguez of Triana around Christmas 1504.

The above-named Admiral Christopher Columbus, of wonderful and venerable memory, a native of the Milan province, discoverer of the Indies, died in May 1506 at the age of seventy while living in Valladolid. May his soul rest in God's glory. His elder son Don Diego succeeded him as Admiral-in-Chief with the royalty income and the honors that through his commitment, his industriousness and luck, he had earned while commanding the ships granted him by the King and Queen.

DIEGO ALVAREZ CHANCA'S *LETTER*

Commentary by
Anna Unali

I. – DIEGO ALVAREZ CHANCA BEFORE HIS VOYAGE TO THE INDIES

The events of Diego Alvarez Chanca's life until 1491, when he is mentioned in a royal decree as Princess Isabela's physician, are scarcely known. There is clear information about neither the place nor the date of his birth. Some historians think he was a native of Seville, basing their opinion on what the friar Antonio de Aspa relates in the introduction to his transcription of the *Letter* in which he refers to Chanca as a native of Seville.

Such a biographical reference, however, cannot be completely accepted since it was made a century after the event, i.e. when information about Chanca's life was hardly verifiable. Also, recent research by C. Varela concerning this subject has led to the determination that neither the last name Chanca, nor any similar surname such as Chanta or Xanta, exist in any Andalusian document. Rather, four places in Spain, again according to the Spanish scholar, carry the place-name Chanca: three in Lugo province and one in the Coruna province.

Morejón and Chinchilla consider him to be a native of Toledo, but their assertion is not supported by documentary evidence. Andrés Bernáldez referred to Chanca in his *Memoirs of the Catholic Sovereigns' Reign,* indicating he was from the vicinity of Seville, revealing therefore his certain Sevillian citizenship and residency, however, he neglected to provide specific information as to Chanca's birth place.

Even if his birthplace remains uncertain, knowing that the city where he mainly lived was Seville does explain Chanca's cultural background. In those years Seville was a multicultural center of great interest not only because of the survival of the Moslem tradition, which endured until the downfall of the Kingdom of Granada in 1492 through constant osmosis between the two civilizations, but also because of the great economic and cultural contributions resulting from, among other things, the presence of colonies of different nationalities,

particularly Genoese and Florentine, which partially determined the world-wide commercial destiny of the Andalusian city.

Chanca's home in Seville, during the period after his return from Hispaniola in 1501, was in the district of San Andrés on a street called *calle de la pellejería* where, as the name suggests, the leather tanners' shops were located.

The artisans' establishments must have caused inconveniences to the residents of the *calle*, as is pointed out by the Seville ordinances of 1527 which regulated these shops, forbidding their presence in the middle part of the street while permitting them only at the beginning and end of the street. It therefore must have been a modest street. Also located on *calle de pellejería* was the *Amor de Dios* hospital, where Chanca had probably provided services as a doctor before the period known to us.

The profession of physician, except for the few especially well known, was not generally considered very prestigious in Spain; many physicians came from "new" Christian families and most of the time received low salaries. They were often viewed as charlatans and very few members of the city's wealthy families devoted themselves to the profession.

Chanca had taken regular university training in medicine, not in Seville which even in the early sixteenth century did not have a medical school, but probably in Alcalá or Salamanca, the main Castilian universities in this field.

In the years just before Columbus's first Atlantic expedition to the Indies, Chanca was able to so make himself known in Spain as one of the best physicians of the time, that he provided medical services to the royal family. How he achieved such fame is unknown due to the lack of documentation regarding this period of his life. The earliest available records cover the central period of his career, when he was already appreciated and sought for his scientific competence.

In addition, the particular scientific field to which he had devoted himself more specifically, his specialization and his basic scholarly bent in the vast and complex field of medicine of that time, can in part be inferred from the medical works he wrote during the years after his trip to the Indies; among those to be mentioned, given the originality of its topic, is the *Tractatus de Fascinatione* which proves Chanca's interest in debating the world of magic and themes intrinsically related to specific aspects of the human psyche. A second element that reinforced his propensity for this specialization is further evidenced, ac-

cording to several historians, in the assistance he provided Princess Juana, the royal family's daughter, nicknamed *la loca*, since she was mentally disturbed. This in turn would also attest to his concern for problems related to the psyche.

Finally, the treatise *Alquímica*, though directly intended to investigate another field, control of and supremacy over nature through the strength of the human mind, confirms the same type of interest. It, in any case, should not be ruled out that these studies may have caused him some trouble with the Inquisition possibly explaining the decision by the Santa Clara de Monaguer convent to reject one of Chanca's cousins, a decision clearly in contrast with the promise to accept her and which had previously been made personally to Chanca by the mother superior.

The period of Chanca's life before his departure for the Indies, the years 1491-1493, is the time better documented by the sources. The extant documentation, five official acts concerning the Catholic Monarchs' authorization for him to make the journey and their interest to facilitate arrangements, yields information of particular significance since it sheds light upon his medical services to the royal family.

In the royal cedula addressed to Queen Isabela's treasurer, Gonzalo de Baeza, dated June 12, 1491, Chanca is referred to as the Princess of Portugal's "physician" i.e., Princess Isabela, daughter of Isabela of Castile and Ferdinand of Aragon, married to Alphonse of Portugal in 1490. At the end of that year the princess, accompanied by Chanca, had reached her husband in Portugal where the plague which had broken out in Evora where she lived was considered over. Her sojourn in Portugal was of short duration, however, because of her husband's death on June 12, 1491, having fallen from a horse. Afterwards, Isabela returned to Castile.

It is not clearly known what Chanca's role with the royal family was during the period immediately following. Different theories have been advanced: Tió thinks he kept tending Princess Juana, the future queen of Spain; of a different opinion are Fernández Repeto, Fernández Ibarra and Juan A. Paniagua who think the physician continued to provide professional service to Princess Isabela, even after his return to Spain. Such hypotheses are based on a controversial interpretation of the July 7, 1492 royal cedula in which the Catholic Queen Isabela mentions the salary owed Chanca for his previous year's medical service to her "dearest and most beloved daughter." The document is inconclusive since the specific name of the princess implied is omitted.

The fact that in 1491 Chanca was indicated as "the Princess of Portugal's physician," whereas one year later the document addresses him more generally as the "princess's physician" without any further specification as though it was an assumed fact, leads one to consider the second hypothesis more probable.

It is evident from this 1492 document, however, that Chanca had not interrupted his service with the royal family during 1491, except, perhaps, for a very short period, i.e. after Princess Isabela's return from Portugal, as inferred from both the explicit reference to "last year" and to the time period "until the end of the year." It is also very likely that he had been retained for the entire year 1492 and, further, was renewed through the following year until May 23, 1493, when the Spanish Sovereigns suggested his journey to Hispaniola.

The expression recorded in the official document granting the Rulers' official consent to Chanca's participation in the second of Columbus's Atlantic enterprises lends some doubts about Chanca's real intentions and will to take part in the expedition as a physician. The document expressly states: "We have learned that you, out of the desire you have to serve Us, want to go to the Indies; and since in doing so you will serve Us and you will be useful to the health of those who by Our order will go there, so that you may do so, in Our service...."

It is therefore impossible to know with certainty whether Chanca himself had requested the authorization to leave in the first place, intending to participate in the Columbian enterprise, or whether he simply submitted to the command of the Spanish King and Queen to accompany the men on the expedition. It may also be concluded that it could have been a combination.

This document in fact shows Chanca's obligation to perform medical services and his willingness to be useful to the King and Queen to be one and the same. Although his desire to go overseas to the islands is not emphasized, it does not mean that Chanca did not make an explicit request to that effect. Indeed, we must not underestimate the euphoria which followed Columbus's first expedition since it might have also affected Chanca, possibly pushing him to forward his request to the Sovereigns.

In any case, Dr. Chanca had been the object of attention from the Spanish royalty, who judged his medical competence to be very useful in the Indies. In fact, two other royal documents, dated May 23 and 24, 1494, the former addressed to the *contador major* of the realm, Gonzalo Chacón, and the other generically directed to the *contadores majores*, express pleasurable anticipation and satisfaction for the work Chanca would do.

In both, the Sovereigns' will to facilitate Chanca's journey and to eliminate every possible impediment is clear.

Two additional notations concerning Chanca's role and the expected length of his stay in Hispaniola seem of interest. In the May 24 document he is referred to as "Our physician," whereas in the earlier one only as "physician." It is possible to conclude that the specific use of the possessive be meant to show consideration for Chanca's services given up to then to the royal family. The same document mentions the remuneration that ought to be paid "every year" proving from the very beginning that the design of this expedition — unlike the first one — implied a lengthy stay in the Indies.

CHAPTER REFERENCES

CHINCHILLA, t. 1, 18.
HERNÁNDEZ MOREJÓN, t. 1, 197.
PANIAGUA, 20-28.
TIÓ, 19, 23.
VARELA, "Diego Alvarez Chanca."
VARELA, "Introducción a la *Carta del Doctor Diego*," 152-55.

II. – MEDICAL SCIENCE BETWEEN 1400 AND 1500

"For those who wish to take advantage of the practice of medicine and so that not only the young but also the old may satisfy their needs by means of these glosses and comments of mine, this most useful work...shall be returned to light." So declares Chanca, referring to the Arnoldian parables, in his *Comentum parabolis Divi Arnaldi de Vilanova*, whose sole purpose was, as he makes clear in the text, to revive for readers the Arnoldian work in its original text duly explained and annotated in Latin.

With respect to its make-up and purpose, the *Comentum* may be considered a typical example of medical literature of the period since it corresponds to the already centuries-old practice of spreading medical science, most often, however, without an accurate verification process or modification of its theories. Chanca's book, a product of a physician of humanistic background, by one who knew Latin and therefore the classical texts, fits in the static conception of medicine which did not deviate in its basic orentation from what had been considered valid by the highest authorities in the field and therefore traditionally accepted over time.

The physician's role, from Galen to Paracelsus to Vesalius, indeed remained almost unchanged over the centuries for lack of substantial changes in medical knowledge. Erudite and expert in all the tenets previously developed in medicine, philosophy, astrology and astronomy, the physician, often referred to as a physicist, carried out his practice by embracing his culturally-acquired beliefs, which, however, were totally devoid of practical experimentation and amounted to untested debatable claims of what had been discussed and asserted.

Although quite slowly, throughout the 1400's and the early decades of the 1500's, awareness of the need for experimental verification, already argued favorably by Leonardo and Paracelsus, was making progress in and outside the medical field. Medicine, however, had not yet overcome the century-old dichotomy of theory and practice sanctioned traditionally

in two distinct professional roles: that of the barber-surgeon, in charge of surgical interventions in the body; and that of the physician theorist, who merely clung to his right to authoritative — ex cathedra — teaching by formulating and disseminating medical knowledge of the past and its crystallized basic assumptions, unchecked by scientific scrutiny.

The physician-theorists functioned in a world of knowledge entirely different from that of the barber-surgeon, who attended wounds, being designated not only to heal wounds literally but also to satisfy all actual necessities. Without university degrees and consequently deprived of an understanding of medical literature written primarily in Latin, he and his class were considered second-class doctors.

Their apprenticeship turned them into people skilled in the treatment of traumatic illnesses, trained for the performance of small operations such as the removal of kidney stones and the correction of hernias, cataracts and bleeding, in addition to completely plain tasks of common occurrence such as giving haircuts, shaving and extracting teeth. Also, being knowledgeable in elementary medical notions allowed them to treat the more usual diseases of the medical sector in which they operated. The implementation of their activity had to be authorized by appropriate officials granting them license to do their jobs.

The scarcity of physician-theorists, especially outside the towns, made the practical physicians' assistance highly sought in several sectors, including the maritime area. Aboard ship, they either performed varied medically-related tasks or merely acted as barbers.

The presence of a physician-theorist on Columbus's second voyage amounts to an extraordinary event. It was not until 1497, when on May 23, a royal memorandum decreeing that aboard all fleets to the Indies "there had to be a physician and a *boticario* [botanist]," that physician-theorists were required to assume such a role.

Medical science, if it can already in that period be called such, had not overcome during the entire fifteenth century the sphere of superstitious reverence for Galen and his theories of the four humors, of the planets, of the loss of equilibrium, and of colors and numbers. Every illness, caused by the lost humoral balance of the individual, was explained as a separate case.

It should also be pointed out that Galen's analysis of the anatomy of the human body in the second century A.D. was mainly based on experiments made on animals, since dissection of the human body was not allowed at that time. Therefore, to study the functioning of the body, Galen made primary use of vivisection of hogs, whose internal apparatus in many respects resembles the human's.

Medicine, passively and in quasi-servile fashion, accepted Galen's postulates well into the 1400's, even when the discordance with objective reality was evident. In such cases, the non-acknowledgement of the error led physicians to think that during the centuries after Galen either an evolution of the human body had occurred or that a decline of the human body in relation to the model described by Galen had perhaps taken place.

Up to Vesalius the teaching of medicine and the treatment of diseases remained nearly unchanged. In his work *De humani corporis fabrica libri septem* [the seven books of the human body machine], Vesalius laid the foundations of the new medicine, asserting the importance, explicated in his *Tabulae anatomicae* [Anatomy tables] of 1538, of learning about human physiology and its natural functioning by dissection of the body.

In his theory, the lifeless body of human beings no longer was a center of visible and sacred powers, but a neutral object, without either life or death. Experimentation implied further changes in the treatment of patients whose symptoms fell within general descriptions derived from the study and analysis of human body functions.

Moreover, the barber-surgeon's previously exclusive competence at surgery would wane when compared to work yielding new medical knowledge. The centuries-old separation between theory and practice no longer persisted since the same individual who held the "body" of knowledge began to experiment and verify his learning through practice.

In a passage of his preface to the *De Fabrica*, Vesalius clarified such evolution and gave examples of the heavy limitations that had conditioned the physician's profession before his time, highlighting that "when the practice of surgery was reserved to barber-surgeons, physicians lost not only their knowledge of the viscera, but soon ended the anatomic practice itself, no doubt because true physicians did not dare perform surgery, whereas those who felt it was their charge were too ignorant to read the books written by the masters of anatomy."

Also Chanca's medical education suffered from this complex and slow evolution of medical science throughout the 1400's and the subsequent role assumed by physician-theorists. Although Chanca did not in general deviate from scholastic medical doctrine, especially for the structural set-up of his works, he nonetheless proved, however timidly, to have in some respects a spirit of observation intent to personally verify already-established knowledge and formulate conclusions based on direct experience.

In the *Tractatus de fascinatione*, for example, though mixed with topics fully taken from tradition, he held — having personally verified it on his trip to the Indies — Avicenna's view concerning the lesser poisonousness

of the animals in humid regions: "Quod ego vidi dum esse in insulis noviter repertis, ubi morsus scorpio(nis)num nihil fere venenositatis habebant propterea quia in illa regione multa abundat humiditas" ["that I saw to be true in the islands recently discovered, where the scorpion(s)'s bite is not as poisonous given the high degree of humidity of that region"].

Even the theory worked out by the great masters of the past could thus be subject to verification, albeit only for marginal issues and not being affected in its substance.

The existence in the New World, under occasionally diverse vegetational form, of products already used in Europe or of products not yet known but whose properties were being discovered, had generally aroused the interest of those who went with Columbus to the Indies. It must be pointed out that pharmacology was totally dependent on botany until Paracelsus introduced chemical therapy.

Chanca, the first physician-theorist to go to the Antilles, took advantage of his scientific knowledge and left behind in his writings a documentation of the vegetative world he encountered and of which he attempts a first classification. His attention to the products of the Indies had, of course, also a commercial implication: there is evidence, early upon his return from the journey, that shows him doing business with chemists whom he probably supplied with medicinal prescriptions based on products found in the Indies; with one of them, Juan Bernal, he had set up a true exchange trade of goods with the Indies.

The formation of the physician-theorist included the study of several branches of learning. In the late 1400's and into the early 1500's, before new ideas in favor of experimentation could take hold, astrology was the physician's primary formal training background as it was commonly held that stars not only influenced the individual but also conditioned the orientation of human behavior before birth.

As a consequence, consideration of such influence featured prominently in the disease prognosis and choice of the related therapy. The knowledge of the astrological data of the individual became indispensable in planning the most suitable time for surgery, for administration of laxatives or for making one bleed, since it provided the physician with some useful elements to initiate a patient's treatment.

CHAPTER REFERENCES

BALLESTEROS-ALCALÁ-ESPINOSA, t. 4, 531-34.
BARRETO, 188-90.
BENEDICENTI.
BOORSTIN, *The Discoverers*, 344-56.
CAPPARONI.
GRANGEL.
GUSDORF, 450-51, 455.
LUNGAROTTI.
PANIAGUA, 17, 114, 122.
PANSERI, 345-51.
PESCE, 3:76-7.
TIÓ, 10-11.

III. – CHANCA'S MEDICAL WRITINGS

The general medical works written by Diego Alvarez Chanca, though concerned with fields of knowledge only slightly related to the discovery voyages and to his formal account of Columbus's second voyage, are undoubtedly relevant not only for scholars and their specific disciplines but also for historians.

In recent decades Chanca's work has been comprehensively examined but only in its totality and not by separate disciplines. The latter approach affords us a better understanding of his cultural and professional world, shedding more light even on his chronicle.

The physicians at the Spanish court around 1500 were quite accustomed to writing medical textbooks. To cite only a few names among the most well-known, we point to Juan Gutierrez of Toledo, the Sovereigns' physician who wrote *Cura de la piedra y dolor de la ijada y cólico renal*; Jerónimo Torrella, King Ferdinand's personal physician, who left a *Comentario ad Avicena*; and finally, Francisco López de Villalobos, the most famous of all, who translated Plautus's *Amphitryon* and devoted himself to the study of syphilis, in his *Tratado de las pestíferas bubas*.

All the medical works by Chanca were written after his voyage, and thus were composed after the report he sent from Hispaniola. We do not know with certainty the reasons that motivated Chanca to concentrate in that period the drafting of his medical texts as we know them. Among the possible conjectures, it might be inferred that this was due either to his longer experience as a physician or to a greater availability of time and money derived from his commercial trade with the Indies, operated mainly by a third party or collaborating partners.

The subjects he discusses concern different fields, very unrelated medically, and intended for different audiences. For example, works in Latin such as the *Tractatus de fascinatione* and the *Comentum* are clearly addressed to the highly learned, whereas *Alquímica* and *Tratado para curar el mal de costado*, composed in Castilian, are for general readers.

The two Latin texts have reached us, whereas very little is known of the other two. Chanca's own identity is even not quite clear in nineteenth-century historiography, which formulated different hypotheses: Morejón in his *Historia bibliográfica de la medicina española* quotes two similar names among the authors he cites, Diego Alvarez Chanca and Diego Alvarez Chacón, maintaining their distinction. On the other hand, in his *Anales históricos de la medicina*, Chinchilla cites only Diego Alvarez Chacón.

Morejón maintains that though the place of birth of the latter is unknown, it may be asserted that he is the author of the work titled *Para curar el mal de costado*, written in 1506. Chinchilla's opinion is that he was probably born in Seville, though he does not exclude the possibility that he may have been from Toledo. During his life in Seville, he likely practiced as a physician, acquiring a fairly good reputation within his profession; Chinchilla also attributes to him the 1506 work *Para curar el mal de costado*.

Among present-day historians, Paniagua asserts that such confusion derives from Nicolás Antonio's error, who, in the first edition of his *Biblioteca hispana nova* of 1662 attributes to Diego Alvarez Chacón a work about pleurisy. But, basing his reasoning on what Bartolomé José Gallardo suggests in his famous *Ensayo*, he maintains that the *Tratado para curar el mal de costado* had actually been composed by Chanca and printed in Seville in 1506 by the German Jacob Cromberger.

Paniagua himself pointed out the ifficulty of finding this text, which he had sought in vain in many European and American libraries, and concluded it should be considered lost. The *Tratado*, written in Castilian, was short and intended to be disseminated among the barber-surgeon's circle.

In the same vein, the only sure data about *Alquímica*, also attributed to Chanca, is that its composition is dated to 1501; the title vaguely addresses the subject of the work, meant to generally investigate alchemical issues. This field of interest itself seems to be a remarkable indication of its author's mentality and his attitude toward a subject that in many respects did not meet the approval of the ecclesiastical hierarchy. Historiography largely focused its attention on a medical treatise entitled *Tractatus de fascinatione*, which allows us to understand Chanca's cultural horizons. Written just before the time preceding Isabela of Castile's death — which occurred in 1504 — as it can be inferred from its "incipit," that reads: *Tractatus de fascinatione* editus a Didaco Alvari Chanca, *doctore atque medico Regis reginaeque dominorum nostrorum...*, this text about sorcery was printed in Spain, perhaps in Seville, by Peter Brun, and therefore not later than 1504.

Among Chanca's works the *Tractatus* is quite important, since, unlike the *Comentum*, it concerns a subject that, although previously assayed by a few great thinkers, is revived by him and examined from a new perspective, as he himself points out, because it had been impossible until then to understand the origin of witchcraft or to deal with it in a completely scientific manner.

Many ancient authors are reported by Chanca to have made reference in their works to the malefic power a few individuals are endowed with. The list of those who studied this subject is very long and it encompasses different periods: Pliny, Plutarch, Avicena, John of Salisbury, Alexander Neckam, Albertus Magnus, Thomas Aquinas, Roger Bacon, Pietro d'Abano and Nicole d'Oresme.

Although reported as a subject not completely ignored in the past, Chanca still justifies himself, on the one hand, for devoting his attention to a topic poorly studied before his time by educated men, while, on the other hand, he shows himself spurred to talk about it out of his desire to explain the disease and therefore share his reflections about causes, prevention and treatment of it.

The "fascinatio" is in this work examined from two perspectives, theoretical and practical. The first part, mainly concerning the disease itself and its transmission, is subdivided into ten "Quaestiones" centering especially on the existence of the "fascinatio," the manifestation of this disease in humans, the emanation process of the malefic fluid, the potential of invasion of any human body or animal and plant, the time and circumstances most likely to bring about the poison, and finally, the most suitable age of the one overtaken by the spell.

The vast interest for the themes he discusses is largely due to their unveiling of his conception of human interaction and his demonstration of the beliefs of his time. Chanca holds some individuals to be in a physically and psychologically dominant position over others explained in terms of innate characteristics as well as age and sex.

In general, weak bodies and those of young boys and girls are more predisposed to the penetration of malefic fluids passed on through the eyes and possibly supported by vapors exhaled through breath or through the pores of the skin. The process begins with the sorcerer, who embodies the spell-binding powers: the vapors spawned inside his body rise toward his head and, unable to exit the skull because of its bony nature, reach the eye socket and through such an outlet spread in the air, thereby penetrating sensitive bodies.

Women, because of their physical constitution, are particularly suited to transferring poisonous vapors, present in their bodies on a monthly

basis every time they experience a boiling of their blood so intense to even steam mirrors. The "fascinatio" does not have, in Chanca's opinion, a diabolic connotation and consequently lies within the realm of white magic.

Though Chanca is still fastened in some respects to the cultural world of centuries past as he emulates traditional authority and its prominent relevance, he is nonetheless well aware of the importance of annotating his personal observations even though he incorporates unverified information merely handed down.

The structure of his treatise falls within the scheme adopted by Thomas Aquinas in his *Summa theologiae*: the posing of the question *(utrum...)* is followed by the formal answer, opposed to what will be stated *(videtur quod...)*; the contrary opinion follows this answer *(sed contra est...)*; and finally, the resolution of the formulated arguments by reaffirmation of the first answer *(ad primum dicendum est...)*.

The second part, regarding prevention, symptoms and treatment of the disease, is less extensive than the first and is divided into three sections. Chanca claims it was more difficult to develop than the first one since only a few authors had previously dealt with this subject. Overall, then, he expresses a degree of anxiety in approaching it ("cum timore ad eam accedo"), possibly out of his perceived fear of contradicting — given the nature of the subject — ecclesiastical dictates, even unintentionally. The first principle he actually expounds is found in his declaration to expose only arguments compatible with the observance of faith and other arguments that may concern common practices previously treated by famous authors.

Among these authorities Chanca probably bore in mind Henry of Aragon, better known as Enrique de Villena, whose *Tratado de aojamento o fascinología*, written in 1411, was an inventory of the superstitions of the time that was subsequently burned by order of King Joao II.

Prevention against spells does not include taking of any medicine, considering also that most of the patients are children, focusing rather on a life style duly regulated by hygienic regimen, such as air purification through vapors and scented waters, or more simply by amulets worn around the neck.

The remedies become even more specific and are of various kinds as well as correlated to the financial means of the patient. For instance, certain precious stones were considered particularly efficient in treating this disease and, especially, sapphires were held to be distinctively powerful, particularly when placed over the heart. The way the stone was cut, in accordance with certain rules, or the way it was set increased its

protective efficacy. Coral and mercury sealed in a capsule are singled out for their positive influence. Even poor people could have at their disposal protective devices against the spell that were simple natural antidotes such as "aquam rosarum vel florum *nenufaris* cum aceto" [rose water or nenuphar flowers water with vinegar].

The symptoms of this disease are observed and quite interestingly described as any other physical illness, thus showing Chanca's intention to adhere as closely as possible to the objective reality of the purpose of describing symptoms as well as establishing scientifically direct result from experience — his medical theory. Consequently, the two most typical features of the time coexist in this work: on one hand, the desire to produce an exhaustive list rigorously based on objective observations of the data, without ever renouncing, on the other hand, constant references to tradition, its errors and approximations included and reexamined.

From a study of his medical work, it appears therefore that Chanca was a typical representative of his time and that its intrinsic inconsistencies are unavoidable because he is culturally connected to both currents: traditional scholastic doctrine versus an incipient trend in favor of scientific experimentation, begun in the last decade of the 1400s and destined to become an established approach in the subsequent century.

CHAPTER REFERENCES

Antonio, 1:204.
Ballasteros-Alcalà-Espinosa, 525-29.
Capparoni, 5, 6.
Doctor Calatraveño.
Coll y Toste.
Gallardo, 1:n.163.
Gallardo Rodriguez.
Gemignani, 35-37.
Gutierrez Colomer.
Luanco.
Manselli, 3, 4, 185.
Menéndez Pelayo, 1:383-403.
Olmedilla y Puig.
Paniagua, 4-5, 65-70, 74, 80, 83-86, 91-94, 114, 122, 129.
Sancho de San Román.

IV. – CHANCA AND THE SECOND COLUMBIAN VOYAGE

Chanca's presence among the men who sailed with Columbus to reach the Indies for the second time is not only confirmed by indirect sources that document the authorization of his departure by the Catholic Sovereigns and that mention his official account of the voyage, but also directly attested in a short passage of his *Tractatus de fascinatione* that says: "Quod ego vidi dum essem in insulis noviter repertis..." [what I saw while I was in the newly-discovered islands].

Their return from Hispaniola, after the first voyage, had aroused enthusiasm and excitement in Spain among all social classes, given the success of the expedition and the prospects for easy profit reported by Columbus and proven by samples of wealth brought back with him from the discovered islands.

In his Letter addressed to Santángel, Columbus does not have doubts about the amount of gold and spices he would be able to bring back on a second expedition: "I will bring," he says, addressing the Sovereigns, "as much gold as could be gathered with the limited help your Highnesses will provide me now, as well as all the spices and cotton that your Highnesses will order to be loaded...." The first trip to Hispaniola had the characteristics of a very quick reconnaissance survey, sufficient nonetheless to nourish great promises and hopes, feelings especially evident in the participants' eager willingness to depart.

As a matter of fact, during the months between the two trips a remarkable number of men decided to leave, with more than 1200 actually authorized to board the ships. As for Chanca's intentions, it was indicated earlier that we do not have hard information, given the nature of the official documents concerning his departure that do not reveal how much he really wished to participate in the expedition, and because it is equally impossible to ascertain how significant a role was reserved by Columbus himself and the Sovereigns for Chanca's presence in the Indies.

At that time the largest ships usually had aboard a barber-surgeon who supplied a minimum of hygienic assistance. We know that in the

first voyage were present master Alphonse, a physician-theorist, and master Juan, a barber surgeon. The latter is the one who remained at La Navidad along with 39 other men. On the second trip, besides Chanca, there was also a barber-surgeon whose name is not known. There were no physicians among the men of the expedition during the third crossing; master Bernal was known to be the physician-theorist for the fourth and final voyage.

Chanca then was probably the only physician with a superior education to sail for the Indies with Columbus. Even without documentary evidence, this fact leads us to think that his participation was not considered necessary to the success of the expedition and that he had not been in any way obliged to join it.

The fleet organized by Columbus for his second Atlantic crossing with seventeen ships and a socially-mixed crew left Palos on September 23, 1493. Most of them were veterans who had participated in the conquest of Granada and who, about two years after the undertaking against Spanish Moslems, were engaging in another important "adventure" that appeared promising at that moment, certainly a successful one. There were royal officers, cadet sons of well-to-do families as well as men charged with minor crimes, traders, soldiers, sailors and all the others who belonged to various social classes but who hoped in this way to guarantee for themselves a profitable way of life.

Before his departure Chanca was already rather well-off financially, especially when compared to the many physician-theorists serving in cities and hospitals. However, his salary — higher than 50,000 *maravedís* — was in any event far inferior to the compensation given other physicians attending the royal family: Fernando Alvarez de la Reina received 90,000 *maravedís* from 1498 to 1504 for his service to Queen Isabela, and Juan de la Parra, Don Juan's physician first and also Queen Isabela's from 1504 on, was given the same amount.

It is not then unrealistic to imagine that the likelihood of easy profits and the positive accounts by the first expedition's participants about the good living conditions and the beauty of the land might also have swayed Chanca. Thanks to his professional knowledge of pharmacology, so closely connected with medicine, he had probably foreseen even the commercial developments of the spice-trade.

In any case, a reading of the report he sent to the Mayor of Seville does not indicate in the least that he considered his leaving an imposition. His writing has a calm tone and is meant to provide mostly an understanding of what was going on around him rather than emphasizing his state of mind or passing judgement on the course of events. His separa-

tion from the city where he led a comfortable and peaceful life has no echo in his report, just as crossing-related events are featured only briefly in a few words, as though uninteresting or perhaps repetitive of the first voyage and therefore not worthy of special remark.

Even the anxiety that preceded the first landfall seems completely absent from this fearless second ocean crossing, at least as far as Chanca is concerned. The experience appears to have been fully tested, foreseeable in all its various stages and therefore deprived even of any particular risk.

The crossing, a relatively short one, is reported favorably but also denounced as a harsh journey over water in precarious living conditions. The entire matter is dealt with concisely, however not without emotions and with some lingering on the men's outburst of joy at the sighting of land. Even if, as already stated, after the first journey there was probably a greater optimism about reaching land, while commenting on the crew's general mood Chanca asserts: "All the people greatly rejoiced that it was wonderful to hear shouts and cries and reasonably so; being very tired from the poor living conditions and the crossing, they were all most anxious to land."

His personal remarks in the description of the trip and stay in Hispaniola are also few; in general, the account does not reveal deep emotions, except for a few passages involving either the extraordinary natural views or unexpected and astonishing events. Chanca rarely uses the first person singular in his account, doing so only when he wants to stress that his opinion was somehow different from that of others.

In most cases the physician from Andalusia reports what Columbus decided and his men executed together at different times, implying that the Admiral's thoughts and actions met with those of the sailors most of the time. Only in connection with topics of interest to him, primarily concerning his professional involvement, does Chanca give way to his impressions, revealing his own presence. For instance, during the visit to Guacanagarí, he must comment, as the one skilled in medicine, about the cacique's wounded leg. "I was present with another from the fleet...," he writes; "it certainly did not look like one leg was hurting him more than the other." Similarly, but this time with respect to the luxuriant vegetation and the ensuing wonder he felt at such a spectacle, he comments: "There was a plant whose leaves released the finest scent I ever experienced...making me think its species to be bay tree [Benzoin odoriferum]."

Because of his distinctive style in reporting always in a most objective and impersonal way about natural surroundings as well as the unfolding events of his stay, it is impossible to learn through his writing

what if any other tasks or roles he might have other than his amply-attested activity as a physician.

Of the historians interested in Chanca, only Tió thinks he had been charged by the Spanish Sovereigns with a second official task, that of recorder on ship. Actually this is not specified in any document, nor does it seem to us to be implied in his *Letter*. Moreover, during the second expedition the fleet's official recorder was Fernán Pérez de Luna whom Columbus formally charged to take down the oath by the crews, on sighting Cuba, documenting their belief that it was mainland and not an island.

It is on the other hand more realistic to think that the fleet's physician in Hispaniola carried out the office of biologist and botanist with formal commissioning since the scientific interest for that field of knowledge fell within the milieu and training of the physician-theorist of the time. Indeed, it must not be forgotten that the most important botanist who, about a century later — much more thoroughly than Chanca — described the Antilles' flora in his famous treatise *About the Things Pertinent to Medical Practice Brought from the Western Indies*, was the physician Nicolás Monardes from Seville.

The life of the men who arrived at the Indies with Chanca turned out to be very difficult during the first period of their sojourn at Hispaniola, especially because of the epidemic which forced many into inactivity and prevented the actualization of their envisioned plan in various sectors: from the search for gold mines to the practice of agriculture that, along with breeding livestock, would have allowed the laying of a strong foundation for a self-sustaining colony. None of that had come about and, a few months after their arrival in the Indies, the situation seemed doomed unless Spain could assure delivery of specific basic provisions, the consumption of which was indispensable for the men to repair their health.

Chanca, in his report, neglects to talk in detail about what was going on from the epidemic point of view; however, his not having stressed how hard it was does not justify us thinking he did not carry out his office and responsibility as a physician in such a circumstance, or that he did not feel in general his heavily increased duties. In fact, while reporting to the Catholic Sovereigns, Columbus very well addresses the seriousness of the situation in a few words: "...the work that Dr. Chanca is faced with considering all those taken ill..."; this proves Chanca had been particularly appreciated for what he had done for "so many ill men..." whom — again, according to Columbus — he had taken care of "with great diligence and charity as he does in all things concerning his office."

Columbus's letter to the Sovereigns, consigned by the Admiral to Antonio Torres as commander in charge of the fourteen-ship fleet that left for Spain on February 14, 1494, praises Chanca's activity considered at that very moment indispensable and explains Columbus's personal intervention with the Spanish Sovereigns in favor of Chanca's request of a salary increase.

Chanca, whose *Letter* was also sent through Torres, ignores really the serious discomfort existing among the men of the expedition. Considering the harsh situation during those first difficult months, it is not improbable that he too wished to return to Spain with Torres. Moreover, the appreciation expressed by Columbus for his medical activity, if on the one hand it does confirm his critical central role, also makes it impossible for Chanca to escape his working commitment or unrealistically pursue any thought of an early return to his country.

CHAPTER REFERENCES

ARANA-SOTO.
BALLESTEROS BERETTA, 2:187-92.
BROTONS PICO.
DE LOLLIS, *Cristoforo Colombo*, 181-92.
MADARIAGA, 372-99.
FERNÁNDEZ DE IBARRA.
FERNÁNDEZ DE NAVARRETE, 2:70, 83-90.
GALLARDO RODRIGUEZ, 17, 19, 24.
GIL, 71.
HARRISSE, 25-67.
HEERS, 238-40.
MONARDES.
MERRIEN, 77.
PALACIO AND DURÁN, 392.
PANIAGUA, 76.
PIEROTTI CEI, 154-56.
TIÓ, 71-72.
VARELA, "Introducción a la *Carta a Santángel*," 145.
VARELA, "Introducción a la *Carta del Doctor Diego*," 152.

V. – READING THE LETTER

The official report Diego Alvarez Chanca sent from Hispaniola has been studied specifically as an important primary source for a reconstruction of events that occurred during Columbus's second trip to the Indies. Due to its significance for Columbian historiography, it logically had to be included in this study both for its primary documentary nature of the enterprise and as a key work in itself of particular interest among the chronicles of the time.

Considering Chanca's cultural and professional background, our review of his *Letter* has focused mostly on those elements that best contribute to an understanding of his personal view of events, his reaction to what he observed and, finally, in view of the existing early mistrust of Columbus's enterprise, any conditions or restrictive circumstances that might have influenced him to take sides with groups for or against Columbus.

Chanca's work is then viewed as the fruit of his sensitivity and personality, his expectations, hopes and disappointments typical of the time and country where he lived. Moreover, the importance of what happened, implicit in his selection and descriptive methodology, has been taken into account because his narrative relegates to second place the chronological order of events.[1]

Chanca indeed appears to shy away from specifying the times of narrated events, showing rather a strong preference to communicate the occasional emotions he felt and the most striking aspects of those events. Above all, he deals with the topics chosen not only because he considers them interesting, but because reporting them satisfied his audience's expectations.

In this regard it must be recalled that the reporter's topical selection used to be heavily influenced by the ultimate recipient, i.e. by the official

---

[1] For a historico-geographical reconstruction of the second voyage, see Nuova Raccolta Colombiana, Vol. II.

to whom the report was written. Historically, discovery literature in the last centuries of the Middle Ages had generated some stereotypes onto which focused the attention of voyage chroniclers who, regardless of their firm claim to scrupulously adhere to the truth of the facts, ended up confusing what they were actually witnessing with what they heard, read and absorbed from the own cultural milieu. Their cultural heritage always played a key role and could not be ignored by these writers, who had to either confirm or disavow what was previously known and often taken for real when it was imaginary but believed to be truthful since it was commonly passed on as real truth. This also explains why these travel-report narratives often sound alike, being a concerted response to the prevailing questions of their time that in a refrain-like process reasserted old information sometimes without any effort at verification.

Moreover, a reading of Chanca's *Letter* cannot be properly done without consideration of beliefs and expectations of the people who surrounded him and had trusted him to the point of organizing the trip and participating in the expedition.

The cultural basis which "scientifically" constructed the geography of that time was, to a great extent, still dependent on *Le livre des merveilles* of Marco Polo, which, by describing the eastern places of China's Mongol empire, had led Columbus to identify the lands he reached as Cipango and the islands near Cathay; to the *Imago mundi* by Pierre d'Ailly, the last great geographer of scholastic tradition, who, for his profound knowledge of Arabic culture, the classics and geographical works derived from their writings, provided learned elements of Biblical and Aristotelian education, though admittedly with very few references to great travelers; and to the travel narrative of John Mandeville — later declared imaginary — which was frequently referred to by Bernáldez as widely known in the Columbian environment.

A traveller, as Mollat rightly stated, cannot "neutralize what he knows, his beliefs, his 'civilized' state of being when confronted by what is different and essentially strange." Thus, Columbus and the chroniclers of his enterprise, Chanca included, were a natural outcome of their time, embodying the notions then prevalent and enriched by their personal and professional experience.

As earlier stated, Chanca was a physician-theorist at the Castilian court sent officially to the Indies by the Catholic Sovereigns as physician of the Columbian expedition. In analyzing his *Letter*, Chanca's professional role has to be considered, because his scientific specialization cannot but influence the contents and the style of his narration. However, our greatest interest is not in this aspect of his account, filled with detailed

investigations or observations concerning medical science (which incidentally were not the focus of his report to the Seville officials), but rather in the fact that even as he divulged specialized news of interest to a restricted audience concerned mainly with concrete and practical aspects, he exudes his "learned" formation personally acquired through his training as a physician. He appears to be a well-educated man whose knowledge of Latin permitted him direct involvement in the major controversies debated in all the disciplines of his time, disciplines that were not yet delimited in narrow, specialized sectors.

Thus, the *Letter* is important among the reports of the discovery of America, not only as a historical source of Columbus's voyage or direct testimony of what happened during the first difficult months of the sojourn in Hispaniola, but rather as a distinctive economic and cultural signal of the mentality, knowledge and expectations of one of the most prominent physician theorists of the Spanish domain, who had left behind the old narrow European world to plunge into a totally new and different environment which could be only partially understood and accepted.

The presence of this newness in the writings of Columbus and those who followed him could provide the measuring stick for what was changing in Western Europe then, namely, its economic directions and market demands.

One of the most obvious components, even if moderated by idealistic motivations — as some historians put it — especially in respect to Columbus's actions, is, as we know, the uncontrolled gold rush and quest to secure drugs and spices for an ever-increasing demand caused by the changing patterns in all spheres of life, from pharmacology to clothing. The very high stakes connected to this second trip, after a promisingly positive enterprise experienced by those who took part in the first Atlantic crossing, demanded at the same time a radical change of one's life as well as implied the risk of being personally defeated in facing every sort of danger.

Chanca, simply on account of his formal education and profession, was probably more aware than many others of what likely awaited them during the voyage and their time in the Indies. He had consented to leave, or might even have sought to go, knowing that in the luckiest of circumstances he would return only after a long period of time from a land where, in any case, much was yet to be done. The explorer's principal hoped-for achievement was establishment of profitable trade relations with the Grand Khan's territories, colonization of the discovered islands which would become the central base of their trading as well as a source of wealth, and, finally, subjugation of the population, a new structure which would have in any case required a good deal of energy.

It is not possible, as some historians tried to do, to measure the degree of courage shown by Chanca in accepting the challenge of the trip and so determine his desire to get rich, because the information on which to base such conclusions is very slim and fragmentary, especially with respect to the period preceding the trip.

More realistically, however, one can attempt an evaluation of his ability to adhere to the reality of the facts he reports by comparing two apparently antithetical data: the first being his wish to suggest, after all, a positive image of their stay, despite the numerous difficulties, including the diseases which had killed some of the people and even struck Columbus himself; the other being the request addressed to the Spanish Sovereigns for an increase in Chanca's salary forwarded by Columbus. Concerning the first point, Chanca could be considered a dreamer who does not give up, even in the face of actual evidence. Such an optimistic attitude, present throughout the whole work, can effectively be explained by considering mainly his overall appreciative attitude toward Columbus that, combined with other contingent reasons, prevented him from very openly denouncing a strongly negative situation.

On the other hand, the request for a salary increase clearly points instead to his awareness of a situation less favorable than originally thought, with the easy profits he had envisioned being now uncertain, to say the least. Only the labors and the hard work as a physician would have allowed him to enjoy, no doubt, more benefits. Had he not realized this so late, his request for a higher salary would have been brought up before departing, at the time all other agreements about his services were drawn up.

Early on, during the first months of his residence in the Indies, in fact, although the general tone of the *Letter* is rather positive in regard to their expectations concerning the quest for gold and other valuables, Chanca is already less optimistic about getting rich easily and rapidly, despite all promises and hopes.

CHAPTER REFERENCES

Bernáldez, *Memorias*, ch. 6.
Charcot, 15-21.
O'Gorman, 22-24.
Guerra.
Mollat, 9-10.
Parry, 60, 65, 66.
Rico Avello y Rico.
Roux, 222-26.
Taviani, *I viaggi*, 2:134-35.
Tió, 20, 30.

VI. – THE NEW WORLD'S NATURAL ENVIRONMENT

The second ocean crossing to the newly discovered land is described by Chanca quite summarily, as though the subject would be uninteresting to those in his country to whom his letter was addressed. Indeed, the news he gives about this is limited to a few matters relating to the voyage-the stops to resupply, the ships' speed and the number of leagues traveled, the general weather conditions, and the number of days the journey took. Of his personal thoughts about the trip, the dangers it could hide, the sudden and difficult change of life-especially for a physician from Andalusia not used to sea life-there is surprisingly not a single note.

Keeping in mind, however, the official nature of his document and the need to address ongoing events as required, Chanca felt inclined to omit any description of the crossing-with the anxiety and hope that characterized it-and thus focus mainly on the living experience in the Indies. This would allow him to stress either the expedition's accomplishments or the disappointments that followed, keeping in mind what prompted the enterprise and the definite expectation that, back in Spain, surrounded voyages to the west.

From All Saints day, when the first islands were sighted, Chanca's description begins to provide more details. Yet, a more intense emotional involvement of the physician with what he was observing-and therefore also his personal participation in the narrative-can be noticed only in a few cases, especially at the beginning of his report, that is, when his emotions vís à vís nature were stronger because of the novelty of the situations and while a total positive feeling for the outcome of the expedition endured. The luxuriance and beauty of nature is to Chanca one of the first pleasant sensations he stresses at seeing landfall. The many islands sighted in the first days aroused wonder in him, along with a sense of rejoicing, because, as he himself says, "in that period of the year there is hardly anything green in our country." Furthermore, his amazement is increased by the variety of the species of trees found there,

different from those previously seen, "some with fruits, others with flowers." He tries to classify one of them, remarking first on the scent of the leaves, similar to the laurel or bay tree, and then on the height of the plant, which is shorter than laurel.

In some cases his remarks express through images both a feeling of spiritual well-being and, at the same time, of incredulity, as in the case, for example, of his description of the splendid, tall waterfall of La Soufrière on Guadaloupe when he adds that it seemed to descend from the sky. The sight of such a distinctive spectacle leads Chanca to elaborate on the scene, to communicate the emotion he and his companions felt at such a sight, underscoring the general wonder-struck feeling they all experienced. He tells us, as if to willfully recapture the child-like joy of observing nature, that wagers had been made on the ships over the nature of such a phenomenon, not being yet able, because of the distance, to establish what it really was: some men thought it was snowy peaks, others that it was water.

The differing natural scenery in relation to that of his own country, while eliciting general enthusiasm and appreciative contemplation for what was observed, in a few cases also worries him since it embodies the dangers of the unknown, possibly bringing about unforeseeable circumstances and therefore adversities. This feeling is consistently present in his narrative.

An example of the hidden perils of nature in the environment of those lands that seemed so extraordinarily beautiful and luxuriant is the discovered toxicity of some of the unknown fruits that turned out to be particularly poisonous. The slightest touch of the tongue would cause serious troubles, as those who unwisely had tasted them found out; Chanca relates that their intense pain was equal to being struck by rabies.

His wonder at natural spectacles never before seen wanes, however, as does the richness of details of their beauty, decreasing as the narrative goes on, only to be replaced by attention to situations stressing presumed or real dangers.

After the initial amazement experienced in looking at the unusual landscape and especially following their confrontation with the cacique Guacanagarí, who had not been able to remove the suspicion of his guilt for the Christians' deaths, Chanca's writing yields primarily information meant to illustrate in a peaceful tone what was going on and reflects a spirit of truthful reporting which stresses the features of the landscape.

When he later turns to providing topographic information about Hispaniola and the location where the new city of La Isabela would be built, although he refers briefly to the presence of a quite diversified and luxuriant nature, including two different-sized rivers and a cliff area which

will become an excellent protection for the future settlement, he is indeed doing so to reveal the colonization plan intended by Columbus, showing very little interest in the impressive landscape.

The same personal detachment and objective reflection is further evident in his concise description of the "more than forty islets" which the fleet sailed along before arriving at Hispaniola. Their outer beauty, certainly inspiring, is all but secondary as he merely hypothesizes that such lands, as far as he could tell, "were likely to contain metals."

The various descriptions of what he observed during the explorations carried out throughout the area before arriving at the settlement of La Navidad constitute his way of summarizing the surrounding realities to allow the addressees of the letter an articulate appreciation of the main accomplishments of the expedition. As the account becomes more purposeful, the enthusiastic tone partially subsides, foreshadowing the emerging difficulties. Consequently, one perceives a growing consciousness of a new situation that was becoming, day by day, anything but idyllic. Against all previously optimistic thinking that had survived major tests there surface realizations concerning problems with the natives, the lack of some basic foods and the increase in disease which together had prevented development of the original plans.

Their suspicion of Guacanagarí's betrayal is the turning point in Chanca's reported outlook, signaling the deterioration of the situation. This became apparent from Chanca's words-"that the chief had no more pain in that leg than in the other one"-spoken after he examined the "wounded" leg the Indian chief showed him bandaged to prove his own suffering following the attack of those natives who, according to him, had killed the Christians. Such a statement represented an incontrovertible opinion because of Chanca's competence as a physician.

His personal narrative of a contemplative sort is therefore quite brief; what follows is a more stylized chronicle where every subject covered is instrumental in providing answers to questions of practical import.

His certainties seem to be slowly dying. The overriding factor which aggravated his specific responsibilities (even though, as was earlier stated, he provides few clues in regard to it) was the disease that struck many men, giving him, professionally speaking, a much heavier load. His consequent description of events revolves then around practical issues and their resolution. His prose thus becomes, even when he is observing nature, a chronicle as objective as possible, to the point of shrinking in the last part of the *Letter* to a mere list of the spices found, briefly detailed in their features, and the procedures involved in their skilful identification.

The profound lyricism, albeit quite brief, at the beginning of his writing has essentially experienced a metamorphosis and become a list of more or less valuable products which could be exported to Spain. The desire for and novelty of the exploration and discovery of new lands have been replaced by a purely economic calculation that would eventually lead Chanca, upon returning from the Indies, to exploit his findings by initiating an intense and prosperous commercial trade with those territories.

CHAPTER REFERENCES

DE MADARIAGA, 376-78.
HEERS, 231-34.
MORISON, *The European Discovery*, 106-17.
PESSAGNO.
REVELLI, 26-30.
TAVIANI, *I viaggi*, 2:146-49.
TIÓ, 118.

VII. – THE NATIVES

It is apparent from his report that Chanca's attitude in providing different profiles of the natives he observed during the first months of his stay in the Indies proves to be a very unfavorable one, conditioned negatively by the first contact.

All of it was in contrast with the totally enthusiastic first impressions about the native people reported by Columbus, who, at his return, characterized them as meek and easily subdued, anticipating not only the possibility of their conversion to Christianity but also an easy program of colonization justified in terms of their disposition, for they were "easy to be ruled, [and it would be easy] to have them work and sow and do whatever would be needed...."

Chanca, less prone than Columbus to idealize what he observed, had come into contact with Hispaniola's inhabitants, who had been favorably judged by the participants of the first journey only after they were forced to experience the cannibals in the Carib islands. And later too, at La Navidad, where they expected to find the men left by Columbus some months earlier, the immediate suspicion that the cacique Guacanagarí had betrayed them and was involved with their killing led the Andalusian physician to doubt the acclaimed simplicity and friendliness of this population and convinced him, on the contrary, that they were not, in this case as well, friendly people.

The first contact with the cannibals had taken place on Guadaloupe, when the men gone on a reconnaissance of a deserted village had the opportunity personally to verify their custom — described as "bestial" by Chanca — of eating human flesh. In their dwellings they actually found human bones, arms and legs and, boiling in a pot, a human neck. They had, moreover, been able to see that the inhabitants of the island, rather than showing themselves affable, hospitable and eager to meet the Christians, as previously happened, regularly abandoned their dwellings and fled as soon as they saw the Christians arrive. The situation therefore appeared totally opposite from the one experienced by Columbus on his

first journey when he related that "more than 2000 of them came and approached the Christians, putting hands over their heads, which was a sign of great reverence and friendship...."

Another element which contributed to an increased condemnation and a stronger sensation of alienation toward the Caribs was Chanca's detection among the natives of a remarkable number of women from other islands who were kept prisoners. Such women demonstrated extreme fear for their condition to the point of being terrified by the presence of Caribs even after being taken aboard the vessels under the protection of the crews. These women showed particular fear for the cannibals' cruel custom of sacrificing the children born of their relationships, after having castrated and raised them until adulthood, because the Caribs thought only men's flesh was good to eat.

Obviously, it is understandable how such a first contact with a population looking hostile from the very beginning could fail to put the men of the second expedition in a favorable mood, notwithstanding their early acceptance of the view that the natives were "commendable for their customs" and of "good disposition."

For the men of the first expedition, cannibalism, rather than a real problem, was an abstraction well removed from their direct experience and, indeed, a more imaginary reality that they associated in their fantasies with monster-like beings, reported by Columbus of the first voyage to have "a single eye on their forehead...." Thus, any awareness of eventual danger was enormously mitigated by such "distance," which explains also Columbus's lack of discernment of any truth in the information offered him and which he did not take seriously, convinced as he was that they were only rumors reported by those natives.

Chanca and the men who faced for the first time such experiences, having verified directly and feared the dangers, were strongly influenced — unlike those who had been there before — by what they saw in the Carib islands as well as by the accounts of the women prisoners. There is evidence in his *Letter* to the Mayor of Seville that they had over-estimated the ferocity and courage of those populations and not properly estimated their fighting ability and the effectiveness of the Christians' weapons.

Fear of being devoured by the cannibals had them believe that the men who had lost their way in crossing a mountain of a Carib island had been captured by those people and eaten.

Chanca's unfavorable reports about the Caribs' bloody customs are, however, moderated by other positive considerations of some aspects of their existence. In fact, he highlights the care they take in building their dwellings in comparison with the natives of nearby islands; although

they are also made of straw, "these people built them better, appear to keep them stocked with more food, and both men and women give the impression of having a superior type of resourcefulness." The Andalusian physician goes on to highlight the fact that such populations own "much yarn and unspun cotton and many cotton blankets so well woven that they have nothing to envy of those from our country." His overall judgement on the quality of life of the populations of those lands, at least in that respect, is then a comparatively good one, making him conclude that "these people seemed to us more civilized than those living in the other islands...."

The inhabitants of Turuqueira, Ceyre and Ayai, in Chanca's opinion, were also of the same ancestry as the Caribs: they did not fight each other but fought the inhabitants of the other islands, reaching them with boats made out of a single tree trunk, like those of the Caribs', and using primitive weapons such as bows and arrows whose tips were made of toothed bonefish or turtle shells, since they had no iron.

As for their defensive capability, we read in Chanca's writing that Carib men and women both used weapons with quickness and skill and did fight with the last ounce of their strength until captured. They showed, incidentally, "great boldness" in fighting even when they happened to be considerably inferior in number.

Chanca and his companions already knew how the natives looked because of accounts by participants of the previous trip. Chanca, surely aware of such descriptions, still shows a surprised curiosity for their looks and, while identifying their unique features, dwells in many instances upon the way they embellished and adorned themselves.

The various ways of arranging their hair gave the natives a chance to differentiate themselves from one another. Some wore their hair long, others had their heads fully shaved and painted with different kinds of symbols, and still others cut it in a curious way, showing shaved strips and preserved locks "in many ways hard to describe," adds Chanca. As an aside, the oddity of this latter hair style led the Andalusian physician to smile and scoff at what he observed to the point of comparing some of the natives' heads to those of mentally ill men.

All of them were beardless; the Caribs, unlike the other natives, particularly emphasized some parts of their faces by painting the area around their eyes and eyebrows in order to appear frightening.

Their common distinctive feature, however, was their nudity. This is the first aspect Chanca notices even when he barely catches a glimpse of the first ones seen on Guadaloupe fleeing at the sight of the Spaniards. His remark that "they were naked people like those the Admiral had

seen during his previous trip" is not intended, in this specific case, as a single notation since he wants to pass on to the reader to whom his report was addressed their disappointment for being in the wrong place rather than in Cathay with the Grand Khan or on the island of Cipango; they were in a land still inhabited by primitive people and not in a place where there were "gold and spices and big ships and traders" as Columbus had dreamed.

From this perspective Chanca reports on nudity as the uncivilized element that puts all the natives on the same level of inferiority and barbarity. The observed differences in appearance become irrelevant compared to this characteristic trait of their way of being and are only of little importance for their life-style and totally unrelated to the civilized Spanish.

The main expectations of the Columbian expeditions to the Indies, not only Chanca's but also those of all the participants of the first two expeditions, were clearly focused on achieving another goal, one much more meaningful and expected to yield precedent-setting economic results and to which the Spanish Crown gave its consent in the first place: to reach the east by going westward across the Ocean to the Grand Khan's regions, rich in gold, spices and precious stones.

In his writing, Chanca devotes pa ticular attention to the relationship with the cacique Guacanagarí, presented as "one of the most important kings of this island," that is, Hispaniola. He builds on several details before leading to the disclosure of the deaths of the men of La Navidad. And these people's customs are "so savage that they show no rationality in choosing where to live." Their huts are located near the sea and are so "fully overtaken...by humidity" that the expedition's physician wonders how they can possibly survive in such conditions. Additionally, his evaluation of their primitive existence is definitely influenced by his determination that, besides their nudity, they showed no intelligence in failing to cover up even when the temperature was cooler.

By declaring his near certainty of Guacanagarí's betrayal of the men committed to his protection by Columbus, the doctor reiterates his conviction that the Indians were dangerous. From that point on, more sharply than ever, there rises in his mind the belief that their relationship would be filled with difficulties as they proceeded with their plans for colonizing and exploiting those islands.

Similarly, Columbus reached that timely conclusion as he confronted the tragedy of La Navidad and when the need for gold-gathering became urgent. His attitude toward the natives during the first voyage, when he still believed the importance of causing them no harm and protecting

then from exploitation, was changed. The impossibility of learning the truth about the men's deaths had made him cautious and contributed to modify his early convictions concerning their expected submissiveness and complete cooperation. In his official report sent to the Catholic Sovereigns, contemporaneous with Chanca's *Letter*, he strongly suggested the opportunity of a policy of repression toward those opposing his directives, practically discriminating between the natives who did and those who did not show total compliance with the Admiral's orders. What was being introduced in Columbus's own words was "the good treatment to be reserved for good people and the punishment that will strike bad people," giving way to an atmosphere of hostility that would endure unchanged afterwards to the point of badly characterizing the Spanish colonization of the New World.

CHAPTER REFERENCES

COLOMBO, *Il Giornale di bordo*, 1:75, 163, 187.
COLÓN, *Memorial*, 154.
ASENSIO, 1:543-45.
MORALES PADRÓN, "Andalucía."
TAVIANI, *I viaggi*, 2:142-47.

VIII. – GOLD AND SPICES

Though symbolic, the gold and spices Columbus had brought to the Spanish Sovereigns upon returning from his first trip to the Indies as a sign of the wealth attainable from those lands and the enthusiastic accounts about living conditions and easy profits must have aroused a general euphoria in Spain, especially among wealthy people, generated by the unanimity of the participants.

The departure of about 1200 men, eager to accomplish a precise and long lasting colonization plan as well as to establish trade relations with some Asiatic region and in the already discovered territories, such as Hispaniola, should be considered a direct consequence of the successful first voyage. The Indies still left to be reached were the mythical Golden Peninsula, Cathay and Cipango Island, which in Marco Polo's description were territories "in which can be found gold in large amounts."

Another big attraction for those interested in participating in the expedition was the importation of spices widely used in several economic sectors from small businesses to pharmacology. It is known that the European market was at that time experiencing some supply difficulties for such products coming from the Orient because of the Turkish conquest of the Byzantine Empire's territories. This new situation produced greater expectations for the new oceanic route predicted to be a guarantee of their supply needs. In other words, the general conviction based on the information received from people returning from Hispaniola was that this second expedition would first and foremost result in the importation of a significant amount of gold and spices, besides achieving other ideals such as the natives' conversion.

Gold, in particular, had been focused on since the first trip, with Columbus himself giving it much attention. It now had become even more important for the Admiral of the Ocean Sea during his second voyage because of the generalized expectations of the Spanish Sovereigns as well as those of the participants in the expedition.

As soon as he realized the seriousness of the situation that had arisen in the first months, Columbus had a vigilant attitude toward what was happening. He worried about having to guarantee collection of an amount of gold large enough to compensate the heavy expenses of equipping the fleet and he worried about proving his promises.

Like many others, even Chanca must have been attracted by prospects of easily obtaining gold in the Indies and therefore was driven by a desire to achieve a much better living condition. Since his report deals, however, with the first months of residence in Hispaniola, at the time of the rise of major difficulties, Chanca only a few times gives prominent attention to this theme. Indeed, after the initial enthusiasm for the landfall and the already mentioned beauty and peculiarity of the discovered islands, Chanca essentially is absorbed in trying to understand the reasons for the Spaniards' deaths, to learn the truth about the events which unfolded and to determine the best policy that could be adopted toward the natives.

In these opening considerations he does not convey any feeling of special priority for the search for gold and the verification of its quantitative availability. A few occasional remarks simply indicate it was one of their concerns.

The references to gold become more frequent, instead, after his arrival at La Navidad, stimulated by two facts: the gifts of the cacique Guacanagarí and the added urgency in connection with the departure of part of the fleet for Spain, which should have carried back to their country the largest amount of gold possible to satisfy expectations.

With respect to the gold the Indians wore as ornamental jewelry — as he emphasizes, not to show off wealth — Chanca addresses the crafting process of this precious metal that from worked thin layers makes masks, belts, and head pieces. As reported by Guacanagarí, the gold had been one of the primary causes of the killing of the Christians by Caonabó, a cacique of the Caribs. Columbus had in fact ordered the men, before leaving the fortress, "to hide the gold in the ground after taking substantial amounts of it" in order that it not be easily found.

The last part of the report is the most interesting as far as the descriptions of gold and spices are concerned. Chanca wants to justify unconditionally Columbus's inability to send to Spain large amounts of the precious metal, maintaining that its search and mining had been prevented by the sickness that in epidemic proportions had struck more than one third of the men and adding that the amount sent to Spain was merely gathered during the reconnaissance of two groups of men who had reached the internal regions of Cibao and Niti on Hispaniola.

The information reported by two captains, Hojeda and Gorvalán, leaders of the groups, was extremely reassuring on both counts, the quantity of gold available and the ease of its recovery. In fact, the Sevillian physician reports, gold was found in more than fifty brooks in Cibao, besides being "on land" and "in so many other places that no man could ever count." Chanca is optimistic even about the amount of gold. In his opinion it could be found using deep mining techniques; "through digging...larger pieces of gold will be found."

Similar were the results of the expedition to Niti: much gold could be found in three or four areas; the samples Gorvalán brought back for the Sovereigns were meant to be a mere demonstration of the type and quantities that could be secured in the subsequent site exploitation.

Thus, the gold appeared to Chanca to be a totally favorable asset to the Spanish Crown, a clearly established economic resource. In Chanca's own words, "our sovereign lords can now consider themselves to be the most prosperous and wealthiest princes in the world." The ships which will be returning to Spain, he continues, "will be able to gather such a large quantity of gold that it will amaze anyone who shall hear of it."

As it was the case with the gold, Chanca reports about the spices only at the end of his letter — and hastily at that — meaning to provide only a list of them, rather than making them an integrated part of his daily account. The spices he gives information about are, in his opinion, far less than the total existing in those regions, but he justifies the incompleteness of his list, saying that "the little time we spent on land has been consumed more in finding a place to settle and in looking for what was needed, than in discovering what things were in that territory." He nonetheless concludes by saying that "in spite of the short time, many worthy and amazing things have been seen...."

Each bit of information in regard to the spices entails his surprise about the abundance and diversity, especially in the case of known products, of the plants which produced them. Cotton, for example, classified then under the generic heading of "spices," grew in Hispaniola on evergreen trees as high as peach trees. And wax was produced by trees, though its "color, taste and burning characteristics" were entirely similar to bee's wax, making for no difference between one and the other. Also, turpentine could be found on trees and, Chanca says, "it is very distinctive and of fine quality."

Among the spices produced in large amounts and fine quality there is the tragacanth, which comes from the trunks and branches of the tragacanth tree, used to prepare pharmacological products and to tan leather. Moreover, Chanca wrongly believed to have found nutmeg trees:

by not examining the fruit, since it was out of season, he had drawn inferences on the basis of tasting and smelling the bark of the trees. This information shows the care with which plants were examined, highlighting Chanca's botanical research.

The general information reported in his letter is at times only indicative of the products which could be imported, for instance, when with respect to ginger he declares to have seen a native wearing a root of that plant around his neck. Medicinal plant derivatives are also of interest, as in the case of aloe, used to prepare digestive drugs and, in stronger doses, purgative drugs. Chanca points out that the aloe found, though qualitatively different from that generally used by physicians, still qualified as one of the kinds that can be used to treat patients.

The last two spices of observed plants that he singles out are cinnamon, used to flavor dishes, and myrabolans from which is obtained a substance for tanning leather. Both of them appeared to be of a quality inferior to those used in Spain, but Chanca maintained that it could possibly be explained by the fact that they were observed out of season.

In conclusion, the spices too are judged to be potentially valuable importation products and projected as a profitable trade made evident throughout Chanca's narrative that foresees developments likely to take place in the upcoming months of residence in Hispaniola.

CHAPTER REFERENCES

COLOMBO, *Carta a Luis de Santángel.*
POLO, 262.

GALLARDO RODRIGUEZ, 17.
GARCÍA DEL REAL, 46-47.
GUERRA.
HEERS, 431, 433, 458.
MOLLAT, 120.
MORALES PADRÓN, *Historia*, 128-30.
TANGHERONI AND DI NERO, 143, 152.
TAVIANI, *I viaggi*, 2:165.
TAVIANI, "Schede," 1:351-58.
UNALI, 317, 333-38.
VANNINI DE GERULEWICZ, 34, 38, 69, 94, 136, 142.
VELOZ MAGGIOLO, *Arqueología*, 44.
VILAR, 86-91.

IX. – DIFFICULTIES PRIOR TO THE SETTLEMENT IN LA ISABELA

In his report, Chanca offers some exclusive quantitative data regarding a topic untreated in other works on the second expedition except for the account by Bernáldez, who spoke of it later. It concerns the indication of the number of miles and length of time it took for Columbus's fleet to travel a short distance along Hispaniola's northern coast, from the fortified site of La Navidad to the site selected for the yet-to-be-built settlement of La Isabela.

Such specific information not only represents an additional important piece for the reconstruction of Columbus's second voyage but also lets us better understand the reasons for the rush of events in the first months of 1494.

Bartolomé de Las Casas, unlike Columbus's son Don Fernando, who gives only a few hints of what happened in those days, lingers at considerable length over the discomfort that the sailing had caused to both men and animals, stressing the consequent illness and death of some of the men without, however, actually revealing the real cause that led to it.

He fails to specify that the events which occurred at La Isabela were directly related to the exhausting sea crossing by a fleet of about 1200 men, horses and other animals, whose food was strictly rationed, because of the impossibility of predicting, as Chanca emphasizes, "what kind of weather we would have to face and for how long God would want us to continue sailing: out of good prudence we had to ration our food to be able to save our lives regardless how bad the weather would be."

Columbian historiography has barely touched upon this aspect, undervaluing the long crossing at sea without being able to land, an experience which, combined with the nutritional and environmental conditions, could not but negatively affect the health of the men on board.

Chanca specifies that in order to cross a short arm of sea —which he considered to be thirty leagues, confusing leagues with miles (it was

really 33 miles) — it took more time and was "more fatiguing" than the crossing from Castile. Particularly strenuous proved to be their enforced stay on the vessels for that extended period of time throughout which the worsening conditions at sea prevented their returning to land and a well-planned or more adequate diet.

This unfortunate event described by the Andalusian physician caused various changes, consequently affecting the original plan: the hurried creation of the La Isabela settlement in a territory not chosen through a considered evaluation of the natural characteristics of that environment, but merely forced on them due to the fact that the fleet had to land there in bad weather conditions that did not permit otherwise; they had to delay planting also, which therefore postponed the certainty at least of food self-sufficiency to some extent. And the risk of a major financial drain because of the long period of time during which the large number of men could not work on such intended tasks as gathering gold was an expenditure that the Spanish Crown could hardly afford beyond a certain length of time.

Such unfortunate happenings, however, do not amount in Chanca's account to a negative reporting against Columbus's enterprise, nor do his various analytical considerations amount to a systematic denunciation of poor leadership or blatant errors on the part of the Admiral. The frank revelation about the difficulties during that very short sailing in that part of the sea is countered by the totally favorable description of the place Columbus selected to found the city of La Isabela. Chanca indeed made clear in that regard that the place and the environment Columbus chose for the settlement were the best "that we could possibly find." And this praise appears more deserved when Chanca then stresses both the harshness of the environment and the ease with which the site could be turned into a natural fortification.

Still, even when showing optimism for the settlement which will be built, he cannot suppress his constant worry about the type of life the Christians shall face in those lands. He expresses doubts in regard to the healthiness of the area given the climate's high humidity, though only lightly denouncing it for the observed rapid perishability of the food. Such information is all the more of interest because it is reported by the official physician of the expedition, who more than the others, by profession, had to be aware of the importance of guaranteeing an adequate diet to the men, whose physical conditions had already been tested by a tormented sailing. The very lack of some essential foods did indeed aggravate the dietary problems so well focused on by Chanca. Throughout the optimistic parts of the unfolding account, perhaps like tiny fleeting re-

flections, his anxieties about a difficult human living condition in Hispaniola, which day by day appeared more precarious and for which he also felt greater responsibility since he was not able to contain the spread of disease, do surface and show the increased sense of responsibility he felt to cure the sick, helped only in his task by the one barber-surgeon, who performed menial functions.

Chanca does not give in his *Letter*, as could logically be expected as a result of his professional background, an accurate and comprehensive treatment of the diseases that had struck the men and that are merely dismissed as a consequence of the terrible sailing off the coast of Hispaniola. The Andalusian physician, instead of reporting on the precarious conditions prevailing during the days right after their landing, indirectly refers to them but goes on and repeats once again that the voyage was long and disastrous and mentions how on that occasion "living conditions were the most difficult ever borne by men."

This constant refrain is also manifest in the kind of considerations that follow. It clearly emerges many times as one of the main causes of the failure or partial success of the expedition, especially in connection with the search for gold. Because of it a small number of men were sent to the gold region and for a limited period of time, thus preventing a large expedition which would have allowed them to gather and send to Spain remarkable quantities of the precious metal. The living conditions, he explicitly claims, "have been basically, I think, the cause of all our problems — together with the harsh work and the crossing, as well as the distinctive difference of this land...."

In essence then, for the Andalusian physician, this is how the initial failure of Columbus's plan is to be explained: it is the reason, maintains Chanca, "the Admiral decided to renounce the idea of finding the mines before sending off the ships that were to leave for Castile."

This underlying unfavorable evaluation of what happened, however, is not a denial by the official physician of the enterprise of his hope for a quick and general improvement of the men's condition and the prospected, still realistic, achievement of the original goals of the expedition. A constant oscillation can be noticed in the account between his denunciation of what happened and his prediction that all difficulties would be overcome. Chanca's intent in taking such a contradictory stance should perhaps be ascribed to the fact that he did not want to let the results of those first months of exploration appear definitive since that could have damaged the reputation of Columbus in Spain.

The illness that "struck so many people" including, as Don Fernando asserts, the Admiral himself, and the tormenting 33-mile crossing

before that are seen as the origin of all their subsequent calamities, but they are counterbalanced in Chanca's report by a few certainties expounded in the last part of it which anticipates the solving of contingent problems as well as the fulfillment of the plan to gather the gold.

The gold-related aspect of the expedition is, then, salvaged by the Andalusian physician in his writing and this banishes those suspicions that would have been formulated against Columbus's behavior by those returning to Spain. Indeed, he lends credence to the fact that the Admiral will soon be able to send an amount of gold so great that the Spanish Monarchs from that very moment could "consider themselves to be the most prosperous, wealthiest princes in the world."

CHAPTER REFERENCES

COLOMBO, *Historie*, ch. 50.
LAS CASAS, *Historia*, ch. 88.
DA CUNEO, *Lettera a Gerolamo Annari*, 15-28 October 1495.
BERNÁLDEZ, *Memorias*, ch. 120.

MARTÍNEZ HIDALGO Y TERÁN, 218-22.
TAVIANI, *I viaggi*, 2:156-57.

X. – CHANCA'S *LETTER* AND OTHER CONTEMPORARY REPORTS

The writings on the discovery voyages should be classified as either chronicles written at the same time as the events themselves by authors personally involved or other writings by those who subsequently reported what happened from direct or indirect sources.

Extant descriptions of events must necessarily be identified for what they are. Except for cases of primary documentation, all sources must naturally be scrutinized for possible distortions that were introduced. And, even when dealing with contemporary sources, any historical reconstruction cannot ignore the motivations at the base of different accounts responsible for varied versions and different interpretations.

The accounts by those who took part in the second Columbian expedition to the Indies may be compared to one another as testimonies of the same experience producing common emotional, psychological, and cultural reactions. The resulting multiple points of view complement each other and contribute substantially to shedding light on a reality quite complex and not yet fully deciphered precisely because it is difficult to distinguish between the actual events and their interpretations.

Moreover, the different times the reports by the participants in the undertaking were composed have to be verified. Chanca's *Letter*, of interest to us in this study, is complemented by only two other contemporaneously-drafted documents which urvived subsequent manipulations: Columbus's own *Letter-Report* and *Memorial*. Both of these were written in 1494 and were sent via Antonio Torres to the Spanish Sovereigns in order to inform them of the overall situation endured by the men of the expedition, its accomplishments to date, the unforeseen difficulties, the epidemic which occurred, their relationship with the natives and the particular meritorious actions of a few men of the expedition, including Chanca.

Guillermo Coma's report, sent to Spain at the same time as the two just mentioned, has not been preserved in its original form, but only in

the Latin translation by Nicola Squillace, done, as he states in the introduction to his work, a few months after Torres's arrival in Spain and, in any case, before December 13, 1494 when it was sent to Alfonso de la Caballería.

Finally, another participant in this second trip, Michele da Cuneo — although he remained in Hispaniola until February 1495 — is the author of another second expedition chronicle, finished on October 15 of the same year.

These works differ in the way they describe some details as well as in their approach, due not only to their personal way of perceiving reality but also in their intended objectives. Leaving aside Columbus's work, obviously biased, two main tendencies in interpreting events can be singled out, even at the risk of excessive simplification: the more objective one focuses on both the positive and negative aspects, expounding on considerations for and against; the other appears to be a demonstration of the positive value of the undertaking.

Michele da Cuneo's work, which belongs to the first category, reveals the most independence in its approach and variety of themes discussed, as most historians have recently agreed.

Da Cuneo, Columbus's friend from Savona, wrote his report about the voyage and the time spent in the Indies, in the form of a letter, in Italian, while staying in his home town of Savona, having been urged to do so by Geronimo Annari, also of Savona, to whom the letter is addressed. The major characteristic of his work, in addition to the personal ideas set forth by the author, is his complete openness in treating a few themes completely neglected by the other chroniclers.

The picture that emerges from his report seems multi-faceted thanks to the variety of the themes discussed and its focus on illustrating neglected details of events described also by other sources.

Da Cuneo's writing, for example, includes the theme of the relationships with native women, and gives his personal reflections. This topic was also hinted at by the two Spanish chroniclers, Chanca and Coma, but only in connection with the killing of the men at La Navidad. The serious results of the unfortunate practice of the white men, of keeping for each one as many as three or four native women, is not stressed but rather reported as unsubstantiated information.

Actually, the citizen from Savona frankly describes the Spaniards' relationships with local women, who are violently abused, and he narrates almost naively and in a quite unprejudiced way this aspect of the colonization which was entirely avoided by the other cited authors. The indirect involvement of Columbus in this kind of behavior toward the native

people — that is, allowing the citizen from Savona rights over a native woman — does not make Da Cuneo hesitate to reveal it (and with the same crude realism and particulars with which he describes his lovemaking to her).

This does not justify thinking that the two fellow countrymen were on strained terms because of Da Cuneo's independent thinking. On the contrary, a passage in his chronicle ("...having found beyond a cape a most beautiful though not too large island, which I had been also the first to sight...and even on account of my love for it, the Admiral named the island 'Beautiful Savonese' and donated it to me") on one hand shows a feeling of gratitude toward Columbus for his munificence and on the other bears witness to the existing friendship between the two men from Liguria.

In the final passage of his work, the esteem he feels for the Admiral's human qualities and navigational skills appears very evident when he asserts: "I want everyone to know that, in my humble opinion, since Genoa has been Genoa, no man so magnanimous and gifted in navigation as the named Admiral was ever born...." The praise is not, however, limited only to Columbus' skills as a sailor as it extends to his determination exhibited in dealing with the most difficult situations to the point of sparing the rest of the crew some heavy labor in intense moments, such as the time when... "once the storm was over, he raised the sails while the others slept."

Michele da Cuneo also reports some rumors regarding Columbus's love life untold by either Coma or Chanca. When he describes the love Columbus had early on for Beatrice de Bobadilla, the first lady of Gomera, he does so with great ingenuousness and without evident malice.

The chronicler from Savona, unlike Chanca, describes events in a personal way, often giving his impressions and his own opinion, so much so that he forces himself into the action with the others even when he is not an actual participant. As stated earlier, Chanca on the other hand rarely expresses his own thoughts and actions, which no doubt had remarkable importance and impact on their daily life, owing particularly to his profession and the serious epidemic that took hold in Hispaniola not long after the fleet's arrival.

The details given by Da Cuneo in some cases also reveal not-at-all edifying aspects of certain situations. For example, when telling about the lost group of men gone ashore on Guadaloupe, he faults their rapacity and intent to pillage the natives' villages, whereas Chanca legitimized their departure from the fleet by order of superiors with the task of obtaining information about the natives and the route to take.

Moreover, about gold the man from Savona seems quite unequivocal in expressing the important role that finding it had as an incentive for that expedition, "so long and full of dangers," and he emphasizes Columbus's hope of being able to send to the Spanish Sovereigns an amount of gold equal to the iron retrieved from Biscayan mines.

Similarly, he describes a situation that developed in Cibao. While telling what happened after the building of the fortress of St. Thomas, he highlights how "many times we sought for gold in the above-mentioned rivers but never could anyone find a single gram of it." The precious metal destined for Spain, he says, came from the gifts of the numerous visiting natives that — from as far as ten leagues away — brought in large quantities.

Chanca, on the other hand, dwells instead on the results achieved by the exploration of the Cibao and Niti regions as well as the future enrichment of the Catholic Sovereigns who would thus become the wealthiest in the world.

Guillermo Coma in his report sides, as does Chanca, with Columbus's actions and therefore the undertaking. This common characteristic, however, should not lead one to conclude that their accounts were related; in fact, they do not concentrate necessarily on the description of the same events nor give similar interpretations.

Because we do not have reliable information about Coma's life, some scholars have even maintained he did not exist at all. Others surmised that he should be identified with a physician from Barcelona still alive in the years 1513-15. If this were so, another physician besides Chanca would have participated in Columbus's second voyage to the Indies.

In Coma's writing, so thoroughly rewritten by Squillace and titled *De insulis meridiani atque Indici maris nuper inventis*, there is no indication of his alleged activity. The only reference to physicians that can be found in it is in regard to *aje*, fruits that he claims physicians prescribed "since it caused improvements from ailments in sick men."

It is therefore impossible on the basis of his report to ascertain whether he was really a physician or, in fact, what his actual profession was; nor, on the other hand, is there any biographical data in his chronicle. His writing about events during the first months in Hispaniola, however, gives some indication of his sensitivity and his lively interests in the many curiosities relating to nature and the natives.

In expressing any kind of evaluation, however, it should always be remembered that the report that came to us was substantially worked over by Nicola Squillace of Messina, a culturally well-versed Italian humanist with a good classical education that explains his spontaneous

mythological digressions as well as citations of works and authors of the past. Basically, his cultural background includes references to a major extent to Pliny and his *Historia naturalis* and also to Apuleius, Horace, Ovid, Vergil, Hesiod, mixed in with biblical allusions, all in a style similarly erudite.

Occasionally doubts arise, mostly in reference to already-known topics; whether along with these erudite references the author possibly introduced more substantial modifications cannot be proven. For example, with respect to the outward voyage, it is amazing, as I stated earlier, that in Chanca's *Letter* this subject is almost completely neglected, yet, equally hard not to imagine, in the same way Guillermo Coma has minute descriptions of the Canaries.

Such indulgences, compared to the peaking curiosity that must have surrounded all that was reported about the discovery of the Indies, seem irrelevant. The meticulous description of the characteristics of the flora and fauna and, in general, of the more or less favorable conditions of the first colonizers of a few of the Canary Islands, where the expedition made an intermediate stop, is quite superfluous in the overall context.

Underneath it all, after singling out the likely additions, one recognizes the Spanish chronicler's original story and thinking, thanks also to the resemblance to a few themes treated by Chanca. In any case, there are many details in the account interpreted in a different way.

In general, unlike Chanca, who seems more detached in his description and no doubt more concerned with unforeseen events and the natives' betrayal, Coma writes a report rich in positive details. Many are the episodes described from which surfaces a favorable impression of the state of affairs.

Regarding Columbus, Coma emphasizes his gifts of far-sightedness, determination and equanimity, which prompted him — a piece of information completely left out by Chanca — to grant a share of the gold "to his companions of labor on earth and at sea." The Indians to him are colorful, relaxed during their dances performed with songs and other sounds, and unaffected in their daily life by either wealth or property, since what they have does not seem to belong to anyone, and no one apparently desires what does not belong to him. The cannibals' huts (which Chanca, as stated earlier, also finds to be better built than those of other natives, though he stresses repeatedly their custom of building them out of straw) are described by Coma as "magnificent" since the building technique reminds him of country-side construction in his homeland.

Only in rare instances, for instance the cannibals' custom of eating human flesh, does Coma resolutely disapprove of their habits. His attitude

even in this matter is more detached; he uses less strong expressions than Chanca, who is more likely to accent their way of life, which, in his opinion, is "bestial."

Despite their concurring positive judgements on the outcome of the undertaking, it cannot be denied that these two Spanish reports differ from one another in their commendations. Chanca seems to express his thoughts more freely, though within a pattern determined by his feeling of gratitude for Columbus, who had, indeed, as earlier stated — in his *Memorial* sent to Spain at the same time as Chanca's *Letter* — urged the Catholic Sovereigns to increase Chanca's salary for "the great diligence and instant availability in all that concerned his office."

Coma seems to exceedingly maximize his attitude, making it, at times, outright flattery, as in the final passage of his work, when he addresses the overall sovereignty achieved by the Spanish Monarchs thanks to Columbus: "Because of his efforts the Spanish dominions were greatly enlarged, new lands were discovered, and innumerable populations in the South were met and subjugated, way beyond the Equator and the heat of the Zodiac, people spread out without any rule...."

Coma's text, compared to the other contemporary reports of the second voyage and the Letter of Columbus himself to the Sovereigns, is more affected by external factors. Possibly, such an attitude did, directly or indirectly, depend upon Columbus's desire to protect himself, allowing the most positive information possible to reach the Spanish rulers in support of what he intended to achieve and of the actual unfolding of the undertaking, as a way of offsetting much of the negative reporting. Columbus really knew what kind of charges he would have to face for sending back to Spain a part of the ships and the crews. Many of them, especially those of the upper class, had become hostile toward him during the first difficult months of their stay in Hispaniola because of his methods and his dictatorial approach. Only in this way could the slanders weigh less with the Crown and therefore be silenced and overcome.

Among Columbus's own writings, the *Letter-Report* of January 1494 expounds upon the salient moments of the first months of the expedition while dealing with matters already described by Chanca. Between the two letters, however, there is a sharp difference in the way some of the most important aspects of their stay in Hispaniola are viewed. Specifically, unlike Chanca, Columbus is inclined to clear the cacique Guacanagarí and his natives of the crime, pointing to the bad behavior of the men left in the stronghold of La Navidad, the real cause for the killings.

As a source for the second voyage, Columbus's *Memorial* is, no doubt, more interesting, for, unlike the other writings of the Admiral

and of other authors on the same matter and of the same time, it not only intended to illustrate the achieved goals but to denounce the existing inadequacies in the different sectors and thus justify his request for help. The newly born colony of La Isabela needed food supplies, men skilled in metal mining, and animals for slaughtering and for work in order to survive and carry out the discovery of new lands as well as find gold and spices.

Paradoxically, then, in such an account Columbus seems more objective than other chroniclers in presenting the actual situation before Torres's departure. Each single request had to be justified and explained within the context of the newly developed situation. Thus, the epidemic is viewed as the origin of most troubles that arose at that time: the impossibility of sowing and thus of being able to guarantee a harvest of wheat and barley as planned, as well as the inability to send but small groups of men to the regions thought to be laden with gold so as not to risk leaving unguarded the sick men and their supplies.

In Columbus, much more than in Chanca and the other chroniclers, who do not dwell extensively on it, the widespread disease is the negative backdrop of the whole situation. Every subsequent decision is intrinsically related to the disease — for example, the very departure of the ships in February 1494 was determined by the food supply need, considered fundamental to the healing of the sick and to ensuring everyone's survival.

As in other writings on the second enterprise, Columbus's *Memorial* also positively highlights the importance of finding gold, given the abundance of the metal found very easily on the ground and in the river waters, and enthusiastically addressing his own anticipation of an improvement in the near future of the emporarily difficult situation.

Like Chanca, who nonetheless projects in not too many words the richness of the precious metal laying in that land, anticipating substantial changes in the financial situation of the Spanish monarchy from the moment the vessels "will be able to gather large quantities of gold," Columbus links the success and the importance of the undertaking to the presence of gold. But, also in this case, Columbus transforms Chanca's general statement into a meticulous analysis of every aspect of the situation in a realistic and concrete way.

The description of the results of the two expeditions sent in search of gold — which, as claimed and reported to the Sovereigns, could be gathered even with bare hands — denotes an almost childish expectation, whereas, in stressing the extraordinariness of the situation that came to be, Columbus reveals a certain "embarrassment in saying and writing so to Their Highnesses." He is therefore glad that one of the two captains

who had gone to Niti will be able to report personally what Columbus is unable to report by letter.

The hope and the promise of realizing considerable profits, however, contrasts with the awareness, repeated in his writing, of the small amount of gold sent to Spain on that occasion, for which he apologizes. Altogether, Columbus's own *Memorial*, riddled with justifying excuses, shows the Admiral in trouble, trying too hard to explain.

Strange as it may seem, it is not out of place to hold that Chanca's and Coma's reports had succeeded, more than Columbus's own, in creating a positive aura around the expedition while conveying the sense of a situation under control of which Columbus was the undisputed leader ready to continue carrying on that policy of persuasion he exhibited during the first voyage, being fully certain of actualizing his projects on that expedition and future ones.

At the same time as the two Spanish chroniclers, Michele da Cuneo, a non-Spanish source, reported the events he experienced in the Indies from a more critical perspective. This increased the strongly negative judgements by Columbus's detractors, who from that moment would considerably increase in number and who finally gained, as we know, ascendancy over public opinion, depriving Columbus of the heretofore unconditional trust of the Spanish Sovereigns.

CHAPTER REFERENCES

COLÓN, *Manuscrito*, 2:447-67.
DA CUNEO, *Lettera a Gerolamo Annari*, 15-18 October 1495.
SQUILLACE, *De Insulis*.
BALLESTEROS BERETTA, *Cristóbal Colón*, 2:187-92.
BOSCOLO, 81-86.
FIRPO, 37-56.
GIL, "Introducción," 177-81.
GIUNTA.
GUERRINI, 110.
MORISON, *Admiral*, 441, 442, 477-78.
RUMEU DE ARMAS, *Libro*, 1:114, 170-71.
VANNINI DE GERULEWICZ, 47-50, 83-86.

XI. – THE LAST YEARS OF CHANCA'S LIFE

The only sources concerning Chanca's life in the period subsequent to his report from Hispaniola are a few documents of a private nature covering the years 1501-1515, found over the last decades in the General Archive in Simancas, in the General Archive of the Indies in Seville and in the Archive of Protocols, also in Seville, in addition to sporadic information contained in medical works. The oldest documents we have refer back only to 1501 and therefore it is not known what happened to Chanca between February 1494 and May 1501.

The only two indications which allow us to establish with certainty that Chanca was in Hispaniola after February 1494 are two references to the salary Chanca should earn during his stay in the Indies after most of the fleet headed back to Spain, the first in Columbus's *Memorial* and, the other the reply from the Spanish monarchs to the questions submitted by the Admiral about that matter. We do not know, however, when he returned to his country, whether at the end of the second expedition in 1496, or some time before that date.

As for the years after 1501, the documentation covers three areas: his family life, his activity as a writer of medical works, and his trading with Hispaniola.

Regarding his family life, we know of two marriages Chanca had contracted during this period: the first in 1501 with a widow, Juana Fernández, and the second six years later, on October 1, 1507, a few months after the death of his first wife, with a young orphan, Ana de Zurita, who had brought him a considerable dowry for a total value of 300[,00?] *maravedís*, including houses, wheat, jewels, house furniture and livestock. Three notarized documents illustrate the implications of this second marriage contract.

Chanca's medical works give some information about his activity as a writer, though very little about his being a physician. Only the *Tractatus de fascinatione*, written after his return from Hispaniola, by mentioning his service to King Ferdinand and Queen Isabela could let us suppose that

he had another appointment as the Spanish Sovereigns' personal physician. The continuation of his medical service with the royal family in that period seems evidenced also by a notarized document of November 1501, referring to the payment of 40,000 *maravedís*, an amount that had to be paid to Chanca by Diego López of Seville, the bursar of their Highnesses and "bookkeeper of the king and queen."

The lack of a specified period in which such service took place, however, leaves doubts, being possibly evidence of the service Chanca had performed previously. For Paniagua this interpretation confirms his idea that the document reflects the time when in 1491 Chanca had followed princess Isabela to Portugal as her personal physician. He is further convinced by the indication Chanca gives in the *Tractatus de fascinatione* about a clinical case in a stronghold he was called to as physician by the King's order. He recalls checking on a soldier on that occasion with two Jewish physicians. Since it is known that the Jews were expelled from Spain by the Catholic Sovereigns in 1492, the reported incident should therefore be understood to have taken place during the period of his life spent in Portugal.

The most interesting subject, it seems to me, among those described by the sources concerns his numerous trade relations established with the Indies, since they provide elements which characterize, beyond his profession, the last years of Chanca's life, spent in Seville. In order to carry out such trade he employed a negro, his "servant," Juan de Zafra. A notarized document of February 19, 1509 says that the imported goods traveled aboard two ships, one owned by Cristóbal Valles, the other by Juan de Jerez; "in the port of Santo Domingo" the merchandise was received by Juan de Zafra, who was engaged to sell it in Hispaniola.

As early as March 23 of the same year a second assignment is given, as always to Juan de Zafra, to sell a cargo of wine and flour which traveled aboard the same ships "bound for Hispaniola to the port of Santo Domingo."

The trade set up with the Indies secured as Chanca's compensation, in the agreement drawn up, half the sum earned with the sale. Moreover, the agent pledged to send back promptly Chanca's compensation aboard the first ship bound for Spain. Such trade had begun with an initial capital of 2,000 *maravedís*, granted by Chanca to his "servant" at no interest.

The trade remained constant during 1509. In another document of that year, we find as partner of the Andalusian physician in a commercial company the pharmacist Juan Bernal, a resident of Seville. He pledged, in front of the Sevillian notary Manuel Segura, to send "to the island of

Hispaniola 150 crates of *membrillo* meat." This time Juan de Zafra again was charged with selling the merchandise at its arrival.

Throughout 1509, Chanca appears engaged in the practice of such trade for which he appointed a successor to Juan de Zafra for the selling activity while the latter was still alive. Appointed by him to succeed De Zafra in the post in the Indies was Diego de Ocena, the king's scribe, just in case — as the document specifies — "his servant died." This way, the Andalusian physician could have relied on a person "to sell goods that he would send to the island of Hispaniola."

It is impossible to learn whether this precaution by Chanca was justified by a sickness of his "servant" or the physician's excessive concern in preparing to face any possible contingency. In any case, the implication is that Chanca watched over the state of his trade business carefully, to the point of taking precautions, before Juan de Zafra's death, to avoid any business interruption.

Actually, such measures soon proved unnecessary. Juan de Zafra still had his assignment as Chanca's agent in Hispaniola for many years, as is shown in a document of 1515, which is also the last one to give us information about the Sevillian physician. Further details about his life before this date are in the testament he issued on October 19, 1510, during a serious illness. This document provides some information related to the sale of goods and loans that he had effected in Seville.

Numerous payments indeed were owed him for various reasons; often, though, the amount that Chanca was to receive in such transactions was not indicated. Thus, we read in his will that a wine buyer owed him money for the selling of such product; that two pharmacists had a debt that they would have paid as a residual of previous trade business; that a physician also owed Chanca a sum for an unspecified reason; and, finally, that a woman owed him some money for a loan she contracted.

Chanca survived a few more years after signing this will and, as I stated earlier, he carried on his trade with the Indies as before. In fact, we find him on October 6, 1513, associated again with the pharmacist Juan Bernal, to whom he sent drugs and medical products in Santo Domingo. The tie with pharmacists, also true in the previous period, showed Chanca's interest in selling products generally related to his profession; however, this is the first explicit instance documenting a shipment of drugs to the Indies by Chanca.

The last document we have about Chanca's life and that gives us an idea of the year of his death is dated 1515. On April 25 of that year, we find him still engaged in his commercial trade with Santo Domingo, where his "servant" Juan de Zafra sold the goods the physician sent

him across the ocean. Since no document concerning the date of his death exists, it is impossible to know when it occurred and equally impossible to establish whether the lack of notarized documentation for the subsequent period reflects a cessation of his business trade or whether the latter coincided with his death, which soon after supervened.

CHAPTER REFERENCES

VALVERDE AND HIDALGO.
PANIAGUA, 48-59.
TIÓ, 25-29.

ANDRES BERNALDEZ
MEMOIRS

Commentary by
Anna Unali

XII. – ANDRES BERNALDEZ'S LIFE

Andrés Bernáldez, referred to as "prelate of Los Palacios" in seventeenth century historiography, has been rightly considered one of the most authoritative and reliable writers on the Columbian voyages to the Indies, especially for his description of the second voyage. His account fits into a broad historical work, the *Memoirs of the Catholic Sovereigns' Reign* which he wrote to illustrate the most important events that unfolded during the reign of the Spanish Sovereigns.

The numerous editions of this work in the decades subsequent to his death show that his work was widely known. It must be pointed out, however, that Bernáldez's work was not thought particularly worthy of mention by contemporary historians, as can be inferred from the absence of references to historical themes he treated or to the author himself.

Two reasons might explain the absolute lack of citations: the non-official character of the *Memoirs*, written without having been commissioned by the Sovereigns, and also the fact that it is a secondary source thus chiefly reliant on indirect experience. In addition, the information about the life and activities of this prelate of Los Palacios is obtained almost exclusively from the frequent personal notations contained in his own writings.

Both the autobiographical notations and his historical reporting are in the first person and of particular interest since, besides supplying items of information which allow us to reconstruct a few events of Bernáldez's life, they also illustrate his thoughts in connection with various aspects of what he describes. In any case, since it is hardly possible to determine the extent to which the sources at his disposal were used by him and to what degree his writing reflects his personal experience, all references must be taken as a mixed indication for a correct interpretation of his work.

From time to time he gives a few pieces of information about his life, making him a presence in the work but one that does not seem to result from a preordained scheme, appearing rather as the product of

accidental considerations originating from an association of ideas related to the discussed topic.

With the *Memoirs*, Bernáldez intended to work through the history of events of his time, i.e. happenings that unfolded during the years in which he lived. As a matter of fact, the work begins chronologically with the reign of Henry IV of Castile, not because Bernáldez particularly wanted to memorialize his actions, which, on the contrary, are presented with numerous shortcomings, but precisely because, as he points out in the introduction, "his fortunes, misfortunes and troubles occurred during my days." Thus, his desire to describe the events of his own lifetime reflects a personal approach which intentionally shows how what happened had to some extent influenced his life.

A good amount of biographical data awaits clarification. We do not have reliable information about his date of birth. It is possible, however, to guess it by relying on the very reference Bernáldez makes to Henry IV when he asserts: "I want to begin writing the memoirs of the extraordinary events which occurred in my time, starting with an account of his life." From this indication, then, it could be inferred that he was born around the time Henry IV ascended the throne, that is, 1454.

The place of his birth and his childhood are documented by him instead as he relates events of the first period of Ferdinand and Isabela's reign. We learn in an early passage of the *Memoirs* that he was born in Fuentes (Encomienda Mayor de León) near Seville.

Additional personal information that he supplies concerns his family. Intending to let it be known what caused him to devote himself to the writing of a historical work about the reign of the Catholic Sovereigns, he pictures himself at the age of twelve, intent upon reading the work his grandfather, the public clerk of the town of Fuentes, had compiled by recounting and commenting on the main events of his time.

In describing the beginning of his formation as a writer, Bernáldez continues by recalling an alleged conversation he had as a boy with his grandmother. Having noticed the young boy's interest in historical narratives, she urged him to consider undertaking, as he grew older, a work similar to his grandfather's in which to record "the good things that will occur in your days, so that they be known to the later generations."

Among the inspiring drives that urged him toward this goal, central was his desire to tell about the liberating conquest of Granada by the Christians, which he therefore must have foreseen and imagined possible in a not too distant future.

In addition to the place in which Bernáldez was born, the *Memoirs* also testifies to his position as parish priest of Los Palacios, near Seville.

This information about his profession is given in connection with the events happening to the Jews as a result of their 1492 banishment from Spain, ordered by the Catholic Sovereigns. The Andalusian curate proves actually how closely, because of his ecclesiastical role, he followed the entire event involving the Jewish population: he was directly engaged with baptizing all those who chose to submit to this forced solution in order to remain in their country. He first mentions having baptized "ten or twelve" of them, but afterwards, after their failed attempt to move to Morocco, "here in the town of Los Palacios I baptized more or less a hundred of them."

A very important event in Bernáldez's private life concerns Columbus's stay in his Los Palacios home in 1496 after his return from the second voyage. From Bernáldez's own words, Columbus's attitude toward the parish priest appears friendly and it is confirmed by the very fact that the Admiral of the Ocean Sea chose Bernáldez's residence as the place in which to rest after his voyage before visiting the King and Queen in Barcelona.

By Bernáldez's own acknowledgement, he had at his disposal on that occasion a few of Columbus's writings from which he drew much information about the first expeditions to the Indies. Besides having personally met the Admiral, this incident likely also meant for Bernáldez an improvement of his own geographical knowledge, for he learned from Columbus's own lips the account of the Admiral's experiences.

Rodrigo Caro, a scholar of the first decades of the seventeenth century, is another source for biographical information that complements the *Memoirs*. Caro tried to secure more information about the Andalusian ecclesiastic's life, intending to edit a version of one of his works.

Caro, in his introductory presentation, offers information about his scholarly attempts to verify the name of the author of the *Memoirs*, who, as I stated earlier, was at that time known generally as "the prelate of Los Palacios," but also sometimes wrongly referred to as "Bachiller Medina." Caro tells of his research in the parochial archive of Los Palacios where he had the opportunity, thanks to having been named ecclesiastical inspector of all the localities in the Sevillian archbishopric, to visit Los Palacios and examine the parish records. From the books covering the period 1488-1513, it appeared that the then parish priest recorded year by year the names of those who were baptized, including the name Andrés Bernáldez or, sometimes, Bernal. The scholar adds further that in the margins of those baptismal registers he found annotations of various sorts inserted by the parish priest and related to the events of those years.

In presenting the *Memoirs*, Rodrigo Caro considered its contents, thus its author, trustworthy. He maintained that Bernáldez "wrote this story because he was a witness to what occurred." As for the part of the information he could not personally verify, Caro holds that Bernáldez made use of his contacts with famous people of his time such as Christopher Columbus and Rodrigo Ponce de León, marquis of Zahara, duke of Cádiz, who had both been his guests.

Moreover, Caro highlighted the Andalusian parish priest's contacts abroad, which allowed him to report also on events that took place in other countries. Finally, Caro concludes that Bernáldez also acted as the chaplain of the archbishop of Seville, Don Diego de Deza, in addition to his duties as prelate of Los Palacios.

The information supplied by Caro cannot be found in contemporary or later sources nor double-checked, since the parochial books of the years Bernáldez carried out his office at Los Palacios were lost, as early as 1870. That year two Spanish scholars, Fernando de Gabriel and Ruiz de Apodaca, who were editing the *Memoirs*, searched in vain the parish archives of Los Palacios for such registers, seeking to obtain further information about the parish priest's life.

Many decades later, in 1955, the Cuban historian Filiberto Ramírez Corría, citing the total lack of documentary and narrative sources about Bernáldez's life, claimed that a chronicler by that name never existed during the period of the discovery of America. Moreover, in his opinion, the *Memoirs* were to be considered the work of many authors and written in a time subsequent to the presumed date of the death of the person identified as Andrés Bernáldez.

In 1962, the year of the last edition of the *Memoirs*, Gómez-Moreno and Carriazo maintained Bernáldez's existence against the theory formulated by Corría without being able to supply determining evidential documentation. The question that has provided historians with some excitement in the last few decades is today completely resolved thanks to the finding of an important document.

Juan Gil, a Spanish scholar, has found in the Archive of Protocols in Seville a notarized document dated March 27, 1504, which he published in 1986. In this document, a certain Andrés Bernal, curate of Los Palacios, appears three times as the debtor of an unspecified quantity of wheat and barley. The name, the office and the date of the notarized deed remove all doubts concerning the identification of the curate of Los Palacios with our Andrés Bernáldez.

Regarding the name Bernal, which appears in the document for Bernáldez, it is still in doubt whether the former really coincides with

the author of the *Memoirs*. Gil thinks the parish priest's name was Bernal, trusting the evidence of the notarized deed. In supporting his hypothesis, he also recalls Rodrigo Caro, who, as stated earlier, did determine that among the signatures on the parish registers there was a Bernal, although he pointed out its lesser frequency.

The reason the form Bernáldez rather than Bernal was adopted in fifteenth-century Seville is mainly, in Gil's opinion, that the latter had a Jewish connotation.

As for his official charge as chaplain of Don Diego de Deza, archbishop of Seville-which the curate had for many years-historiography commonly considers it mostly an honorific title, in view of the fact that the prelate never gave up his job as parish priest.

There is no reliable information about the date of his death. Only the post-quem date can be inferred on the basis of two different pieces of information, both pointing to 1513: one reported in Caro's introduction to the *Memoirs* and the other being the year of the last events Bernáldez describes as the account ends in September 1513.

The abrupt interruption of the *Memoirs*, whose story awaited conclusion, allows further speculation that Bernáldez did not voluntarily end his work then. Death must have come unexpectedly upon him sometime after September 4, 1513. This is only a hypothesis, however, since no documentary evidence has been found to prove it.

Nineteenth-century historiography tried, comparing the texts of various chroniclers of Columbus's voyages, to determine the date of the composition of the *Memoirs* and establish the year of Bernáldez's death. Cesare de Lollis, who had noticed considerable similarities between Peter Martyr of Anghiera's work and Bernáldez's, emphasizes with amazement that there is no reference to him among the authors cited by Don Ferdinand Columbus, the Admiral's son, in his list of 1538, the one in which he listed all the works of importance concerning his father's enterprises.

Logically then, should one think that the Andalusian parish priest's death was later than 1538? De Lollis himself, however, in presenting such a consideration, was well aware of the improbability of maintaining it, since Bernáldez would have been too old then.

Hence, Ferdinand Columbus's failure to mention the *Memoirs* opens a new question which shall unfortunately remain without definitive solution, together with the unknown dates of the Andalusian parish priest's work and that of his death.

CHAPTER REFERENCES

Bernáldez, *Memorias*, ch. 72, 113, 193.

Amador de los Rios, 7:329.
Ballesteros Beretta, *Cristóbal Colón*, 1:17-20.
Fernández de Navarrete, 1:66-69.
Gil, "Noticia."
Gil and Varela, 20.
Gómez-Moreno, and De M. Carriazo, v, xiii-xvii, xxi, xxii.
Jane, *Select Documents*, 1:cxlvi-cl.
Jane, *Voyages*, 87.
Menéndez Pelayo, 8:81.
Mollat, *Les explorateurs*, 71, 72.
Pelayo y Del Pozo, 1:132.
Ramírez Corría, 14.
Rosell, 3:567.

XIII. – *MEMOIRS OF THE CATHOLIC SOVEREIGNS' REIGN*: SOURCES, METHODS, AND PURPOSES

The document that Andrés Bernáldez wrote reporting the events of his time has been handed down with no title. During the centuries that followed the first edition it has been known as either "Memoirs," "History," or "Chronicle." The selection of a different title by different editors always has reflected a focus on one of the aspects of his work to highlight, in each instance, a particular feature of Bernáldez's writing.

In opting for the first of the three titles, already adopted in the edition by M. Gómez-Moreno and J. de H. Carriazo, I chose to emphasize the idea of a memoir, which is often mentioned in the work as its goal as well as being the dominant aspect of the narrative, and also chose to highlight the subjectivity of its personal recollection.

The most important events of the times in which the Andalusian parish priest lived were, in other words, selected and "interpreted" by him before being handed down to future generations as an inheritance of positive and negative experiences, surrounding various aspects of everyday living. For Bernáldez, preserving the "memory" of events was a way to ensure the likelihood of progress. This way, at a time when experimentation was timidly beginning to hold sway, Bernáldez strived to provide a means of seriously preventing further social and economic scourges which had tormented humanity for centuries, while, at the same time, making sure that key events marking the progress of the history of mankind be known. One of the distinctive contributions of Bernáldez's work is his clear aim to educate posterity by preserving factual information.

Many times, being unable to report information on subjects derived either from other authors or from news received from participants in the described events, Bernáldez emphasizes selected aspects by weaving together different sources as an ever-present narrator enriching them with personal and cultural considerations out of his own experience.

In a few instances, he quotes quite literally the works consulted, even imitating the grammatical structure of sentences, whereas he normally

conveys the essential. By slight modifications, though occasionally even of little relevance, he avoids the outright repetition of quoted writings.

The Andalusian prelate does not then consider all information worthy of presentation. His selections indicate to us what, in his opinion, was most significant or considered of extraordinary prominence in his time. Detailing the methods and purpose of his historical work, he openly states that since it is "impossible to describe all that happened in Spain during the reign of King Ferdinand and Queen Isabela, I shall limit myself to reporting worthy items of particular interest."

Such words addressing the main purpose of his effort could be narrowly interpreted to mean he will describe only the major positive developments of the two Spanish monarchs' reign. However, a reading of the *Memoirs* proves Bernáldez did not have predetermined ideas or a limiting perspective when he chose some events rather than others. He wanted to record extraordinary events even if negative ones, thus ensuring objectivity to his work. Remarkably, unlike other chroniclers, he did not need to adjust his style and thoughts to a pre-established scheme or distinctively encomiastic goals and consequently produced a chronicle characterized by unencumbered argumentation and balanced judgement.

Bernáldez did not even enjoy an official appointment as a chronicler of the Catholic Sovereigns to write the *Memoirs*. He merely presents his work as a result of his own willingness to engage in a task without the implications of a formal commitment. He realistically shows a dual attitude toward the official chroniclers: on one hand he feels the limitations and narrowness of the range of information supplied by the "chroniclers of Their Highnesses" who "by not keeping in touch with the common people, forget many of the events which occurred, when they occurred and those who took part in them...." On the other hand, he displays humility as he nonetheless acknowledges his difficulty in having undertaken a task for which he does not have sufficient competence and which has, as he manifestly asserts, "nothing to do with my profession."

Moreover, Bernáldez is keenly aware that the chroniclers in the Sovereigns' service were in a privileged position, as he points to the wealth of data at their disposal and to their ability to "send timely letters from their offices in order to inquire about what is happening in other kingdoms, and to receive answers and to learn through them — crucial for their job — of note worthy events and news concerning nearby kingdoms." Their office is by him also evaluated in relation to their function: being political intermediaries, in their letters "by means of prudent wording they need to strive to avoid hostilities and wars between kings and lords and to promote peace and harmony...." Numerous are

the sources that the parish priest of Los Palacios bears in mind for the part of the *Memoirs* related to Columbus's expedition to the Indies, by him considered a subject of great interest among the many events that unfolded during the time of the Catholic Sovereigns. Except for the most obvious sources that Bernáldez specifically refers to in his work, such as Diego Alvarez Chanca's *Letter* and Columbus's *Letter-Report*, it is impossible to determine on which additional writings he based the account of the *Memoirs*. In other words, it should be emphasized that while the actual contributions of Chanca's *Letter* and Columbus's own reports can be verified against their preserved testimonies, it is not, however, possible to ascertain how much Bernáldez actually owes to the reports of "other gentlemen who were with him on the above-mentioned voyages."

The use Bernáldez makes of the *Letter* Chanca had sent through Antonio Torres to the Mayor of Seville, covering necessarily only events from the second expedition until February 1494, clearly shows the importance that the parish priest ascribed to this report, both for the evident incorporation of many passages, as we earlier discussed, and also by his very acknowledgement that it was among the principal writings he consulted.

The only surprising element comes from the greater relevance and preference given to the physician's work, despite the fact that the Andalusian parish priest had at his disposal Columbus's own writing, which he indeed uses in his description of the second part of that voyage. There is no convincing explanation for the reason behind his preference for Chanca's report as the basis for the description of the first months after their arrival at Hispaniola.

The few elements not taken from Chanca's writing should not be forgotten in our analysis of the *Memoirs*, because they contribute further information that is added to the original text as well as contribute to a better understanding of the thinking of the parish priest of Los Palacios.

The *Memoirs'* testimony about Chanca's participation in the second Columbian expedition, even though reported partially in the third person that Chanca used, is in any case important as a proof of the actual participation of the Andalusian physician in the voyage to the Indies.

For numerous other topics in his work, Bernáldez made use of pieces of information that came to him directly from Columbus's experience. In fact, not only did he have at his disposal Columbus's writings, but also, having personally met the Genoese who had been his guest, he probably obtained information verbally. Indeed, one should think that the Admiral on that occasion was likely stimulated to talk about his undertakings by the interest the parish priest of Los Palacios showed toward such events.

It is equally natural to believe that during his stay in Los Palacios Columbus regaled Bernáldez with his geographical convictions and many other aspects of the first two voyages.

In Bernáldez's *Memoirs* there are also analogies, affinities and, in a few cases, parallelisms both in form and in content with Peter Martyr of Anghiera's *Decades* concerning the second Columbian voyage. In his fundamental study about Columbus and the chroniclers of the Columbian expeditions, De Lollis documented, as has been noted, the similarities existing between these two writings. He is inclined to believe that such similarities do not stem from the Andalusian ecclesiastic's reproduction of the *Decades*, in 1493-1494, written almost ten years before the *Memoirs*, but from Columbus's journal, the common basis of their account. If anything, the scholar thinks that Peter Martyr's work was for Bernáldez a narrative model he followed in organizing the material he incorporated.

Another source that Bernáldez held to be of great value, especially in confirming some of his information, is *The Voyages* by John Mandeville. Written in the fourteenth century, this work had as many as forty editions in several languages during the 1400s and 1500s. As late as the three decades of the nineteenth century, Mandeville was believed to have actually gone to the places in the Middle East and Far East he described when in fact he wrote his work relying on previous travel literature, primarily the work of Oderico da Pordenone, as well as on his imaginary interpretation of reality.

Although not to be considered a primary source, Mandeville's writing is nonetheless of great historical interest, both for its testimony to the geographical and commercial knowledge of his time and also for the popularity it enjoyed among contemporaries and in the following centuries influencing the thinking of men still bound to tradition, as was, in some respects, the Andalusian parish priest himself.

Bernáldez cites *The Voyages* especially in connection with Columbus's geographical ideas, his description of Cathay and some odd beliefs about the Indians. These references show a thorough understanding by Bernáldez of this fourteenth century work, which he utilizes as a reinforcement of Columbus's way of thinking. He thus proves Columbus was right in believing the earth could be wholly travelled by land or sea by showing out that such an idea coincided with what had been asserted by the fourteenth-century author in his work.

As for Cathay, defined in the *Memoirs* as "the richest region in the world with respect to gold, silver, all metals, silks, cloths, wheats, fruit and livestock," Bernáldez explains that his main source was the account of Mandeville who indicated that he had "gone there, saw and lived

with the Grand Khan," thus deferring to Mandeville's writing for "all those who wish to know the truth." Mandeville's description of Cathay is lengthy and detailed, defining this land as "wonderful, good, rich in many types of merchandise and wealthy," while describing a splendid court and other riches of the kingdom of the Grand Khan, and finally dwelling on the customs practiced at the Chinese court.

As for the alleged news concerning the widespread report among the Indians that the people of the territory of Magón had tails, the Andalusian parish priest declares not to believe in such odd rumor, basing his conclusion on his reading of Mandeville's account.

The *Memoirs* must be regarded as a unified work although it includes different subject matters. Actually, the correlation between its parts is so strong that none of it should be taken up separately. This is why also the chapters related to the figure and the work of Columbus in the Indies must not be considered independently, as was frequently done in the nineteenth-century or even in contemporary historiography, keeping in mind that the topics are related. The retelling of Columbus's undertakings takes on a different dimension when viewed in the context of other exploration voyages, both Spanish and Portuguese.

Chronologically, Bernáldez's historical work encompasses the period between the ascension to the throne of Henry IV, which, as has been noted, occurred in 1454, and the events that took place in 1513, with particular reference to the reign of Isabela of Castile and Ferdinand of Aragon. Bernáldez wrote the first chapters after the year 1500, as is implied by the fact that he sets in the first part of his writing a few passages — dated 1500 — from the work *Claros Varones*, by Fernando del Pulgar, official chronicler of Ferdinand and Isabela.

The subjects dealt with by Bernáldez cover several areas ranging from Italian events of the second half of the 1400's and the first decades of the 1500's to the relationship between Spain and Portugal in the same period, and from the conquest of the West African territories by the Portuguese to the exploration of the Indies undertaken by Columbus. Overall, the latter topic is predominant in the organization of the work, not simply in terms of the amount of information supplied but also and primarily for the relevance the subject enjoyed at the time.

In his approach Bernáldez insists upon the truthfulness of the arguments submitted and frequently proclaims his firm intention to adhere to the truth, pointing out that the account can be confirmed by those who know and who lived through the described events ("some gentlemen and nobles who saw this and others who did not see this"), and that the narration is due to reliable pieces of information, "things

I myself saw and which were open and public, that happened, developed and came to pass."

As for the sources he used, the parish priest of Los Palacios in a few instances clarifies the origin of his information, wanting to support his descriptions with enhanced evidence and thus appear more trustworthy. Even for news of little relevance, such as the finding in Rome in 1498 of a body of a young girl, well preserved in the eyes of those who found it and which decomposed only three days later, he indicates that the information was supplied by trustworthy persons and further checked against news contained in letters arriving from Rome. For this as well as other episodes, his attention to details of events discussed — occasionally to the point of including repulsive data — must be stressed.

The scruple of showing that his account certainly conformed to the truth becomes for him in a few cases pedantic, as when for instance, while reporting on Mandeville's *Voyages* he even indicates the numbers of the chapters. Bernáldez feared being considered too prolix a writer and making mistakes, admitting his "readiness to stand corrected...."

He has a voracious curiosity, even for aspects of daily life, dwelling at times on peculiar events characterizing Andalusian social and economic history, such as, among many other things, the extraordinarily numerous locusts who invaded in 1508 and caused a serious famine. This subject is discussed extensively, although Bernáldez considers it unique and extraneous to the general interest of his readers.

The importance of the *Memoirs* lies in Bernáldez's desire to identify among the events important for mankind those traditionally underestimated or generally viewed as unworthy of mention. By so doing, extraordinary events of all kinds took on a new importance of their own, therefore becoming, as the parish priest of Los Palacios underscores, more relevant for their preservation in the memory of posterity.

CHAPTER REFERENCES

DE PORDENONE, 15-71.
BERNÁLDEZ, *Memorias*, ch. 1, 7, 14, 214, 238.
MANDEVILE, 87-129.
DE GABRIEL AND DE APODACA, 1:vii.
DE LOLLIS, "Introduzione," 1:lxxxvi-lxxxviii.
DELUZ.
HERNANDO DEL PULGAR.
FERNÁNDEZ DE RETANA, 11, 15.
GIL AND VARELA, 21.
GÓMEZ-MORENO AND DE M. CARRIAZO, v, xiii-xvii, xxi, xxii.
JANE, *Voyages*, 87.
ROUX, 224-25.
TIÓ, 9.
VARELA, *Diego Alvarez Chanca*, 32.

XIV. – THE *MEMOIRS* AS A DOCUMENTARY SOURCE OF THE TIME: NATURAL DISASTERS AND EXTRAORDINARY EVENTS

"It seemed right to me at this time to record extraordinary and prodigious things which occurred during this reign (of the Catholic Sovereigns), so that those who live and shall see similar events in later years may not wonder and may be better equipped to provide remedies." Thus Bernáldez ended his long account of the devastation by the locusts that happened "in the year 1508 in Andalusia and in many areas of Castile."

Such a formal memoir of events was itself a pedagogical tool able to affect those who might relive similar situations in later times and particularly important when it referred to very serious and dangerous situations involving entire communities.

In the parish priest's conception, any teaching arising from recollections of past events would allow people, as soon as the phenomenon repeated itself, to take precautions and suitable measures to confront, as far as possible, similar emergency situations.

While relating events which characterized the years of his life, Andrés Bernáldez pays constant attention to the social environment in which he lived, choosing to describe the major natural disasters taking place then and their heavy consequences, which affected, more or less generally, his country.

Thus, besides the *Memoirs*' passages devoted to a description of the great events that marked Spain's internal history under the Catholic Sovereigns — among which we recall the expulsion of the Jewish people from the Iberian peninsula and the Christians' conquest of the Andalusian cities that were still under the rule of the Sultan of Granada — we find further this other aspect of the same reality, namely, the retelling of numerous natural calamities such as floods and famines which occurred in those years and the frequent serious plagues which followed, weighing heavily upon the general social and economic situation of many Spanish regions, in some cases for several decades.

The narration of such events is significant in itself for the uniqueness of the themes introduced and the many interesting episodes connected or discussed, but in particular because of its data about daily life mainly provided by, or emerging from, the direct experience of the author who, in some cases, put it forward to exemplify what was being narrated.

The engaging descriptions of these calamities takes on a particular relevance in the *Memoirs*, equal to that given to positive events flattering the Sovereigns. As a matter of fact, one of the most engaging aspects of his work is precisely this balanced approach, offering on the same level the best, i.e. what gave fame and wealth to the Spanish Crown, as well as the worst, what turned out to have disastrous consequences for social life.

In the work by the parish priest of Los Palacios the period of time more heavily affected by a sequence of calamities stretches from 1478-1508, with a single intermission between 1495 and 1502. Bernáldez also writes about years before the period he examines, but does not treat any natural phenomena of those years.

He describes situations that developed as a consequence of those catastrophes with rich detail that does not correspond to any literary scheme; his description appears to be in close touch with the lives of humble people and sensitive to the exigencies and abrupt changes brought about in the economic and social life of the affected communities.

The geographic range of the *Memoirs* mainly extends to the territories of Andalusia, but in some cases also of Castile and León. And since the account is less detailed when it refers to other Spanish regions, it leads us to suppose that Bernáldez limited his reporting to what he could personally verify or to news he could gather from those places.

We cannot determine how realistically accurate the figures are that Bernáldez quotes for the number of deaths or the cost of basic food items, which in that period of time was most unstable and varied with the quantity of imported goods. The data is generally noteworthy given the fact that his analysis covers nearly two decades and treats all events objectively without distinctive emphasis on any of them. In his narration of each event, always analyzed retrospectively, he correlates facts and situations which in his view are analogous.

In terms of time, Bernáldez occasionally focuses on the time of the year in which most of the phenomena he examines took place, creating a panoramic view that emerges from his post-factum consideration of events, probably based upon his personal notes. Thus he is able to group together phenomena fully described as they unfolded over a longer or shorter period of time but also set in an analytical framework.

The actual danger in many Andalusian localities during the years he indeed examines is unconnected in Bernáldez's work to other important events of the time, to the point of creating the impression that, despite the intensity of each phenomenon examined and its consequences, their almost regular occurrence diminished the sense of danger, making the events he considers appear to be almost normal. The unavoidable shock usually associated with the death of so many people or other critical aspects of daily life does not produce complications on the political level.

The little connection in his work between social and political issues or between the decisions taken by political authorities concerning the major events of the reign and the emergency situations constantly arising because of the many natural calamities in all spheres of life — from living conditions to the basic necessity of food — shows he used a diversity of sources.

In reporting the principal calamities that occurred during his lifetime, Bernáldez highlights his astonishment vís à vís the monstrous proportions of these phenomena and their consequences, while, at the same time, he feels great sympathy toward the appalling conditions of the poorest people, caught at the very edge of subsistence.

The most violent disasters which characterized some periods showed a domino effect in an almost indissoluble cycle: floods caused famine, which often in turn generated epidemics. After all, the Andalusian places Bernáldez most frequently refers to lay mainly along rivers and were exposed to yearly flooding.

The first catastrophe Bernáldez mentions is that of 1481, the year of a plague and of heavy rains that led to the swelling of rivers and then to floods. The plague was so widespread that Bernáldez says "in all the Andalusian towns, countryside and localities, an enormous number of people died; in Seville, more than 1500 people died and as many also in Cordoba; in Jerez and in Ecija 9000 people died and this went on in all the other rural localities."

According to the prelate, during the month of August that year an intensification of the plague occurred and lasted a long time, with a notable virulent reoccurrence lasting "over eight years with a varying intensity...now in one part of Andalusia, now in another."

The flood which followed such a serious epidemic, as if the Andalusian people had not been tested enough, took place over Christmas 1481: because of heavy non-stop rains lasting three days, the Guadalquivir, swollen to the highest level, overflowed, causing heavy damage to many localities all along the river's banks. In Seville throughout the flood there was fear the entire city would be submerged.

The river's devastating fury recurred as a constant threat every year in which the rains were particularly abundant. According to the *Memoirs*, the most dangerous time of year for floods of the Guadalquivir valley was around Christmas.

Andrés Bernáldez recalls how only four years after the floods of 1481 there were heavy rains again for six weeks on end, and a similar situation developed in 1485. The Andalusian parish priest supplies greater details about this flood than about the previous one, dwelling on the situation in Seville, the damage caused to the dwellings of many areas of the city and its suburbs. This time the danger lasted eleven days, turning the city into a lagoon with boats being the only way to haul people from place to place.

The parish priest of Los Palacios emphasizes that the Sevillian people very much feared being unable to face such a catastrophe after many city dwellings were lost and "a large part of Triana" destroyed. Moreover, the water "flooded the convent of Las Cuevas; the nuns were saved using boats but the convent suffered severe damages." According to the *Memoirs*, Seville "was totally surrounded by water" and consequently was deprived of basic necessities.

His account continues with a list of the Andalusian localities struck by the flood. In some cases they were the same locations previously affected, and suffered serious consequences. Some Castilian localities were also beset by violent thunderstorms which caused the death of a great number of people, a large amount of livestock and the destruction of houses and other buildings, vineyards and orchards.

The 1485 flood disasters were such that their memory lasted for a long time. Bernáldez says that the 1488 flood, involving the Andalusian region but especially Seville, though just as violent, was shorter than the ones previously recorded. This time the Andalusian ecclesiastic, rather than stressing city damages, comments on agricultural devastation: it was so serious that it caused the destruction of a quantity of sowed wheat equal to 150 *cahices*.[1]

Floods were the main danger those years until 1488. And, afterwards, in all likelihood, the situation was much the same since the parish priest of Los Palacios mentions, every now and then, floods without giving them the same importance as in the past.

Throughout the second period, 1502-1508, most similar to the first in terms of its constant sequence of calamities, Bernáldez gives much

---

[1] Dry measure of grains equal to 666 litres.

consideration to the precarious conditions of the Andalusian communities. In each instance he analyzes the consequences of poverty, hunger, disease and death as the elements that had altered the normal pattern of life. The most common causes of calamity were, mainly, unfavorable weather conditions, bad harvests, the destruction caused by locusts and, last but not least, the worst effects of the plague which occurred again and again, alternately, in one place or another, every few years.

Among the many scourges of the time, Bernáldez particularly lingers upon the earthquake of 1504 which had primarily struck Andalusia. The earthquake was felt in Los Palacios where it caused serious damage. It was followed by an extremely heavy famine in 1505 because it prompted an outbreak of serious diseases.

"On Good Friday, April 5, 1504, between nine and ten a.m., the Spanish land shook, causing great fear: it was the largest earthquake Andalusia ever had." Thus wrote Bernáldez, who was in Los Palacios when the earthquake's shocks were felt and who described what happened during those moments of terrifying trembling: "Fear ran so high that people were collapsing and lay on the ground as though they had fainted."

The Andalusian parish priest's prose catches people's anxieties about being annihilated and their fear of imminent disaster which followed the earthquake, when "all the reinforced buildings, churches and houses shook, swaying both ways, first toward the south and then back up the other way."

The passage that embodies the greatest overall significance in his narration, however, is his description of the incident that he himself witnessed inside the parish church of Los Palacios during a religious function. The account of what happened, reported in the first person, affords us a glimpse of his own life while it is certainly a product of his own perceptions and a sample of his subjective writing style. As indicated earlier, our incomplete knowledge of the sources he used for the *Memoirs*, which prevents a full understanding of the extent to which they were used, necessarily leads us to value the most those passages which indisputably convey the Andalusian ecclesiastic's own personality.

"What I wrote is what I saw happening in the church of Los Palacios." The collapse of the bell-tower, the plaster coming off the walls, the loud noise that began just as a hiss the squeaking of the church roof "as if scores of people were running over it" convey with great intensity Bernáldez's state of mind. He adds that he wanted to leave the church by crossing over by the main altar, but the entire building was shaking from side to side while the floor surged and cracked. The cries for help

addressed to the Madonna and Christ by those inside the church, the random rush by some to the exit and the immobility of others — mostly women unable to move because they were stunned by fear — are but some strokes that with other elements depict a most vivid emotional representation (and the same happens elsewhere in his work). And, anxiously wishing to confirm his personal involvement, Bernáldez concludes with a classic statement: "quod vidimus testamus [I witness what I saw]."

Another memorialized period of such calamities extends from the beginning of 1505 until April of the same year when the Andalusian people experienced serious troubles due to heavy rains and floods so close together "that one was not over yet when the next began." Bernáldez supplies interesting indications about the cost of grain which, he maintains, did not increase sharply, despite the loss of most of the harvest.

This market stability, which lasted until Queen Isabela's death in 1505, was due to high fines: 500 *maravedís* per *fanega*[2] were levied against those who sold wheat or other grains at a higher price than the established one. The parish priest of Los Palacios details how by the King's and Queen's order, starting on December 22, 1502, "a *fanega* of wheat could not be sold for more than 110 *maravedís*; nor one of barley for over 60 *maravedís*; and one of rye over 70 *maravedís*."

The harvest in 1506 was still miserable; however, this time it was caused by a lack of rain which prevented the crops from ripening. In his long account about this matter, the ecclesiastic of Los Palacios examines the situation prevalent in many areas of Andalusia and Castile and supplies to us the most important information item as he reports the request of wheat, forwarded by the Council of Seville to Flanders and Sicily, for quantities capable of resolving the gravity of the situation. Equally significant are his indications concerning the ships, loaded with wheat, which in that year moored in Seville: 800 of them, coming from Flanders, Brittany, Sicily, the Italian peninsula, the Black Sea and Barbary.

The following year, in addition to the hunger caused by famine there was plague. In Andalusia, Castile and León the population was halved. The mortality rate was widespread and struck all indiscriminately: "An extremely high number of old people died along with numerous clerics, priests, friars, nuns, doctors and skilled people in every craft...." In this case, even more than in the past, his realistic descriptions show desolation and the inability to react in such a widely precarious situation.

---

[2] Dry measure of grains equal to 22.5 or 55.5 liters, depending on the region.

Famines, floods, earthquakes, destruction of crops and plagues were therefore the dominant elements in the life of people about to expand their radius of action into faraway lands. The account by the parish priest of Los Palacios shows that the Columbian undertakings were not exempt from serious diseases which had far-reaching consequences for the course of the expeditions. All these precarious situations are to be taken into consideration for a more proper understanding of the environment in which such an enterprise was prepared, virtually determined and actualized.

CHAPTER REFERENCES

BERNÁLDEZ, *Memorias*, ch. 44, 78, 91, 201, 202, 214, 215.

BRAUDEL, 203-220.
MCNEIL, 185-216.

XV. – THE PORTUGUESE VOYAGES OF EXPLORATION

In his *Memoirs* Bernáldez attentively considered the expeditions conducted by the Portuguese during the 1400s with the dual purpose of exploring the western coasts of Africa and of reaching India. Actually, the parish priest of Los Palacios shows a parallel interest, along with describing Columbus's expeditions aimed at reaching the Indies through a western route, in paying attention to the Portuguese navigators and their most important stages of exploration.

Portugal had officially entered the ranks of the great sea powers during the first decades of the fifteenth century, thanks to the conquest of Ceuta in 1415 by the Infante Don Enrique, successfully surprising, with a brand new and unexpected plan, Mediterranean "nations" known by tradition as great sea and trading powers. Until then it was unthinkable that a rapid nautical development by the Portuguese could bring about the realization of an ambitious plan programmed for the exploration of the African coast south of Cape Bojador, for centuries the insurmountable limit of all traders — Italians included — interested in securing Western Sudanese gold.

Bernáldez does not offer readers a stage by stage account of the Portuguese Atlantic explorations from the very first attempts to their circumnavigation of Africa and arrival in the Indian region of Malabar. The first notation he makes concerns one of the most important moments of the Portuguese enterprise, the reaching of the Mina de Ouro on Guinea's coast. Despite its name, it was not a gold mine but a coastal location where the native populations gathered, coming from all over the interior to barter the precious metal for goods imported from Portugal.

The event, for its remarkable economic and political repercussions, undoubtedly aroused great interest even for Bernáldez, who was interested in oceanic journeys. He points out in his writing that they reached Mina in 1471, a good decade before building the fortress designed later to become the major gold-supply base for the Portuguese Crown.

Besides becoming a possession of the Sovereigns of Portugal, this locality came to represent the Portuguese monopoly on the African gold of Mina (see note about gold and spices in the African and Asiatic voyages).

The news generally reported in the *Memoirs* in connection with the Portuguese expeditions is rather summary. Notwithstanding Bernáldez's tendency to select only the most relevant elements, he does show great fascination with reporting the exploration of the territory of the Mina and the events which took place as well as balanced objectivity by dwelling more upon the positive results, rather than the negative, ensuing from these long expeditions to African lands. Thus, he stresses Portugal's huge profits from the importation of gold that enriched the royal treasury and was seemingly "increasing day by day."

Any negative implication connected to expeditions along the Atlantic African coast, although at first characterized by serious sanitation problems which led to the death of many sailors as properly reported by Bernáldez but without particular insistence upon this aspect of the Portuguese voyages, is actually, after their initial difficulties, minimized for the subsequent expeditions. Bernáldez does not explain exhaustively such a change of situation that ensured the continuation of the Atlantic journeys, bringing forward, as its sole reason, their acquired experience which led to a general improvement in the living conditions for the crews.

The second event related to the Portuguese discoveries that the prelate of Los Palacios dwells on is the expedition Vasco da Gama made to Calicut ten years after Diaz, in 1487, had reached the Cape of Good Hope, an undertaking that required more than 70 years of continual attempts, over difficult routes that varied depending on set goals and contingent environmental conditions.

This achievement, a critical stage for voyages to the Indies, permitted the Portuguese to achieve control of Indian territories in a short time. The navigation of the Indian Ocean would be far easier than the crossing of the Atlantic, and could also count on the blossoming trade of Indian and Chinese merchants that for centuries charted those seas. It is common knowledge that Da Gama profited by the skill of an Arab pilot who guided him and made his way to Calicut possible.

Bernáldez shows a key consideration for this event and, in giving views of it, he highlights the June 10, 1499 return to Lisbon of Da Gama's vessel as "one of the ships the king of Portugal had sent to discover," using in this case also the verb "to discover" normally applied to the still then unknown African territories and to Columbus's voyages to the Indies.

Da Gama's journey lasted two years from the time he left Lisbon. In compiling a list of the most important economic places touched during the voyage along the Atlantic coast of Africa, Bernáldez again cites the Mina de Ouro, confirming the importance of such a stronghold as a center for gold trade that would ensure regular exchanges with the mother country. While following its route southward and then east toward India, the fleet travelled 1800 leagues beyond the discovered territories.

Calicut is presented as a big city, larger than Lisbon, with a population "made up of Christian Indians, who own churches, lands and houses made of stone, in Moorish style, and with straight roads." Bernáldez uses the urban features of Calicut common to western cities and above all the similarity of religion as key indicators for the understanding of a remote geographic reality about which little was known. His appreciation of the lifestyle of the local sovereign, of his palace impressive for its great order and of all the different types of body guards, provides a positive undertone to his account.

The economic factor figures in the *Memoirs*, appearing indeed to be a predominant aspect of the narration. In the city of Calicut, Bernáldez says, "there are many very rich Moorish merchants who have the monopoly trades with the king, who rules by relying on their support." Trading was very active in those seas that were filled with a great number of ships. These, however, generally lacked on-board artillery and weapons, showing an underdeveloped technique of ship-building. The many vessels, seemingly around 1500 in number, were small, never exceeding 60 tons. Each had only one mast and could navigate only in one direction.

Trade connections were made possible by many ships inside the big gulf off Calicut, the one crossed by the fleet of Da Gama, as the Andalusian parish priest points out.

Moreover, wishing to illustrate in more detail the Indian situation, Bernáldez states that in the gulf there were many populated places: cities, towns, and castles, all controlled by the power of the Moors. The region was rich in every sort of goods including, as he points out, some products brought from the Mediterranean coasts such as clothing material from Lucca or malmsey wine from Crete.

According to the author of the *Memoirs*, the presence of such merchandise from the West in Indian lands showed the existence of a well-organized trade between the Mediterranean, principally Cairo, and the Indian territories. Similarly, the presence in the Indian markets of Mediterranean coins is also reported with particular mention of, besides the golden seraphs of the sultan of Cairo "which weigh two or three grains less than a ducat," Italian coins such as "Venetian and Genoese ducats."

The impression one receives from reading these pages of Bernáldez's work is twofold. On the one hand, he expresses wonder about the intense commercial trade internal to the Indian region, its variety and quantity of products (his list, besides gold and spices, includes wheat, oxen and cows, different sorts of fruit and many types of plants and dyes); on the other hand, he implies great interest as well in the position of the Indian peninsula as an international commercial point with important consequences tied to the trade which that region could have for Portugal.

The opening by Da Gama of the Indian route is particularly emphasized by Bernáldez, since, as he himself states, "I wanted to put such an event in this book of memoirs because it happened right at the beginning." It seems that with these words he wishes to justify why he was writing, at times enthusiastically, about the accomplishments of a nation that was in competition with his own country with regard to trade expansion and the exploration of unknown, or very little known, territories to the west.

In his opinion, the breakthrough substantially consisted in the actual opening up of a new route which not only inaugurated new trade prospects for Portugal but also constituted a turning point in the history of mankind.

As for the voyages that followed, continuing the discovery of the Indian Ocean by the Portuguese — who during the reign of Manuel I expanded "still more in those regions, taking possession in his name of those territories and establishing a monopoly on trade" — Bernáldez gives a few thoughts on the new international situation that was launched on the commercial level.

Like the Portuguese chroniclers of the time, for instance João de Barros, who highlighted the economic advantages of the mid-fifteenth century Portuguese explorations, so Bernáldez emphasizes the importance of the Lusitanian voyages in terms of the commercially altered balance in the Mediterranean, although tending at the same time to exalt the Columbian discovery of the Indies, which would have equalled the Portuguese imports from Africa and India.

Even though the principal aim of the *Memoirs* was to expound on the most important happenings taking place during the reign of Ferdinand and Isabela, the curate of Los Palacios, by the mere fact of being an unofficial writer for the Crown was able to present an overall picture of the Portuguese explorations during the 1400s and the first decades of the 1500s very favorable to Portugal for their exploration of the African territories, the opening of the new Indian route and, also, its commercial implications. Bernáldez's major achievement lies in the wider perspective

of his work, which, having taken into account the accomplishments of the rival Iberian nation and having presented in his writing a vaster panorama — not limited to internal affairs or restricted for the purpose of a self-serving eulogistic account — did thus broaden the picture to include the most important events of his time, even those concerning other countries. He consequently was able to pick up on the most disparate news coming from different countries, simply capitalizing on what was of curious interest, odd, and in any case, extraordinary for the history of mankind and which happened to occur during his lifetime.

CHAPTER REFERENCES

DE BARROS, 2:1049-50.

DA GAMA.

BOORSTIN, *The Portuguese Discoverers*, 22-28.

BRULEZ.

CHAUNU, *La expansión*, 68-96.

A. CORTESÃO, "Discobrimento."

J. CORTESÃO, *Los Portugueses*, 502, 520.

DE MATOS PROENSA, 7-17.

DEVISSE, 4:725.

FERNÁNDEZ-ARMESTO, 217-22.

FERRO, 75-197.

MAGALHAES GODINHO, *L'économie*, 535-65.

MAGALHAES GODINHO, *Les grandes découvertes*, 46-49.

MONOD, *et al.*

MORALES PADRÓN, *Historia*, 51-61.

TAVIANI, *Cristoforo Colombo*, 1:70-84; 2:92-96, 103-07, 161-68.

XVI. – SPANISH JOURNEYS OF EXPLORATION: THE CANARIES

The islands of the Canary archipelago in ancient times were called *Insulae Fortunatae* ["Fortunate Islands"], though we do not have any information about them from that time. During the early Middle Ages and especially by the second half of the thirteenth century, the Genoese, lured mainly by African gold and Indian spices, often visited the ports of the Mediterranean and Atlantic Maghrib. And, thanks to the undertaking of the Vivaldi brothers in 1291, who had ventured, as is known, into the Ocean still farther southward than the already-known territories, in an attempt to reach India.

During one of these voyages along the Atlantic coast of Africa during the first decades of the 1300s, the Genoese Lanzarotto Maloncello rediscovered the Canary archipelago. Evidence of this trip can be found in Dulcert's 1339 map, which along with the contour of a few islands of the archipelago records the name of this Genoese. Between 1341 and 1342, the Canary Islands were reached by Portuguese, Majorcan, French, Castilian, English and Genoese expeditions without territorial conquest claims made by any of them. This situation lasted until 1344 when the Castilian Luis de Cerda claimed possession. In 1402 the Canary Islands were the goal of Norman and French nobles under the command of Jean de Béthencourt and Gadifer de la Salle who occupied them and presented them, in 1403, to the King of Castile. A few more decades would have to go by, however, before such discovery would turn into colonization and exploitation of the territory.

The situation becomes more complex when Enrique, the Infante of Portugal, resolved to take over the islands, indeed taking possession in 1448 with the title of "Senhor" [Lord]. The conflict with the Spanish starts in the years immediately following with the Portuguese capturing some Castilian ships which had been sent to the islands. This situation lasted through the years 1479-1480 when a treaty between the two Iberian nations was signed and ratified as the Alcacovas Treaty, leading to the

cessation of hostilities and the sharing between the two crowns of the territories and zones of influence.

The agreement settled that Spain owned "the Canary Islands and all the other islands of the area, either conquered or yet to be conquered," according to Bernáldez. The Azores, Madeira, the Cape Verde Islands and "the territories discovered and yet to be discovered and all the other islands that could be found and conquered beyond the Canary Islands toward Guinea," on the other hand, were to be under Portuguese authority.

The parish priest of Los Palacios devotes four chapters of the *Memoirs* to the overtaking of the Canaries by Ferdinand the Catholic; the description of the physical and geographical characteristics of the archipelago; the customs of its inhabitants; and, finally, the new situation after the conquest. The purpose of his reporting, aimed mainly at illustrating the time period in which the dispute for possession of the Canary Islands (protracted for decades against Portugal and the inhabitants of the islands) had been decided in favor of the Spanish monarchs, seems to be no different from the one that inspired his description of Columbus's accomplishments for the first two voyages. In both cases, Bernáldez's underlying desire to identify the most important events of his time and commit them to posterity is evident.

The events preceding the conquest of the archipelago had not produced a positive image of the Spanish. Overall, in different ways and times the Spanish are depicted by Bernáldez as being in a position of inferiority compared with the natives, who, on the contrary, are essentially fair and defiant in battle.

Bernáldez's conquest description is a reconstruction of the major turns in the struggle for possession of the Atlantic islands by the various rulers who held them since the early years of the fifteenth century. The bits of information he provides in his work are sometimes incomplete. With respect to the date of the conquest ascribed to "Mosen de Betancurt," for example, not only does he set it "more or less" around the year 1400, but in trying to clarify further, he actually refers to the ten-year reign of "King Enrique III, or to the inception of his son King Joao II's rule under guardianship begun in 1407 when he was 20 months old."

In recounting what happened, the *Memoirs* starts from the expedition of the "French captain" Béthencourt, who with his fleet would eventually take possession of Lanzarote, Fuerte Ventura, (La) Gomera and Hierro islands, after subjugating them. As it can be seen, the archipelago experienced various occupations before becoming the Catholic Sovereigns' possession.

Bernáldez narrates that the sale of the islands from the French captain to the Count of Niebla, Don Juan Alonso, and from the latter to Ferran Peraza, who ruled them until his death, allowed Castilian influence to begin, which continued under Peraza's daughter and her husband, Diego de Herrera, who assumed the title of Lords. Their descendants also became Lords of the Four Islands, but would be unable to conquer the three remaining islands of the archipelago due to the strong reaction of the natives, who tried to retain their independence.

Still according to the *Memoirs*, the Catholic Sovereigns Ferdinand and Isabela, being interested in conquering the islands in order to set up profitable plantations, sent a 500-man fleet to the archipelago under the command of Juan Rejón and Pedro de Algarve, who had serious disputes between them, causing the expedition to fail. Only later, with the captains Pedro de Vera and Alonso de Lugo, would the three islands be subjugated and Spanish rule imposed upon the remaining four islands.

The conquest of the Canary Islands, described by Bernáldez in its main stages, is enriched by interesting descriptions of the natives' customs and their reactions against the Spanish and of the natural environment of the islands and, moreover, by explanations of their geographical location: news that supplies the reader with an opportunity to understand the geographically far-away reality, which because of the Crown's desire for colonization, did, however, appear of interest to those who wanted to test their luck. Before its conquest, The Grand Canary was divided into two regions, Galda and Telde, each ruled by two authorities who, as Bernáldez explains, corresponded respectively to the king and the bishop. The king of Telde, aggressive and a champion of the independence of his territory, was the most important sovereign on the island and ruled a population more numerous than the rest of the region's.

The sovereign of Galda, on the other hand, soon showed his openness to yield and become a "friend of the Christians and...a vassal of the king of Castile," with whom he established a friendship later strengthened during the time he spent in Castile. Received with "great honors" by the Spanish Sovereigns, the Canarian chief promised them to reciprocate such friendship with his loyalty and support against the king of Telde.

Bernáldez seems quite interested in reporting the details of the events that took place on The Grand Canary in 1483 and led to a violent confrontation between the two regions. Of the information the Andalusian parish priest presents, most surprising to us is the situation of military inferiority of the Spanish compared to the natives, who — it is emphasized — are impressive for their courage as well as their arms, though primitive. The Canarian natives' superiority on the battle field is

in sharp contrast with the image of Spanish superiority over the Caribbean natives emphasized in the *Memoirs* throughout Columbus's voyages.

While narrating the various stages of the fight against the Canarians loyal to the king of Telde, Bernáldez does not hesitate to show the Spanish weakness. At first they had prevailed over their enemies only to be later ferociously attacked and suffer casualties, either killed by stones or forced to flee. Bernáldez stresses how a massacre was avoided only with the help of the king of Galda and his people. Two hundred people died, including the second officer in command, the Biscayan Michel, while the natives suffered only half that number of casualties.

Although in the end the Spanish prevailed, their lack of courage seems to be the basic theme of the entire account. The judgement, on the other hand, that the Andalusian parish priest voices toward the local people is definitely positive, on account of the strength shown, their honesty in keeping their agreements, their perseverance and skill in battle.

Bernáldez clarifies also that the episode of their deportation to Spain after they surrendered occurred only through deception. In June 1483, captain Pedro de Vera, letting the Canarians believe he was taking them on the caravels to Tenerife to supply them with clothes, deported them to Spain, landing in Cádiz. Actually, the parish priest points out, "had Pedro de Vera not taken the elder men of that island by deceit, it would have been an amazing feat subjugating them." Moreover, the territory's natural defenses would have almost guaranteed their resistance.

The Canarian community ruled by the king of Telde included women who were also subsequently sent to Spain, living at first in Seville in the Mijohar city-gate area. Subsequently, after the Castilians had already partially populated The Grand Canary, the original natives wishing to return were taken back to their home island. Those who returned, however, were forced to participate, side by side with the Spanish, in the conquest of Tenerife where, Bernáldez underscores, "many of them died."

The *Memoirs* then tersely concludes: "in such a way Don Ferdinand and Isabela took possession of The Grand Canary," certainly not a triumphant conclusion.

After outlining the basic features of the difficult and long fight of the Spanish against the natives, the parish priest of Los Palacios reports on the situation that developed in the island soon after the Spanish repopulation. Bernáldez supplies a detailed list of the names of the island territories and continues then with some considerations on the customs and habits of the Canarian people, once again in positive terms: indeed, they appear rather civilized, with their own "laws" and customs.

Even from the perspective of existing resources, Bernáldez points out that The Grand Canary transformation which followed soon after the Spanish conquest was also a result of the hard work of its inhabitants. The economic picture of the island is shown as particularly flourishing, rich in farms breeding lambs, goats and rabbits as well as with a well-developed agriculture, new vineyards and extensive sugar-cane cultivation. Overall, the results for the Spanish were finally positive: the Spanish Crown effectively initiated, with the possession of the Canarian archipelago, its program of exploration and colonization of new lands. A decade later, Columbus would reach, to use Morales Padrón's expression, the other "Canary Islands" which lay across the ocean.

CHAPTER REFERENCES

Gran Canaria, 43.
CHAUNU, *Sevilla*, 43, 44.
CIORANESCU, *Colón y Canarias*, 165-88.
DE MADARIAGA, *Vida*, 212-13.
DIFFLE AND WINIUS, 92-95.
FERNÁNDEZ - ARMESTO, 168-95.
FERRO, 68-70.
JULIEN, 4-8.
MORALES PADRÓN, *Historia*, 15-63.
MORALES PADRÓN, *Canarias*, 22, 67.
OTTE.
TAVIANO, *I viaggi*, 2:36-37.
VIERA Y CLAVIJO, 1:593-97.

XVII. – GOLD AND SPICES FROM THE AFRICAN AND ASIATIC VOYAGES

The Portuguese desire to reach various Western Sudan and Guinea locations in order to ensure their gold supply underscores a centuries-old precious metal supply problem for the West, a problem which during the late Middle Ages was confronted mainly by the Italian seafaring cities and by the Aragonese along the Mediterranean and the Atlantic coasts of Africa that were then known.

The Portuguese trade throughout the fifteenth century, characterized by the principal need of securing gold from the African coastal area south of Cape Bojador, is to be considered a direct consequence or derivation of the contemporary trading by Mediterranean merchants with the ports of Northern Africa. In reality, there were no substantial changes in the Portuguese methods of securing gold other than their getting closer to its areas of production.

For the trade, then as before, the gold was mined and hauled to the coast by the natives where it was exchanged for a variety of merchandise. Actually, the Portuguese had no intention, no more than they had later in the Americas, of reaching the inland gold-producing areas or directly exploiting them through the natives.

The only real difference or novelty in the Portuguese expeditions was their much-improved profit, obtained by avoiding all the dangers posed by a long and costly supply-caravan through the Sahara, which the merchants had to face before reaching the Mediterranean ports.

Reporting on the expeditions ordered by the Kings of Portugal along the Atlantic coast of Africa, Bernáldez considers exclusively the importation of gold. He does not mention any other motivation or consequence achieved by the Portuguese trade, for instance, the slave trade, which nevertheless was fundamental to contemporary Portuguese chroniclers. The slavery issue and, in general, all the economic advantages related to Portuguese exploration are better understood within the framework and attention the author of the *Memoirs* devotes to the theme of the quest for

and subsequent finding of gold by Columbus during his first two voyages to the Indies.

The statements Bernáldez makes with regard to the Portuguese discoveries do not at all diminish the importance he attaches in his writing to the wealth the Spanish Crown stood to gain from the gold found by Columbus in the Indies. The author views the two discoveries, the Columbian and the Portuguese, as arising from the same curiosity about faraway lands and countries as well as the inherent economic profits connected to them.

With regard to the goals and the methods employed to get the precious metal from Guinea, Bernáldez stresses that they were not expeditions aimed at the colonization of new lands as was the case with the Spanish in the Canary Islands and even later in the Antilles. As stated earlier, the Portuguese did not intend to conquer the interior of Africa, the regions where the gold was mined, nor did the Portuguese sovereigns want to improve their authority over the gold mining in those areas.

The gold imported simply reflected the *rescate*, i.e. the amount of gold obtained "from the black population in all those regions...who brought it to make exchanges." The trading took place without any imposition or pressure and, referring to the native traders, Bernáldez explicitly states that the exchange was made "out of their spontaneous will and desire." The Portuguese usually exchanged goods of little value to Western people but which, on the contrary, "the natives valued highly."

In order to secure the gold supply for Portugal — whose profits, as the curate does not conceal, brought "the highest wealth and fame" — the Portuguese rebuilt a fortress, their São Jorge da Mina stronghold, in which to gather the gold destined for importation. This fortress, in addition to those already built, actually became the center of the Portuguese gold trade on the African coast. The import of gold from the Mina (as it was generally referred to by the chroniclers) reached its peak between 1480 and 1521.

This Portuguese monopoly, sanctioned by a bull of Pope Nicholas V in 1454, is illustrated — from different perspectives — starting as early as the time of the building of the previous Portuguese fortress in Arguim, according to the reports of the Venetian merchant Alvise da Ca' da Mosto and the Portuguese Diego Gomes. Both had personally participated in some of the expeditions ordered by the Portuguese Crown in the years 1455-56 along the African coasts.

The activity that took place at the Mina, discussed in detail in the *Memoirs* because of the amount of gold it provided for the Portuguese

Crown, did permit the Portuguese expansion in other territories where they could establish their gold monopoly. It seems unimportant to Bernáldez to linger upon the many expeditions made in those decades and to remember the names of the main figures who participated in them. In treating the question of Portuguese gold his unique reference is to the Sovereigns who supervised the important African undertakings. Likewise, in describing the Columbian expeditions, he mostly describes the events that occurred in the Indies, only to stress the ultimate wealth that would come to the Spanish Crown.

The Lusitanian expeditions, on the other hand, had only one other focus of interest for the parish priest of Los Palacios: the spices. As is known, because of their variety and use in several economic areas, from the food industry to textiles, spices had become during the late Middle Ages one of the most commercially valuable cargos for ships that crossed the Mediterranean.

When in 1368 China's Ming Dynasty enacted an isolationist policy, closing its trade with the West, importing spices from the Indian peninsula, both those produced there and those which arrived there from regions more or less distant, became quite more important to the European markets than previously. And, the opening up by the Portuguese of a new route to India which would allow a direct supply of the precious oriental products became all the more urgent, as it is commonly acknowledged, after the total Turkish conquest of the Byzantine Empire that created new customs problems far more severe than in the past, greatly disturbing trade for Italian cities.

Bernáldez claims that Calicut, Da Gama's landing place in the Malabar region and the most important commercial center of a vast resupply and trading area, "has every sort of spice" and that its market price is particularly low: "a five-quintal weight of cinnamon costs only ten or twelve golden ducats. And, there are pepper and cloves for the same price and ginger for less than half that."

A great many flat and small boats hauled spices there from the surrounding islands many leagues away. As already indicated, with his words the Andalusian parish priest highlights the existence of an intense mercantile trade in the Indian Ocean directed toward the West through the Red Sea, Mecca and Cairo.

Bernáldez shows little interest in the Portuguese permanence in India and his description is confined to a few hints relating to how well-received were the Lusitanians by the local authorities.

The Red Sea route remained the principal route followed by the spice traders coming from India until the new Portuguese route along

the African continent became established. Though attributing fair importance to Da Gama's undertaking, Bernáldez still points to the traditional route followed, highlighting its importance (see note on Portuguese explorations). From his account, the city of Cairo seems to be the place where "most of those spices, as well as many other kinds of merchandise, converged," and he gives a detailed list of them.

After noting the importance retained by the Red Sea route for a certain period of time, the ecclesiastic of Los Palacios describes the period following the first Portuguese journeys to India, confirming what he had already hinted at in a previous chapter. Namely, he stresses how in that period arose the first serious difficulties in the importation of the spices destined for the northern cities of Egypt. Cairo and Alexandria experienced then a commercial collapse, caused by the scarcity of supplies coming from the Orient which also involved other cities depending on the same traders. Bernáldez explicitly states that Manuel II, King of Portugal "sent his army many times through that way [the African route]. The spice-related wealth was greatly damaging to the sultan of Cairo and Babylon, the enemy of the holy Catholic faith; it caused a collapse of his revenues...."

Thus, the precarious situation that ensued in the Mediterranean supply is recognized as a negative consequence directly linked to the stabilization of the Portuguese trade in India. With respect to this point Bernáldez is quite explicit when he maintains that the Mediterranean cities, primarily Italian ones, were commercially penalized by the newly established mercantile center of Lisbon, which obtained Indian products at lower costs. This damaged the trade of the "merchants of Venice, Genoa and Florence, the richest in the world, who went to Alexandria to load the above-mentioned spices and merchandise to distribute throughout all of Latin Christianity, that is France, Germany, Spain, England, Flanders...." Thus, Bernáldez recognizes that Spain, like the other European nations, experienced negative economic consequences from the increased Portuguese trade with India.

Although describing the wealth acquired by the Spanish through the Columbian discovery of gold in the Antilles, contrasting the African gold and Indian spices imported by the Lusitanians, Bernáldez's in his thinking is exempt from hostile feelings about the resulting disputes regarding the Atlantic hegemony. Overall, however, his description of the first two Columbian voyages shows a comprehensive evaluation of the economic advancement of the two Iberian nations, and anticipates a new balance against the previously greater Portuguese power; thanks to Columbus's gold, the Catholic Sovereigns shall become, as we read in the *Memoirs*, "the richest and most influential sovereigns on earth."

CHAPTER REFERENCES

DA MOSTO, 24-27, 32-36.
BENASSAR, 109-10.
BLOCH, 151.
BRAUDEL, *La Méditerranée*, 361-69.
BRULEZ, 314, 315.
CHAUNU, *L'expansión*, 270, 271.
A. CORTESÃO, "Espionagem," 1:41.
DE LA TORRE.
DE MEDEIROS, 176.
FERNÁNDEZ - ARMESTO, 141, 144, 146.
FERRO, 192-97.
HEERS, *Christophe Colomb*, 108-22.
MAGALHAES GODINHO, *L'économie*, 173-217, 535-37.
PICOLO.
RICH, 357.
UNALI, 317-43.
VILAR, 63-77.

XVIII. – THE FIGURE OF CHRISTOPHER COLUMBUS

From the beginning of his account concerning the Spanish voyages of exploration to the Indies, Bernáldez focuses on the figure and actions of Christopher Columbus, emphasizing more his character than any accomplishment. Columbus is portrayed by the parish priest of Los Palacios, who knew Columbus as his house-guest, to be the very symbol of the Spanish discovery and first colonization of the "recently-found islands." The most detailed part of Bernáldez's account of what took place in the Indies is the embodiment of the most important moments of the Admiral's activity: the first two voyages.

Indeed, Columbus's last two voyages do not have in the *Memoirs* the same prominence as the two earlier ones, not because the former should not be considered equally noteworthy in their consequences for the Spanish Crown, but because they were already part of the decline of the Genoese's glory. Thus, the Andalusian parish priest identifies the years of Columbus's highest success with the zenith of the Spanish discoveries.

Bernáldez's interest in recounting events occurring in the Indies falls to nearly nothing for the last two expeditions, when his only considerations are limited to following the key events involving Columbus. Moreover, in his work, the parish priest of Los Palacios merely hints at other voyages that paralleled those of Columbus — except for a single instance — whereas he had described in great detail the previous Spanish expeditions aimed at the discovery and conquest of the Canary Islands. Although his writing encompasses events up to 1513, his account regarding the voyages actually ends with the Admiral's inglorious demise in 1506.

The issue that the curate presents first in describing the characteristic moments of the navigator's life is his Genoese origin.

Actually, in all of the manuscripts of the *Memoirs* that have reached us, the phrase "man from Genoa" is reported, except for the one reference which is reproduced in this volume, where he is indicated as being "from Milan." Such variance, corroborated by the testimony of other

manuscripts and other parts of the *Nuova Raccolta*, can be historically explained by events taking place in Genoa in the second half of the 1400s. The Ligurian Republic was at that period experiencing a rather uncertain political moment during which the protection by the Milanese *Signoria* alternated with its own rule.

The same manuscript, within the part announcing the Admiral's death, reports the same expression a second time.

In two other passages of the *Memoirs* there are indications about Columbus's home country. The first one does not explicitly mention Genoa, but the Admiral's origin foreign to the Spanish world is seen by the parish priest of Los Palacios as the reason for the hostile attitude of many of those who participated in his third expedition to the Indies. In fact, Bernáldez maintains that misunderstandings about Columbus's enterprise derived from "the fact he was from another country."

The second passage instead specifies his Genoese birth, thus clarifying which nation Bernáldez was referring to in the first one. The episode in which such biographical information is given concerns the accusations brought forward by the Spanish during the third voyage. A few of his opponents, motivated by their hatred of Columbus, went so far as to consider the possibility, in the parish priest's words, that Columbus intended to betray the Spanish Sovereigns, imagining he "hid gold, wishing to become Lord of the Island (Hispaniola); others believed he wanted to donate it to the Genoese...." This detail in the *Memoirs*, which was certainly not written to clarify his birthplace, is a further indisputable attestation of the Genoese origin of the Admiral of the Ocean Sea.

The date of birth of the Genoese, which historians commonly place in 1450-1451, is not reported by the Andalusian curate specifically in his writing and he erroneously holds (perhaps due to Columbus's prematurely white hair) that Columbus was 70 years old at the time of his death.

That Columbus was Genoese probably meant, also for the Andalusian parish priest, in light of a generalization popular in the late Middle Ages, that he possessed the two basic characteristics ascribed to the people from that Ligurian city: skills in the art of navigation and trade. Columbus is presented by Bernáldez as personifying this double quality, and in the *Memoirs* only the most important moments of his life are recalled: early on as a book merchant without formal training, though a man of great intelligence who studied the problems of his culture with determination and used the experience he acquired as a mariner and cartographer — to the point of being able to, later on, take advantage of his gifts and skills together with knowledge from his reading of different authors, such as Ptolemy and John Mandeville, and seize the opportunity to be heard by

the Spanish Sovereigns as well as to be able to carry out his plan, elaborated from intuition and objective data accumulated over time that gave him the certainty he would fulfill his expectations.

Moreover, the parish priest underscores Columbus's "reasoning ability" as the element which allowed him to interconnect issues being debated in his time while pointing out how the Portuguese, who had also tried to achieve the same objectives by travelling westward in the ocean, did not reach any land, notwithstanding their skill. Bernáldez frequently highlights Columbus's genius, making him out to be the author of a world map to which, he claims, Columbus devoted "much study" and which he used to trace the plan he conceived and that "aroused in them [Ferdinand and Isabela] the desire to know more about those lands."

The arguments given to understand his early convictions and the plan later elaborated are based on the spherical nature of the earth, which "is steady in the center of the globe" and can be "fully circumnavigated." In addition to such rudimentary cosmological enunciation, which Bernáldez says is a product of the Genoese's thinking, we find a practical purpose: among the reasons that prompted men to sail and reach the unknown lands across the ocean is the quest for gold, as the parish priest of Los Palacios maintains. After presenting Columbus's claim to be able to reach the Asiatic continent also by sailing west, he makes him say that "by so doing a land with much gold would be found."

The connection between these two points, seemingly opposite, appears in another passage of his work: "and he was convinced that by sailing or crossing the ocean sea in whatever direction, he would not fail to find land and believed much gold would be found in such land." Columbus's speculative intuition thus appears to be interpreted by the Andalusian ecclesiastic as a direct outcome of economic motivations and, quite specifically, his quest for gold.

The *Memoirs'* meager reconstruction of the events which led Columbus to obtain the authorization by the Catholic Sovereigns to start his voyage westward across the ocean reflects the traditional version of those events. Columbus's proposal to the Portuguese Sovereign, Joao II, who "very much liked to discover"; the King's refusal, after consultation with the skilled seafarers of his kingdom and who disagreed with a plan they considered impractical; the request presented to the Spanish Catholic rulers, Ferdinand and Isabela, who were at first reluctant to consider his plan viable, but were later convinced by "learned men, astrologists, astronomers and cosmography scholars" that Columbus "was speaking the truth" — all these are topics related to events that preceded the Columbian enterprises and are commonly found in the chronicles of the time.

The ensuing account of Columbus's life is thus nothing more than an impersonal and concise retelling of events which, surprisingly, Bernáldez, who had met the Admiral, does not seem to enrich with a commentary on the difficult years that preceded Columbus's journeys to the Indies and that would have revealed the friendship he had with Columbus. In any case, we must keep in mind that since his account is based on works by several authors, it is therefore conceivable that even in regard to this period Bernáldez preferred to use only information coming from them.

The opinion of the parish priest of Los Palacios on Columbus's activity is generally positive throughout the entire work. Only in a few instances does he wear the cloak of a severe judge, criticizing some of the Admiral's decisions and ideas. With respect to the possibility of reaching the lands of the Grand Khan, the Andalusian ecclesiastic, using the writings of John Mandeville (see note on sources), once more rejects Columbus's belief that he could reach Cathay as planned. This observation concerning the time period of the Genoese's return from his second voyage shows a latent disagreement between them wider than its specific geographic issue, indeed encompassing an entire plan that in some ways was not only unconvincing but so badly formulated as to appear quite impossible to fulfill.

Another episode that possibly leads us to consider Bernáldez to be leaning to a certain extent in favor of Columbus's detractors is his description of the meeting of the Admiral with an old Indian where the author's expressions of apparently affable reproach are addressed to the Admiral. Though the source of this passage turns out to be a literal quotation of Columbus himself, it seems interesting that Bernáldez included it in his work. Its mere presence is in any case, though unintentionally for the parish priest of Los Palacios, indeed a permanent criticism as it was brought forward against the Admiral's actions right at the end of his second voyage.

Specifically, Bernáldez tells how Columbus and his men arrived, after sailing a part of the White Sea to the Ornofay region, in "a mountainous and most fertile land, mainly inhabited by very mild people." There, the Admiral met a local cacique, "who was a very respected man and chief of numerous people and of a large family." The description of various moments of this encounter are related with particularly emotional involvement.

The image of the Genoese being welcomed by the cacique, who held his hand while "another Indian, more than eighty years old, held his other hand showing great excitement," and, again, the atmosphere of serenity conveyed by their walking while holding one another's hands with "all

the other Indians walking behind them" are building to a moment in which Bernáldez reports the cacique's speech to Columbus in which the cacique himself — fully aware of being "daring," basically makes two points — he tells Columbus not to be boastful and not to think himself immortal.

Essentially this matched the thinking of the Admiral's detractors. The Indian reminded him not to be "boastful, for although all the people feared him, still he remained a mortal being like all other men" and, like everyone else, he would die. Further, he was charging Columbus with a flight from reality, of no longer being able to correctly evaluate what was happening around him.

The words used by Columbus to reply to the charges of considering himself an extraordinary man, thus able to strike at will those he thought were in the wrong, fall quite short of removing the suspicion of guilt of what he was accused of. Columbus's answer is an attempt to defend himself from the accusations brought forward against him. He maintains he had not "harmed anyone nor intended to harm good people, but only punish the bad ones." But in so stating he merely inspires a new element of repression with his words.

Advocating for himself the authority to distinguish between bad and good people in order to punish the latter while rewarding the others was unacceptable to many people. This attitude of rejection and rebellion against Columbus's behavior on the part of those who had previously believed in the realization of his plans and their own personal enrichment signals the beginning of a new dissatisfaction, leading to Columbus's growing isolation and loss of trust, even on the part of the Sovereigns, which will constitute the determining factor of his fall out of grace.

CHAPTER REFERENCES

COLÓN, *Carta-Relación de 26 febrero 1495*, 2:487-515.
D'AVEZAC.
HEERS, *Gênes*, 193-206.
MANSELLI, "Cristoforo Colombo."
Raccolta Colombiana, pt. 2, 1:112.
TAVIANI, *Cristoforo Colombo*, 2:24-27.
TAVIANI, *La genovesità*, 67-78.
THACHER, 4, 6.

XIX. – CHRISTOPHER COLUMBUS'S FIRST TWO VOYAGES TO THE INDIES

The events which took place during the four voyages that the Genoese navigator undertook in the period 1492-1504 do not enjoy a balanced presentation in the organization of Bernáldez's work, since their treatment varies both in terms of richness of details provided and importance of interpretation. In fact, the events of the second voyage have far more weight than those reported on the other expeditions, both for length and degree of interest shown. The part devoted to the first voyage, presenting the figure of Columbus and introducing the westward expeditions across the ocean has a certain prominence also in the work, though it leaves the impression of being considered less important than the second crossing.

The first two parts of the account of the Columbian enterprise have not been thought of in the same way as those that chronologically follow and which Bernáldez deals with quite briefly, limiting himself to concisely treat some essential events.

With respect to this it must be remembered that, by admission of the author as well as from an objective comparison of the sources, Bernáldez's description of the second voyage sometimes contains passages that very slavishly reproduce Diego Alvarez de Chanca's report. Chanca had personally taken part in the expedition and left in writing his impressions about the early Spanish stay in Hispaniola up to the time Antonio Torres left on a mission to Spain to obtain supplies.

Even though the period of time covered was short, the importance given to what happened in those months in relation to the natives, the quest for gold and the founding of La Isabela — to cite only the most important moments spent on the island — is evident in its lengthy exposition. It must in any case be underscored that the second part relating the settlement of the new city, the finding of gold in Cibao and the exploration of other islands in the Antilles and encompassing chronologically a two-year period until 1496 is equally lengthy. And, though

necessarily differing from the first in the general tone of the narrative, given the different sources examined, it proves accurate and especially rich in emotional involvement for the events recounted.

The main source used by Bernáldez for the second part of his work is the account of the voyage by Columbus himself, which the parish priest claims to have had at his disposal when Columbus lived with him.

His knowledge of Columbus's *Letter-Report* is also confirmed another time in the *Memoirs* in connection with subjects foreign to men like the parish priest of Los Palacios, unskilled in navigation, namely, the various speeds of a caravel and the skill of a good pilot. According to Bernáldez, his sources for these topics were the sailors themselves, who talked to him about the leagues that can be travelled "on long and on short days... in accordance with what they themselves were saying and the Admiral himself... wrote in the book that deals with it."

In Bernáldez's account of the first Columbian expedition to the Indies, Christopher Columbus is constantly praised for his gifts of firmness, intuition and determination, which made him persuasive and reassuring in the most difficult moments and which are commented on without particular emphasis. On the contrary, the positive events and the descriptions of nature are reported with plenty of details, often with superlatives, as is noticeable from one of the passages on Hispaniola's beauty: "this island appeared far more beautiful than all the others, since there are many incomparably better ports along the coast, among the best that can be found in Christendom, and many wide rivers amazing to see."

The natural description of the regions observed, however, was in many cases accompanied by utilitarian considerations for "their luxuriance and fertility," in other words because "those lands would prove to be of great utility and profit, suitable for cultivation, seeding and production of wheat, trees and breeding livestock brought here from Spain."

The narration is normally flowing and unencumbered by the author's judgements or reflections. The only episode on which Bernáldez lingers to show some of its implications involves the reported rumors concerning his reason for leaving some people in Hispaniola while the fleet set out to return to Spain after the first crossing. Bernáldez says that the Admiral's decision was not caused, as he wanted it to be believed (pointing out that the reason "was kept secret"), by a desire to begin populating and colonizing the island, but because "having lost a ship, it was not possible to take all of them back."

At any rate, the overall evaluation of Columbus's actions during this first expedition is positive and it is even more evident in the warm

welcome the Spanish Sovereigns reserved to the Genoese and their awarding him the title of Admiral, which not only gratified him for accomplishments in his first undertaking but also generated in him great expectations for the future.

With regard to the second expedition from its beginning to Torres's return trip, Bernáldez's observations provide variations to Chanca's text. It is revealing to dwell on two of them. The first concerns the causes of the Christians' deaths, on which the curate insists on elaborating the different hypotheses formulated to explain this crime: on the one hand, the general disagreement which occurred because the men were having relations with several Indian women, thereby provoking the natives' reaction, who had therefore killed out of jealousy; and, on the other hand, those unspecified "unreasonable actions" that were allegedly committed by the Christians in Hispaniola.

His desire to determine the truth on this subject must have led Bernáldez to expound on these formulated guesses.

The second digression from Chanca's report concerns the setting up and the goals of the second voyage, which is mainly shown in its economic aspect: "the Admiral took with him on this voyage seventeen vessels... four ships and thirteen caravels, with 1300 soldiers to settle there in order to continue the conquest; and brought 24 stallions, ten mares, three mules, hogs, sows, calves, goats, sheep and all they needed for breeding...." In the same passage Columbus's position toward the exploitation of gold is shown as well: one reads in the *Memoirs* that he intended "to take it for the king and queen, either with the consent of the inhabitants or by force." Throughout his description Bernáldez is still inclined to agree with and approve of Columbus's attitude and actions, understanding his aims and the means used to achieve them.

In his account of the events that took place after February 1494, based on Columbus's own writings, generally one notices an increased attention, besides that given the Admiral's decisions and opinions, to the contemplation of nature which in a few passages stands out for its magnificence, occasionally reaching poetic tones.

More frequent, however, are also references to Columbus's behavior, which as time went by became more and more difficult due to the generally changed environmental and humanly complex situation, compared with that at the end of the first voyage, which had aroused in the expedition's participants radically different expectations.

The punishments adopted in Hispaniola by Columbus's uncompromising attitude against those who were found guilty of disobedience led in some cases to forced returns in chains to Spain, and they are approved

and supported by the parish priest of Los Palacios as fair conduct. This happened, for example, also to Formin Zedo, the gold expert who had underestimated the value of the gold found in Hispaniola to maintain it was melted gold. Relying "upon the truth that came to light later," in reporting Columbus's stand, Bernáldez is still of the opinion that the censures against him were unfounded.

His description of the events concerning the second expedition ends in the *Memoirs* with a list of the products Columbus had brought back after a nearly two-year stay in the Indies: objects used by the natives; necklaces and other decoration; the Taino men, including a certain Don Diego — Caonabó's brother, baptized with a Spanish name — who, at Columbus's request, wore a huge golden necklace weighing 600 *castellanos* around his neck, and displayed it whenever they entered a city. Bernáldez gives testimony to having held this necklace in his own hands at the time the Admiral stayed with him in Los Palacios.

Columbus lived in Castile and Aragon for one year, waiting for the appropriate moment to sail again. The Andalusian ecclesiastic explains that the Catholic Sovereigns' indecision before granting authorization to leave was mainly due to the war against France. So, once again, Bernáldez avoids mentioning any charge leveled against the Admiral without, however, hiding some shortcomings of the Columbian enterprise that was dotted with human and economic difficulties: scarcity of gold, excessive costs compared to profits, lack of food supplies and, finally and most serious of all, the by now rampant general hostility toward Columbus's record.

With such recognition, the evaluation by the parish priest of Los Palacios of the Genoese's undertakings begins a gradual mutation that clearly acknowledges the controversy raised by the adversarial positions, without renouncing his fundamentally balanced, independent judgement through the voicing of appreciation. The proof of a changed situation and of his own reservations about Columbus is in Bernáldez's underscored reference to the Catholic Sovereigns' surprising decision "to grant license to many captains who decided to go discovering new lands...." The situation that had evolved, was now more difficult for the Admiral in many respects and — as Bernáldez himself concedes — this moment marked the beginning of an irreparable decline of Columbus's fortune.

CHAPTER REFERENCES

Colón, *Carta-Relación de 26 febrero 1495*, 2:511-12.
Ballesteros Beretta, 2:22-31.
De Madariaga, 361-78.
Morales Padrón, *Historia*, 133-38.
Morison, *Admiral*, 447, 451, 474-76.
Morison, *European Discovery*, 99-139.
Palacio and Durán, 391-92.
Parry, 204-5.
Taviani, *I viaggi*, 1:92-102.

XX. – THE NATIVES

Among the subjects discussed in reports of voyages of exploration, chronicles and other similar writings involving the same topic, the aspects commanding greatest attention are the physical appearance, customs and habits of the natives in the newly discovered lands. The curiosity and imagination of all writers — those reporting their first-hand impressions and thoughts about what they saw; those whose accounts relied upon oral or written primary sources; as well as, finally, those authors who used total fiction — were especially aroused by the distinctive behavioral and physical characteristics of the natives in the territories under scrutiny and by the substantial differences from western civilization clearly detected in most aspects of their living.

The attitude of the writers toward these peoples, even though they all were dealing with the same reality, was never consistent, showing instead a high degree of variation depending on their subjective way of observing the natives, reflecting the feelings and intentions of each author.

In addition to these personal considerations, which varied according to the individuals and the purposes of their works, many other contributing factors must be taken into account which, over time, modified the explorers' attitudes and consequently altered the relationships they established with the natives in the final analysis. For instance, the good will or the aggressiveness exhibited by the natives toward them in their first encounters would condition, for better or for worse, their exchanges with the local people.

In describing the Indians the curate employs two methods, generally common to the travel literature genre. Through the first method are presented some behavioral aspects of the natives in an uninvolved way, as if dealing with objective information while detailing their main characteristics. The second method weaves these characteristics into the narrative context, making them an integral part of it.

Bernáldez gives a portrait of naive, mild and cooperative Indians; others are seen as ferocious, aggressive and bestial in their habits. They

are generally presented positively except in the case of the cannibals of those regions, the Caribs, who are branded with an essentially negative judgement.

One of the habits reported immediately, as if it were a common denominator of the natives of the various islands observed, is their nudity. The description of both men and women gives much attention to physical details and the different sorts of decorations which adorned their bodies. Bernáldez exhibits repeated amazement, in several passages of his work, in noticing that such nudity did not arouse in them any shame and that they acted just "like Castilians who go around dressed."

His assertion concerning nakedness will become a topos in the travel literature and, occasionally, amount to an exaltation of the natives' bodily characteristics. The Portuguese Pero Vaz de Caminha, for example, in his *Carta de achamento* of 1500, in describing Brazilian women, highlighted the beauty of their bodies, which he considered far superior to that of women in his country.

Bernáldez, too, relying on what he had learned from those returning from the Indies and Columbus's own writings available to him, lingers on Indian beauty, especially upon the women's features as well as their way of adorning themselves.

His account is clearly sensitive to some memorable responses of these people. For instance, in reporting on the second voyage, the Andalusian ecclesiastic, who used as a source the Admiral's February 26, 1495 *Letter-Report*, tells a story of the cacique whom Columbus had met and who wanted to take his family and go to Castile aboard one of the Spanish ships, having been lured largely either by what the Indians who had previously gone to Spain had told him or, as he himself admitted, out of fear his own land would be conquered by Columbus.

The description of the arrival of the canoes of the Indian who was in this way planning to leave his island is full of lyricism. The passage is suggestive in its many details concerning the physical appearance and the embellishment of the people. Bernáldez is fully taken by this event, responding quite positively. He takes considerable pleasure in detailing astonishing elements, which gives this passage an underlying literary unity enhanced by lovely images and the incorporation of elements normally neglected.

The observations, clearly showing emotional involvement, had to have been borrowed from one of the members of the expedition, perhaps Columbus himself, who so intensely believed in the undertaking to the point of being capable of rendering through poetic images the reality he experienced. Also in this case one is reminded of his Journal for the

previous voyage, given the similarity here to the narrative contained in his description of nature as observed during the first expedition. Bernáldez's *Memoirs* is enriched by this episode, although it happens too frequently here that his account repeats Columbus's own descriptions without substantial changes.

Both Indian men and women are described while taking part in a ceremonial event. The most colorful canoes, the flag bearer who "stood alone on the first boat," his outfit made "of many-colored feathers shaped as a tabard," the huge plume head-piece he wore and "the plain white flag" in his hand, the adornment of two Indians also with big plumes over their heads and "a painted tablet on their forehead," and of two other ones also similarly made up and bearing primitive musical instruments and "little wooden trumpets, extremely well worked in the shape of birds or other elaborate shapes..." (to cite only some of the most suggestive images) give the impression of being in "cultural" situations that, though far from western ones, had their well-established rituals and responded to not-at-all primitive symbolism.

His description of the cacique, his wife and their two daughters becomes even more detailed. Bernáldez, in describing the necklace the man wore, reports about its shape as well as the metal with which it was made and the place where it had been mined, commenting even on the jewel which hung from it. "Shaped like a giant flat lily flower," the necklace in the *Memoirs* was "worn on his neck with a string of big nuggets like marble stones they also highly valued."

Describing the wreath the man wore on his head, Bernáldez highlights "the minute green and many-colored stones" as well as the large size of the stones on the inside and the fact that "in the central part, some were white...." As for the ear jewelry: "from his ears hung two golden tablets and strings of smaller green nuggets," and, finally the belt, "worked like a wreath," whereas the rest of the body was bare.

An equal attention to detail characterizes, in this parade of images, his illustration of the women. To make some elements of their adornment more recognizable, Bernáldez compares them to the clothing used by western women. For instance, "the thick cotton bands" the cacique's wife wore "around her arms near the armpits" recall for the writer the "sleeves of ancient bodices of French women."

The nudity of the cacique's daughters is also referred to in all its beauty in the *Memoirs*: "the elder daughter, the most beautiful, walked completely naked, except for a string of small black stones worn as a belt from which hung, at the end, a leaf-like ornament in the shape of ivy, made of green and other colored stones, sewn onto a cotton fabric."

In regard to the Indians' custom of going around naked, the *Memoirs* remarks that the Spanish accepted nudity or, at least, that it did not amount to an obstacle in their exchanges. According to the Andalusian parish priest, such a tolerant attitude was later preserved when 500 Indians, men and women, were taken prisoners and sent to Spain the second time Columbus sent the vessels back to Spain in 1494, where they "arrived, in accordance with the country's custom, naked as at their birth, showing no greater uneasiness than animals do."

Obviously, Bernáldez's acceptance of the naturalness of their nakedness should not be misinterpreted as licentiousness; he is mere offering a display or "sample" of novelties found in those distant lands, just as he would any other objects and animals brought from the Indies.

This consideration leads one to suppose that the positive evaluation of the natives was quite circumscribed. They were generally viewed simply as products of those lands to be displayed as proof of achievements by the Columbian enterprise or as a source of labor to be exploited for the mining of gold. This judgement seems confirmed when Bernáldez says shortly afterwards that "all of them were sold, but they turned out to be a poor investment...."

The subject of nudity surfaces once again in the *Memoirs* in connection with an odd belief reported by Columbus to be alive among the Indians of Ornofay: according to him the natives maintained that in Magón "all the people had tails and for that reason they wore clothes."

The curate of Los Palacios compares this rumor to another one gathered — as he testifies — from John Mandeville's work, which reported that "all the people of the Indies, in the Mori province, go around totally naked and they make fun of those who dress up, saying that those people do not believe in God, He having created our progenitors Adam and Eve naked and claiming that nobody should be ashamed of what is natural." Bernáldez does not take a position on the subject of nudity so treated by Mandeville but merely repeats without commentary what is reported by him.

The detailed characterization of the physical appearance of the Antillian people — "broad faces and brows, round heads as wide, from side to side, as from front to back, with very black and loose hair," medium height, dark complexion, "more white than black" — is a great improvement over the general description of the natives made on the first voyage. The hair-styles and the dyes used to adorn their bodies and faces to make them look more frightful were of different sorts depending on the tribes. Beardlessness was a common characteristic. All of the above features, taken partly from Chanca's report, are mentioned several times by Bernáldez in his work.

The women's "dress" was quite limited given their near complete nudity, amounting to merely tiny pieces of cloth or tree leaves held by strings to cover "out of prudery... their lower part." According to the parish priest of Los Palacios, there was a difference between the girls and the women who had already given birth: the latter "wore a cotton band around their hips down to the middle of their thighs," as was mentioned in the report of the first expedition.

The opinion that Bernáldez has of these people, gathered as it was from travelers' reports and impressions concerning the physical appearance of the Indians brought to Spain (we must remember that when Columbus was his guest, Caonabó's brother, called Don Diego, was with him), is not general or uniform, but it varies depending — as I said — not only on the sources used but also on the narrative context. At the beginning of the second voyage it is noticeable how he simply follows more closely Chanca's approach with an attitude of detachment reaffirmed by the realization that the men left at La Navidad were murdered.

Chanca's suspicion does not change, because he is describing an encounter that covered a brief period of time. Bernáldez, instead, besides including considerations taken from the Sevillian physician, reports some positive remarks about the natives in his narration following the foundation of La Isabela.

The parish priest of Los Palacios, following Columbus's account in listing the natives' limitations, does not view the latter in terms prejudicial to their intellectual capability. Their primitive way of life, the mindless inability to protect their bodies, the ignorance of their own territory, unaware as they were whether it was an island or mainland, as well as their nudity are all elements coloring his account and are meant to be an unbiased consideration of their intellectual capacity.

A proof of this is the already-cited episode involving the elderly cacique, who, showing wisdom and abstract reasoning capability, typifies a native awareness of spirituality. He advised Columbus to behave accordingly, reminding him he was a mortal being with an immortal soul and that "the latter suffered as a consequence of the ill behavior from each mortal part," having to "meet either the heavenly king or the ruler of the earth's abyss, depending on the good or evil accomplished throughout one's lifetime."

This Indian's awareness of important issues surrounding death convinced Bernáldez and earlier Columbus himself that the people of those lands, "thought seemingly primitive and practicing nudity," had "remarkable reasoning power." The curate further develops this conviction by stressing that the Indians went "for learning new things," provoking

in "all of them great pleasure and enduring satisfaction." Bernáldez thus points out their thirst for knowledge, which cannot but originate "from a lively intellect and sharp perceptual ability."

His praise of the Indians of those regions, at least in this case, no longer shows detachment or intellectual condescension, nor an implied statement of the Christians' superiority, which is nonetheless generally present in other passages of his work. Though Bernáldez addresses also the cultural limits of their intellectual curiosity, given the natives' "lack of education, unawareness of law, history, reading, writing and therefore their great ignorance," he still — despite all of this — appreciates their desire to learn. Bernáldez further documents the natives' desire for knowledge when he recounts, once again relying on Columbus's description, the meeting between Columbus and the cacique who wanted to go aboard his ship in order to go to Castile. The conversation between the two consisted mainly of "well-detailed" answers Columbus gave to the cacique's questioning about "our country." Columbus did not hesitate to give his time to an Indian who had no understanding of traditional culture; on the contrary, the story proves that a relationship had developed between the two of them, who, through an interpreter, "kept talking well into the night."

The conversation between Columbus and the wise cacique shows that the Indians were curious to know who the Admiral really was, where he and his people came from and how the Admiral's authority, which they felt was absolute and despotic, could relate to that of the Spanish Sovereigns, the superiors to whom Columbus kept referring in his speeches. For the Indians it was difficult to understand the meaning of a hierarchy and what was meant by the fact "that this Admiral has and obeys another lord... [and] that the King and Queen of Castile are the world's most important lords."

In addition, the Indian interpreter offered the cacique and his people information related to "what he had seen in Castile and the Spanish wonders." This fact allows us to understand the type of interest aroused in the Indians about the Spanish world. The things remembered are "the great cities and fortresses, churches, people, horses and other animals; the nobility, the wealth of the monarchs and the great lords; the food, feasts and contests he had seen, the run of the bulls and what he had learned about wars." Bernáldez repeats even in this case Columbus's expression ("that all of this [the Indian] conveyed very well and correctly"), intended by the Admiral to signal the natives' predisposition to understand reality.

Among their positive traits, Bernáldez insists upon an important element of the Antillian's customs, namely that they were great sailors

and travelled that sea with good vessels. The *Memoirs* tells us that these canoes "are and were boats the same length as the fustas, some small, others large...." Their main characteristic was that they were carved out of a single tree trunk and, therefore, although they reached a remarkable length with up to eighteen rows, their width was limited.

Bernáldez stresses above all the communication these canoes were able to guarantee, allowing as they did crisscross trading among the islands. For him, this was responsible for the fact that all of the people spoke the same language, unlike the inhabitants in the Canary Islands, who did not understand one another simply because they were not able to sail each others' islands. Moreover, according to the parish priest of Los Palacios, their ability to reach the other islands allowed the Indians "to sail ...among the peoples of those islands and throughout all those seas trading their possessions for others." Thus, among these people, although primitive, did exist a system of trade.

The canoes had enough capacity to carry up to "eighty oar men" and, as Bernáldez reports, Columbus had measured "one of them to be 96 feet long and eight feet wide." The canoes, the author of the *Memoirs* says, rewording the Admiral's testimony, had for the Indians who owned them a far more important meaning over and above the utilitarian one. In fact, the owners showed great pride in them just as "a gentleman feels proud to own a big and beautiful vessel." They were therefore eager to adorn their canoes to the point that they appeared to have quite elaborate "embellishments in the bow and stern areas, filled with ornaments and paintings producing amazement for their beauty."

The canoes were common to all of the people of the islands Columbus visited, but some tribes, such as the Caribs, used them mainly to reach other territories where they could obtain human flesh. This realization is responsible for one of the greatest obstacles to the Indians' establishing relations with the Spanish.

In fact, in Bernáldez's analysis the eating of human flesh was one of the principal causes of incompatibility and hostility. As stated earlier, based on Chanca's report, during the second voyage the presence of cannibals had conditioned relations with all the natives. For example, it was common knowledge that when some men of the fleet had been sent ashore to gather information from the Indians about where they were, and these men, unable to find their way back, having gotten lost in a vast forest of thick trees, the Spaniards immediately interpreted their absence — given the existing psychosis of cannibalism — as the result of their having being killed to be eaten.

The gradual decrease of feelings of alienation and total differentness from the Indians experienced by the Spanish, as a better mutual understanding developed over time, did not apply to the cannibals for whom rejection remained unchanged. Their habits are eerily described, often with gruesome details; one time the Spanish found in a village a pot where a human neck was boiling; another time they discovered bones from which, says Bernáldez, taking the episode from Chanca, "all that could be gnawed had been eaten."

Another habit which showed the Caribs' ferocity and aggressiveness toward other people — taken again from the Andalusian physician's report — is mentioned in the account by the women-prisoners who claimed the cannibals were accustomed to indiscriminately capturing men, women and children, but showing preference for men's flesh and displeasure in eating other kinds. They consequently used to castrate the boys and let them grow to ensure a supply of victims when they felt like having them.

From similar descriptions their cruelty seems boundless, when one considers reports from women of other tribes depicting the cruelty they personally endured: "the children conceived with them were eaten, whereas the ones born from their women were raised."

The weapons of the people of the islands of which Bernáldez learned were rather primitive and differed from one another in only a few, though rather important details. All weapons, reeds or wooden sticks, bows, and arrows, had no iron since in those islands there was no iron ore. The main difference among the weapons of the various tribes was that the Caribs used as points of their arrows a very hard fish bone or, sometimes, tips made of turtle shell instead of wood. The Andalusian parish priest, who takes such information from Chanca, comments that they "can clearly wound and kill naked people ut would hardly endanger people from Spain."

The items of information reported in the *Memoirs* by Bernáldez about relations developed between Columbus, the Spanish and the Indians during the third expedition are very scanty, becoming completely non-existent for the fourth voyage. The parish priest of Los Palacios, in line with the already-explained scope of his work, wished to avoid narrating the sad event (unlike Las Casas, who does report it) of the cruel exploitation of the natives in order to mine the gold. The total subjugation of the Indians not only will eliminate any previously established friendly relation, but shall bring about, as we know, a brutal dependent relationship.

In describing the later Columbian expeditions the Andalusian parish priest mentions the Indians only once, when he talks about the capture

of the cacique Caonabó, who was brought aboard, along with his brother, to be taken to Spain. All considered, the episode involving Caonabó is an example of Bernáldez's tendency to minimize Spanish cruelty; Bernáldez clarifies how the feared chief of the Caribs "had not been captured in combat, but after having heard words of reassurance." Considering the Indians' repression, carried out by Columbus for the purpose of securing gold, an established practice by the third voyage, this talk of "reassurance" emerges from Bernáldez's wishful thinking to give those events, in spite of everything, a positive flavor. Caonabó was taken to Spain but died during the crossing "from illness or precarious living conditions." He probably still did not like the voyage very much even if he had been promised, according to the *Memoirs*, that after meeting the King and Queen, he and the other Indians "would be taken back home to their original life." The inheritance he will leave to the Spanish will be his heavy golden necklace, this too a symbol of the developing situation in the Indies; upon entering cities and villages, Columbus insisted on showing it off, on Don Diego's neck, as the highest display of acquired power in the Indies.

CHAPTER REFERENCES

COLOMBO, *Il giornale*, 21 dicembre, 22 dicembre, 24 dicembre.
COLOMBO, *Carta a Luis de Santángel*, 1:201, 205.
COLOMBO, *Memoriale ad Antonio Torres*, 147-62.
COLÓM, *Carta-Relación de 26 febrero 1495*, 2:514-15.
ALVAREZ CHANCA, *Carta al Cabildo de Sevilla*.
DA CUNEO, *Carta a Geronimo Annari*.
DE MADARIAGA, 309-10.
MORALES PADRÓN, *Fisionomía*, 1-2.
TAVIANI, *I viaggi*, 2:142-44.
TODOROV, 41-61.

XXI. – GOLD AND THE COLUMBIAN EXPEDITIONS

Gold was of key importance for the West's economy in the second half of the fifteenth century, not only that which was obtained traditionally in African [Egyptian] ports, where gold arrived from western Sudan, but especially because in those decades an imbalance in the gold supply was taking place due to the Portuguese imports of this metal from the western African coast just then being explored (see note about the Portuguese gold).

In the exploration of Africa the Spanish Crown had fallen behind Portugal, limiting its conquest to the Canary Islands colonized during the Catholic Sovereigns' reign. The Portuguese monopoly on the importation of African gold from Arguim and Mina de Ouro caused new expectations for the Spanish, who initially opposed Portuguese imports given the fact that, traditionally, gold was secured through the trans-Saharan route.

Moreover, the Portuguese Crown seemed determined to reach a further goal, that of acquiring the Indian peninsula. The Spanish had no plans for the Orient, involved as they still were in their ancient war against the sultan of Granada, intending to definitively drive the Moors out of their country.

The removal of this obstacle, which had exhausted the Spanish royal finances because of this centuries-old fight, in any case made possible the start of their westward expansion, the remaining uncharted direction. Common knowledge has it that after the conquest of Granada the Crown's plan and Christopher Columbus's coincided, leading to the royal consent to Columbus's departure.

This authorization of the Columbian enterprise implied an expansion of Spain's commercial horizons through the colonization of new lands. As Bernáldez often highlights, however, Cathay remained the aim of all Spanish expeditions to the West. Gold, silk and spices of the Grand Khan's China were controlled by a class of merchants who had flourished for centuries. The Spanish intended to establish direct contacts with them, without depending on intermediary agents of other regions.

The projections concerning gold and spices were a high priority in the last decades of the 1400s for both the new attempts at opening up trade with the East pursued by the Portuguese who continued it until the last years of the fifteenth century and also for the unfriendly international trade situation in the western countries. It can be safely asserted that the Turks' victory against the Byzantine Empire with the conquest of Constantinople and the consequent strengthening of their dominion over the Near East were among the main reasons for an expansionist policy in the Iberian countries and in which merchants from various Italian cities did participate but, despite their mercantile and financial prestige, played only a supporting role; Ca' da Mosto, for instance, did it for the Portuguese voyages and Columbus for the Spanish.

Bernáldez's writings in reference to the Columbian undertakings are set against this historic time, at a moment in which the quest for a way to secure gold was particularly felt by the Spanish Crown. Gold was considered one of the primary objectives of the expedition to the Indies in view of what Columbus himself noted and it was also reflected in the many consequences that its finding and gathering caused. So in the *Memoirs*, this is one of the key narrative lines of the whole Columbian event.

The first time Bernáldez mentions gold and the possibility of reaching a land where it could be found in large quantities is in connection with Columbus's geographical conception and the inherent possibility, he upheld, of circumnavigating the globe to arrive back at his point of departure. The parish priest of Los Palacios emphasizes that this idea, which he culled from Columbus's writings, was an original one not shared by contemporary sailors, who thought that "with the west astern...it would be impossible to find land," while at the same time acknowledging that "in the opinion of many people, in that direction lay lands very rich in gold." Whereas a generalized expectation to find gold in those faraway regions did exist, Bernáldez maintains that only Columbus was able to plan an undertaking which would encompass those two objectives.

The curate says that there actually was gold in Hispaniola, insisting that great wealth would be derived from the island since, according to the Indians, it lay in large quantities both in the river sands and in mines. According to Bernáldez, what the Indians had at first related by gestures was soon confirmed by the gold they offered to the Spanish in exchange for small, worthless objects. Since they were able to gather gold consistently in this way, it became the basis of a firm belief that on the island there was plenty of this precious metal.

Moreover, the parish priest reaffirms the importance of reaching Hispaniola not only for the gold mines that lay there, but also for the trade that could be established thanks to the favorable position of the island, "in the middle of two worlds." Though showing in this way his ignorance of the geographic position of the islands reached, Bernáldez does highlight the fact that Hispaniola satisfied a double objective: it supplied gold and represented at the same time an important link between two continents, the European and the Asiatic.

Next to gold, of which there were at first mere clues but of which much was later discovered first hand in rivers and mines, Bernáldez poses another priority, repeatedly-pointed out, of the Columbian voyages: the desire to establish a flourishing trade with the territories and the cities of the Grand Khan, whose riches are many times featured.

The finding of gold will turn out to be much more difficult than ever was expected on the first voyage. Chanca and Bernáldez are fully conscious of this when they report the events of the first months of resistance in Hispaniola during the second voyage. The serious situation which occurred was strictly connected to adversities they had to overcome (as is well documented in Chanca's work). The critical moment in the quest for gold at this time was a double expedition to Cibao and Niti right before Antonio Torres's departure for Spain.

The result was proof of the actual existence of large deposits of gold, as proven by the samples sent to the Catholic Sovereigns.

The gold, in Bernáldez's account, will have from now on a higher significance than before, for it will greatly influence events leading to Columbus's success and decline, and the related events of a worsening rapport with the Indians, which will deteriorate out of this frenzy to accumulate large amounts of the precious metal.

About a month after Torres's fleet left, the problem of gold was still pressing and Bernáldez states that Columbus "hurried the fortification of the city" of La Isabela. He then decided to go "along with all the required people, some on foot, others on horseback, to the region of Cibao" in order to personally oversee the acquisition of gold and set in motion an organization which would control its mining.

The description of their arrival in the Cibao region, "a quite rough land with the highest peaks and mountains, many rocky and steep areas," rich in especially curative waters, culminates with the confirmation that "in those brooks and on those peaks there is much gold, all of it in nuggets." The two events which would, in part, change the situation in Hispaniola were "the fortress the Admiral ordered built in Cibao... called Saint Thomas" and the reaction against the Indians "who were denied

everything, unless they brought gold." From then on the control of the men of the expedition and of the Indians by Columbus became totally dependent on the gathering of gold which was to be sent to the Spanish Sovereigns.

Bernáldez follows step by step Columbus's actions in enforcing his plan without evaluating the actual consequences of his actions: a conduct which will prove laden with negative consequences when his actions will undergo scrutiny. The most telling moment concerning Columbus's difficulties in meeting the request for gold to be exported to Spain as promised to the Spanish Sovereigns is shown in the curate's account of the Admiral's return to Hispaniola, along with some of the men, after the long trip, during which they attempted to reach the mainland of Cathay.

The events that Bernáldez describes in connection with the gold are even more dramatic in light of the ongoing disorder in Hispaniola that complicated things for Columbus on the island and also had repercussions in Spain. Having been considered lost for a long period of time, during which they did not have any news of him (and for that "those who wished him well cheered his return, whereas those who did not like him were unhappy"), the Admiral upon returning to the island "did not find any accumulated gold, nor anyone who worked to that purpose or anyone with knowledge of where to find it, or even daring to look for it out of fear of the Indians, and this throughout his absence."

This passage proves the seriousness of what had happened during the whole episode, not only in reference to the gold which now could not be guaranteed to the Spanish Sovereigns, but also in regard to the Indians, toward whom a very hostile attitude had lately been setting in, thus preventing the men that remained on the island from performing the duties as ordered by the Genoese before his departure.

Also on the third voyage Columbus will not be able to keep the situation under control because of the feeling of rebellion which spread and sometimes blew up among the men. We read in the *Memoirs* that during that period of time Columbus "as he arrived in Hispaniola set order in the gold mines." Once again order meant intolerance and authoritarianism, irrespective of existing agreements: "he did not allow any trading to take place except for a very few things as samples. The sailors were very disappointed by this, since he had told them that whatever God would offer during that trip he would have shared with them."

The charge of not keeping his word, which Bernáldez levels against Columbus, sums up the numerous disparaging rumors about him which by now were accepted as true by many of those who, like Bernáldez himself, had excused and defended him on many occasions.

Despite these indications of doubt about Columbus's actions, however, the Andalusian ecclesiastic still defends the Admiral's good faith and far-sightedness in certain respects. In fact, according to Bernáldez, Columbus had been right about the existence of "rich gold mines, such as he had thought and claimed there would be, although not believed by many people, gentlemen, sailors, esquires and common people alike who used to scoff at what he said."

Bernáldez therefore felt a need to defend Columbus in a moment in which he had been totally isolated and abandoned by confirming the truthfulness of his theory about finding a land with much gold. In this way the author of the *Memoirs* once again emphasizes the positive nature of the Columbian expeditions to the Indies which left Spain an acquired inheritance of great wealth despite the sad epilogue of the Admiral's life.

CHAPTER REFERENCES

COLOMBO, *Carta a Luis de Santángel.*
COLOMBO, *Memoriale ad Antonio Torres.*
F. COLOMBO, *Historie*, ch. 50, 51, 52, 54, 61.
COLÓN, *Carta - Relación de 26 enero 1495*, 494.
ALVAREZ CHANCA, *Carta al Cabildo de Sevilla.*
DE CENEO, *Lettera a Geronimo Annari.*
BRAUDEL, 374-76.
CADDEO, 15.
CHAUNU, *L'expansión*, 268-70.
DE MADARIAGA, 134-35, 148-49.
GIL, "Colón."
HEERS, *Christophe Colomb*, 444-89.
LANDSTROM, 135.
ORTWIN SAUER, 122-26.
PARRY, 32.
TAVIANI, *I viaggi*, 2:94.
TAVIANI, "Notes."
TODOROV, 8-11.
VILAR, 79-83, 87-91.

XXII. – SPICES AND THE COLUMBIAN EXPEDITIONS

The importation of spices had become very important in the western world during the age of geographical explorations, to the point that it rose to be one of the prime topics in the travel literature. The slow progress of Portuguese exploration along the African coasts throughout the fifteenth century which culminated with the 1497-99 Da Gama expedition to Calicut had among its most important stimuli the attractiveness of the Indian spice market. Until then, as Bernáldez himself indicates, Indian spices were reaching for the most part Egyptian ports, passing through the Indian Ocean and the Red Sea.

Regarding the spices that the participants in the Columbian expeditions found in the Indies, it must be stressed first of all that Bernáldez gives a special prominence to pepper. This was not done accidentally, since this product, as is known, occupied a primary position in trade during the late Middle Ages. The *malagueta* pepper found by Portuguese explorers along the African coast of Benin in the second half of the 1400s had been considered of inferior quality compared to Indian pepper.

It is perhaps for this very reason that the parish priest of Los Palacios devoted special attention to the qualities of the pepper found in the Antilles, in an attempt to overcome any negative evaluation of its properties.

Bernáldez expounded on the necessary qualities of good pepper which, above all, must be characterized by a strong burning sensation. The parish priest of Los Palacios reports that the type of pepper found in Hispaniola is very good and burns twice as much as the one we have here, whereas the type found in the Carib islands is "four times stronger than the pepper we use in Spain." This detail shows a particular sensitivity to this issue, perhaps due to the presence of African pepper in the Spanish market in those decades.

Bernáldez adds new information about the spices observed and described in Hispaniola during the first months of the second expedition by Chanca in his report. In fact, in his hurried list in the final part of his report the Sevillian physician had omitted including pepper among the

337

spices, emphasizing rather the existence of certain medicinal plants in the islands directly connected with his profession and of basic importance to pharmacology, such as aloe, and pointing out specifically that the kind of aloe found in Hispaniola was "one of those we physicians use."

The parish priest of Los Palacios, on the contrary, is mostly interested in giving information about the pepper of the Indies, describing the kind of plant ("bushes similar to vegetables") and that the consistency and size of the fruit "is soft and not as hard as the Indian... and bigger," characteristics that made it different, as we read in the *Memoirs*, from the type grown in India and sold in Spain, imported from the port of Alexandria.

Bernáldez states also that the natives of the Antilles considered it a very useful product since they used it as a medicine and for that the curate specifies "they sow and harvest it."

Among the spices found on the first voyage to the Carib islands, besides pepper and aloe, the Andalusian parish priest lists mastic and ginger. Presumably, however, this information about the finding of such products is to be attributed to a time subsequent to the first expedition given the fact that during the first voyage it was impossible for the Spanish to establish contacts with the Caribs, who were feared for their viciousness and aggressiveness, and therefore even more unlikely for them to learn about their products. We do not know when this passage of the *Memoirs* was written. In any event, we must assume it refers to the moment in which Columbus had subdued the Carib tribe and Caonabó, one of their most important chiefs.

The news reported by Bernáldez about the other spices noticed during the first period of their stay in Hispaniola is for the most part taken from Chanca's work and his related comments in another part of this volume. The only difference between the two reports concerns cinnamon. The Andalusian parish priest specifies how, as was true for pepper, cinnamon commonly came from the Orient to the Mediterranean port of Alexandria.

Given the similarity of these two works, the variation introduced by Bernáldez must be particularly worthy of notice. He must have had the feeling that Chanca's reporting about spices was not exhaustive. Although taking Chanca's text as the basis for his *Memoirs*, Bernáldez, in other words, felt free to add data in his writing from other works and other reporting participants of the expedition to the Indies.

CHAPTER REFERENCES

COLOMBO, *Carta a Luis de Santángel*.
COLOMBO, *Memoriale ad Antonio Torres*.
F. COLOMBO, *Historie*, ch. 50, 51, 52, 54, 61.
LAS CASAS, *Historia*, bk. 1, ch. 47.
ALVAREZ CHANCA, *Carta al Cabildo de Sevilla*.
DE CUNEO, *Lettera a Geronimo Annari*.
PETER MARTYR, *De Orbe Novo*, dec. 1, bk. 1.
BERNÁLDEZ, *Memorias*, ch. 118, 120.

HEERS, *Christophe Colomb*, 431-33.
PESSAGNO.
REVELLI, 26-30.
TAVIANI, *Cristoforo Colombo*, 2:65-67.
TAVIANI, "Notes," 347-49.

XXIII. – ACCOUNTS OF THE THIRD AND FOURTH VOYAGES

According to Bernáldez the events of the final two Columbian expeditions constitute the sad epilogue of a heroic adventure which had led to the exploration of faraway lands and seas, procuring for the Spanish Crown, with the extraordinariness and magnificence of the undertaking, glory and fame in the eyes of the learned people of the time, in and outside Spain.

The echo of this portentous event, immediately following the return from the first voyage, generated bewilderment and stupor as a high achievement for mankind which foreshadowed a new world, where reality and imagination seemed still blurred together. Moreover, the news of the finding of a large amount of gold in those islands helped to increase the mythical notion of the riches of those lands which in the travel literature had been characterized by fantastic descriptions of wealth, leading to confusion between what was actually found and what was merely dreamed of. Reaching the Indies became an inescapable reality greeted with great exultation. Peter Martyr of Anghiera, who was at that time at the Catholic Sovereigns' court, wrote numerous letters documenting the extraordinary event. His December 29, 1494 letter to Pomponio Leto, an Italian man of letters, can be considered an example of the general enthusiasm that accompanied the announcement of the successful expedition. The letter says: "My most kind Pomponio, you disclosed to me that you jumped for joy and barely kept yourself from tears of happiness at the reading of my letter in which I was informing you about the world of the Antipodes, not previously discovered."

The third Columbian expedition actually left for the Indies about three years after the happy return which had signaled the realization of the expectations of the Spanish Crown which had adopted a cautious stance during those decades of exploration of the new lands. In the short period between the first and the third voyages in various social circles there had arisen the awareness that the expeditions across the ocean could indeed be carried out even without Columbus's participation. Out of the

341

experience of the previous undertakings, other vessels were then sent to the Indies. Bernáldez lets it be understood that the Spanish Crown, considering Columbus no longer indispensable for the accomplishment of its plans, had begun a series of expeditions entrusting to other captains the task of "going on to discover new lands" by retracing the Columbian routes across the Atlantic.

The reality of this substantial change is contained in a few words by the parish priest of Los Palacios, who stresses that in the year in which Columbus was forced to stay in Spain "they went and discovered new islands."

Bernáldez recounts the departure of the third voyage not only without fanfare, merely presenting its major achievements without commentary ("he set course for certain islands which he had not previously reached... [and] found and discovered the Island of Pearls"), but also above all, in describing what happened, he constantly refers to the struggles Columbus had to face. The men's discontent with the decisions of the Admiral dominates the narrative. "He did not want them to make exchanges in trade, and this greatly disappointed the sailors," reads the *Memoirs*.

The Genoese's repression and lack of sensitivity made increasingly difficult his rapport with those who should have helped him carry out the "gold plan" that called for him to mine large amounts of it. Moreover, Bernáldez reports that Columbus's problem was worsened by the vituperative charge that he was not keeping his promises.

Columbus's answers to the men's anticipation of wealth were discipline and order. Disappointment and distrust was in turn the response of those who had sailed with him. The Admiral, according to the parish priest of Los Palacios, kept on declaring that he rightly imposed order because of the responsibility given him by the Catholic Sovereigns, for whom the entire amount of gold was destined, maintaining they "sent him on that course to discover, not to make exchanges." Columbus meant to very firmly control the men's behavior, above all in regard to gold mining, a task "he lived up to with great commitment."

The mines, continues the parish priest of Los Palacios, had been found to be very large and abundant. Once again, Bernáldez highlights the positive outcomes of Columbus's action. His attitude toward the Genoese, however, becomes more ambiguous: on the one hand, he continues to acknowledge the positive value of his concept and plan while, on the other hand, he shows Columbus's organizational inability in the face of an evolving situation in the Indies. The unplanned natural misfortunes that had taken place during the previous voyage were respon-

sible for what was going on, above all for the murder of the men who had been left behind at La Navidad and the malaise which, since the first months, had worn out the discoverers' level of resistance and effectiveness and weakened the dissatisfied men of the expedition, thus giving rise as well to the repression of the Indians who during the first two voyages had proven to be well-disposed and inclined to spontaneous collaboration.

Gold is the sole topic upon which the Andalusian ecclesiastic lingers while telling of events covering the two years after the departure of the third expedition in August 1497. This subject, as already stated, appeared decidedly crucial for both its economic consequences and the inglorious end of the Admiral. According to Bernáldez's testimony, during the early period Columbus "was not able to find gold in great abundance." Only in the next year "he began to find it in large amounts and in 1500 started collecting it." However, the opposition to the Genoese's decisions grew at Hispaniola, so much so that it appeared as an unbearable situation to the Spanish Sovereigns. The gold was being sent late to Spain and Bernáldez reports that Columbus himself was irritated and explained that this was actually tied to the "many rumors against him."

Bernáldez still defended Columbus's action, asserting that "absolutely it shall not be trusted that he has acted in such a way." Despite their support for his decision, there appears, in Bernáldez's description of those events, however, also the fact that he is blamed by the Sovereigns. "Because of the Admiral, the King sent to Hispaniola a governor named Bobadilla who sent back Columbus as a prisoner with the gold the Admiral had collected." Though uttered with regret by the parish priest, these words in the *Memoirs* end the period of admiration, fame and glory "for having reached the Antipodes" and inaugurate the vituperation which was disseminated and actually accepted as true by those who had once supported and defended Columbus.

The Catholic Sovereigns' decisions in the following years are presented by the Andalusian ecclesiastic as the unavoidable consequence of what had occurred.

His description of the fourth expedition is totally abbreviated and inaccurate. He does not spell out which lands were reached nor how long Columbus had to stop for storms at sea. The items of information provided seem only to be the result of a desire to end the account of the Columbian enterprise rather than a sign of the original intention to record for readers all the remarkable moments of the expeditions.

The last events of the fourth voyage show a Columbus weakened by the great misfortunes that had befallen him, unable to react or to be as decisive in acting as he wanted to be. Bernáldez describes him as

deprived of a plan, under the control of the natural elements; sea-water and wood-eating worms cost him the ship on which he was sailing and forced him to take refuge aboard the only remaining vessel.

The ensuing situation in the Antilles becomes then the sole topic of information surfacing from the account of the curate of Los Palacios and is irrelevant to Columbus's action; it focuses rather on the beginnings of the Spaniards' settlement and the networking of their various groups. It was no longer a situation without an organized purpose, as was true previously; now the colonization of Hispaniola was taking hold under the control of a governor sent by the Catholic Monarchs.

Ending his account of Columbus's undertakings with the discoverer's death in 1506, Bernáldez memorializes him as "the one who discovered the Indies" while defining him worthy "of the wonderful and honored memory" he enjoyed. The farewell comments of the *Memoirs* to the Admiral are unmistakably positive and whatever honors and income Columbus would pass on to his son, Diego, are then emphasized.

Finally, Bernáldez does not forget to name the Spanish King and Queen among those responsible for the actual outfitting and realization of the Columbian fleets; they are the ones who did gain as direct inheritance from the Genoese's undertakings the wealth and glory which very soon would symbolize their world power.

CHAPTER REFERENCES

BALLESTEROS BERETTA, 2:543-46.
DE MADARIAGA, 471-74, 566-86.
HEERS, *Christophe Colomb*, 593-602.
GIL, *El rol*, 1-10.
MAHN-LOT, 147-72.
MORALES PADRÓN, *Historia*, 141-49, 184-90.
ROMEO, 21-22.
RUMEU DE ARMAS, 307.

XXIV. – BERNÁLDEZ'S UNDERSTANDING OF THE WORLD'S GEOGRAPHY AND THE PROSPECT OF CIRCUMNAVIGATING THE GLOBE

According to modern historians, Bernáldez's *Memoirs* is less important as an account of Columbus's expeditions than as a source of information on various other topics. This is so for subjects clearly considered most noteworthy by the author himself — and for that reason taken into account with all their developments throughout the period of time examined — as well as for those topics treated only indirectly, associated with other issues.

The multiplicity of subjects and encyclopedic references to all the places in the world then known unintentionally turn Bernáldez's work into a major source for different kinds of information about the most heterogeneous localities. Geographic knowledge was not a specific object of study for the Andalusian parish priest, who lacked proper competence in this field, yet it amounted to a by-product of a series of considerations he formulated in relation to general or specific topics.

It is obvious that the importance which the author of the *Memoirs* ascribes to various events in his account depends on the varying amount of personal knowledge of the facts and situations he analyzed, on the sources at his disposal and on his interest for what he was reporting. In his writing, he offers then an assortment of news concerning more or less distant places which become of interest to us as a way of learning the limitations and particulars of the author's geographic knowledge as well that of others of his time, affording us in this manner a compendium of localities which were then known and that for various reasons had contacts with the western world.

The mention in the *Memoirs* of places far from the Iberian peninsula gives an idea of the territories more or less connected with Spain during the Catholic Monarchs' reign. The number and names of regions, cities and places referred to is considerable. Sometimes they are mere citations, more often they are fuller descriptions giving a precise picture of the

cultural and geographical understanding of educated Spaniards of the time as a whole.

The interest in analyzing ongoing events concerning more or less distant places directly depended on the repercussion they had, whether in terms of political, economic or social consequences, as well as the cultural implication they held or, finally, their exceptional and extraordinary quality. In the Andalusian parish priest's geography, real and non-existent places or imaginary entities derived from handed-down traditional lore and prevalent opinions of the time are mixed together.

Bernáldez observed nations closest to Spain, such as those of Western Europe, especially in the Mediterranean, where Spain had established frequent political and economic contacts, and at the same time he evidences interest in the Moslem world of North Africa's coasts, areas closely related to the history of the Iberian countries as well, and he describes its gradual alternating conquest, until 1513, by Portuguese and Spanish powers.

In addition to this more direct knowledge, explained by the closeness of these territories and their connection with the Iberian countries' political orientation and ties developed in the late Middle Ages, the *Memoirs* contains information about distant regions. The reaching of lands unknown to the Occident by the Portuguese and Spanish in those decades compels Bernáldez to narrate the main events involving the exploration of Africa and Asia, thus necessarily providing geographical details.

On the Portuguese discovery of the Mina de Ouro (dealt with in a previous note) the Andalusian parish priest gives very imprecise information. As for its position on the African coast of the Gulf of Guinea, he says vaguely that the Portuguese stronghold "is located on the Ocean coastline opposite, south of our country," without more precise details on its location. In trying to better identify it, Bernáldez adds that La Mina was located in a territory "beyond the coast [inhabited] by blacks known as *gelofes*, and beyond their boundaries lay much, much more."

This assertion alone sufficiently documents the inadequate preparation for expressing the geographic co-ordinates of the Occidental part of Africa south of Cape Bojador. Similarly, in attempting to better specify the distance between the southern tip of the Iberian Peninsula and the territory of La Mina, Bernáldez resorts to using the parameter of the earth's curvature, asserting that "for those living in the north" that territory "is practically hidden, given the roundness of the earth." Moreover, the use of adverbs stressing approximation contributes to highlighting even more the scantiness of information in identifying the geographic location of the territories on the Atlantic African coast.

This kind of overt geographical imprecision, however, does not generally affect all the matters treated by Bernáldez. According to Jaime Cortesão, besides revealing that era's limited objective knowledge of those African regions, in all probability this shortcoming must also be attributed to Portuguese guarded secrecy for technical and scientific information. They were very careful not to let such information leak out, especially when it dealt with navigation and the exploration of new lands. The detailed description of the geographic location of the Canary Islands, conquered by Spain's Catholic Sovereigns, may be interpreted as a further confirmation of the Portuguese secretive attitude in matters concerning the explorations.

Bernáldez devotes a chapter of his work to the environmental and human conditions of this Atlantic archipelago at the time before the conquest, supplying as well some geographical facts. For instance, we read in the *Memoirs* that "located in the Ocean Sea, the Canary Islands are seven and closer to Africa than to any other land. Leaving Cádiz to reach them, land always lies to the left. They are near the land that borders the Small Sea, some five, others thirty, still others fifty leagues away, more or less. The Small Sea borders the Tagaos and Mesa lands." Thus, in sharp contrast to his previous total inaccuracy, we have sufficient geographic elements and a few parameters of reference about the Canary Islands' location to identify the archipelago along the Atlantic coast.

The curate relates with many details the Spanish conquest of Grand Canary Island (see note), showing the subdivision of its entire territory before its colonization. Given Bernáldez's particular interest in the organization of the natives (to the point of listing by name all their 35 villages), expectations concerning the exploitation of the land must have been favorable in the eyes of the Spanish, who had to plan on establishing enduring settlements.

For the later period, nearly 30 years after the discovery of La Mina by the Portuguese, the parish priest of Los Palacios recounts in the *Memoirs* the story of Lusitanian explorations from Da Gama's 1497-9 voyage to India. This time, as earlier in the description of Portuguese explorations along the western coast of Africa, the scarcity of information is confirmed. A single exception of geographic information is his indication of the distance between La Mina and the city of Calicut, calculated by the Andalusian parish priest to be 1800 miles.

In the same chapter in which Bernáldez briefly mentions the Portuguese route of the spices coming from India, he gives a much more detailed account of the traditional route for spices that, through the Egyptian ports, ensured delivery of these Oriental products to the

Christian Occident. After providing a few specifics about Portuguese mercantile navigation in the large gulf opposite Calicut, Bernáldez does not develop the theme of Portuguese importation of spices, focusing rather on the route followed for centuries by Moslem merchants.

In the *Memoirs* one finds well documented the difficult commercial situation facing Portugal, which had to compete with these traders who took Oriental products into the Mediterranean through the Red Sea. Bernáldez follows the entire course of the ships which set out from Calicut, in the Indian region of Malabar, bound for Cairo: "And so, at the end of the above-named gulf, they pass through a strait, like the one of Gibraltar, and enter another gulf with the Red Sea at its right. There they transfer the above-mentioned spices onto other boats, smaller because of the shallows, thus taking the spices to other ports close to Mecca, a city located in the Arabian desert...whence they finally leave for Cairo by camel, passing the foot of Mount Sinai."

Although amounting to brief indications, these statements by the Andalusian curate seemingly stressing the importance of the traditional route rather than the Portuguese circumnavigation of Africa, do justify our thinking that, even though Bernáldez does acknowledge the extraordinary nature of the Lusitanian voyages, he was most concerned with the priorities of the Spanish market to which most of the Indian spices were directed after crossing the Indian Ocean, the Arabic Gulf, the Red Sea and Egypt.

In the *Memoirs*, there still is a final mention of the Portuguese route in the reference to the distance traveled by ships in order to reach India, as we read "that the voyage from Portugal to there is about 3000 miles including detours." The lack of additional information about the Cape of Good Hope route can perhaps be inferred as further evidence of the difficulty of securing information outside Portugal about Orient-bound Lusitanian voyages.

The geographical information offered by Bernáldez with respect to the Canary Islands and the routes of the Indian spices do complement that derived from Columbus's expeditions.

The attention he pays to describing the first two expeditions and the stress given to the Genoese's elaborate cosmographical conception of reaching Asia by sailing westward affords him the opportunity also to specify some of his ideas as they match Columbus's.

Never throughout his whole work, though his account continues until 1513, does there surface any awareness that Columbus mistakenly thought he had reached the Asian mainland. Following the voyages and the Admiral's death, which occurred in 1506, he neither re-examines nor

modifies his account in the last part of the *Memoirs*, maintaining unvaried his position regardless of the new awareness in the Occident of the existence of another land that interfered with the reaching of Asia.

In this regard, Bernáldez expounds with great evidence his idea of the location of the Chinese territories of the Grand Khan, maintaining that Cape Alfaeto "located at the beginning of Cuba...was the outermost cape of the Orient, just as Cape San Vicente in Portugal is the outermost cape in our continent, in the West." He goes further, making clear his position that "between the two capes lay all the populated lands of the world. So much so that whoever left San Vicente eastward by land could, without crossing the Ocean at all, reach Cape Alfaeto, and vice versa, one could likewise come from there to Cape San Vicente."

Being so adamant in his ideas, it could safely be assumed that the Andalusian parish priest wrote his work on the Columbian expeditions as they unfolded and that afterwards, because of the lack of interest toward explorations beyond the Ocean, he did not have to rectify his thinking, notwithstanding the new evidence. This hypothesis, however, cannot explain away the fact that, while describing the second voyage, he indicates that he wrote subsequent to the described events.

Columbus's intent to reach Asia and indeed to sail "through his desired route with the purpose of getting to the region and city of Cathay" is repeatedly highlighted by Bernáldez in his description of the trip Columbus made to discover the mainland on the second expedition. The interactions that in the Andalusian parish priest's thinking would quickly come about with the people of the Asiatic territories, had Columbus's plan been realized, even led him to imagine possible successive developments. Thus he writes that the Genoese actually thought of being able "to return to Spain by way of the Orient" when he was "quite close to the Golden Chersonese, which he was forced to leave behind due to unfavorable conditions, an endless voyage and the scarcity of provisions." Columbus's idea of circumnavigating and arriving at the same place he left, after travelling around the entire earth's circumference by land or sea, is repeated many times and amounts to one of the most interesting elements of Bernáldez's work concerning the Columbian voyages. In fact, the Andalusian parish priest is the only one who points out this intention of Columbus, having probably learned it from the Admiral's own lips. Presenting the Columbian plans and elucidating the various ways of implementing such an undertaking, Bernáldez shows it was possible to achieve the same result following one of these routes either wholly by land or by sea, or again partly by sea and partly land. The Andalusian ecclesiastic asserts that leaving from Cape San Vicente, at the

extreme occidental boundary of the Iberian peninsula, to return on Portuguese soil by land one would go through the cities of Jerusalem, Rome and Seville.

Another route, also mentioned in Columbus's February 26, 1495 *Letter-Report*, foresaw the eastward crossing of the Indian Ocean "reaching the Ganges, the Arabic Gulf, Ethiopia" and after that who ever had faced such a journey "could reach," Bernáldez maintains, "Jerusalem by land, then Jaffa, where on a ship one could reach the Mediterranean Sea and arrive finally at Cádiz."

The third option consisted of "doing the whole trip by sea and reaching Calicut... by coasting all of Libya, a land of African people, and returning subsequently by the way the Portuguese come back from Calicut."

These plans must have been deemed very ambitious since at the same time in the *Memoirs* it was pointed out that the demonstrations of their usefulness depended first on reaching Cathay.

When he reaches the territories of the Grand Khan, Bernáldez shows some perplexity concerning the distance calculated by Columbus: Bernáldez considers it greater. He reports that "to find those lands would necessarily take a long period of time..," adding, while clarifying his thinking, that "I am of the opinion that even by sailing another 1200 leagues around the infinity of sea and land one could not get there."

This statement, written by Bernáldez allegedly after Columbus's return from the second voyage, shows that the credibility of Columbus was doubted. The idea Bernáldez expresses is indeed not corroborated by evidence since he explains that a longer period of time was required than that figured out by Columbus himself, and he implies that the distance between Hispaniola and Cathay was greater because of the fact that "in ancient times the Grand Khan ruled the Tartars as far as the grand Tartar land bordering on Russia and Valia. It could be claimed that the Tartar region actually begins with Hungary and that all Tartar lands lie directly where the sun rises as one looks toward them from our region of Andalusia." This lack of an acceptable explanation in support of his idea proves how Bernáldez only really voiced his own doubts concerning Columbus's undertakings, rather than some original, personal conviction about the duration of the journey to Cathay.

The Andalusian parish priest thus, for the first time in his *Memoirs*, clearly disagrees with Columbus on a geographic point and reports that when the Admiral was a guest in his home at Los Palacios he had the opportunity to personally convey to him how he thought differently. The curate actually states: "I told him so and had him understand in

1496, when he first came to Castile, after returning from his second discovery voyage, while he was my guest."

This criticism levelled against Columbus, whom he had previously considered a great expert on geography and cosmography, a subject so removed from his own specific competence, was both a confirmation of rumors regarding the lessened credibility with which the Admiral would carry out future expeditions to the Indies, and was a proof of Columbus's weakened position and an acknowledgement of the shortcomings of one who had previously been considered an expert.

CHAPTER REFERENCES

COLÓN, *Carta-Relación de 26 febrero 1495*, 494.
CORTESÃO, *Los Portugueses*, 523-27, 543-55.
DIFFIE AND WINIUS, 175-86.
FERNÁNDEZ-ARMESTO, 192-95.
MAGALHAES GODINHO, *Les grandes découvertes*, 46, 47.
O'GORMAN, 21-24.
TAVIANI, *I viaggi*, 1:218-21.

BIBLIOGRAPHY

of the

EDITIONS AND MANUSCRIPTS
OF THE *LETTER* OF DIEGO ALVAREZ CHANCA
AND OF THE *MEMOIRS* OF ANDRES BERNALDEZ

by Anna Unali

Diego Alvarez Chanca's *Letter* was first published in Spanish by Fernández de Navarrete in 1826 (see M. FERNANDEZ DE NAVARRETE, *Colección de los viajes y descubrimientos que hicieron por mar los españoles, desde fines del siglo XV*, Vol. II, Madrid 1826, 198-224).

The subsequent Spanish editions are: A. FERNANDEZ DE IBARRA, *The Letter of D. Diego Alvarez Chanca, dated 1494, relating to the Second Voyage of Columbus to America*, Smithsonian Miscellaneous Collections, XLVIII, Washington 1907; C. COLL Y TOSTE, *Carta del físico Diego Alvarez Chanca al cabildo de Sevilla, dándole cuenta del segundo viaje, en el qual se descubrió la isla de San Juan*, Boletín Histórico de Puerto Rico IV, San Juan de Puerto Rico (1917); A. TIÒ, *Doctor Diego Alvarez Chanca*, Biographic study, Barcelona 1966; S. ARANA SOTO, *Los médicos en el descubrimiento del Nuevo Mundo y homenaje al doctor Chanca*, Burgos 1967; F. PORTUONDO, *El segundo viaje de descubrimiento*, Havana 1977; J. GIL y C. VARELA, *Cartas de particulares a Colón y Relaciones coetáneas*, Madrid 1984.

For English translations of the *Letter*, see: NICOLAUS SYLLACIUS, *De insulis Meridianis atque Indici maris nuper inventis*, translated by the Rev. John Mulligan, Appendix A, Translation *of Chanca's Letter*, New York 1858; J. B. THACHER, *Christopher Columbus*, New York 1902; C. JANE, *The Voyages of Christopher Columbus*, London 1930.

The original manuscript of the report sent to the Sevillian magistrates by means of Antonio Torres's fleet was lost. We know the work because the Spanish historian Martín Fernández de Navarrete found a XVI century manuscript copy.

The codex was among the writings concerning the Indies collected by Fr. Antonio de Aspa in the monastery of Majorada, near Olmedo. Friar de Aspa, in a brief introduction to the transcription of Chanca's report (reproduced in Navarrete's edition) reflects the importance of the Andalusian physician's *Letter*, which is a direct testimonial of events. De Aspa proves the value of Chanca's work by comparing it to Peter Martyr of Anghiera's *Decades*. De Aspa maintains that the latter, reporting the undertaking without having taken part in it, gives "worthless information," unlike Chanca, who "does not contradict himself," since what he writes is the result of his own observations.

The codex, now kept in the Biblioteca de la Historia of Madrid, consists of 33 manuscript folios. The first 17 take in the Castilian translation of Peter Martyr of Anghiera's I and II *Decades*, while the remaining 15 folios reproduce Chanca's *Letter*. In 1807 Martín Fernández de Navarrete had obtained a copy of the *Letter* from Don Manuel Avella.

Andrés Bernáldez's *Memoirs*, like Chanca's *Letter*, was published for the first time more than three centuries after being drafted. There are four Spanish editions of the Andalusian parish priest's work as well as a selection:

1) *Historia de los Reyes Católicos D. Fernando y Da. Isabel*, Crónica inédita del siglo XV, escrita por El sachiller Andrés Bernáldez, Cura que fue de Los Palacios, Vol. I-II, Granada 1856;

2) *Historia de los Reyes Católicos D. Fernando y Da. Isabel*, escrita por El Bachiller Andrés Bernáldez, Cura de Los Palacios, y Capellan del Arzobispo de Sevilla D. Diego Deza, Vol. I-II, Seville 1869;

3) *Historia de los Reyes Católicos del Bachiller Andrés Bernáldez, cura de Los Palacios*, in *Crónicas de los Reyes de Castilla desde Alfonso el Sabio hasta los Católicos Don Fernando y Doña Isabel*, Colección ordenada por D. Cayetano Rosell, Vol. III, Madrid 1878;

4) *Historia de los Reyes Católicos D. Fernando y Da. Isabel*, Selección prologo y notas de Luciano de la Calzada, Madrid 1946;

5) *Memorias del reinado de los Reyes Católicos*, Edición y estudio por M. Gomez-Moreno y J. De M. Carriazo, Real Academia de la Historia, Madrid 1962.

Gómez-Moreno and Carriazo's edition is reproduced in this volume, having served as the basic text for the Italian translation.

Numerous are the extant manuscripts of the *Memoirs*. These 22 manuscripts can be categorized into two groups or families. The first group is made up of those derived from Rodrigo Caro's manuscript, known as the *familia Caro*. They are complete and rather similar, taken from a copy of a lost original made in Seville, in the XVII century, by Rodrigo Caro. According to Gómez-Moreno and Carriazo it seems that the main manuscript of this family is *Ms*. n. 1359 of the Biblioteca Nacional of Madrid.

The second-group consists of those manuscripts still unpublished when Gómez-Moreno and Carriazo elaborated the comparative edition of the codices. Their edition is here reproduced but without the notes containing all the manuscript variants.

These manuscripts known therefore as *familia inedita* include *Egerton* 303 of the British Library; *num*. 99 of the Duke of Gor's Library in Granada; and *num*. 1355 of the National Library of Madrid. Gómez-Moreno and Carriazo hold that the most important of these three codices is the British Museum's *Ms*. 303, which belonged to Zurita and which is to be ascribed to a time before 1520, that is, soon after Andrés Bernáldez's death.

According to the two Spanish scholars, its very early dating as well as the excellence of its text account for the fact that this manuscript was preferred to all the others known. The first 99 chapters of it are missing and are replaced with the corresponding chapters from Diego de Valera's *Crónica de los Reyes Católicos*, up to the end of the Vera campaign in the war of Granada, the summer of 1488.

Reported below is the complete list of the 22 manuscripts.

1) Manuscript *Eg*. 303, British Library;

2) Manuscript *28,490*, British Library;

3) Manuscript *Eg*. 306, British Library;

4) Manuscript *num*. 99, the Duke of Gor's Library, Granada;

5) Manuscript of the Marquis of Montealegre's Library;

6) Manuscript *A*-83 (2-7-4), Biblioteca de la Real Academia de la Historia;

7) Manuscript *A*-81, Muñóz collection (9-23-3), Biblioteca de la Real Academia de la Historia;

8) Manuscript *D*-81, Biblioteca de la Real Academia de la Historia;

9) Manuscript *D*-80, Biblioteca de la Real Academia de la Historia;

10) Manuscript 83-7-28, Biblioteca Capitular y Colombina, Seville;

11) Manuscript 83-6-36, Biblioteca Capitular y Colombina, Seville;

12) Manuscript *V. II*. 6, the Escorial, Madrid;

13) Manuscript 8207, Biblioteca Nacional, Madrid;

14) Manuscript 1355, Biblioteca Nacional, Madrid;

15) Manuscript 1359, Biblioteca Nacional, Madrid;

16) Manuscript 8272, Biblioteca Nacional, Madrid;

17) Manuscript 619, Biblioteca Nacional, Madrid;

18) Manuscript 18215, Biblioteca Nacional, Madrid;

19) Manuscript 1272, Biblioteca Nacional, Madrid;

20) Manuscript of the Marquis de Villapanés, personal library in Jerez de la Frontera;

21) Fragments of the *Memoirs* preserved in *Ms.* 170 (Saint Germain franc., n. 1583), Biblotèque Nationale, Paris;

22) Manuscript of the *Fundación Hispánica*, Library of Congress, Washington, D. C.

INDICES

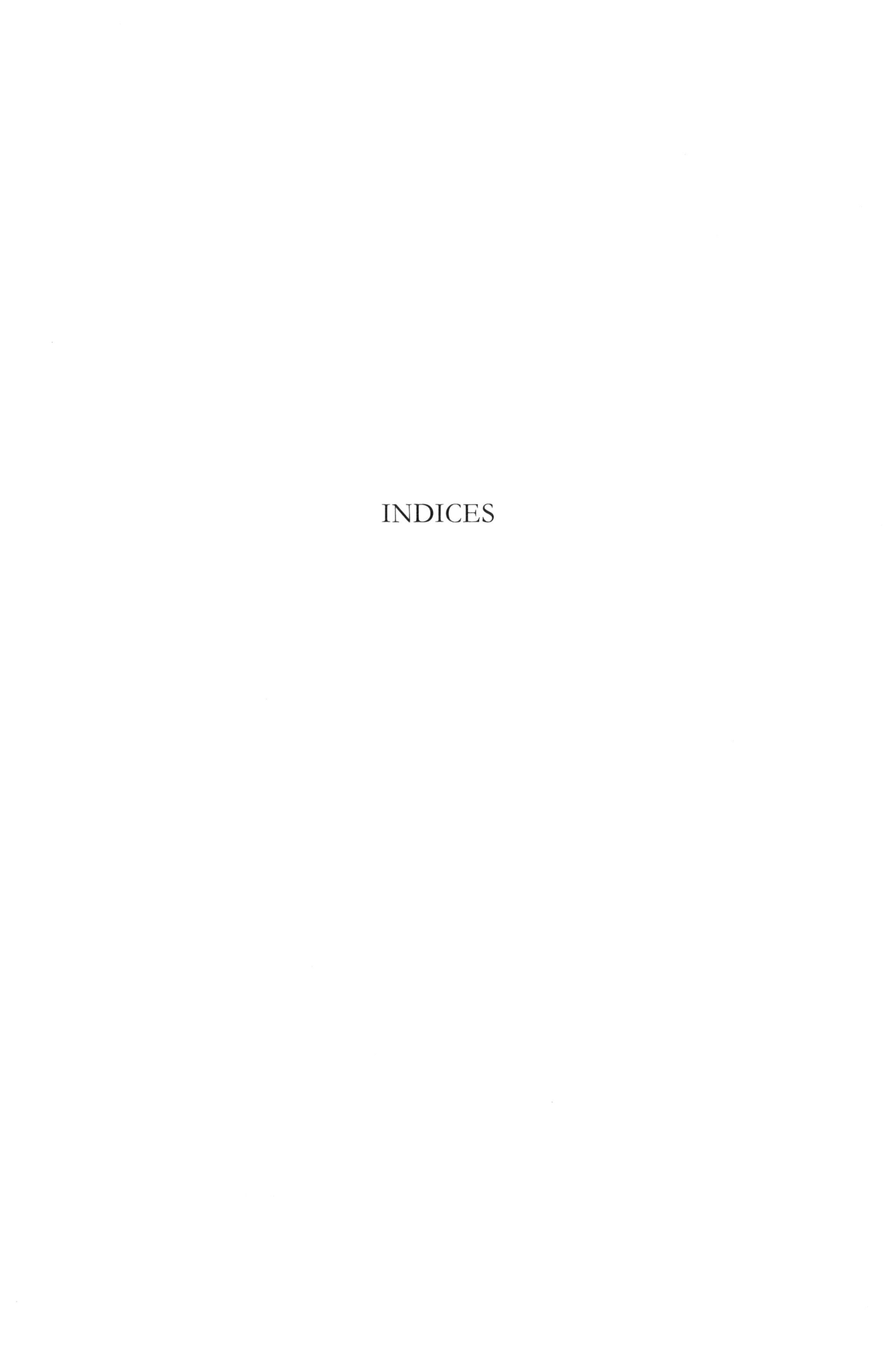

The indices were prepared in the Cultural Office
of the *Istituto dell'Enciclopedia Italiana* – founded by G. Treccani – Rome

INDEX OF PERSONS

(The names of Diego Alvarez Chanca, Andrés Bernáldez and Christopher Columbus, appear on nearly every page and therefore are not included in this index)

AILLY, PIERRE D': 232

ALBERTUS MAGNUS: 221

ALPHONSE OF PORTUGAL: 209

ALPHONSE, [MASTER]: 226

ALGARVE, PEDRO DE: 299

ALONSO, JUAN (COUNT OF NIEBLA): 299

ALVAREZ CHACÓN, DIEGO: 220

ALVAREZ DE LA REINA, FERNAND: 226

ANNARI, GERONIMO: 256

ANTONIO, NICOLÁS: 220

APOCADA, R. DE: 272

APULEIUS: 259

ARANA-SOTO, J.: 355

ARAGON, HENRY OF: 222

ASENSIO, J.M.: 245

ASPA, ANTONIO DE: 207, 355

AVELLA, MANUEL: 355

AVICENNA: 215, 221

BACON, ROGER: 221

BAEZA, GONZALO DE: 209

BALLESTEROS BERETTA, A. 344

BARROS, JOAO DE: 294

BEATRICE DE BOBADILLA: 257

BERNAL, JUAN (MASTER): 216, 226, 265, 266

BERNALDO DA PISA: 129

BÉTHENCOURT, JEAN DE: 297, 298

BOBADILLA: 201, 343

BRUN, PIETRO: 221

CÁ DA MOSTO, ALVISE, *see* DA MOSTO, A.

CABALLERIA, ALFONSO DE LA: 256

CABILDO OF SEVILLE: 8, 242, 277

CALZADA, LUCIANO DE LA: 355

CAONABÓ, (CAPTURE OF): 197, 199, 329, 338; [INDIAN CHIEF]: 39, 57, 127, 318, 325; (NAVIDAD): 41, 43, 45, 47, 51, 53, 107, 109, 111, 113, 115, 119, 248

CARO, RODRIGO: 271, 272, 273, 355

CERDA, LUIS DE LA: 297

CHANCON, GONZALO: 210

CHANTA: 207

COLL Y TOSTE, C. 355

COLOMBO, DIEGO: 203, 344

COLUMBUS, FERDINAND, DON: 251, 273,

COMA, GUILLERO: 255, 256, 257, 258, 259, 260

CORTESAO, J.: 347

CROMBERGER, JACOBO: 220

DA CUNEO, MICHELE: 8, 256, 258, 329

361

DA GAMA, VASCO: 292, 293, 305, 306, 337, 347

DA MOSTO, A.: 304, 332

DA VINCI, LEONARDO: 213

DE LOLLIS, CESARE: 8, 273, 278

DEZA, DIEGO DE: 272, 273, 355

DIAZ, BARTHOLOMEW: 292

DIEGO, DON (BROTHER OF CAONABÓ): 197, 199, 318, 325, 329

DULCERT: 297

EMANUEL I OF PORTUGAL *see* MANUEL I

ENRIQUE III OF CASTILE: 298

ENRIQUE IV OF CASTILE *see* HENRY IV OF CASTILE

FERDINAND THE CATHOLIC II, OF ARAGON: 7, 13, 83, 85, 129, 141, 165, 183, 185, 191, 195, 197, 201, 208, 219, 254, 258, 264, 271, 300, 306, 311, 326, 341, 299

FERDINAND THE CATHOLIC & COLUMBUS: 65, 67, 229, 261, 262, 263, 317, 318, 355

FERDINAND THE CATHOLIC, CONTRASTING COLUMBUS: 203, 312, 343, 344

FERDINAND THE CATHOLIC & PEOPLE, GOODS OF INDIES: 79, 127, 135, 173, 199, 329, 329, 333, 334

FERDINAND THE CATHOLIC & CHANCA: 209, 210, 225, 232, 245, 260

FERDINAND THE CATHOLIC & HIS REIGN BY BERNÁLDEZ: 269, 271, 276, 277, 280, 283, 288, 294, 298, 299, 301, 307, 311, 344, 333, 342, 347

FERNÁNDEZ, JUANA: 263

FERNÁNDEZ REPETO: 209

FERNÁNDEZ DE IBARRA, A.M.: 209, 355

FERNÁNDEZ DE NAVARRETE, M.: 355

FONSECA, JUAN DE (COUNT OF PERNIA): 79, 127, 129, 141, 197, 199

FORMIN, ZEDO: 129, 135, 318

FRANCIS, ST.: 197

GABRIEL, FERNANDO DE: 272

GALDA, SOVEREIGN OF: 299, 300

GALEN: 213, 215

GALLARDO, BARTOLOMÉ JOSÉ: 220

GAMA, VASCO DA *see* DA GAMA, VASCO

GOMES, DIEGO: 304

GORVALÁN: 249

GRAND KHAN: 137, 139, 141, 233, 244, 279, 312, 349, 350

GUACANAGARÍ: 35, 39, 45, 47, 49, 51, 105, 107, 109, 111, 113, 115, 117, 119, 135, 227, 238, 239, 241, 244, 248

GUTIERREZ DI TOLEDO, JUAN: 219

HEERS: 344

HENRY IV OF CASTILE: 279

HENRY THE NAVIGATOR, (PORTUGAL): 291, 297

HERRERA, DIEGO DE: 299

HESIOD: 259

HIDALGO, J.: 266

HOJEDA: 249

HORACE: 259

INFANTE DON ENRIQUE *see* HENRY THE NAVIGATOR

ISABELA PRINCESS OF SPAIN: 207, 209, 210, 264,

ISABELA THE CATHOLIC: 7, 13, 65, 67, 79, 83, 85, 127, 129, 135, 141, 165, 173, 183, 185, 191, 195, 197, 199, 201, 203, 208, 209, 210, 219, 220, 225, 226, 228, 229, 232, 245, 254, 258, 260, 262, 263, 269, 270, 276, 277, 280, 283, 288, 294, 298, 299, 300, 301, 306, 307, 311, 311, 312, 317, 329, 333, 334, 341, 342, 344, 347, 355

JANE, C.: 355

362

Jerez, Juan de: 264

Joanna the Mad *see* Juana la Loca.

Joao II of Castile: 222, 298

Joao II of Portugal: 65, 292, 311

John II of Portugal *see* Joao II of Portugal

John II of Castile *see* Joao II of Castile

John of Salisbury: 221

Juan, don: 67, 131, 155, 226

Juan, [master]: 226

Juana la Loca: 209

Las Casas, Bartolomé de: 125 (n. 28), 251, 329

Leto, Pomponio: 341

López de Villalobos, Francisco: 219

López de Seville, Diego: 264

Lugo, Alonso de: 299

Madariaga, S. de: 329, 344

Mahn-Lot, M.: 344

Mairení *see* Marlení

Maloncello, Lanzarotto: 297

Mandeville, John: 63, 139, 141, 157, 165, 232, 278, 280, 310, 312, 324

Manuel I of Portugal: 294, 306

Marlení: 39, 41, 43, 45, 107, 109, 111, 113

Mayrení *see* Marlení

Mc Neil, W.H.: 289

Melchior, sailor with Columbus: 43, 111

Michel, biscayan captain: 300

Mollat, M.: 232

Monardes, Nicolás: 228

Morales Padrón, F.: 245, 329, 344

Morison, S.E.: 93 (n. 16)

Mulligan, John: 355

Neckam, Alexander: 221

Nicholas V, [pope]: 304

Nicola d'Oresme: 221

Niebla, Count of *see* Alonso, Juan

Ocena, Diego de: 265

Oderico da Pordenone: 278

Ovid: 259

Paracelsus: 213, 216

Parra, Juan de la: 226

Peraza, Ferran: 299, 299

Pérez de Luna, Fernán: 228

Peter Martyr of Anghiera: 273, 278, 355

Pietro d'Abano: 221

Pinzón, Martín Alonso: 65

Plautus: 219

Pliny: 221, 259

Plutarch: 221

Polo, Marco: 232, 247

Ponce de León, Rodrigo: 272

Portuondo, F.: 355

Prester, John: 141

Prince of Spain, *see* Juan, don

Ptolemy: 63, 310

Pulgar, Fernando del: 279

Ramírez Corría Filiberto: 272

Rejón, Juan: 299

Rodriguez, Diego: 203

Romeo, R.: 344

Rosell, C.: 356

Rumeu de Armas, A.: 344

Salle, Gadifer de la: 297

Santángel, Luis de: 225

Scillacio, N. *see* Squillace, N.

SEGURA, MANUEL: 264

SPAIN, PRINCE OF *see* JUAN, DON

SQUILLACE, N.: 256, 258, 259, 355

SYLLACIUS, NICOLAUS *see* SQUILLACE, N.

TAVIANI, P.E.: (n. 8) 79, 121 (n. 25), 245, 329

TELDE, [KING OF]: 299, 300

THACHER, J.B.: 355

THOMAS AQUINAS: 221, 222

TODOROV, T.: 329

TORRELLA, JERONIMO: 219

TORRES, ANTONIO: 8, 131, 135, 229, 255, 256, 261, 277, 315, 317, 333, 355

VALERA, DIEGO DE: 357

VALLES, CRISTÓBAL: 264

VARELA, C.: (n. 6) 29, 355

VAZ DE CAMINHA, PERO: 322

VERA, PEDRO DE: 299, 300

VERGIL: 259

VESALIUS, A.: 213, 215

VILLENA, ENRIQUE DE *see* ARAGON, HENRY OF

XANTA: 207

ZAFRA, JUAN DE: 264, 265, 266

ZURITA Y CASTRO, JERÓNIMO: 357

ZURITA, ANA DE: 263

INDEX OF PLACE-NAMES

Africa: 7, 279, 291, 292, 293, 294, 297, 303, 304, 331, 337, 346, 347, 348

Ahia (Hispaniola): 103

Alcalá: 208

Alexandria (Egypt): 123, 306, 338

Alfa et O, Cape [Alfaeto]: 139, 143, 175, 349

America: 8, 233, 272

Andalusia: 63, 81, 83, 141, 280, 283, 284, 285, 286, 287, 288, 350

Andes: 121 (n. 25)

Antigua, Island: 97 (n. 17)

Antilles: 216, 228, 304, 306, 315, 337, 338, 344

Antipodes: 343

Arabia: 348

Arabia, Gulf of: 143, 348, 350

Aragon: 199, 318

Arguim: 331

Asia: 141, 311, 346, 348, 349

Atlantic Ocean: 8, 77 (n. 7), 292, 342

Azores: 298

Babylon: 306

Bahía De Santiago (Cuba): 147 (n. 33)

Bahía (Puerto Rico): 101 (n. 22)

Barbary: 288

Barcelona: 79, 258, 271

Baxa (Jamaica): 189

Benin: 337

Biscay, Cape: 77

Biscay, Mines: 258

Black Sea: 288

Bohío (Hispaniola): 33, 103

Bojador, Cape: 291, 303, 346

Borique, Island: 29, 31, 49, 101, 117

Brittany: 288

Cabo Cruz (Cuba): 147 (n. 34)

Cabra, Island: 125 (n. 27)

Cádiz: 13, 15, 83, 85, 127, 143, 201, 300, 347, 350

Cairo: 293, 305, 306, 348

Calicut: 143, 292, 293, 305, 337, 348, 350

Canaries: 13, 75, 83, 85, 259, 297, 298, 299, 300, 301, 304, 309, 327, 331, 347, 348

Cape Haïtien: 43 (n. 11)

Cape Verde: 298

Cape Verde, Islands: 65

Caribs, Islands of the: 17, 25, 27, 29, 49, 51, 53, 75, 79, 87, 89, 91, 99, 101, 117, 195, 197, 201, 241, 242, 338

Castile: 41, 49, 51, 57, 63, 79, 91, 109, 111, 117, 119, 121, 123, 125, 129, 141, 147, 155, 163, 165, 171, 173, 181, 183, 185, 195, 197, 201, 203, 209, 252, 253, 283, 284, 286, 288, 299, 318, 322, 326, 351

CATALONIA: 75

CATHAY: 137, 139, 141, 143, 232, 244, 247, 278, 279, 312, 331, 334, 347, 349, 350

CEUTA: 291

CHILE, NORTHERN: 121 (n. 25)

CHINA: 232, 305, 331

CIBAO (HISPANIOLA): 53, 57, 103, 127, 131, 135, 137, 248, 249, 258, 315, 333

CIENFUEGOS (CUBA): 165 (n. 39)

CIPANGO, ISLAND: 232, 244, 247

COLIBRE (*see* ALSO COLLIOURE): 75 (n. 6)

COLLIOURE (*see* ALSO COLIBRE): 75 (n. 6)

CONSTANTINOPLE: 332

CORDILLERA, CENTRAL (HISPANIOLA): 53 (n. 17)

CORDOBA: 285

CORSICA: 175

CORUÑA, PROVINCE: 207

CRETE: 293

CROOKED ISLAND: 67 (n. 3)

CUBA (*see* ALSO BAHÍA DE SANTIAGO, CABO CRUZ, CIENFUEGOS, ENSENADA DE CORTÉS, GUANTANAMO BAY, HANAN, JARDINES DE LA REINA, JUANA ISLAND, MACACA, MAGÓN, ORNOFAY, POINTE MAISÍ, PUNTA GORDA, QUEEN'S GARDEN): 67 (n. 4), 75, 179 (n. 42), 228, 349

CUEVAS, LAS, MONASTERY: 286

CURRUQUIA, ISLAND: 33

DOMINICA, ISLAND: 21 (n. 3), 29 (n. 5), 85 (n. 10), 93 (n.16), 243

DOMINICAN REPUBLIC: 35 (n. 10)

EAST INDIES: 139, 157, 165, 291, 324

ECIJA: 285

ECUADOR: 121 (n. 25)

EGYPT: 306, 337, 347, 348

ENGLAND: 75, 306

ENSENADA DE CORTÉS (CUBA): 175 (n. 40)

ETHIOPIA: 143, 350

EUROPE: 216, 233, 346

EVORA: 209

FAR EAST: 278

FAROL, POINTE (JAMAICA): 189

FERNANDINA, ISLAND (*see* ALSO LONG ISLAND) (BAHAMAS): 67

FLANDERS: 288, 306

FLORENCE: 306

FRANCE: 199, 306, 318

FUENTERRABÍA: 77

FUENTES DE LA ENCOMIENDA MAYOR DE LEÓN: 270

FUERTE VENTURA, ISLAND: 298

GALDA: 299, 300

GALICIA: 75

GANGES: 143, 350

GENOA: 257, 306, 309, 310

GERMANY: 306

GILBRALTAR, STRAIGHT OF: 348

GOLDEN PENINSULA (CHERSONESE): 143, 175, 247, 349

GOMERA, LA, ISLAND: 13, 83, 298

GOOD WEATHER, GULF (JAMAICA): 189

GOOD HOPE, CAPE OF: 292, 348

GRANADA, KINGDOM OF: 75, 207, 226, 270, 331, 357

GRANDE ANSE, BAY (*see* ALSO GUADALOUPE, ISLAND): 91 (n. 15)

GUADALOUPE, ISLAND (*see* ALSO GRANDE ANSE, BAY): 19 (n. 2), 21 (n. 3), 87 (n. 12), 91 (n. 15), 93 (n. 16), 238, 241, 243, 257

GUADALQUIVIR, RIVER: 285

GUANAHANÍ, ISLAND: 67 (n. 1)

GUANI, ISLAND: 193

GUANTANAMO BAY (CUBA): 145 (n. 32)
GUINEA: 291, 298, 303, 304

GUINEA, GULF: 346

HAITI, ISLAND (*see* ALSO HISPANIOLA, SAINT NICHOLAS PORT, SAMANA): 33, 75, 77, 101, 127

HANAN (CUBA): 75

HIERRO, ISLAND: 13, 15, 83, 85, 298

HISPANIOLA (*see* ALSO AHIA, BOHÍO, CIBAO, CORDILLERA, HAITI, LA ISABELA, MARTA, MONTE CRISTI, MONTE JUAN, MORI, NITI): 7, 8, 19, 25, 31, 35 (n. 10), 53 (n. 16), 63, 67, 69, 75, 77, 89, 97, 101, 103, 117, 127, 139, 185, 189, 197, 199, 203, 208, 210, 211, 219, 225, 227, 228, 231, 233, 238, 239, 241, 244, 247, 248, 249, 250, 251, 253, 246, 257, 260, 263, 264, 265, 277, 310, 315, 316, 317, 318, 332, 333, 334, 337, 338, 343, 344, 350

HUNGARY: 141, 350

INDIA (*see* ALSO MALABAR): 291, 293, 294, 305, 306, 337, 338, 347

INDIAN OCEAN: 292, 294, 305, 337, 348, 350

ISABELA, LA (HISPANIOLA): 51 (n. 14), 119, 131, 137, 238, 251, 252, 261, 315, 325, 333

ISABELA, LA, ISLAND (CROOKED IS.): 67

ITALY: 8

JAFFA: 143, 350

JAGUA, RIVER [MESSE, RIVER] (JAMAICA): 189 (n. 44)

JAMAICA (*see* ALSO BAXA, GOOD WEATHER GULF, JAGUA RIVER, MESSE RIVER, MONTEGO BAY, MORANT POINTE, SAINT ANNE'S BAY, SANTIAGO): 143, 145, 147, 151, 155, 177

JARDINES DE LA REINA (CUBA) (*see* ALSO QUEEN'S GARDEN): 159 (n.38)

JEREZ DE LA FRONTERA: 285, 358

JERUSALEM: 63, 143, 350

JUANA, ISLAND (*see* CUBA): 63, 67, 69, 75, 139, 141, 143, 155, 157, 169

KINGSTON (JAMAICA): 191 (n. 46)

LANZAROTE, ISLAND: 298

LAXAR, RIVER: 189

LEÓN: 284, 288

LIBYA: 143, 350

LIGURIA, REGION OF: 310

LISBON: 293, 306

LONG, ISLAND (*see* ALSO FERNANDINA, ISLAND) (BAHAMAS): 67 (n. 2)

LUCCA: 293

LUGO, PROVINCE: 207

MACACA (CUBA): 155, 189

MADEIRA: 298

MADRID: 356, 357, 358

MAGHREB: 297

MAGÓN (CUBA): 163, 185, 279, 324

MAJORADA, MONASTERY: 355

MALABAR (INDIA): 291, 305, 348

MARIE GALANTE, ISLAND: 21 (n. 3), 85 (n. 11), 93 (n. 16), 243

MARTA (*see* ALSO ISABELA, LA - HISPANIOLA): 51

MECCA: 305, 348

MEDITERRANEAN SEA: 143, 293, 305, 338, 348, 350

MESA: 347

MESSE, RIVER (NOW JAGUA, JAMAICA): 189

MIDDLE EAST: 278

MIJOHAR, PORT (DISTRICT OF SEVILLE): 300

MILAN: 63, 203, 309

MINA DE OURO: 291, 292, 293, 304, 331, 346, 347

MONTE CRISTI: 33, 35 (n. 10), 125 (n.28)

367

Monte Juan, Port (Now Monte Cristi, Hispaniola): 105, 125 (n. 28)

Montego Bay (Jamaica): 155 (n. 37)

Montserrat, Island: 95 (n. 17)

Morant Pointe (Jamaica): 189 (n. 45)

Mori (Hispaniola): 165, 324

Morocco: 271

Mount Castalino: 189

Mount Sinai: 348

Navidad, La: 77, 115, 226, 239, 241, 244, 248, 251, 256, 260, 325, 343

Near East: 332

Nevis, Island: 97 (n. 18)

Niti (Hispaniola): 53, 57, 59, 248, 249, 258, 262, 333

Ocean SEa: 63

Olmedo: 355

Ornofay (Cienfuegos, Cuba): 165, 169, 181, 187, 189, 312, 324

Pacific Ocean: 121 (n. 25)

Palacios, Los: 7, 269, 270, 271, 272, 278, 287, 318, 350

Palos: 65, 79, 226

Paris: 358

Pearl, Island: 342

Perpiñán: 75 (n. 6)

Peru: 121 (n. 25)

Pinos, Los, Island (Pine Island): 179 (n. 42)

Pointe Maisí (Cuba): 139 (n. 31)

Portland Bay: 191 (n. 46)

Portugal: 75, 143, 209, 210, 264, 279, 291, 292, 294, 298, 304, 331, 348, 349

Puerto Rico (Bahía): 29 (n. 7), 101 (n. 21)

Puerto [Muy] Grande: 145

Puerto Bueno: 151 (n. 36)

Punta Gorda (Cuba): 175 (n. 41)

Pyrenees: 75 (n. 6)

Quaruqueriá, Island: 93

Quayrique, Island: 93

Queen's Garden (Cuba): 159, 169, 171, 181, 189

Red Sea: 305, 306, 337, 348

Rome: 63, 280, 350

Russia: 141, 350

Sahara: 303, 331

Saint Anne's Bay (Jamaica): 151 (n. 35)

Saint Nicholas, Port (Haiti): 139

Saint Thomas: 333

Salamanca: 208

Samana (Region of Haiti): 33, 103

San Salvador: 67

San Andrés (Seville): 208

San Sebastián: 77 (n. 7)

San Vicente, Cape: 63, 143, 349

San Juan Evangelista (Peninsula): 179

Santa Maria, Island: 67

Santa Gloria: 151

Santiago (Now Jamaica): 177

Santiago Bay: 147 (n. 33)

Santo Domingo: 264, 265

Sao Jorge Da Mina: 304

Savona: 256

Scotland: 75

Serafin Pointe: 173, 171 177

Seville (*see* also Mijohar, Port): 7, 8, 63, 65, 79, 81, 115, 129, 207, 208, 220, 233, 263, 264, 270, 272, 273, 285, 286, 288, 300, 350, 356 207

Sicily: 147, 288

SIMANCAS, ARCHIVE OF: 263

SMALL SEA: 347

SOUFRIÉRE, LA, VOLCANO: 17, 238

SPAIN: 13, 17, 21, 31, 51, 53, 69, 75, 79, 83, 85, 89, 93, 101, 103, 143, 183, 185, 207, 208, 209, 220, 225, 228, 229, 237, 240, 247, 248, 249, 250, 253, 254, 255, 256, 258, 260, 262, 263, 264, 271, 276, 279, 283, 287, 298, 300, 306, 315, 316, 317, 322, 325, 326, 329, 331, 333, 334, 335, 337, 338, 341, 342, 343, 345, 346, 349

ST. THOMAS: 135, 258

ST. CROIX: 25 (n. 4), 93 (n. 16), 97 (n. 20)

SUDAN: 291, 303, 331

TAGAOS: 347

TARTAR, GRAND: 141, 350

TELDE: 299, 300

TENERIFE: 300

TOLEDO: 207

TRIANA: 286

VALENCIA: 151

VALIA: 141, 350

VALLADOLID: 203

VENICE: 306

VERA: 357

WASHINGTON: 358

WEST INDIES: 8, 13, 63, 73, 77, 83, 85, 127, 137, 139, 141, 199, 203, 208, 209, 210, 211, 214, 215, 216, 219, 225, 228, 231, 232, 233, 234, 237, 240, 241, 244, 247, 248, 255, 256, 258, 259, 262, 263, 264, 265, 269, 271, 277, 279, 293, 304, 305, 309, 310, 315, 318, 322, 324, 329, 332, 335, 337, 338, 341, 342, 351, 355

WHITE SEA: 169, 177, 181 (n. 43), 312

BIBLIOGRAPHY

J. AMADOR DE LOS RIOS, *Historia crítica de la literatura española*. Madrid: Joaquim Muñóz, 1865.

N. ANTONIO, *Biblioteca hispana, sive hispanorum qui usquam unquamve sive latina sive populari sive aliam quamvis linguam scriptio aliquid consignaverunt...* Rome, 1672.

J. ARANA - SOTO, *Los médicos en el descubrimiento del Nuevo Mundo y el homenaje al Doctor Chanca*. Burgos: Aldecoa, 1967.

J. M. ASENSIO, *Cristóbal Colón: su vida, sus viajes, sus descubrimientos*. Barcelona: Espasa y Compañía, 1891 [1st ed. 1886-88].

A. BALLESTEROS BERETTA, *Cristóbal Colón y el descubrimiento de América*. Barcelona-Buenos Aires: Salvat Editores, 1945.

BALLESTEROS - ALCALÁ - ESPINOSA. "Médicos y farmacéuticos españoles en América." *Anuario de Estudios Americanos* 4 (Seville: 1947): 531-4.

L. F. BARRETO, *Descobrimentos e Renascimento: Formas de ser e de pensar nos seculos XV e XVI*. Lisbon: Imprensa Nacional-Casa de Moeda, 1983.

G. DE BARROS, "Dell'Asia." In *Navigazione e viaggi*, vol. 2. Edited by G. B. Ramusio. Turin: Einaudi, 1979.

B. BENASSAR, *La América española y la América portuguesa*. Madrid: Akal bolsillo, 1980.

A. BENEDICENTI, "Cristoforo Colombo e la medicina." In *Studi Colombiani*. Atti del Convegno Internazionale di Studi Colombiani (Genova: 1951), vol. 3. 119-21. Genoa, 1952.

M. BLOCH, *Lavoro e tecnica nel Medioevo (Il problema dell'oro nel Medioevo)*. Bari: Laterza, 1981.

D. J. BOORSTIN, *The Portuguese Discoverers*. Lisbon: The National Board for the Celebration of Portuguese Discoveries, 1987.

D. J. BOORSTIN, *The Discoverers*. New York: Random House, 1983.

A. BOSCOLO, *Saggi su Cristoforo Colombo*. Rome: Bulzoni, 1986.

F. BRAUDEL, *La Méditerranée et le Monde mediterranéen à l'époque de Philippe II*. Paris: Armand Colin, 1949.

J. BROTONS PICO, "Un médico en el Descubrimiento de América." *Revista General de Marina* (Madrid: July 1980): 3-11.

W. BRULEZ, "Les voyages de Cadamosto et le commerce guinéen au XVe siècle." *Bulletin de l'Institut Historique Belge de Rome* (1968): XVII-XXX.

R. Caddeo, "Il grande viaggio." Introduction to *Giornale di bordo di Cristoforo Colombo (1492-1493)*. Milan: Mondadori, 1973.

P. Capparoni, "Il *Tractatus de fascinatione* di Diego Alvarez Chanca." *Atti e Memorie dell'Accademia di Storia dell'Arte Sanitaria* 35 (Rome: 1936): 30-6.

J. B. Charcot, *Christophe Colomb vu par un marin*. Paris: Flammarion, 1928.

P. Chaunu, *La expansión europea (siglos XIII al XV)*. Barcelona: Nueva Clio, 1977 [1st ed. in French 1972].

R. Chaunu, *Sevilla y America Siglos XVI y XVII*. Seville: Publicaciones de la Universidad de Sevilla, 1983.

A. Chinchilla, *Historia de la medicina española*. Valencia: López, 1841.

A. Cioranescu, *Colón y Canarias*. La Laguna de Tenerife: Instituto de Estudios Canarios, 1959.

C. Coll y Toste, "Carta del físico Diego Alvarez Chanca al Cabildo de Sevilla, dándole cuenta del segundo viaje, en lo cual se descubrió la isla de San Juan." *Boletín Histórico de Puerto Rico* 4 (San Juan de Puerto Rico: 1917): 97-125.

C. Colombo, *Il Giornale di bordo: Libro della prima navigazione e scoperta delle Indie. Nuova Raccolta Colombiana*, vol. 1. Rome: Istituto Poligrafico e Zecca dello Stato, 1988.

C. Colón, *Carta-Relación de enero de 1494*. Transcription by A. Rumeu de Armas. In *Manuscrito del Libro Copiador*, vol. 2. Madrid, 1989.

A. Cortesão, *Los Portugueses*. Barcelona: Salvat Editores, 1961.

A. Cortesão, "Descobrimento de Guiné e de Cabo Verde." In *Acta Universitatis Coninbrigensis*, vol. 1. 3-38. Lisbon, 1974.

A. P. D'Avezac, "Canevas chronologique da la vie de Christophe Colomb." *Bulletin de la Société de Géographie* (Paris: 1872): 5-25.

A. Da Mosto, "La navigazioni atlantiche." In *Il Nuovo Ramusio*, vol. 5. Edited by T. Gasparrini Leporace. Rome: Istituto Poligrafico dello Stato, 1966.

V. Da Gama, *Roteiro da primeira viagem de Vasco da Gama (1497-1499)*. Lisbon: Agência geral das Colónias, 1940.

A. De La Torre, "Los castellanos en Guinea y la Mina del oro después del Tratado de 1479." In *Congreso Internacional de História des Descubrimentos*. 2-7. Lisbon, 1961.

C. Deluz, "Le livre de Jean de Mandeville, autorité géographique à la Renaissance." Actes du Colloque de Tours. 205-20. Paris: Maisonneuve et Larose, 1987.

J. Devisse, "L'Afrique dans les relations intercontinentales." In *Histoire générale de l'Afrique*. Vol. 4, *L'Afrique du XIIe au XVIe siècle*. Paris: Unesco-Nea, 1985.

B. W. Diffle, and G. D. Winius. *Foundations of the Portuguese Empire 1415-1580*. Minneapolis: University of Minnesota Press, 1977.

Doctor Calatraveño. "Hechos médicos relacionados con el Descubrimiento de América." *Revista de España* (Madrid: 1892): 47-74.

A. M. Fernández de Ibarra, ed. "The Letter of D. Diego Alvarez Chanca, dated 1494, relating to the Second Voyage of Columbus to America." *Smithsonian Miscellaneous Collection* 48 (Washington: 1907): 428-57.

M. Fernández de Navarrete, *Colección de los viajes y descubrimientos que hicieron por mar los Españoles, desde fines del siglo XV*. Madrid: Imprenta Nacional, 1958 [1st ed. 1825-37].

R. P. L. Fernández de Retana, *Isabel la Católica*. Madrid: Editorial El Perpetuo Socorro, 1947.

F. Fernández-Armesto, *Before Columbus: Exploration and Colonization from the Mediterranean to the Atlantic, 1229-1492*. Hong Kong: MacMillan Education, 1987.

G. Ferro, *Le navigazioni lusitane nell'Atlantico e Cristoforo Colombo in Portogallo*. Milan: Mursia, 1984 [1st ed. 1974].

L. Firpo, ed. *Colombo, Vespucci, Verrazzano: Prime relazioni di navigatori italiani sulla scoperta dell'America*. Turin: UTET, 1966.

F. Gabriel, de and R. de Apodaca. "Introducción." In *Historia de los Reyes Católicos Don Fernando y Doña Isabel, escrita por el Bachiller Andrés Bernáldez*. Seville, 1870.

F. Gallardo Rodriguez, "La medicina y el descubrimiento." *Sevilla 92* no. 19 (Seville: 1986): 17-9.

B. J. Gallardo, *Ensayo de una biblioteca española de libros raros y curiosos*. 4 vols. Madrid, 1863-69 [Facsimile in Biblioteca Románica Hispánica, vol. 1. 163. Madrid: Gredos, 1968].

E. García del Real, *Historia de la medicina en España*. Madrid: Ed. Reus, 1921.

P. A. Gemignani, *La scoperta di Colombo e la medicina*. Genoa: Ecig, 1988.

F. Giunta, "La scoperta colombiana e l'umanesimo del Mezzogiorno." In *Saggi sull'età colombiana*, edited by A. Boscolo and F. Giunta, 60-72. Milan: Cisalpino-Goliardico, 1982.

J. Gil, *Mitos y utopías del Descubrimiento, Io: Colón y su tiempo*. Madrid: Alianza Universidad, 1989.

J. Gil, *Noticia de Andrés Bernáldez, cura de Los Palacios*. In *Temas colombinos*. Seville: Escuela de Estudios Hispanoamericanos de Sevilla, 1984.

J. Gil, "Introducción a la *Relación de Guillermo Coma, traducida por Nicolas Esquillache*. In *Cartas de particulares a Colón y Relaciones coetáneas*, edited by J. Gil and C. Varela, 177-81. Madrid: Alianza Editorial, 1984.

J. Gil, "Colón y la Casa Santa." *Historiografía y bibliografía americanistas* 21 (Seville: 1977): 125-35.

M. Gómez-Moreno, and J. de M. Carriazo. "Introducción" to *Memorias del reinado de los Reyes Católicos*. Madrid: Real Academia de la Historia, 1962.

Gran Canaria en la órbita de la Hispanidad, 1492-1957, España descubrió América. Las Palmas: Patronato de la Casa de Colón de Las Palmas, 1957.

L. S. Grangel, *El ejercicio de la medicina en la sociedad española renacentista*. Cuadernos de Historia de la Medicina española, vol. 10. Salamanca, 1971.

F. Guerra, "La política imperial sobre las drogas de las Indias." *Revista de Indias* 103-4 (Madrid: 1966): 31-58.

F. Guerra, *Historiografía de la Medicina Colonial*. México: El Abastecedora de Impresos, 1953.

O. Guerrini, *Michele da Cuneo. Relazione del secondo viaggio di Cristoforo Colombo*. Atti e memorie della R. Deputazione di Storia Patria per le province di Romagna, 3d. ser., vol. 3. Bologna, 1885.

G. GUSDIRF, *Les sciences humaines et la pensée occidentale, II: Les origines des sciences humaines*. Paris: Payot, 1967.

H. GITIERREZ COLOMER, "Isabel la Católica y los fármacos del Nuevo Mundo." *Medicamenta* 11 (Madrid: 1951): 120-3.

H. HARRISSE, *Christophe Colomb: sa vie, ses ouvrages et ses découvertes*. Paris: E. Leroux Editeur, 1884.

J. HEERS, *Gênes au XVe siècle: Activité économique et problèmes sociaux*. Paris: S.E.V.P.E.N., 1961.

J. HEERS, *Christophe Colomb*. Paris: Hachette, 1981.

A. HERMÁNDEZ MOREJÓN, *Historia bibliográfica de la medicina española*. Madrid: Impr. de la viuda de Jordan e hjos, 1887.

C. JANE, *Select Documents Illustrating the Four Voyages of Columbus*. London: The Hakluyt Society, 1930.

C. JANE, *The Voyages of Christopher Columbus*. London: The Argonaut Press, 1930.

A. JULIEN, Ch. *Les voyages de découverte et les premiers établissements*. Brionne: Gerard Monfort Editeur, 1979.

B. LANDSTROM, *Colón*. Barcelona: Juventud, 1971.

C. LOLLIS, de. "Introduzione a *Scritti di Cristoforo Colombo*." In *Raccolta Colombiana per il Quarto Centenario della Scoperta dell'America*, vol. 1, pt. 1. Rome, 1892.

C. LOLLIS, de. *Cristoforo Colombo nella leggenda e nella storia*. Rome: Treves, 1923 [1st ed. 1892].

J. R. LUANCO, *La alquimia en España*. Madrid: Tres, Catorse, Diecisicte, 1980.

R. LUNGAROTTI, "I medici di Colombo." *Rivista del medico calabrese* 3.23 (Reggio Calabria: 1988): 2-4.

S. MADARIAGA, De. *Vida del Muy Magnífico Señor Don Cristóbal Colón*. Buenos Aires: Editorial Sudamericana, 1973 [1st ed. in English 1939-40].

V. MAGALHAES GODINHO, *Les grandes découvertes*. *Coimbra:* Coimbra Editora, 1953.

V. MAGALHAES GODINHO, *L'économie de l'empire portugais au XVe et XVIe siècles*. Paris: S.E.V.P.E.N., 1969.

M. MAHN-LOT, *Portrait historique de Christophe Colomb*. Paris: Editions du Seuil, 1988.

G. MANDAVILLA, da. *I viaggi*. Edited by F. Zambrini. Bologna: Gaetano Romagnoli, 1870.

R. MANSELLI, *Magia e stregoneria nel Medioevo*. Turin: Giappichelli, 1976.

R. MANSELLO, "Cristoforo Colombo tra fede e scienza." In *Histoire économique du monde mediterranéen 1450-1650*. 359-68. Toulouse: Privat Editeur, 1973.

J. M. MARTÍNEZ HIDALGO Y TERÁN, "La naves de los cuatro viajes de Colón al Nuevo Mundo." In *Scritti in onore di P. E. Taviani*. Genoa: Ecig, 1986.

J. MATOS POENSA, de. "Portugal nos mares." In *Pedro Alvarez Cabral: 500 años*. 7-17. Porto Alegre: Edioes da Universidad Federal do Rio Grande do Sul, Facultade de Filosofía, 1969.

W. H. MCNEIL, *Plagues and Peoples*. Middlesex: Penguin Books, 1979.

Medeiros, F. De. *L'Occident et l'Afrique (XIIIe-XVe siècle)*. Paris: Karthala, 1985.

M. Menéndez Pelayo, *Historia de los heterodoxos españoles*. Mexico: Editorial Porrúa, 1983.

M. Menéndez Pelayo, *Estudios y discursos de crítica histórica y literaria*. Obra completa. Santander, 1942.

J. Merrien, Christophe *Colomb*. Paris: Denöl, 1955.

M. Mollat, *Les explorateurs du XIII*e *au XVI*e *siècle: Premiers regards sur des mondes nouveaux*. Paris: JC Lattes, 1984.

N. Monardes, *Delle cose che vengono portate dalle Indie Occidentali pertinenti all'uso della Medicina*. Venice: Giordan Ziletti, 1582.

T. Monod, R. Mauny, and G. Duval. *De la première découverte de la Guinée, récits par Diogo Gomes (fin XV*e *siècle)*. Bissau: Centro de Estudios da Guiné Portuguesa, 1959.

F. Morales Padrón, *Fisionomía de la conquista indiana*. Seville: Consejo Superior de Investigaciones Cientifica, 1955.

F. Morales Padrón, *Canarias: crónicas de su conquista*. Las Palmas: Ayuntamiento de Las Palmas, 1978.

F. Morales Padrón, "Andalucía y América." *Asociación europea de profesores de Español* 15.8 (special issue): 17.

F. Morales Padrón, *Historia del descubrimiento y conquista de América*. Madrid: Editora Nacional, Cultura y sociedad, 1981.

F. Morales Padrón, *Historia del descubrimiento y conquista de América*. Madrid: Editora Nacional, 1981.

S. E. Morison, *Admiral of the Ocean Sea: A Life of Christopher Columbus*. Boston: Northeastern University Press, 1983.

S. E. Morison, The European Discovery of America: The Southern Voyages. New York: Oxford University Press, 1974.

E. O'Gorman, *La invención de América: El universalismo de la cultura de Occidente*. México: Fondo de Cultura Económica, 1958 [1st ed. The Invention of America, 1961].

J. Olmedilla y Puig, *Breves consideraciones históricas acerca del médico español de los siglos XV y XVI, el doctor Alvarez Chanca accompañante Colón en su segundo viaje a América en 1493*. Madrid: M. Ricardo Fé, 1892.

C. Ortwin Sauer, *Descubrimiento y dominación española del Caribe*. Mexico: Fondo de cultura económica, 1984.

E. Otte, "El comercio exterior andalus a fines de la Etad media." In *Actas del II Coloquio de Historia Medieval Andaluza (Sevilla 8-10 abril 1981)*. 193-240. Seville, 1982.

A. Palacio, and L. Durán. "Segundo viaje del Almirante Colón." *Revista General de Marina* 131 (Madrid: 1946): 392.

J. A. Paniagua, *El doctor Chanca y su obra médica*. Madrid: Ediciones cultura hispánica, 1977.

G. Panseri, "Medicina e scienze naturali nei secc. XVI e XVII." In *Storia d'Italia,* vol. 3. 345-51. Turin: Einaudi, 1980.

J. H. Parry, *Le grandi scoperte geografiche*. Milan: Il Saggiatore, 1971.

H. Parry, *La conquista del mare*. Milan: Gruppo Editoriale Fabbri Bompiani Sonzogno, 1984 [1st ed. *The Discovery of the Sea,* 1981].

M. Pelayo y Del Pozo, "El cura Bernáldez." In *Memorias de la Sociedad Arqueológica de Carmona*. Seville, 1888.

G. Pesce, "I medici di bordo ai tempi di Cristoforo Colombo." In *"Studi colombiani": Atti del Convegno Internazionale di Studi Colombiani (Genova 1951)*, vol. 3. 76-7. Genoa, 1952.

G. Pessagno, "Questioni colombiane." *Atti della Società Ligure di Storia Patria* 53 (Genoa: 1926): 65ff.

G. Pessagno, "Questioni colombiane." In *Atti della Società Ligure di Storia Patria*. Genoa, 1926.

H. I. L. Picolo, "Os fondamentos economicos dos descobrimentos." In *Pedro Alvares Cabral: 500 años*. 33-45. Porto Alegre: Edioes da Universidad Federal de Rio Grande do Sul, Facultade de Filosofía, 1969.

L. Pierotti Cei, *Isabella di Castiglia regina guerriera*. Milan: Mursia, 1985.

Polo, Marco. *Il Milione*. Edited by R. Allulli. Milan: Mondadori, 1982.

O. De Pordenone, *Le livre de sa peregrination de Padoue à Pekin au Moyen Age*. Paris: Editions Hots, 1982.

F. Ramírez Corría, *Reconstrucción crítica del segundo viaje cubano de Colón: La ficción colombina del Cura de Los Palacios*. Archivo Histórico Pinero, 2. Havana, 1955.

P. Revelli, *Colombo*. Turin: UTET, 1941.

E. E. Rich, "Gli insediamenti coloniali e i problemi della manodopera." In *Storia economica di Cambridge*, vol. 4. Turin: Einaudi, 1975.

C. Rico Avello y Rico, "Patología en la conquista de América." *Asclepio* 30-31 (1978-79): 337-87.

R. Romeo, *Le scoperte americane nella coscienza italiana del Cinquecento*. Bari: Laterza, 1989.

C. Rosell, "Introducción a la *Historia de los Reyes Católicos Don Fernando y Doña Isabel,* de A. Bernáldez." In *Crónicas de los Reyes de Castilla*, vol. 3. Madrid: M. Rivadeyra, 1878.

J. P. Roux, *Les explorateurs au Moyen Age*. Paris: Fayard, 1985.

A. Rumeu de Armas, *Libro Copiador de Cristóbal Colón: Correspondencia inédita con los Reyes Católicos sobre los viajes a América*. Madrid, 1989.

R. Sancho de San Román, "Indices de las obras de Hernández Morejón y Chinchilla." In *Seminario de Historia de la Medicina Española*, pt. 2. Salamanca, 1960.

M. Tangheroni, and L. Di Nero. *Commercio e navigazione nel Mediterraneo Medioevale*. Rome: Scholastica, 1978.

P. E. Taviani, *La genovesità di Cristoforo Colombo*. Genoa: Ecig, 1987.

P. E. Taviani, *Cristoforo Colombo: La genesi della grande scoperta*. 3d ed. Novara: Istituto Geografico De Agostini, 1988 [1st ed. 1974].

P. E. Taviani, "Schede per la ricostruzione storico-geografica della *Prima navigazione e scoperta delle Indie*." *Nuova Raccolta Colombiana,* 1:351-8. Rome: Istituto Poligrafico e Zecca dello Stato, 1988.

P. E. Taviani, *I viaggi di Colombo: la grande scoperta*. 2 vols. Novara: Istituto Geografico de Agostini, 1984.

J. B. Thacher, *Christopher Columbus: his Life, his Work, his Remains*. New York: Putnam's, 1904.

A. Tió, *Dr. Diego Alvarez Chanca*. Publicaciones de la Asociación Médica de Puerto Rico, Instituto de Cultura Puertoriqueña. Barcelona: Universidad interamericana de Puerto Rico, 1966.

T. Todorov, *La conquista dell'America: Il problema dell'altro.* Turin: Einaudi, 1984 [1st ed. in French 1982].

A. Unali, "L'oro nei primi due viaggi di Cristoforo Colombo nelle Indie." In *Scritti in onore di P. E. Taviani,* vol. 3. Genoa: Ecig, 1986.

L. J. Valverde, and J. Hidalgo. *Documentos médicos farmacéuticos conservados en los Archivos de Sevilla.* In *Ist. de Hist. de la med. esp.* Salamanca, 1971.

M. Vannini De Gerulewicz, *El mar de los descubridores.* Caracas: Publicaciones de la Commissión organizadora de la III Conferencia de las Naciones Unidas sobre el derecho del mar, 1974.

C. Varela, "Introducción a la *Carta del doctor Diego Alvarez Chanca al cabildo de Sevilla.*" In *Cartas de particulares a Colón y Relaciones coetáneas,* edited by J. Gil and C. Varela, 152-55. Madrid: Alianza Editorial, 1984.

C. Varela, "Diego Alvarez Chanca, cronista del segundo viaje colombino." In *Historiografía y bibliografía americanistas.* Escuela de estudios hispanoamericanos, vol. 29. Sevilla, 1985.

C. Varela, "Introducción a la *Carta a Santángel.*" In Cristóbal Colón, *Textos y documentos completos.* Madrid: Alianza Universidad, 1982.

M. Veloz Maggiolo, *Arqueología prehistórica de Santo Domingo.* Singapore: McGraw-Hill Far Eastern Publishers, 1972.

J. Viera y Clavijo, *Noticias de la historia general de las Islas Canarias.* 6th edition, with an introduction and notes by A. Cioranescu. 2 vols. Santa Cruz de Tenerife: Goya Ediciones, 1967-71 [1st ed. Madrid, 1772-83].

P. Vilar, *Oro y moneda en la historia, 1450-1920.* Barcelona-Caracas-Mexico: Editorial Ariel, 1981 [1st ed. Paris, 1969].

GENERAL INDEX

Introduction . . . . *Pag.*	7
Diego Alvarez Chanca *Letter to the Mayor of Seville* . . . . »	11
Andrés Bernáldez *Memoirs of the Catholic Sovereigns' Reign* . . . . . »	61

INDEX TO COMMENTARIES
FOR CHANCA'S LETTER

I) Diego Alvarez Chanca Before His Voyage to the Indies . *Pag.*	207
II) Medical Science Between 1400 and 1500 . . . . »	213
III) Chanca's Medical Writings . . . . »	219
IV) Chanca and the Second Columbian Voyage . . . . »	225
V) Reading the *Letter* . . . . »	231
VI) The New World's Natural Environment . . . . »	217
VII) The Natives . . . . »	241
VIII) Gold and Spices . . . . »	247
IX) Difficulties Prior to the Settlement in La Isabela . . . . »	251
X) Chanca's Letter and Other Contemporary Reports . . . . »	255
XI) The Last Years of Chanca's Life . . . . »	263

INDEX TO COMMENTARIES
FOR BERNALDEZ'S MEMOIRS

XII) Andrés Bernáldez's Life . . . . *Pag.*	269
XIII) *Memoirs of the Catholic Sovereigns' Reign*: sources, methods, and purposes . . . . »	275
XIV) The *Memoirs* as a Documentary Source of the Time: natural disasters and extraordinary events . . . . »	283
XV) The Portuguese Voyages of Exploration . . . . »	291
XVI) Spanish Journeys of Exploration: The Canaries . . . . . »	297

XVII) Gold and Spices from the African and Asiatic Voyages	*Pag.*	303
XVIII) The Figure of Christopher Columbus	»	309
XIX) Christopher Columbus's First Two Voyages to the Indies	»	315
XX) The Natives	»	321
XXI) Gold and the Columbian Expeditions	»	331
XXII) Spices and the Columbian Expeditions	»	337
XXIII) Accounts of the Third and Fourth Voyages	»	341
XXIV) Bernáldez's Understanding of the World's Georgaphy and the Prospect of Circumnavigating the Globe	»	345
Bibliography of the editions and manuscripts of the *Letter* of Diego Alvarez Chanca	»	353
Index of Persons	»	361
Index of Place Names	»	365
Bibliography	»	371

PRINTED IN THE SECURITY PRINTING PLANT
OF THE ISTITUTO POLIGRAFICO E ZECCA
DELLO STATO, IN ROME, 1993, ON
SPECIAL WATERMARKED PAPER
PRODUCED BY CARTIERE
MILIANI FABRIANO
PAPERMILLS